Crafting Anatomies

Crafting Anatomies

Archives, Dialogues, Fabrications

Edited by Katherine Townsend, Rhian Solomon, and
Amanda Briggs-Goode

BLOOMSBURY VISUAL ARTS
LONDON • NEW YORK • OXFORD • NEW DELHI • SYDNEY

BLOOMSBURY VISUAL ARTS
Bloomsbury Publishing Plc
50 Bedford Square, London, WC1B 3DP, UK
1385 Broadway, New York, NY 10018, USA
29 Earlsfort Terrace, Dublin 2, Ireland

BLOOMSBURY, BLOOMSBURY VISUAL ARTS and the Diana logo are trademarks
of Bloomsbury Publishing Plc

First published in Great Britain 2020
This edition published 2022

Cover art direction, layout, type design by Adriana Brioso
Cover concept: Ian Cutmore
Cover image: Documentation illustrating seams on the body after dissolution of the
garments during the shooting of "*An Impossible Wardrobe for the Invisible*", 2011.
(© Lara Torres)

A catalogue record for this book is available from the British Library.

A catalog record for this book is available from the Library of Congress.

ISBN: HB: 978-1-3500-7547-4
       PB: 978-1-3502-4243-2
       ePDF: 978-1-3500-7548-1
       eBook: 978-1-3500-7549-8

Typeset by RefineCatch Limited, Bungay, Suffolk
Printed and bound in Great Britain

To find out more about our authors and books visit www.bloomsbury.com
and sign up for our newsletters.

In loving memory of

Barry John Briggs (1944–2017)
Carol May Solomon (1945–2018)
Geoffrey Roy Townsend (1933–2018)

Contents

Illustrations

Figures

Tables

Foreword

This *Crafting Anatomies* book developed out of the *Crafting Anatomies* exhibition curated by all three of its editors at Nottingham's Bonington Gallery in 2015. An important and timely book, its principal premise is that the human body is essentially an "available site" for conceptual, creative, scientific, digital, and performic examination across the multidisciplines of fashion and textiles, and through the lens of history, psychology, biology, and craft. Its span is complex and diverse, representing the work of significant practitioners, creators, innovators, designers, scientists, medical researchers, materialists, engineers, and biotechnologists, with global reach, relevance, and responsibility. Thematically organized, the body is seen via its archives, its dialogues, and its future fabrication, providing methods by which to access its past, its present, and what is yet to come…

The preserved and documented progress of the body through time is a subject of fascination. From cloth and clothing debris, detritus, and ephemera to the formal artifact, text, and material evidence of fashion, craft, and textile culture, the body's existence is mapped through its proxies (shoe lasts, pattern blocks, toiles and armatures, smart accessories and intelligent prostheses, disruptive innovations and somatic augmentations, bio-regeneration, modular garments, and interactive wearable technologies) as well as its substances (cells, flesh, skin, hair, bones, sexes, brain impulses, electrical rhythms, sanguinary flow, and biofabricated simulacra), its vapors (emotions, intelligence, sensations, embodied and ethereal knowledge, genders, absences, impressions, relations, and affects), and its legacies (anthropological and data traces, memories and memorials, waste footprint, intellectual impact, genetics and genealogies, phenomena, intuition, holographic and digital ghosts). All this—and more—is captured, categorized, shaped, and interrogated by the editors and authors in the pages following, and I am honored to expose a little of it in this invited foreword.

The actively articulating and passively narrated body intrigues, engages, and inspires. Users experience the crafted anatomy and feed back into the loop of learning. Co-designers collaborate, and then tell their stories onwards into textile, fashion, and craft communities. Aesthetes and designers of their individual discipline's look and language correspond and collude, create, and critique, building their canon. Assistive communication technology transmits speech and tonality, conversation, and translation, helping to spin the yarns and weave the webs. Circular systems, supply chains, sustainable successions, and sequences of concept-to-disposal turn and tell tales. Those who curate, choreograph, cut, and craft the textiles and garments that clothe the body seek verbal, written, broadcast, and virtual means by which to spread their words, their manifestos, and their ideologies. They traverse and intermingle their disciplines, constructing even greater complexity and manifesting multi-meanings from past, present, and future.

And that future body, of course, is the much quested and questioned holy grail, with its miraculous powers to provide happiness, eternal youth, or infinite sustenance. In the final third of this book, the elusive future fabricated body is conjured and imagined. Future-focused technologies manufacture new sensory and mechanical humanity through bioinspiration and biomimicry. Materials are manipulated, while new means of complex fabrication, new methods for personal customization, and newly emergent technologies seek and find increasingly additive and synthetic solutions to the problems of human frailty.

But remember that those frail humans—me, you, us—are soft, responsive, tactile. We feel, we love, and we die. *Crafting Anatomies'* ultimate hypothesis rests on the will to enhance and extend our capability, performance, and longevity. To succeed, body hackers know that design must be human-centered, machines must be soft, actuation must be multisensory, and robots must be authentic. These are tall orders, demands on design, craft, and the anatomy of the human that will test and challenge for decades to come. This book's ultimate contribution and impact is to map with care the work so far, respecting the trajectories that have formed the status quo, and shining a sharp white beam of light into the shadows of the future of that frail human body, which must also be the future of our frail humanity.

Professor Catherine Harper
Deputy Vice-Chancellor
University of Chichester, UK

Acknowledgments

To all who kindly contributed to the *Crafting Anatomies* Exhibition and Project

The exhibition selection panel: Deborah Dean (Exhibitions Manager at Nottingham Castle Museum and Art Gallery), Kashif Nadim Chaudry (Artist), Liz Ciokajlo (Concept Development Footwear Designer).

Bonington Gallery Curators: Tom Godfrey, Joshua Lockwood-Moran.

Exhibiting Artists: Richard Arm • Boudicca • Anne Brennan • Lucy Brown • Margaret Bushby • Jon Clair • Laura Clarke • Nuala Clooney • Amy Congdon • Jo Cope • Amanda Cotton • Colin Cork & Tilak Dias • Marisa Culatto • Kathy Dickenson • Julian Ellis • Sandra Fruebing • David Gates • Shelly Goldsmith • Fiona Hamblin • Karen Harrigan • Karen Ingham • Adriana Ionascu • Lauren Kalman • Sarah Kettley • Julie Light • Di Mainstone • Lee Mattocks • Emma Montague • John Pacey-Lowrie • Lois Pittman • Veronica Ranner • Ana Rajcevic • Ania Sadkowska • Julia Schuster • Juliana Sissons • Marloes ten Bhömer • Alana Tyson • Aminder Virdee • Sarah Walker • Hannah White • Jessie White • Alexa Wright.

Nottingham Castle Museum and Art Galleries for the loan of artifacts and documentary films from their historic collection.

The Wellcome Trust for use of their archival film footage.

NOTTINGHAM
TRENT UNIVERSITY

BONINGTON
GALLERY

1

Introduction

Crafting Anatomies

Katherine Townsend, Rhian Solomon, and Amanda Briggs-Goode

Introduction

Crafting Anatomies places the human body at the centre of a transdisciplinary exploration, revealing how it acts as a catalyst for craft-based collaborative research, using archives, creative dialogues, and technologically advanced fabrications. As the book demonstrates, nothing happens without collaboration in fashion and textiles, which involves intense, creative dialogues at all stages of the process (Anderson 2017). Increasingly, this applies to all contemporary artistic design practice—where the tradition of the "isolated auteur" and mastery of a specific discipline is challenged by the provocative and disruptive nature of information and technology (Mower 2017).

This collection of illustrated narratives seeks to highlight how critical making and conversation around the contemporary body is manifest through a range of material and immaterial responses. The contributors, drawn from a network of creative thinkers and practitioners based in Europe, North America, and Oceania, exploit methodologies that resonate with wider transnational philosophies, "[paying] no attention to the boundaries between fine and applied art, high and low culture, gendered and racial identity, let alone, fashion, textiles and craft"[1] (Hemmings 2015: 157). So, through the shared lens of *crafting anatomies*, researcher/practitioners in materials (textiles) and product (fashion) design are united with artists, writers, scientists, and curators to demonstrate how their/our response to the corporeal is constantly flexing and changing.

Figure 1.1 Ana Rajcevic, "Animal: The Other Side of Evolution" (2012). Photograph by Ana Rajcevic.

Craft

While many of the contributors to this book could be described as "designers," the term "crafting" is adopted, both literally and metaphorically; revealed through the unique relationships makers have with the fabric of, and for the body. Adamson (2007: 1) asks provocatively "Isn't craft something mastered by the hands, not the mind? Something consisting of physical actions, rather than abstract ideas?" Skilled making, or craftsmanship, is widely understood as "expertise in technique"; the result of a learned repertoire of refined gestures informed by hand and mind, sustained through supplemental material-based practice (ibid.: 4; Sennett 2008). However, the influence and impact of craft is no longer tied to the Western constructed definition or terrain of "the crafts," following new insights into the role, value, and "power of making"[2] to the creative economy and culture.

The authors within this book demonstrate an inherent understanding of craft's capacity for collaboration; to communicate across distinct ideologies, domains, and cultures (Niedderer and Townsend 2019; Solomon 2013). The reconceptualization of craft, in parallel with other practices[3] has resulted in the melding and dissembling of different genres of making (Ravetz, Kettle, and Felcey 2013). Exchanges between individuals across disciplinary boundaries are shared and through joint endeavor leave one or both sides significantly changed; haptic and reflective dialogues leading to the generation of new and unexpected ideas (Schön 1984). In *Crafting Anatomies*, therefore, we define craft as a holistic "approach" to the body, realized through the actions and concepts of practitioners who utilize it as a form of "material intelligence" (Adamson 2019).

The body

In *Shapeshifters*, Francis (2019: 3) discusses our evolving understanding and treatment of the human body from ancient history to the present, observing that "it is in constant flux, with porous physical and psychological borders that are shaped by the environments we inhabit." Francis also makes connections between the systems of the natural world and humankind's biological capacity to grow, recover, and adapt based on a continual process of metamorphosis.[4] As this study demonstrates, skin,[5] the body's largest organ and regenerative frontier between the inside and outside of the human form, is the source of groundbreaking textile advances. What goes on "beneath the skin," how our internal organs appear, function, and influence the human condition (Lynch in Alderman et al. 2018) also represents an expanding territory for hybrid practitioners to intervene in.

"The singular, bounded, carbon-based body is being replaced by the proliferation and emergence of technologies and practices which enable the enhancement, alteration and invention of new bodies" (Blackman 2008: 2).

Designer/makers are adapting their existing toolkits and mindsets toward hybrid approaches to the corporeal, drawn from different domains. Consequently, the repair and transformation of the body is no longer restricted to medicine and surgery, with the crafting of its internal and external architectures increasingly located at the intersection of technology and biology (Oxman 2015). The merging of mechanized and natural systems, via hand, augmented and virtual realities are extending the engineering of "the digital body";[6] through the employment of biotechnologies and robotics to enhance its capabilities and ontology.

A plethora of temporary exhibitions and permanent gallery spaces dedicated to the body have also appeared globally (e.g., the Wellcome Collection, Science Gallery, Cité du Corps Humain, and Deutsches Hygiene Museum), stimulating new dialogues and perspectives.

Crafting the body

As Turner (2008: 1) identifies "humans both have bodies and are bodies" the exception being, as Entwistle expands, that "humans are dressed bodies" (Entwistle 2015: 31). Thus, the body, in both its natural and clothed state, has continued to intrigue artists and designers since the beginnings of classical Western culture.[7] Cloth and clothing "represent the body as a fundamentally liminal phenomenon by stressing its precarious location on the threshold between the physical and the abstract, the literal and the metaphorical" (Wilson 2003: 273). It is therefore difficult to consider the concept of "crafting anatomies" without contemplating the codes, matrices, and materials of the system in which the body is fashioned (Barthes 2010).

Entwistle (2015: ix) observes "how much the field [of fashion] has massively complexified and breached discipline boundaries" since the beginning of the new millennium. Similarly, the "end of fashion" has been proclaimed and debated by theorists and practitioners alike, acknowledging that its "former paradigms have been exhausted" (Geczy and Karaminas 2019: 1). This is evidenced by changes to the conceptualization, processes, and dissemination of fashion, resulting in a more critical design environment "which has its core in the body and its way of being in the world, of its representations, its masking, its disguises, its measures, and its conflicts with stereotypes and myths" (Calefato 2019: 33). Such change has led to a more focused exploration of the somatic through "corporeal design," involving subtle and spectacular modifications using decoration and accessories (Zellweger 2011).

One of the most critical issues relating to the crafting of the fashionable body is how fashion and textile products are resourced, designed, and made; the bodies and labor involved (von Busch et al. 2017). Resultantly, a growing number of organizations, including Fashion Revolution[8] and the Union of Concerned Researchers[9] are attracting international membership and affecting change in the fashion system. Sustainable design is acknowledged by the contributors to this book both implicitly and explicitly; via methodologies that utilize craft as both method and philosophy toward enhancing human expression, health, and well-being, and reducing human impact on the environment.

As the collated examples illustrate, craft-based methodologies often engender slower, co-creative, human-centered models, "away from assembly and closer to growth" (Oxman 2015). Some contributors are materially orientated, e.g., regenerating historical artifacts, growing natural biomaterials, making use of the whole cloth, and dematerializing the current fashion system. While others question the values associated with the industry, including the wasteful nature of mechanized garment production, how a closer affinity with the human body, its natural assets, materiality, and functionality can inform how we design, manufacture, and consume, for a better future (Solanki 2018; Franklin and Till 2018).

Viewing the disciplines of fashion and textiles through alternative lenses challenges established perceptions and practices within the field. Access to laboratories to engage with new methodologies and techniques, usually reserved for scientists, is creating innovative material and technological applications to benefit body and society. Residencies and cross-sector ventures are enabling practitioners to cast fresh eyes on the corporeal through interdisciplinary interactions facilitated by those who are the "other to each other in their views, their disciplines, or their cultures" (Ginsberg and Chieza 2019).

By crafting both subject and substance of the body designers are evolving a more fluid perception of how the human form is materialized and philosophized in contemporary culture, which the contributing authors seek to convey through this text.

The exhibition

The concept for *Crafting Anatomies* emerged from an exhibition[10] staged at Bonington Gallery (2015) in the School of Art and Design, Nottingham Trent University. The project was the outcome of two years' work by the editors, who were invited to curate an exhibition to anticipate the School's 175th anniversary.[11] The aim of the curators was to explore how the body is interpreted and reimagined through historical, contemporary, and future contexts. Following a call for participation and an independent panel selection process, forty-five artworks by international researchers and practitioners were curated via the themes of: Material, Performance, and Identity. The contributors employed a variety of contrasting craft approaches to reconceptualize, speculate upon, and frame the body through art, design, and medical practices. Selected artists from the exhibition have also contributed to chapters in this book.[12]

Material

Artifacts employing advanced textile and surgical imaging technology to visualize the hidden, internal structures and systems of the human body, were employed to develop solutions in clinical settings. These included embroidered

Figure 1.2 View of the *Crafting Anatomies* exhibition at Bonington Gallery, Nottingham Trent University (2015). Artifacts by various artists including "Embroidered Implants" by Ellis Developments; "Gendered Postures" by Julia Schuster; "Material Compulsion" by Marloes Ten Bhömer; and "Dress Block" by Jo Cope. Image reproduced courtesy of Bonington Gallery / Nottingham Trent University.

implants for orthopedic surgery by Julian Ellis (Ellis Developments[13]) and hand-modeled and 3D-printed "phantom" human hearts (to train surgeons) by Richard Arm[14]. Together with other examples, these artifacts demonstrated the importance of hand and digital craft knowledge to create pioneering devices for, and of, the body.

The embracing of biotechnologies and their application to fashion were further interrogated by projects that blurred the boundaries between skin, cloth, the body, and dress and which conceptualized skin as a symbolic interface between the self and the world (Paterson 2004).

Speculative works by designer Amy Congdon, proposed a "future where materials are not made, but grown, where luxury goods are fashioned from skin

Figure 1.3 Richard Arm, "Synthesizing the Human Heart" (2014), 3D-printed heart, cross-sectional internal anatomy study. Photograph by Richard Arm.

cells, not fabric" (Congdon 2016). The fabrication of biodegradable scaffolds for human hearts (constructed by silk worms) was investigated by Veronica Ranner—"shifting our understanding of industrial and bio-technological manufacturing from 'hardware' to novel 'wetware.'" (Ranner 2018).

Designers exploring the deconstruction of traditional fashion approaches also featured within the Material section of the exhibition. Fashion film *The Liquid Game* (2013), by avant-garde studio Boudicca, emphasized the transitions for designers working between physical and digital material constructs; preempting the increasing permeability of fashion and art (Calefato 2019). This project acted as an example of the dematerialization of fashion through the hybrid use of computational material languages, which are now challenging established understandings of surface and skin (Solanki 2018; Harris 2013).

Performance

In the context of performance, the body was explored by exhibitors through the development and testing of fabrications as second skins within fashion, sport, and science. Interactive accessories, controlled through the performative actions of the wearer, were presented alongside projects that monitored emotional responses and connectivity through such devices.

The "Human Harp" project[15] developed by Di Mainstone transformed its wearer into an instrument. When attached to the wires of a suspension bridge, the body accessory enabled the wearer to "play" the bridge, translating the structure's vibrations into sounds.

Marloes Ten Bhömer's series of films entitled *Material Compulsion* (2013) illustrated the mechanics of the accessorized body through systematic experiments, documented using high-resolution motion capture techniques. Here, the intricate physiology, form, and movement of the foot were meticulously recorded to inform experimental approaches to future footwear design.

In her film *The Choreography of Making* (2015), Fo Hamblin visualized the unspoken languages of embodied knowledge; capturing reflective conversations

Figure 1.4 Katie Raine playing the Human Harp on Bob Kerrey Suspension Bridge, Omaha, Nebraska, USA, by Di Mainstone (2018). Photograph by Miguel Cedillo.

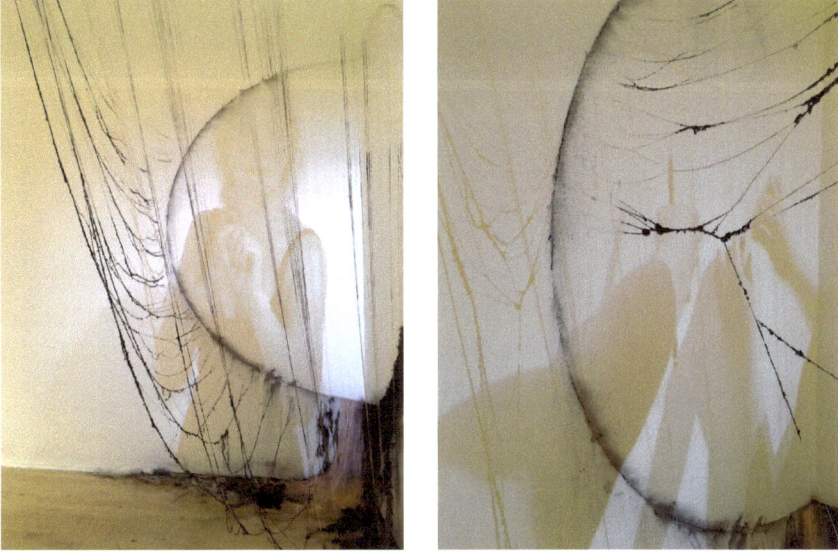

Figure 1.5 Fo Hamblin, installation "Choreography of Making" (2015) integrated with *Choreography of Making* film by Fo Hamblin and R&A Collaborations (2015). Images and photographs, F. Hamblin.

occurring between materials and maker "along multiple paths of sensory participation" (Ingold 2011: 18).

Julia Schuster exposed the gendered nuances, present in intuitive bodily actions, by recording playful interactions with ceramic objects, visualizing the often very subtle and overlooked gestures of physical expression. These and other examples reinforced the diverse ways and contexts in which bodies express their biomechanical, haptic selves.

Identity

Divergent approaches to the construction of identity were communicated through interpretations that reflected on how our characters are crafted through objects of material culture. Exhibits were selected to illustrate how worn objects and prostheses enable us to concurrently expose and conceal our individuality, "materialising questions of identity in particularly intimate ways" (Woodward 2007: 3).

The work of John Pacey-Lowrie reinforced craft's role in the sensitive reconstruction of the self; conveying both the skill of the ocularist in creating prosthetic eyes, and the resultant close relationships forged through regular consultations with patients.

Individual biographies embedded within clothing were investigated within *Every Contact Leaves a Trace*, by Shelly Goldsmith, who applied different textile processes to reclaimed garments and accessories to create forensic objects exploring the human traces left at crime scenes perpetrated by female serial killers. Amanda Cotton also exposed the evidence of blueprints assumed by artifacts crafted from human biological matter, including ear wax, hair, and urine. Her work served to critique our bodies' material make-up, its relationships with commercial goods alongside deeper ethical concerns surrounding the use of living matter in design. These exhibits stretched the definition and agency of the craft practitioner and what their chosen materials might comprise, pre-empting the use of human biological waste as radical sustainable matter (Franklin and Till 2018).

Evolving the concept

The *Crafting Anatomies* exhibition highlighted a return to "the body" within contemporary culture, accessing technologies to understand how "the body is

Figure 1.6 View of the *Crafting Anatomies* exhibition, Bonington Gallery, Nottingham Trent University (2015), showing "Every Contact Leaves a Trace" by Shelly Goldsmith, and screen, photography, and material-based artifacts by Emma Montague, Amy Congdon, Aminder Virdee, and other artists. Image reproduced courtesy of Bonington Gallery / Nottingham Trent University.

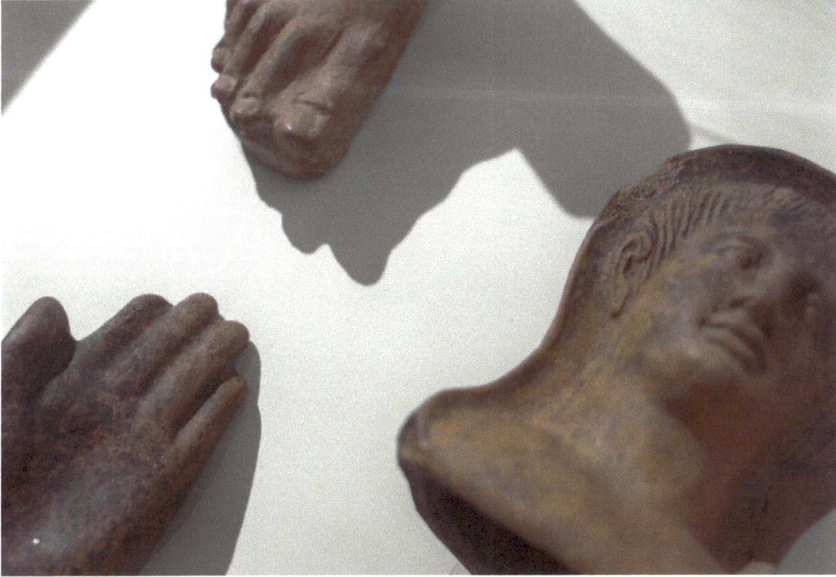

Figure 1.7 Anatomical votives, *c.* sixth century BCE, loaned by Nottingham Castle Museum and Art Gallery for the *Crafting Anatomies* exhibition, Bonington Gallery, Nottingham Trent University (2015). Image reproduced courtesy of Bonington Gallery / Nottingham Trent University.

moving into a complex array of entangled, material, social and historical forces" (Blackman 2008: 12). The project also celebrated the diversity of contexts that contemporary designers and makers were operating in at the time and, in doing so, opened up debate around the future role of creative fashion and textile practitioners within scientific, technological, and engineering fields.

The migration of the domains of fashion and textiles into radically different fields has rapidly progressed since the exhibition in 2015, suggesting a need to document such developments in this book. The initial emphasis for the curation of items within Material, Performance, and Identity has since morphed into themes that relate more specifically to each of the editors' area of research interest—"The Archived Body," "The Body in Dialogue," and "Fabricating the Body," as outlined in the following sections.

The Archived Body—Amanda Briggs-Goode

An archive may indeed take in stuff, heterogenous, undifferentiated stuff … texts, documents, data … and order them by the principles of unification and

classification. This stuff, reordered, remade, then emerges—some would say like a
memory—when someone needs to find it or just simply needs it, for new and
current purposes.

Steedman 2001: 68

Intrigued by the thrill of a potential discovery from the past, contributors to "The Archived Body" focus on the transformation of these objects into contemporary creative works. The aim: to enlighten our understanding of our current and future relationship with objects, our bodies, and materiality.

The chapters offer perspectives on approaches that artists and designers take to archives and the body as well as their seductive effects: Derrida talks of "archive fever" (Checinska and Watson 2016: 284), Foster (2004) of "archival impulses," and Huizinga of "historical sensation" (Jefferies et al. 2016: 193). These nouns are all connected by an active, palpable, and instinctual response to material culture but equally to sensuality and the body. It is this intersection that offers such a rich opportunity for artists to explore the body through archives, as well as the fashion and textiles which cover it.

The section opens with a chapter by **Amanda Briggs-Goode** and **Gail Baxter**, "The Archived Lace Body: Contemporary Artist Designer Responses," which focuses upon the rich potential for creative practice offered by exploring lace heritage. The chapter considers the enticing effects of the archive and lace as a fabric loaded with connotation and meaning. This synergy becomes even more expressive when it is worn on the body. Unpacking these concepts, exploring their relevance and significance to creative practice, the authors examine the seductive efficacy, sensorial value, and the ritualized meaning of archives, lace, and the body. The creative practice of Joy Buttress, Cal Lane, Mal Burkinshaw, and Danica Maier offer a new perspective, of the "stuff" that Steedman (2001) refers to, but also exposes new insights into our personal and collective histories, challenging our biases and assumptions, and revealing some of the narratives that inform them.

Clothes form part of our memories; both our personal embodied narratives and the skill and traditions of their makers. Clothes talk about "us"—and therefore the material culture of both cloth and clothes and how they restrain or liberate our bodies offers possibilities to interrogate their meaning. In "Disarmed: Lasting Impressions," **Johannes Reponen** uses an "in conversation" approach to elicit from artist **Jo Cope** her use of archives and past narratives to explore a conceptual fashion design language. In the chapter we begin to understand how Cope is fascinated by speculative objects that sit at the boundary between art, craft, and fashion. This is explored by her use of both craft skills and new technology to make work that has been informed by past narratives and future potentials. Born out of frustration with the "standardization" and sterile environment of commercial fashion, Cope explains how she focuses upon the body's interactions. The playful and surreal artifacts that Cope creates explore the sensory and practical aspects of wearing and moving in clothes. Craft skills are key to unlocking these narratives and she describes the development of a language to communicate with the skilled "last makers" from Northampton, as well as a new visual language that she uses to articulate fashion in motion.

Narratives of identity can be reflected upon through our own personal physical, documented clothing and photographic archives. As Entwistle states (Entwistle and Wilson 2001: 16) "We are invited to play this game of fashion and perform our identity through our choices of dress." It is in this context that **Ania Sadkowska** proposes a phenomenological approach to explore the experience of aging, fashion, gender, and identity.

This research develops a deeper understanding of the role of clothes as the communicators and mediators between self and society and our understanding of older male identities. As Entwistle positions "dress, as both a social and personal experience, is a discursive and practical phenomenon … thus requir[ing] understanding of both the socially processed body which discourses on dress and fashion shape, as well as the experiential dimension" (2010: 16). The work addresses this experiential dimension as a way of understanding and reflecting upon bodily practices over time. Sadkowska produced and exhibited three responses in the form of customized jackets, to reflect the themes emerging from her case studies: "Pioneering," "Nonconforming," and "Rematerializing." These she has identified as key male behavioral traits that reflected her research participants' previous fashion "desires" in a contemporary context to create alternative insights into their lived experiences through making. Sadkowska observes that it is precisely in the context of mundane everyday practices that phenomenological understanding of the lived body can emerge.

The final chapter, "The Electric Corset and Other Future Histories," explores an experimental and collaborative research project aimed at speculative design for wearable technology. **Katherine Townsend**, **Sarah Kettley**, and **Sarah Walker** were inspired by Dr. Scott's electric corset, designed in 1883 using "medical and scientific principles" to enhance the health and well-being of the wearer. Dissecting not only the subtle languages of the performing body but that which is embedded within its construction led the team to consider this historical fashion accessory as a metaphor for speculative, future "wearables" design.

Through their selection of garments from historical dress collections, it became apparent that wearables are not solely developments of the late twentieth and early twenty-first centuries but are present as concepts integrated into historical artifacts. They communicate and represent the ensuing practice-led research, as an integral, choreographed aspect of the creative design process, involving numerous iterative stages, actions, and technologies.

The project uses a craft-based methodology, looking back to move forward, by studying objects across time to inform the way we design and connect with future wearables. As Pierce (2017) proposes an "archive can have relevance to contemporary design by stimulating design and material innovation." The aim of this work is to conceptualize the future potential of wearables through an imagined ontology.

These chapters demonstrate how viewing archives and the body can stimulate new concepts, practices, and approaches to material investigation and exploration, which in turn offer new insights to our view of our past, present, and future selves.

The Body in Dialogue—Rhian Solomon

"The Body in Dialogue" is considered from multiple perspectives from contributors to the second core section of this text, each of the authors exploring the "body as a meeting place"[16] to invoke discussion across diverging ideologies.

In Chapter 6, "Fashion and Participation in the Hands of X," **Andrew Cook** and **Graham Pullin** explore the materiality of collaboration. Here, the role of material libraries at The Institute of Making[17] provides a platform to forge new conversations between prosthetics wearers, designers, prosthetists, and engineers, during the redesign of prosthetic hands and associated services. Their Hands of X project[18] poses a shift from a medicalized model of design, production, and supply to one that is democratically co-produced; facilitating the involvement of the wearer throughout the design process, as specialist of their own life and experience (Cottam and Leadbeater 2004; Donetto et al. 2015).

Using carefully crafted participatory design methods, the duo connect distinct cultures who are working with and designing for the body (and wearer). Their approach not only serving to challenge subject-specific boundaries but confronting the cultural and biological borders of the self. By repositioning prosthetic hands as understated fashion items, not medical devices, Cook and Pullin are able to challenge engrained perceptions of disability, shifting the role of the user from patient to wearer, designer, and collaborator; advocating for "disability-led design to ultimately become more nuanced."

In Chapter 7, "Tissue Engineered Textiles: Craft's Place in the Laboratory," **Amy Congdon**, **Lucy Di Silvio**, and **Carole Collet** evidence how the specialisms of tissue engineering and constructed textiles collide; sharing technical craft skills across disciplines, identifying a need for translating conventional design techniques, in order to accommodate new ones.

Dialogue in this context is centered on the "cellular body"; serving as a site for conversation and collaboration. The trio also highlight the importance of recognizing both similarities and differences between science and design approaches and between the spaces in which "practice" is undertaken—the laboratory and textile studio.

Craft in these circumstances is "relational, adaptable and influential in modes of cross fertilisation" (Ravetz et al. 2013: 10) allowing for boundaries between disciplines to be disrupted. Congdon has since extended her approach, to apply craft's role in the laboratory, to a recent position as Associate Director of Materials Design, at Modern Meadow,[19] her abilities in tissue engineering and cell culture facilitating the development of biomaterials, to produce sustainable leather alternatives for the fashion industry.

In Chapter 8, "Mind–Body–Garment–Cloth," **Holly McQuillan** and **Timo Rissanen** propose a holistic approach to designing for the body, confronting complex and wasteful fashion manufacturing practices "that have given rise to new and pernicious forms of power" (Rocamora 2015: 191). Emphasizing the complexity of the fashion system, made up of individual and collective agents, the pair introduce creative projects that facilitate global and local discourses concerning the sustainably clothed body.

In select examples of practice, dialogues between objects, people, and institutions are navigated (machine, factory worker, wearer, designer, and manufacturer) in divergent contexts and at various speeds (Brand 1999) and are explored conceptually by the authors as a complex interplay between the themes of Mind–Body–Garment–Cloth. McQuillan and Rissanen celebrate the role of the designer as catalyst for systemic change, rethinking established Fordist systems of production that have dominated manufacturing in the fashion industry to date.

In Chapter 9, the final chapter in this section, "Empowerment and Self-Care: Designing for the Female Body," **Giulia Tomasello** and **Teresa Almeida** consider the female body as a political site in medical thought and practice, taking inspiration from feminist theorists and activists of the 1960s and 1970s

(Women's Health Movement).[20] Responding to a distinct lack of knowledge that is available to women about their bodies in medical practice, the duo have developed DIY toolkits (employing digital and biotechnologies) to promote "bodily awareness," ultimately enabling women to hold intimate dialogues with their own bodies and enhanced conversations with clinicians (and others).

Tomasello and Almeida draw upon the ubiquity of clothing in daily life (particularly underwear), exploiting its intimacy with the body to foster dialectics between body and self. Woman-Centered Design approaches (Almeida 2017) such as these not only serve to confront gendered positions of authority and power within institutional care, they also widen societal discourse on "taboo" subjects related to gynecological health, and lived experiences of gender and of the female body in contemporary society.

As each of the chapters in "The Body in Dialogue" identify (and indeed within the *Crafting Anatomies* book), a major shift is repositioning the role and skills of designers (Thackara 2013; Manzini 2015), who are no longer responsible for designing products and artifacts, but are engaged in the transformation of entire systems and service ecologies (Buchanan 2002; Prendiville 2016). Design is migrating into increasingly complex territories (Conklin 2006), and as a result, designers are responding by developing interdisciplinary, discursive methodologies.

The projects introduced within this section successfully facilitate differences in power, culture, or "language" in order to radically transform practices within the contexts in which they are applied. Dialogue is invested in materials (Binder et al. 2019; Eriksen 2012), in future-focused making (Sanders and Stappers 2014), which provides a conduit to broker meaningful interactions concerning the body. The body becomes a site for potentiality; a place where new discourses can emerge and (in some cases) where hybrid disciplines are formulated.

As the borders of the self are becoming ever more fluid through technological advancement and philosophical debate, should the pursuit of a more holistic, multifaceted understanding of the human body be encouraged—observing the body not as subject *or* object (from the viewpoints of specific communities or disciplines) but as "Body Multiple" (Mol 2003).

"Our bodies are always extending and connecting to other bodies, human and non-human, to practices, techniques, technologies and objects which produce different kinds of bodies and different ways, arguably of enacting what it means to be human" (Blackman 2008: 1).

The Fabricated Body—Katherine Townsend

In the final section of the book, physical and human dimensions are examined through projects that pose questions around mimicry, simulation, and biological experiments with the materials of the body. All of the contributors to this section are post-digital artisans who readily synthesize physical and virtual crafting strategies using hand manipulation with the digital tactility of code, across art, science, design, fashion, and architecture (Solanki 2018; Openshaw 2015).

Each of the four chapters provides a different perspective on how the body acts as both catalyst and armature for fabrications and visualizations that reimagine the fashioned, human form. The resulting experimental *and* experiential prototypes, substrates, performances, and films have been developed by creative practitioners applying research methodologies informed by the paradigms of "technology driven design, sustainable design and human-centred design" (Giacomin 2014: 607). Human-centered design particularly embraces "multidisciplinary skills and perspectives, explicit understanding of users, tasks, environments and experiences" (ibid.) as demonstrated by the following contributions.

In "OurOwnsKIN: The Development of 3D-Printed Footwear Inspired by Human Skin," **Manolis Papastavrou, Liz Ciokajlo**, and **Rhian Solomon** question whether a deeper understanding of how human skin behaves as a material, informs the design of 3D-printed shoes.

OurOwnsKIN is a specialist design consultancy, which seeks to "translate materials for the body"[21] focused on the conceptualization and production of innovative footwear to fashion apparel. The consultancy's work is informed by an interest in materials that can replace traditional substrates, such as leather. Biomaterials offer more environmentally friendly alternatives to impactful oil-based, natural, and animal-based fiber production. This is exemplified by Ciokajlo's collaboration with Suzanne Lee, on the BioCouture Shoe (2013) grown from bacterial cellulose, providing a non-leather biodegradable alternative.

Experiential knowledge of these biomaterials has inspired the OurOwnsKIN team to seek technologically led solutions, by using Additive Manufacturing and biopolymers to construct a new footwear solution; one that blurs the boundary between the biological and man-made material structures of the human foot and shoe.

The company has studied the mobility of the foot and collagen make-up of its skin, to digitally craft a seamless 3D-printed carapace, by tailoring the inherent microstructure of the skin to the shoe. This bespoke, zero-waste approach disrupts conventional footwear design, construction, and sizing. OurOwnsKIN demonstrates that if we are to create better, more sustainable products using bio-design as a philosophy and/or method (Ginsberg and Chieza 2019), we must look not only to nature, but to the materiality of our own bodies.

Amy Winters also creates various skin-like surface constructions, discussed in "Material Robotics: Shaping the Sensitive Interface," where explicit connections are made between the elements and materials from the natural world and her bioscientific approach. Winters' research and development of soft robotic, actuated materials, focuses on their potential to interact with the body; unlocking new categories of immersive experiences in Virtual Reality, Intelligent Mobility, and Fashion.

In her "Skin Series" (2016) Winters reinterpreted different qualities found in human skin, beginning with the pore, to create soft, sponge-like silicone textures that can absorb and dispel liquid—referencing the underlying anatomy of the spleen, breast tissue, and lungs, known as "the light organ" (Nagra in Alderman et al. 2018). Winters discusses the various roles encompassed in her practice, from hacker and bricoleur to alchemist, where she synthesizes textile knowledge and highly developed tactile sensitivity with color chemistry and synthetic biology.

By adapting the medical diagnostic application of "microfluidics"[22] she has created a "soft programmable toolbox" whereby liquid channels are integrated into textile membranes, with the capacity to trigger novel "synthetic sensations" based on body-responsive stimuli. Winters mimics natural materials and systems negotiating the surface fabrication of the body by interfacing between physical making (Ingold 2011) and artificial interaction (Vigneshwara 2018). Her most recent work builds on Lanier's (2011: 190) concept of "post-symbolic" communication through tactile, sensory languages using nonverbal communication.

In "The Genetics Gym," **Adam Peacock** discusses a year-long design residency at The Fashion Space Gallery, London College of Fashion, University of the Arts London, where he investigated how science-based and imaging tech-nologies provide the potential means for us to redesign ourselves, from our DNA upwards. Originally trained as an architect, Peacock speculates on how advances in human genetics, social media, and brand marketing could influence how we personalize our future selves. Peacock's research involved "speculative body design" in collaboration and consultation with experts in fashion, public health, genetics, fertility, psychology, and reconstructive surgery. These included Agi Haines, a surgical artist and synthetic biologist whose work asks: "How might people respond to the possibilities of our body as another everyday material and how far can we push our malleable bodies while still being accepted by society?"[23]

Peacock pushes this concept to the limit through the physical and virtual creative development of five characters, based on participating male and female models, selected for their different physiological and cultural characteristics. By adopting a multimedia approach to body imaging, Peacock envisions his models as post-human avatars, rendered to express a range of imagined brand ideologies. The resulting "Genetics Gym" installation reflected the "undecidable" (after Derrida) nature and influence of photography on the body, and the long-held tradition of "retouching as a cultural act . . . aimed at adapting photographs to the dictates of mass culture" (Vainshtein 2019: 50). The characters in the "Genetics Gym" make uncomfortable viewing; they are familiar, yet alien (even to the models themselves) encompassing an uncanny mix of analogue and digitally manipulated features. The work is raw and powerful and questions the reliability of the imagery of fashion and the need to remain attentive to the impact of emergent technology on the contemporary body (ibid.: 63).

In "The Body as Factory," Lara Torres explores "a post-productivist fashion practice through film," her immaterial response to the unsustainability of the established fashion system (Barthes 2010). Having worked in a garment factory, she witnessed and was subsumed into the manufacturing process, her body becoming lost in the dehumanizing process of mass production. This experience affected her deeply and her approach to the "productive body" (Guéry and Deleule 2014), leading to a theoretical and artistic position from which to interrogate how we make and, indeed, unmake our fashion selves through fashion. By considering fashion as a "situated bodily and social practice" (Entwistle 2015: 40), Torres documents the hidden, but highly skilled, relational gestures (Adamson 2010: 2) of hand sewing, draping, and dressing. The body of the craftsman, therefore is represented in the films in action, as the embodiment of both fashion maker and wearer.

Torres' films capture the residual, immaterial nature of fashion, as a significant form of fabrication in itself. For example, *Mimesis* (2008), an interdisciplinary project, situated between fashion, ceramics, and jewelry, utilizes traditional metalwork and mold-making, to reproduce found clothing and accessories as a critique of their functionality. This is redolent of Margiela's integration of time and memory into his work, the value of the fashion relic (Verhelst and Debo 2008); the referencing of ghosts of past wearers and makers (or indeed machinists). Emphasis is placed on the procedural stages of the fashion fabrication process; the choreography of body through making *is* the material, without which the fashion system cannot exist.

Entwistle and Townsend conclude the book in Chapter 14 with "On Fashioning Anatomy," where they reflect on the contributions by considering how the work reintroduces and reconceptualizes the body into fashion related praxis, "in all its variations and complexities [which has] completely disappeared from the creative chain" (Visceral in Pecorari 2016).

In "working with the material" the authors consider how the book challenges the established parameters of fashion research by prioritizing practices that craft the body. Parallels are raised with the "material turn," which drew attention away from texts toward the materiality and praxiography of bodies (Clever and Ruberg 2014); and the sensory and emotive interrelationships forged between body and cloth (Millar and Kettle 2018; Townsend and Sadkowska 2017).

In "the unarchived body" connections are made between the ghosts of past and future anatomies, located in "museumized" things (Calefato 2019). The body is re-presented through: artworks using lace as pattern and metaphor; performed artifacts, fabricated using historical blocks; deconstructed menswear expressing phenomenological experience; and archived dress objects reanimated as wearables.

"Dialogues between nature and culture" explore the possibilities of collaborative conversations with and around the body, leading to biomedical and biomaterial interventions, the personalization of prostheses by wearers and the use of biophilia to self-heal. The need for a holistic, zero-waste approach to the equating of Mind–Body–Garment–Cloth, champions the needs of nature over global, capitalist culture in the "fashioning the future body." Second-skin-like accessories and membranes for the evolving body use biological blueprints as inspiration, toward the notion of a post-growth, post-petroleum society. Digital crafting is used as a tool for criticality, to decode the fashioned identity by "creating new things through presentation, styling and self-fashioning" to make the world a more inclusive and sustainable place (Quinn in Pecorari 2016).

In *Crafting Anatomies*, the comingling of fashion and textiles with craft, science, medicine, and art make it challenging to ascertain where the materials of the self/body end, and dress/culture begins.

Notes

1   Comment attributed to the multimedia practice and Soundsuits made by the African artist Nick Cave.

2 *The Power of Making* (Charney 2011) exhibition and publication was one of the most visited shows ever held at the Victoria and Albert Museum.

3 In 2014 the Crafts Council Innovation Programme, UK, held the first of its Make:Shift conferences and introduced two projects: "Make:Shift:Do" and "Parallel Practices."

4 Francis (2019: 3) cites Ovid's poem *Metamorphoses* and Kafka's *Metamorphosis* to reiterate the resonance of "bodily transformation" in art and literature.

5 *Skin*, exhibition, Wellcome Collection, June 10–September 26, 2010, London.

6 "The Digital Human," BBC Radio 4. Available online: https://www.bbc.co.uk/ programmes/b01n7094/episodes/player (accessed March 15, 2019).

7 For an historical account of the classically draped to the modern fashionable body, see Hollander (1978).

8 Fashion Revolution is a not-for-profit global organization consisting of 100 member countries founded in the wake of the Rana Plaza disaster, Bangladesh on April 24, 2013, where 1,138 garment workers were killed when a garment factory collapsed. See: https://www.fashionrevolution.org/about/ (accessed August 9, 2019).

9 Following the *Global Fashion Conference: What's Going On?*, Centre for Sustainable Fashion, University of the Arts London, 2018, the "Union of Concerned Researchers in Fashion" was formed by Kate Fletcher, Timo Rissanen, Mathilda Tham, and Lynda Grose. A manifesto setting out actions can be accessed at: http://www. concernedresearchers.org/ (accessed August 9, 2019).

10 *Crafting Anatomies: Material, Performance, Identity* (2015). Available online: http:// www.boningtongallery.co.uk/exhibitions/crafting-anatomies (accessed May 20, 2019).

11 The School of Art and Design was established in 1843 to service the lace industry. See Jones (1993).

12 Selected artists from the exhibition also featured in this book in chapter order include: Briggs-Goode (2), Cope (3), Sadkowska (4), Townsend, Kettley, and Walker (5), Congdon (7), and Solomon (10).

13 Ellis Developments Ltd. Available online: http://www.ellisdev.co.uk (accessed May 20, 2019).

14 BBC News, "3D Printed Body Parts to Help Trauma Surgeons," September 26, 2016. Available online: https://www.bbc.co.uk/news/uk-england-nottinghamshire-37497182 (accessed June 15, 2019).

15 "Human Harp" (2019). Available online: https://www.humanharp.org (accessed June 10, 2019).

16 See Rhian Solomon, PhD: http://ldoc-cdt.ac.uk/designer-facilitator/ (accessed August 3, 2019).

17 "The Institute of Making is a multidisciplinary research club for those interested in the made world: from makers of molecules to makers of buildings, synthetic skin to spacecraft, soup to diamonds, socks to cities" (https://www.instituteofmaking.org. uk, accessed August 9, 2019).

18 See: https://www.instituteofmaking.org.uk/research/hands-of-x (accessed August 9, 2019).

19 Modern Meadow is "pioneering the creation of biologically advanced materials. [They] seek to transform the material world by unlocking the power of nature to inspire design for a healthier planet." Available online: http://www.modernmeadow.com (accessed April 10, 2019).

20 The Women's Health Movement is a feminist movement (originating in the late 1960s) that works to improve all aspects of women's healthcare.

21 OurOwnsKIN (2019). Available online: https://ourownskin.co.uk/ (accessed April 10, 2019).

22 Microfluidics is the science of manipulating and controlling fluids, usually in the range of microliters in networks of channels with dimensions from tens to hundreds of micrometers.

23 Agi Haines (2019). Available online: https://www.agihaines.com/home (accessed April 10, 2019).

References

Adamson, G. (2007) *Thinking Through Craft*, Oxford: Berg.

Adamson, G. (2010) *The Craft Reader*, Oxford: Berg.

Adamson, G. (2019) *Material Matters with Grant Gibson*. Available online: https://podtail.com/en/podcast/material-matters-with-grant-gibson/glenn-adamson-on-material-intelligence/ (accessed February 27, 2019).

Alderman, N., Beauman, N., Kennedy, A. L., Lynch, T., Dharker, I., and Kerr, P. (2018) *Beneath the Skin: Great Writers on the Body*, London: Wellcome Collection.

Almeida, T. (2017) "Designing Technologies for Intimate Care in Women," PhD thesis, Newcastle University. Available online: http://hdl.handle.net/10443/3868 (accessed August 3, 2019).

Anderson, J. W. (2017) *Disobedient Bodies: J. W. Anderson at The Hepworth*, ed. A. Bonacina, Wakefield: InOtherWords / The Hepworth.

Barthes, R. (2010) *The Fashion System*, trans. M. Ward and R. Howard, London: Vintage Classics.

Blackman, L. (2008) *The Body: The Key Concepts*, London: Berg.

Brand, S. (1999) *The Clock of the Long Now: Time and Responsibility*, New York: Basic Books.

Buchanan, R. (2002) "Design Research and the New Learning," *Design Issues*, 17(4): 3–23.

Calefato, P. (2019) "Fashionscapes," in A. Geczy and V. Karaminas (eds.), *The End of Fashion: Clothing and Dress in the Age of Globalization*, 31–45, London: Bloomsbury.

Charney, D. (2011) *The Power of Making: The Case for Making and Skills*, London: V&A Publishing.

Checinska, C. and Watson, G. (2016) "Social Fabric: Textiles, Art, Society and Politics," in J. Jefferies, D. Wood Conroy, and H. Clarke (eds.), *The Handbook of Textile Culture*, 279–92, London: Bloomsbury.

Clever, I. and Ruberg, W. (2014) "Beyond Cultural History? The Material Turn, Praxiography, and Body History," *Humanities*, 3(4): 546–66.

Congdon, A. (2016). *Amy Congdon*. Available online: http://www.amycongdon.com/ (accessed April 24, 2018).

Conklin, J. (2006) *Wicked Problems and Social Complexity*, CogNexus Institute. Available online: https://cognexus.org/wpf/wickedproblems.pdf (accessed August 3, 2019).

Cottam, H. and Leadbeater, C. (2004) *Red Paper 01 Health: Co-creating Services*, London: Design Council. Available online: https://www.designcouncil.org.uk/sites/default/files/asset/document/red-paper-health.pdf (accessed August 3, 2019).

Donetto, S., Pierri, P., Tsianakas, V., and Robert, G. (2015) "Experience-Based Co-design and Healthcare Improvement: Realizing Participatory Design in the Public Sector," *The Design Journal*, 18(2): 227–48.

Entwistle, J. (2015) *The Fashioned Body: Fashion, Dress and Modern Social Theory*, 2nd edn, Cambridge: Polity Press.

Entwistle, J. and Wilson, E., eds. (2001) *Body Dressing*, London: Berg.

Eriksen, M. A. (2012) "Material Matters in Co-Design," doctoral thesis, Aalto University.

Foster, H. (2004) "An Archival Impulse," *October*, 110: 3–22.

Francis, G. (2019) *Shapeshifters: A Doctor's Notes on Medicine and Human Change*, London: Wellcome Trust.

Franklin, K. and Till, C. (2018) *Radical Matter: Rethinking Materials for a Sustainable Future*, London: Thames and Hudson.

Geczy, A. and Karaminas, V., eds. (2019) *The End of Fashion: Clothing and Dress in the Age of Globalization*, London: Bloomsbury.

Giacomin, J. (2014) "What Is Human Centred Design?," *Design Journal*, 17(4): 606–23.

Ginsberg, A. D. and Chieza, N. (2019) "Editorial: Other Biological Futures," *Journal of Design and Science*, 4. Available online: https://jods.mitpress.mit.edu/pub/issue4-ginsberg-chieza (accessed August 3, 2019).

Guéry, F. and Deleule, D. (2014) *The Productive Body*, trans. Philip Barnard and Stephen Shapiro, Winchester: Zero Books.

Harris, J. (2013) "Digital Skin," *Textile: The Journal of Cloth and Culture*, 11(4): 242–61.

Hemmings, J. (2015) *Cultural Threads*, London: Bloomsbury Academic.

Hollander, A. (1978) *Seeing Through Clothes*, New York: Viking.

Ingold, T. (2011) *Being Alive: Essays on Movement, Knowledge and Description*, Abingdon: Routledge.

Jefferies, J., Wood Conroy, D., and Clarke, H. (2016) *The Handbook of Textile Culture*, London: Bloomsbury.

Jones, C. A. (1993) *A History of Nottingham School of Design*, Nottingham: Faculty of Art and Design, Nottingham Trent University.

Lanier, J. (2011) *You Are Not a Gadget*, London: Penguin.

Manzini, E. (2015) *Design, When Everybody Designs: An Introduction to Design for Social Innovation*, trans. R. Coad, Cambridge, MA: MIT Press.

Millar, L. and Kettle, A. (2018) *The Erotic Cloth*, London: Bloomsbury Academic.

Mol, A. (2003) *The Body Multiple: Ontology in Medical Practice*, Durham, NC: Duke University Press.

Mower, S. (2017) "New Eyes on the Establishment," in J. W. Anderson, *Disobedient Bodies*, London: In Other Words.

Niedderer, K. and Townsend, K. (2019) "Celebrating Craft," *Craft Research*, 10(1): 3–15.

Openshaw, J. (2015) *Postdigital Artisans: Craftsman with a New Aesthetic in Fashion, Art, Design and Architecture*, The Netherlands: Frame.

Oxman, N. (2015) *Design at the Intersection of Technology and Biology*. TED.com, March. Available online: https://www.ted.com/talks/neri_oxman_design_at_the_intersection_of_technology_and_biology?language=en (accessed June 22, 2017).

Paterson, M. W. D. (2004) "Skin: On the Cultural Border Between Self and the World," *The British Journal of Aesthetics*, 44(2): 208–10.

Pecorari, C. (2016) "Blocking: Between Composition and Tableau," *Contributor*, 16. Available online: https://contributormagazine.com/16-2/ (accessed August 3, 2019).

Pierce, G. (2017) "The Fabric of the City: Archive Textiles Inspire a Collaborative Project in Contemporary Design and Innovation." In Proceedings of *Intersections: Collaborations in Textile Design Research* Conference, Loughborough University London, September 1. Available online: http://www.lboro.ac.uk/media/wwwlboroacuk/external/content/schoolsanddepartments/aed/downloads/Pierce_INTERSECTIONS2017.pdf (accessed August 3, 2019).

Prendiville, A. (2016) "Connectivity Through Service Design," in P. Sparke and F. Fisher (eds.), *The Routledge Companion to Design Studies*, 40–53, Abingdon: Routledge.

Ranner, V. (2018). *Veronica Ranner*. Available online: https://www.veronicaranner.com (accessed July 24, 2018).

Ravetz, A., Kettle, A., and Felcey, H. (2013) *Collaboration Through Craft*, London: Bloomsbury.

Rocamora, A. (2015) *Thinking Through Fashion: A Guide to Key Theorists*, London: I. B. Tauris.

Sanders, E. B.-N. and Stappers, P. J. (2014) "Probes, Toolkits and Prototypes: Three Approaches to Making in Codesigning," *Codesign-International Journal of Cocreation in Design and the Arts*, 10(1): 5–14.

Schön, D. A. (1984) "The Architectural Studio as an Exemplar of Education for Reflection-in-Action," *Journal of Architectural Education*, 38(1): 2–9.

Sennett, R. (2008) *The Craftsman*, New Haven, CT: Yale University Press.

Solanki, S. (2018) *Why Materials Matter: Responsible Design for a Better World*, London: Prestel.

Solomon, R. (2013) "sKINship: An Exchange of Material Understanding Between Plastic Surgery and Pattern Cutting for Fashion," in A. Ravetz, A. Kettle, and H. Felcey (eds.), *Collaboration Through Craft*, London: Bloomsbury.

Steedman, C. (2001) *Dust*, Manchester: Manchester University Press.

Thackara, J. (2013) *In the Bubble: Designing in a Complex World*, Cambridge, MA: MIT Press.

Townsend, K. and Sadkowska, A. (2017) "Textiles as Material Gestalt: Cloth as a Catalyst in the Co-designing Process," *Journal of Textile Design Research and Practice*, 5(2): 208–31.

Turner, B. S. (2008) *The Body and Society: Explorations in Social Theory*, 3rd edn, London: Sage.

Vainshtein, O. (2019) "Photography and the Body," in A. Geczy and V. Karaminas (eds.), *The End of Fashion: Clothing and Dress in the Age of Globalization*, 47–65, London: Bloomsbury.

Verhelst, B. and Debo, K. (2008) *Maison Martin Margiela "20" The Exhibition*, Antwerp: MoMu.

Vigneshwara, M. (2018) "The Screaming Sun: Choreographing Synesthesia," Proceedings of the *Twelfth International Conference on Tangible, Embedded, and Embodied Interaction—TEI'18*, Stockholm, March 18–21. Available online: https://dl.acm.org/authorize.cfm?key=N43315 (accessed August 3, 2019).

Von Busch, O., Cuba, L., Gatzen, P., Moon, C., Rissanen, T., and Wissinger, E. (2017) *Animal Laborans: The Labor of Fashion*, New York: The Fashion Praxis Collective / Self Passage.

Wilson, E. (2003) *Adorned in Dreams: Fashion and Modernity*, London: I. B. Taurus.

Woodward, S. (2007) *Why Women Wear What They Wear*, Oxford: Berg.

Zellweger, C. (2011) "'26 Stitches': Extending the Definition of Body Adornment Today," *Craft Research*, 2(1): 151–60.

Part One

The Archived Body

Edited by Amanda Briggs-Goode

2

The Archived Lace Body

Contemporary Artist Designer Responses

Amanda Briggs-Goode and Gail Baxter

Archives and lace

In welcoming visitors to the Nottingham Trent University (NTU) lace archive there have been a number of reactions that have fascinated us about how people engage and respond to this space. The archive itself is a repurposed room, its existing low lighting, white walls, gray carpet, and institutional furniture received the addition of a bank of archiving shelves in 2010. The view of this archive shelving system as an initial indicator of what the room holds begins to shape the reactions of visitors—students, scholars, or members of the public—as they enter. We have noted their instant response to the environmental conditions— the low lighting, the unique smell, a combination of aged fabric, paper, and leather, all promising a glimpse into the past. It is a simultaneously seductive and intriguing space in which visitors respond to these sensory codes and the beauty of the lace with "oohs" and "ahs" and flutters of excitement. As Jefferies states, the archive enables: "a process of exchange. Interpretation is coloured by our current values and knowledge and in this way it is permeable to its users" (2016: 102). The objects held within the lace archive, being textile based, also elicit reactions that connect with intimate, bodily sensorial experiences: "cloth is permeated with so many memories in its bodily associations and its haptic sensations: stain, the cut, the feel, the drape, the smell, the sound all of which may activate the erotic through the remembrance of the forgotten" (Millar and Kettle 2018: 5).

Entwistle (2015: 324) articulates dress as "embellishing" the body with each material conveying its own idiosyncratic meaning to the previously unclothed form. Lace might be described as a "concentrated form" of this "embellishment" which, alongside the "eroticism" and "memory" that Millar and Kettle (2018) describe with its ability to simultaneously "reveal and conceal," allows glimpses of flesh, thus leading to intimate connections with our bodies. Lace is therefore "loaded" with this meaning, which has also been mediated by the ritualized contexts in which lace is often used: "Lace plays a part in the significant moments of our lives: marriage, birth and death all resonate with the symbolic use of lace as the erotic and ritualized" (Briggs-Goode 2018: 50).

Defined as luxury fabric since the fifteenth century, lace was "deployed to demonstrate wealth, taste and rank" (St Clair 2018: 143). However, due to progress in terms of mechanization, man-made fabrics, and shifts in society's structures, lace has now become simultaneously ubiquitous, hidden, and classless—there are few women not wearing lace on a daily basis (it can be a challenge to find undergarments without it). All of these factors contribute to our perceptions of lace being quite literally woven into the fabric of our lives.

It is in this context that we investigate how creative practitioners interpret and transform notions of lace and the body from archives, or collections, through a series of critical, metaphorical, or narrative methods. These artists and designers open up spaces for us to engage with discussion about the body, gender, heritage, and memory in contemporary culture.

Archives and the senses

Our experiences within these evocative and sensory environments invoke what Derrida referred to as "archive fever," where he describes the archive as the "place of origins, the place from which order is given, the place where order and knowledge based on 'official' records are to be found" (Checinska and Watson 2016: 284) and which Steedman (2001: 3) interprets as our human need for "inception, beginnings and origins" and ultimately a desire to find the "truth." The "truth" only becomes apparent through our interactions with archives, because archives are full of stuff and "as stuff, it just sits there until it is read, and used, and narrativised" (ibid: 68). Time in archives is often precious and accompanied by fellow travelers who either illuminate the way or chaperone the experience but with whom we: "become entangled in a web of classifications, categories, keywords and so on; archivists and researchers become accomplices in experiencing the traps of the archives, the secret passages and hidden rooms" (Jefferies 2016: 102).

For many of us, this wandering into secret passages and hidden rooms is the joy of visiting archives alongside the mediators of this knowledge as well as the privilege of working with them. In the case of the exhibition *Lace Unarchived* held at NTU in 2018 the curator intended to both reveal the legacy of the art school, established in 1843, and its impact on generations of lace designers who worked within the region and across the globe. The "mood" of the exhibition was intended to create something of the sensory experience of entering the archive, through low lighting, focused upon illuminating six large vitrines, full of samples and ephemera from the archive to reveal its breadth. Significantly it was intended to expose simultaneously the "stuff" from the lace archive alongside recent art and design practice to demonstrate the power of archives to inform and inspire creative practice as well as illustrate that the manufacture of Nottingham lace is still an important part of commercial practice. Therefore businesses such as Cluny Lace, Morton, Young and Borland (MYB), and Sophie Hallette were shown, as well as products from designers and brands who have used these manufacturers to develop their ideas. The lace for Burberry's lace coats was manufactured by Cluny and both Timorous Beasties' Devil Damask and Hobbs' Tijou Lace Dress used MYB for their recent lace collections. The exhibition also included examples from a collaboration between the NTU lace archive and the high street retailer Oasis (to produce a womenswear collection) as well as the work of artist Matthew Woodham who was commissioned to produce a piece of work inspired by the archive which he realized through moving image. These

Figure 2.1 *Lace Unarchived*, Bonington Gallery, Nottingham Trent University, 2018. Photography by Julian Lister.

works demonstrated explicit connections to the lace archive and therefore the relationship between the past and the present enabling a translation of what they found in ways relevant to their contemporary contexts. Jefferies (2019: 254) referencing Steedman (2001) in her review of *Lace Unarchives* states: "there is a 'trembling excitement' that grips the artist-designer-researcher and historian when archive collections are made visible. When made highly visible as in *Lace Unarchived* there is another trembling excitement as the Gallery is awash with lace, color and technical vibrancy, which offer the future of design some exciting possibilities."

Cloth and the body

Our experiences of cloth throughout our life creates a strong affinity to its touch and the relationship between our skin and the layers of fabric we wear becomes ultimately indistinguishable—it protects us and we become vulnerable without the layers of fabric holding, restraining, draping, embellishing. As Goett (2016: 122) states, textiles become the physical manifestation of:

> the tear of pain and happiness, the sweat of anxiety and excitement both part of the self and absorbed by the cloth, perception and affection, inside and out, body and object interwoven in memory. Folds, entanglements and creases, comfort and restraint, interwoven strands, loose ends, unravelling threads, seams and knots, wear and tear, invention and imagination, magic and symbolism, are all embedded in the fabrics of our life.

Textiles' relationship with our embodied selves makes them powerful signifiers of our personal memories and lived experience. They become advocates of the passage of time through our collective memory and via scientific clues identified through the color, fabric type, style, technical details, wear, etc. Roberts (2018: 62) in reflecting on cloth says: "I am seduced by the material, the look, the touch and the hidden narrative and histories of these fabrics ... [clothing] enables us to discover not only how things were made, but to appreciate their lived embodied histories." Cloth, and in particular lace, holds numerous relationships with our bodies. "The glimpsed body is most present when the clothing is made from lace, or contains lace elements. The lace allows for an undefined, a hoped for suggestion, caught for a moment, but not wholly revealed—an intimate space between two surfaces" (Millar 2011: 6).

Entwistle (2015: 327) proposes that "the boundary between self and other, individual and society ... is intimate and personal, since our dress forms the visible envelope of the self" and this "boundary" is subject to social codes and moral obligations. Should we fail to meet these obligations we are often left feeling embarrassed, particularly if what we reveal relates to the more intimate body beneath the outer layer. Lace, a decorative and "luxurious" fabric that brings with it a multitude of diverse and varied weights, scales, and drape qualities and, as such, is able to be used as a delicate binding as in the context of "intimates" or a fabric with less drape, or a denser pattern for outerwear pieces. The "practical pointlessness" of lace was identified by Thomas Fuller in the seventeenth century as he identified lace as a "superfluous wearing because it doth neither hide nor heat" (St Claire 2018: 145). These factors and the potential for the reveal/conceal to "offer" a view of "below the surface" challenge these more typical social conventions and codes and therefore make lace particularly compelling fabric for creative practitioners to explore.

Interpretations of archives, lace, and the body

Foster (2004: 4) describes an "archival impulse" whereby "artists seek to make historical information, often lost or displaced, physically present" and to "distribute ideas" or "liberate activity" (ibid: 7). As Checinska and Watson (2016: 285) argue this enables "counter narratives" to be produced; in this context, the archive is "an active producer of knowledge, as opposed to the archive as a passive receptacle in which knowledge resides." The methods of interpretation that artists might use to explore this "truth" could be explored metaphorically, critically, or literally. Four practitioners have been selected to demonstrate different approaches through their interpretations of archives with literal, narrative, or metaphorical links to lace and connections to the body.

Joy Buttress

New narratives emerged through the work of artist Joy Buttress in 2012–13 in an exhibition held at Nottingham Castle entitled *Lace Works: Contemporary Art and Nottingham Lace*. As Dean (2013: 67), the curator of the exhibition, states, Buttress demonstrates "an interest in the ambiguities surrounding lace and our responses to it." Her piece "Worn" utilized French peasant undergarments that reveal their embodied experiences of labor, alongside the functional requirements of their time. The garments, abstracted through their physical elevation above head height and internal lighting, bring to our attention details within the garments through the use of intricate stitching, beading, wax, and gold foil. While entranced, and momentarily seduced by their aesthetic, we begin to ponder why and where these details are placed, on the internal side of the garments, concluding that this is likely to be at the points where the bodily secretions of everyday life might appear. Buttress stated that she wanted "the viewer to be challenged to search for unseen and concealed interventions on the inner surface of the garments, suggesting intimacy, secrecy and suppression" (Dean 2013: 67). This approach, which explores the duality of the simultaneous experience of beauty and repulsion, is a mechanism that she first utilized as part of her doctoral research which resulted in a solo exhibition in 2012 called *Lacuna*. Of this practice Buttress states: "The qualities of lace as a purely ornamental fabric cover the wearer with decorative patterns that can represent heritage and wealth but which can also add sexual tension and erotic significance, engaging the viewer to judge and connect with the person wearing lace" (2013a: 49). The ambivalence of meanings associated with lace precipitated her interest in forms of practice that instigated ideas around gender, beauty, and sexuality.

Figure 2.2 Joy Buttress, "Worn," *Lace Works*, Nottingham Castle, 2013. Photograph by David Severn.

During her PhD research Buttress developed ideas to enable the visual exploration of these concepts and she began to visit a number of archives around the UK, including: Nottingham Trent University Lace Archive, Nottingham City Museums archive, Dents Glove Museum in Warminster, and The Fashion Museum in Bath. This led to a practice that utilized the "skin" of vintage kid gloves to act as a "canvas" on which the stitch was applied. This resulted in exquisitely ornamented gloves utilizing beads, iron filings, human hair, and threads to create the details, in which, as Dean (2013: 67) states: "these lace inspired embellishments appear to grow from the leather." The "skin" and "stitch" in this context acted as a visual metaphor between "reveal and conceal" duality of "skin" and "lace" and also bring our attention to the labor, mainly female, involved in lace making. Tantalizingly the gloves were placed in sealed tea crates, lit internally and with "peep" holes cut into them at challenging heights—too high, too low. This rendered the beautiful stitching, frustratingly difficult to gaze upon and admire, impossible to touch. Much like the fleeting moment of interaction between skin and lace where as Millar (Millar and Kettle 2018: 12) states: "Always it is in that ambiguous space of between and becoming that the erotic floats."

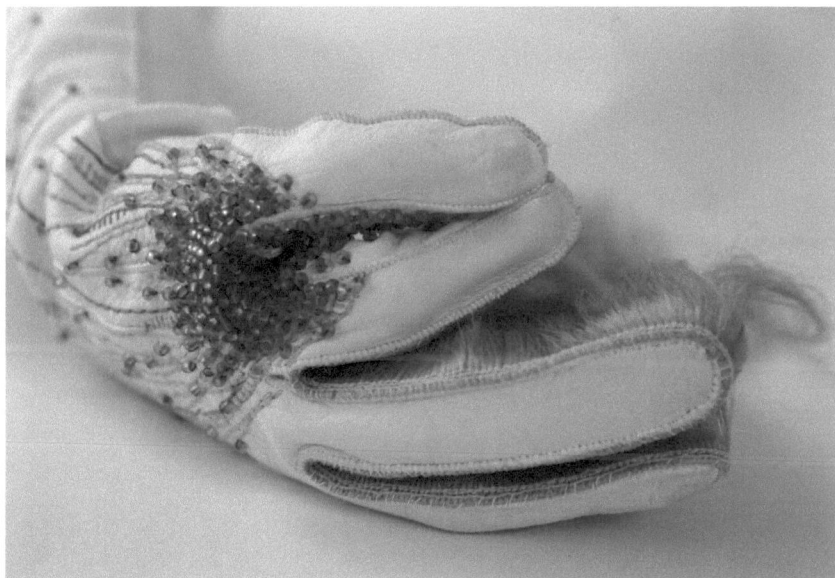

Figure 2.3 Joy Buttress, *Lacuna*, Bonington Gallery, Nottingham Trent University, 2012. Photo courtesy of Bonington Gallery.

Cal Lane

In contrast, artist Cal Lane seeks to produce counter-narratives through her approach to materials and processes that are placed at the antithesis of those associated with the feminine and are read against the highly gendered subject of lace. Lane does this by subverting the tools and materials usually associated with masculinity and rendering them useless. She achieves this through manually cutting lace patterns into reclaimed metal objects using an oxyacetylene torch, which she describes as both drawing and sculpting (Steifle Edwards 2007: 98). Lane reveals a series of challenges to meaning through the change of function of the object when seen in conjunction with a lace pattern. Spades, car hoods, and oil drums, among other industrial objects, are rendered useless by intricate lace patterns cut into their surface. Lane says of herself: "I like to work as a visual devil's advocate, using contradiction as a way to create an empathetic image. By comparing and contrasting ideas and materials my work creates a visual clash but also a sense of balance" (Lane n.d.).

Lane has engaged with archives and historic collections of lace and, after visiting a lace museum in Belgium where she saw how handmade lace is made, she recognized that she "was attracted to the focus and repetitive motion of the work, much like welding and cutting" (The Design Center 2009: 83). Lane also used the archive at The Design Center, Philadelphia University to search the Quaker Lace Collection to find a piece suitable for the commission that she was undertaking for their exhibition *Lace in Translation*, held in 2009–10. The lace was required to have various technical aspects to ensure that it could maintain the structural integrity of the metal through the process of cutting. She noted that: "Searching through the collection of lace pieces and garments was beautifully mysterious. The old tattered bits of lace carefully arranged into books created a detailed study of patterns, like reading a visual novel of texture, colour, pattern" (The Design Center 2009: 83).

Lane's work has often explored large-scale pieces, beyond the scale of the body, however, *Disobedient Virtues* in 2016 finds her inverting her approach to materials, "the absurdity of having opposing extremist stances is there for reaction" (The Design Center 2009: 83). So, instead of inserting found lace imagery into an incongruous object, this time she explores the lace "ready-made." She reverses the shift of meaning from lace patterning rendering a functional, solid, metallic object useless to the use of metal to render our understanding of lace fabric underwear useless. Representing women's lace underwear in solid metal in both two and three dimensions she draws attention to their original

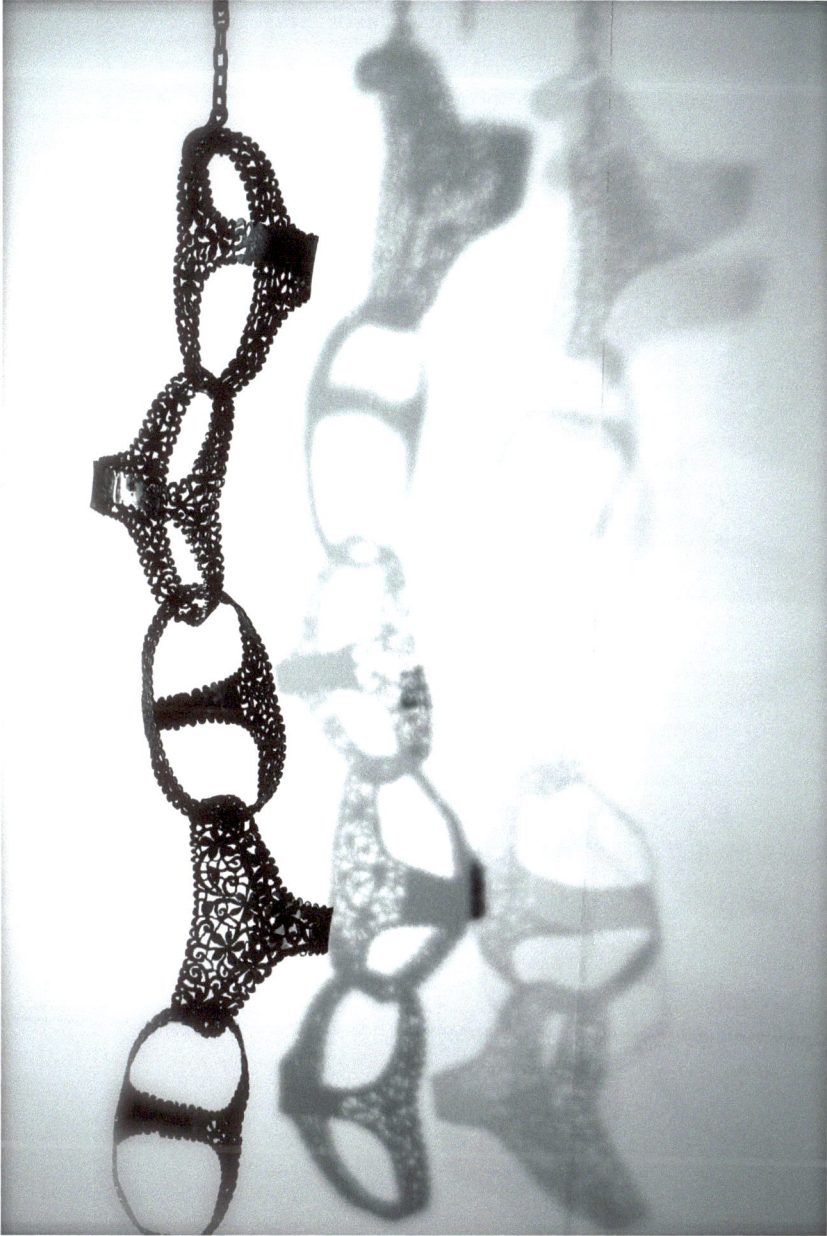

Figure 2.4 Cal Lane, *Disobedient Virtues*, 2016. Photograph by Cal Lane.

flimsy form with the artworks' solid and static materiality. The absence of the body in these "floating" three-dimensional static pieces alerts us to what is missing and inevitably to references regarding chastity.

Figure 2.5 Cal Lane, *Covered*, 2005. Photograph by Cal Lane.

In contrast to utilizing masculine materials and processes, Lane created another more intimate and bodily collection of work in 2005: *Covered*. In this group of images Lane visually evokes the essence of icing sugar stenciled onto a cake, with all of its aesthetic and sensory pleasure. In this artwork, though, her collection of images is created by sifting dirt directly onto a human form through large pieces of lace, thus the bodily form distorts and undulates the pattern of the intricate lace design. Of this practice she comments: "It creates a dialogue of beautiful filth. On the people, it's dirty, sexy, beautiful and morbid. On the floor it relates to ornamental rugs, a temporary form of printmaking to be later swept up" (Steifle Edwards 2007: 98). The piece strongly resonates with the concept of the funeral, the use of earth as the media and lace as a tool echoing the ceremonial effect of the burial.

Mal Burkinshaw

Program Director of Fashion Design at Edinburgh College of Art, Mal Burkinshaw, has used fashion design processes as a creative methodology to question the contemporary fashion marketplace and its approach to body shape in order to challenge contemporary notions of beauty and body image. As part of a wider project called *Beauty by Design* launched by the Scottish National Portrait Gallery and in conjunction with the "All Walks Beyond the Catwalk" initiative, Burkinshaw created *Silhouettes en Dentelle* (see Burkinshaw 2014). Inspired initially by the "Reformation to Revolution Gallery" in the Scottish National Portrait Gallery, where portraits of a number of significant figures from the Renaissance period of history reside, including Mary, Queen of Scots and James VI. This interpretation utilizes lace, one of the key signifiers of wealth, status, and hierarchy during the Renaissance, reinterpreted through exquisite machine-made lace by the French manufacturer of Nottingham lace, Sophie Hallette. Using lace references "the centuries of highly skilled activity involved in making this delicate material" (Beauty by Design 2014). In this work Burkinshaw creates a dialogue between past and present notions of "normalized" body shapes through using a recognizable garment, a jacket, to challenge perceptions of beauty. The jackets do not conform to standard sizes and are non-gender-specific, inviting us to question the shapes and proportions of the body. We are invited to make comparisons about the body ideals of the Renaissance with their "cherubesque" forms that contrast dramatically with our sense of the body ideals of today. The work reflects upon the potential for self-sabotage, which can be the powerful impact of today's visual culture.

The work itself was created painstakingly echoing the labor of the sixteenth-century lace makers. This was undertaken by Burkinshaw using a large light box to collage motifs of lace, which were individually appliqued by hand onto "high performance" netting. In describing the process of creating each jacket he says it "was both reactive and instinctive; in a sense, each jacket has been 'painted with lace'" (ibid.).

Burkinshaw used lace to explore gender, body size, and notions of beauty through the production of seven jackets that develop in scale and grow progressively larger. His making process creates a paradox: lace was developed as an industrialized process in the early nineteenth century to bring speed and efficiency savings in order to make lace affordable to the burgeoning middle classes. Therefore, the overlaying of this product of machine-made skill with the skilled labor of the hand inverses our Western industrial narratives of the machine replacing the hand and this inversion elicits a creative dichotomy that has been beautifully responded to. The process also acknowledges the highly skilled lace makers who would have once made lace by hand to demonstrate the status and wealth of the aristocrats found in the portraits. In 1668, Charles II spent *c.* £80 on lace in one single purchase (St Clair 2018: 148), today this translates to £13,000 (MeasuringWorth 2018).

Figure 2.6 Mal Burkinshaw, *Silhouettes en Dentelle*, 2014. Photograph by Mal Burkinshaw.

Burkinshaw's jackets have been physically exhibited at the Scottish National Portrait Gallery and the Cité International de la Dentelle et de la Mode in Calais, and, more recently, images of the jackets have been projected at large scale in the exhibition *Lace Unarchived* in Nottingham. Presented in this way their appearance, reminiscent of X-rays, drew viewers to poignantly question the absence of the person who might inhabit them. To ask: who would wear these jackets—what size and shape might they be? The concept of the work and indeed the project was to decode the beauty ideals of this era and contrast this with a contemporary, non-gendered silhouette therefore highlighting some of the negative issues around body shape in today's fashion industry.

Danica Maier

Danica Maier has worked with both lace and archives in a number of different ways for over a decade. Through these inquiries she has approached lace both literally and metaphorically. She engages with it as a drawing tool while also referencing contemporary pornography; exploring this through either anamorphically distorted imagery or through handmade lace practices. Maier has also utilized archives, most recently the lace archive at NTU, as part of a wider project called "Bummock," to explore "the undiscovered" through a creative method referred to as "controlled rummaging." This work, resolved in a musical collaboration, draws upon the lace-drafting process as a source of rhythm.

From 2005 Maier has worked with textiles and lace in particular to develop a collection of work through which to explore pornographic imagery from "top shelf" magazines. In her work, as O'Reilly (2005: 1) states, "Pattern and lace in particular has an oddly double-edged set of associations through, from Victorian uprightness and indigenous handcrafts to sluttish ostentation." These dualities and inherent contradictions are explored in a number of works that she has exhibited internationally: *Firelock, Midlands and Tooraloorals,* and *Adam and Eve It.* All of these works use narrow strips of lace ribbon and dressmakers' pins. The lace comes mainly from an archive of lace and textiles which were left to her by her grandmother, and is wrapped around nails, reminiscent of "thread and nail" drawings. These images create multilayered, anamorphic distortions that also present the phenomena of "multistable perception," whereby these 3-D drawings can flip from being patterns, abstract or chaotic images, into a second of clarity when the image comes into perspective and you see clearly what is being represented. The movement implied in this "flipping" is resonant of lace's capacity to conceal and reveal. Lace, Maier proposes, is not being used in this context as a sexually charged fabric, but in pastel colors to counter the

Figure 2.7 Danica Maier, "Have Lunch Downtown," London Printworks Trust, Brixton, as part of the exhibition *Adam and Eve It,* 2005. Photograph by Michael Hinds.

Figure 2.8 Danica Maier, "Flowers of Chivalry," Ñandutí lace made as part of an artist's residency in Paraguay with the Museo Del Barro. These pieces were made with the help of local lace makers, 2005. Photograph by Danica Maier.

pornographic imagery—and as Buttress (2013b: 65) states "the distinction of the two sides of lace underpins ideas found in her work that balance the domestic and decorative with the subversive and unspoken."

Another body of work produced at this time was *Intraducible* which was produced as part of a residency in Paraguay. This work is connected conceptually to the lace ribbon drawings but was interpreted through the handmade lace practice of Paraguayan women. The unexpected nature of the images in the context of product and production created a surprising element, the seemingly decorative and domestic being contrasted with a subversive and sexualized content of the imagery. Vinebaum (2015: 73) comments that Maier's work is "both unsettling and provocative" as it unsettles our understanding of women's domestic, decorative crafts as they become "sites for women's self assertion." A recurring theme evident in the works described is the absence of performance and how the static nature of the images created highlights their rhythmic resonance.

Maier's most recent work (2018) is entitled "Bummock: New Artistic Responses to Unseen Parts of Archives," conducted by artists Danica Maier, Andrew Bracey, and Lucy Renton. This project has sought to challenge the orthodoxy of the accompanied "expert driven" archive visit. Having undertaken a previous project that had included accompanied access to the lace archive, Maier enquired about having unfettered access for a project that, as the title denotes, would enable the artists to "discover" the "hidden depths" of the archive. After relevant instruction on handling objects, and establishing ground rules, the artists were enabled to enter the archive unaccompanied to engage with "controlled rummaging" to seek the unknown and the unpredictable. This project has resulted in an exhibition, symposium, and book, of which the purpose was to explore and establish new or alternative methods of access to archives and collections as well as exploring the ethical relationship between artists and archives. This method elicited a more personal and revelatory exposé of the archive, in contrast with a more typical experience. Vaughan (2019: 81) states: "The tips of the archive collections might more easily enable the archivist to provide access and 'tips' inspire the awe and aura of the archive in the general public through the tropes of fame and the status of official histories." The work that Maier exhibited as a result of this project exposed the lace-drafting process. This explored its pattern and rhythm, enticing the audience to engage in their own performance through the use of a music box. The instrument had been pre-primed with the notations of the draft, hole punched into a paper ribbon. Creating a paper lace ribbon also echoed the Jacquard cards which drove the patterning of lace on Leavers lace machines.

Activating archives

The relationship between lace and the body is not a new one but the artists who have been case studied in this chapter demonstrate new approaches through the methods that they use to explore this material connection. These creatives use this relationship to draw out metaphor and narratives to engage with playful, provocative ideas related to a number of dualities—beauty/repulsion, rhythm/static, and reveal/conceal. They have also explored counter-narratives through subversion, absence, gender, body size, skills, and production. The unique interplays of lace and the body appear to be situated in the fact that lace and the body, through the concept of reveal and conceal, can create duality and dichotomy and in so doing open up the space for dialogue of the space in between these two states.

Buttress examines the unseen, the duality of reveal/conceal and beauty/repulsion through exquisitely embroidered "canvases" in the form of "ready-made" garments. In doing so she requests that you consider the history of women's labor in the production of decorative consumer goods. Lane approaches her work through counter-narratives, her choice of materials and tools enabling you to reflect on these lace objects and in so doing consider the absence of the body. The work also encourages you to focus on assumptions about skill and gender. Burkinshaw's work reflects specifically on contemporary fashion and its polarized view of body shape, gender expectations, and beauty. Maier, by contrast, explores subversion and the unsettling of narratives through provocative imagery and rhythm.

Welcoming artists and designers into archives is a key aspect of maintaining their currency and visibility. These visitors, with their idiosyncratic expectations and curiosity, challenge curators and keepers to locate and explore new contexts and connections between their questions and the material heritage within the archive. The dialogue that occurs in these contexts is facilitated by and through objects, senses, gesture, and spoken language—all of which are absorbed, nurtured, and cultivated to become art works. These pieces offer us an opportunity for reflection and scrutiny of histories, gender, bodies, and materiality in our cultural context but more importantly for us as individuals.

References

Beauty by Design (2014) "Mal Burkinshaw, *Silhouettes en Dentelle—Series 1*, 2013–14." Available online: http://www.beautybydesign.org.uk/mal-burkinshaw/4586840261 (accessed October 2, 2018).

Briggs-Goode, A. (2018) "Black Holes: An Exploration of Absence," *Selvedge: The Fabric of Your Life*, 82: 50–4.

Burkinshaw, M. (2014) *Silhouettes en Dentelle*, Edinburgh: Scottish National Portrait Gallery.

Buttress, J. (2013a) "The Metaphorical Value of Lace in Contemporary Art: The Transformative Process of a Practice-Led Inquiry," doctoral thesis, Nottingham Trent University.

Buttress, J. (2013b) "Worn," exhibited at *Lace Works: Contemporary Art and Nottingham Lace*, Nottingham Castle.

Checinska, C. and Watson, G. (2016) "Social Fabric: Textiles, Art, Society and Politics," in J. Jefferies, D. Wood Conroy, and H. Clark (eds.), *The Handbook of Textile Culture*, 279–92, London: Bloomsbury.

Dean, D. (2013) "Lace Works: Contemporary Art and Nottingham Lace," in A. Briggs-Goode and D. Dean (eds.), *lace:here:now*, 64–75, London: Black Dog Publishing.

Entwistle, J. (2015) "Fashion and the Fleshy Body: Dress as Embodied Practice," *Fashion Theory*, 4(3): 323–47.

Foster, H. (2004) "An Archival Impulse," *October*, 110: 3–22.

Goett, S. (2016) "Materials, Memories and Metaphors," in J. Jefferies, D. Wood Conroy, and H. Clark (eds.), *The Handbook of Textile Culture*, 121–36, London: Bloomsbury.

Jefferies, J. (2016) "Editorial Introduction: Textile, Narrative, Identity, Archives," in J. Jefferies, D. Wood Conroy, and H. Clark (eds.), *The Handbook of Textile Culture*, 97–106, London: Bloomsbury.

Jefferies, J. (2019) "Review of *Lace Unarchived*," *The Journal of Textile Design Research and Practice*, 7(2): 246–54.

Lane, C. (n.d.) "Cal Lane," artist's website. Available online: http://callane.com (accessed October 5, 2018).

MeasuringWorth (2018) "Purchasing Power of British Pounds from 1270 to Present." Available online: https://www.measuringworth.com/calculators/ppoweruk/ (accessed October 10, 2018).

Millar, L. (2011) "Transparent Boundaries," in K. Millar (ed.), *Lost in Lace: Transparent Boundaries*, 5–14, Birmingham: Birmingham Museum & Art Gallery.

Millar, L. and Kettle, A., eds. (2018) *The Erotic Cloth: Seduction and Fetishism in Textiles*, London: Bloomsbury.

O'Reilly, S. (2005) "Undercover," commissioned essay to accompany D. Maier and M. Whall's exhibition, *Adam and Eve It*, London Printworks Trust, London.

Roberts, D. (2018) "The Rustle of Taffeta: The Value of Hapticity in Research and Reconstruction of an Eighteenth Century Sack-Back Dress," in L. Millar and A. Kettle (eds.), *The Erotic Cloth: Seduction and Fetishism in Textiles*, 62–72, London: Bloomsbury.

St Clair, K. (2018) *The Golden Thread: How Fabric Changed History*, London: John Murray.

Steedman, C. (2001) *Dust*, Manchester: Manchester University Press.

Steifle Edwards, J. (2007) "Cal Lane," in D. R. McFadden, J. Scanlan, and J. Steifle Edwards, *Radical Lace and Subversive Knitting*, 98–101, New York: Museum of Arts and Design.

The Design Centre at Philadelphia University (2009) *Lace in Translation*, Philadelphia, PA: The Design Centre at Philadelphia University.

Vaughan, S. (2019) "Artists' Methods in the Lace Archive," in A. Bracey and D. Maier (eds.), *Bummock: The Lace Archive*, 74–81, Waddington: Flipping the Bummock Press.

Vinebaum, L. (2015) "Fxxxing Homework: Danica Maier's Art of Domestic Subversion," in D. Maier (ed.), *Grafting Propriety: From Stitch to the Drawn Line*, 71–9, London: Black Dog Publishing.

3

Disarmed

Lasting Impressions

Jo Cope in conversation with Johannes Reponen

Mannequins and shoe lasts document an imprint onto which new physical realities can be projected. With their uniform appearances, these objects have stamped a multitude of past narratives while offering an opportunity for new, unknown aesthetics to emerge. Central to the work of conceptual fashion designer Jo Cope, who creates speculative objects that blur the line between art, design craft, and fashion, is the presence of these seemingly anonymous body molds.

Drawing from philosophy, psychology, and psychotherapy, and inspired by thinkers such as Maurice Merleau-Ponty, who "identified the body as the hidden source of our ability to construct all meaning within the world" (Trimingham 2011: 112) and Sigmund Freud's theories on the conscious and subconscious mind and human behavior, Cope positions fashion as an extension of self. Starting with the body, she creates clothing artefacts that initially seem recognizable and wearable but on a closer inspection invite the viewer to consider both the sensory and practical implications of wearing them alongside their meaning. For her, an artefact is both functional and surreal, blending the motions of anatomy with logical and potential actions.

Cope's method of abstraction and conceptualization builds on the practice of fashion designers such as Hussein Chalayan, Martin Margiela, and Issey Miyake who have explored fashion's duality as a consumable and object artistically extending far beyond this primary function into realms of performance and installation. Yet, despite her affinity with and understanding of fashion, Cope seeks to reject its very purpose as a commercial commodity in search of its deeper meaning and its potential alternative value within society. In line with practitioners such as Oskar Schelmmer and Rebecca Horn, the body becomes extended as a way to manifest the mental and the physical. The material and the unseen negative space become a way to illustrate relationships between the self and the surrounding environment. It is discussed in *Body Landscapes* that "Rebecca Horn is constantly preoccupied with … things concealed behind their outward appearance" and that "the viewer's interest must be caught by something in these objects that is of deeper human interest" (Horn 2004: 19–20)

Traditional craft techniques collide with new making methodologies and this enables Cope to extend the boundaries of how an object can be experienced in contemporary culture. Personal and social archives act as a catalyst to create symbolic objects that have a direct connection to the body through fit. Much in the same way as artists such as Tracey Emin and Louise Bourgeois, Cope aims to archive life through her practice. It is at these multiple intersections that the dynamism of Cope's work can be found.

In conversation with fashion critic and scholar Johannes Reponen, Jo Cope talks about critical fashion practice, the role of body in performance and the physical craft process of making lasting impressions.

Your bachelor degree is in Fashion Design from Nottingham Trent University and your master's degree is in Fashion Artefacts from London College of Fashion. You create objects one can wear and you call yourself a conceptual fashion designer, yet your work is most likely to be seen in galleries and exhibitions or on stage as opposed to on the streets and in shops. Could you describe how your work evolved from studying a more traditional design discipline into something that is more reminiscent of art?

When I began studying fashion, I realized quickly that it was the relationship between clothes and self that interested me. Commercial fashion did not offer the right type of stimulus and I wanted to situate my practice in a place of breaking conventions, where fashion could talk about "itself" and "the self." From the outset, I began to create garments and accessories that weren't necessarily commercially viable but, instead, could transform and move. "Aerodynamic Dress" (Figure 3.1), exhibited and commissioned by Silverstone racetrack, is an example of this, cut to adapt with the moving body in transformation from a lying to standing position. The fact that they had little purpose on a clothes rail led me to find an alternative reality, initially through performance. Looking to fashion's future, I felt it could have a life of its own with multiple means of existence. I was interested in challenging people's visual preconceptions and started by approaching the design process with questions. The use of conceptual thinking allowed me to start to break down the essence of fashion in order to represent it in less obvious ways, ignoring fixed typography.

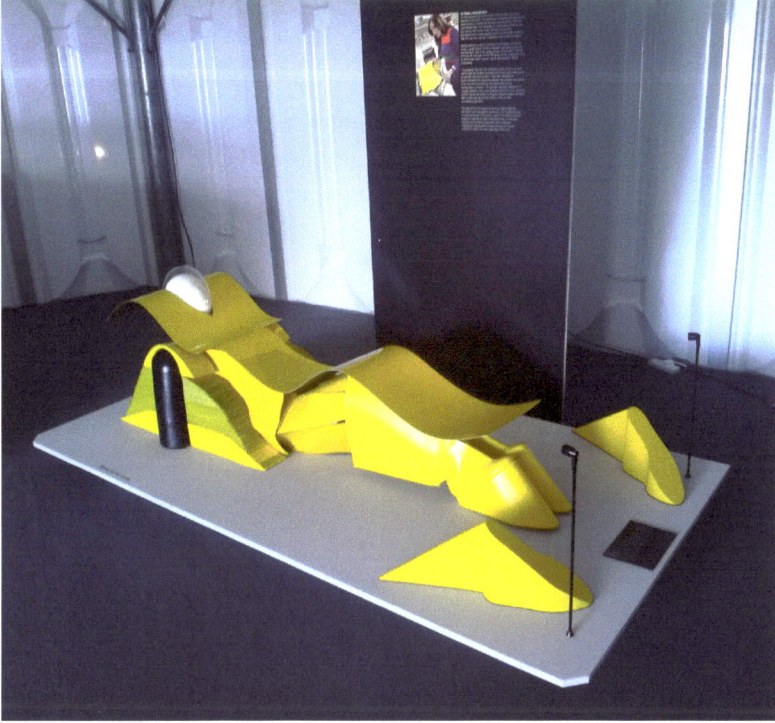

Figure 3.1 Aerodynamic Dress, Jo Cope 2011 for 'Formula Fashion' exhibition commissioned by Northamptonshire council and Silverstone racetrack funded by Arts Council England, exhibited at the British Grand Prix 2011. Photograph by Jo Cope.

From the beginning, I escaped what I perceived to be a sterile environment in the fashion studio; for me the act of flat pattern cutting was completely unnatural because it meant working away from the body in two dimensions. I wandered into departments such as fine art, seeking to develop ways of creating more physical extensions of the body and the self. Plaster casting initially offered a more holistic material connection through touch. The use of plaster and cardboard in prototyping created a more physical interaction between the maker, the material, and the body. I believe in intimate construction methods where the body is central to the three-dimensional construction aiding the viewer in relating more deeply with the work. To give an example of this, the shoes created for the piece "Walking in Circles" (2017) (see Figure 3.9) was originally constructed by first using 3D foot-scanning technology and then building around each foot in CAD [computer aided design], generating wire frame forms which could be milled in any material. When these pieces were CNC [computer numerical control] milled as prototypes they looked soulless, which brought me back to my usual hands-on approach. The CAD method was the most logical but it lacked the emotive quality of human touch. I went back to hand sculpt each piece directly around the foot (see Figure 3.3), I then 3D-scanned the hand-formed shoe objects so they could be milled out of wood as the plaster would not be a stable enough material: it was a type of reverse process. Ian White, a footwear technician at LCF [London College of Fashion], and brilliant craftsman who I worked closely with on my master's collection said something to the effect of: humans are built with the innate ability to visually recognize the human hand in an object even when there is no direct evidence of it.

Studying MA Fashion Artefacts at London College of Fashion allowed me to develop more craft skills, to aid the exploration of traditional and non-traditional fashion and footwear-based techniques and materials. I used this as an opportunity to work around the foot, not studying footwear design directly, but to approach shoes as a more abstract body related object. Throughout my master's I continued to subvert the meaning of the function of shoes, placing them further into the context of art. Eleanor Antin's "100 Boots Turn the Corner" was an important reference point at this time. The boots in this project have a powerful life of their own, taking on humanistic characteristics, and their separation from the body raising intrigue and ambiguity.

Figure 3.2 Jo Cope, "Looking for Love," shoes (2016). Photograph by Nigel Essex.

Throughout my practice, I have purposely created installations in diverse art and fashion venues to ensure dialogue between the two, including concept boutiques, museums, and gallery spaces, and as an official part of London Craft Week 2018, London Design Festival, and the Venice Design Festival that runs parallel with Venice Architecture Biennale 2018.

Craft is central to all types of making. In your case, this covers not just the art of sewing, manipulating materials, and constructing three-dimensionally but also the very act of creating the mold, whether body form or last. In many ways, it seems that you are also crafting new anatomies with these extended forms around the body. Could you talk about the way you see the role of craft in your practice?

In my practice, craft skills have become key in creating beautifully refined artefacts while futurist aesthetics push traditional making methods to the limits. I use labor-intensive hand processes in part to preserve my artistic values.

In conceptual art, the idea rather than the material object is considered the most important, whereas in fashion it is the reverse. The role of craft in my master's project was to create an equal collaboration between mind and hand. After many observations, encounters, and debates with a vast range of people on the subject of conceptual work, I believe that evidence of "skill" in the making of the work is valued by audiences. However, by only focusing on the skill of the hand, what is dismissed is the primary skill in conceptual work: the artistry of the mind. Hence my approach to the work is to attempt to balance the mind and hand. I have also come to the opinion that many believe that fashion shouldn't be anything other than wearable and I have long been interested in challenging this through proposing new ways of seeing and interpreting fashion. There are many exacting rules and techniques relating to the way shoes are made and my aim is to continue to use traditional shoemaking methods while also challenging these methods with new technologies and materials. My perception is that people can more easily appreciate skills of the hand than fathom those created by the mind. It might be hard to put value on conceptual thoughts in the same way that we might appreciate the products of three months of hard labor. I have used craft as a tangible means of creating wonder, which hopefully aids in engaging people into conceptual thinking. By its very nature, craft in this solid state creates its own form of sustainable future as an artefact.

Craft skills have also been utilized to create the purest visual representation of the concept in three dimensions. For example, in the seam-free leather stretched between the male and female conjoined lasts in "Love Triangle" (2016;

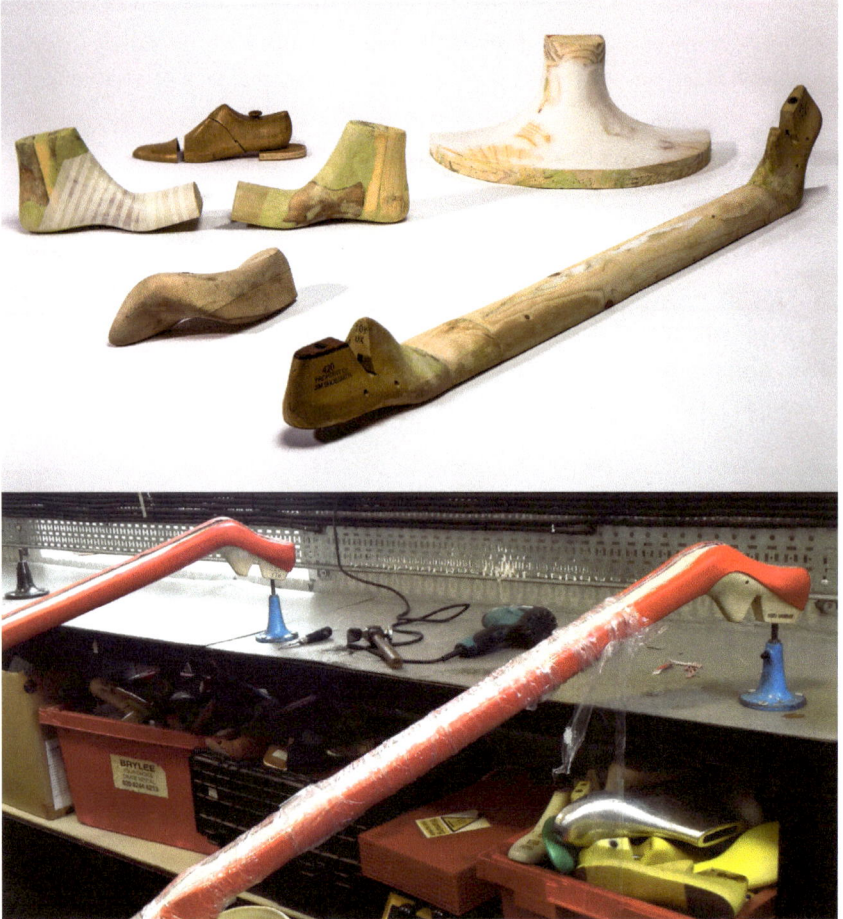

Figure 3.3 Jo Cope, adapted wooden lasts (2015–17). Photographs by Nigel Essex.

see Figure 3.3), the making process would have been far easier if multiple pattern pieces had been used. But this seamless connection between the two sexes allows for no distractions, an essential part of the eyes being able to flow uninterrupted to engage in the fixed situation being suggested between the relating humans in the piece. The craft itself is used to add weight and value to the idea, to elevate it beyond that of transitory fashion trend. Craft is used in the adaptation of the pitch, length, and form of vintage lasts, sometimes recreating them completely. The footwear starts to imitate anatomy as the shoes start to take on human gesturing. The role of craft is often similar to that of my practice, which first looks at the template before considering the alternative direction I want to push it.

Leaving the "last" inside the shoe prohibits the wearing while making the object in many ways static. But movement is also a vital part in your work particularly when you work on performances like the artefacts you created for *The Opposite of Addiction* (2017) with choreographer Lee Griffiths, commissioned by Sadler's Wells and London College of Fashion for the Material Movement Gala. Could you talk about the physical and conceptual challenges of creating objects for a performance?

In 2004, Dr. Michele Danjoux, a fashion designer and educator, and Johannes Birringer, Professor in Performing Arts at Brunel University, invited me to become an early member of DAP lab, a cross-media design space they continue to co-direct today. It was the starting point of playing with fashion in a collaborative environment with performance and narratives. The lab was a space for multiple disciplines to explore fashion in conjunction with the body, assisted by many forms of technology. I used the mediums of dance and performance to question "intention" and "improvisation" in relation to fashion objects. I realized through this process that what I was really interested in was narrating disciplined choreographed actions to use fashion in motion to create visual metaphors. These clean sequences of abstracted actions were embedded within and led directly by the objects.

In working with objects in conjunction with the body, practical implications have to be considered and the degree of function versus form is a balancing act. The most important thing to me is to ensure that the aesthetics are not compromised or restricted by live movement but instead are empowered in that relationship. I was commissioned by London College of Fashion to create a performance in collaboration with choreographer Lee Griffiths for the LCF × Sadler's Wells Material Movement Gala 2017. For an aspect of the performance at Sadler's Wells I created a series of "suggestive" foot objects, the word "suggestive" relating to the partial non-functional interaction between the body and abstract shoe forms. The pieces were intended to push the visual language of shoes into something which resembled a walking landscape. The objects' ergonomics were taken from visualized leg actions and the top circumference opening a space to allow the toe to suggestively dip but not fully enter. In this case I am rejecting the notion of a shoe as something which has to be defined by the physical embodiment of the wearer. These footwear artefacts existed statically on the stage prior to the dancers' entry, intentionally being ambiguous until brought to life through physical interaction. The objects in this collaboration played the central role in creating the framework concept and theory which led to the development of the choreography. It was important to me to define the shoes as having their own rich symbolic language to remove old preconceptions of fashion as a secondary performance costume or a prop. During the choreography the performers had to work together to bring the two individual more "wearable" shoes together as one full circle (Figure 3.4). Floor sliding motions and lifting actions replaced classic walking motions.

In a four-minute performance there is no time for "putting on," but at the same time the shoes needed to hold around the foot. The "Full Circle" shoes went through a lot of prototyping processes to find a solution, which was internal wooden profiles of the foot made to loosely grip the toe and the heel. A moving anatomy is more of a challenge to craft than a static one, for obvious reasons; this is made harder by creating rigid rather than fluid flexible forms. The two-part body piece which accompanied the shoes connected the two dancers as one through concave and convex leather body forms which slotted into each other. This piece had to be continually fitted and adapted during prototyping and tested and altered during rehearsals. It would have taken half the time if built for mannequins, but then I like a challenge. When creating for performance, the challenge for me was to maintain my minimalist construction methods which often include clean glued leather joints rather than sewing, while not compromising its stability as a working object.

You brought up the fact that, most often, fashion, and indeed footwear, is constructed around a static and standardized form and yet our bodies are anything but static or standardized. In your practice, you are challenging this approach by creating objects using non-traditional methods for garment construction. However, at the same time, you rely on these standardized forms to guide your practice as a template and a starting point. Could you expand on the relationship your practice has to mannequins as well as lasts?

There is a relationship I have with the body that I think goes beyond fashion. It is an intrigue that relates to human connections explored physically and mentally through touch as well as social and self-observation, and the use of psychoanalysis to capture bodily acts driven by issues faced by the mind. Before fashion, I studied human anatomy and moved around the body massaging the form. It was much like rhythmic dance: one static person, one moving. In this way, massaging is very similar to sculpting around the mannequin. I transmit some of the things I continue to learn about people and myself onto lifeless objects so that my fashion can speak. In looking to extend fashion's parameters, the body is the constant feature and the mannequin or last acts as a starting point. It is something

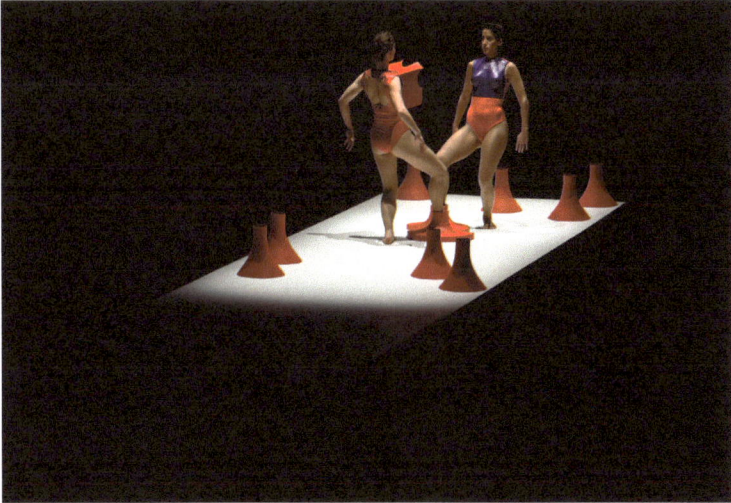

Figure 3.4 Jo Cope, "Full Circle" shoes (2017), *The Opposite of Addiction*, Sadler's Wells Theatre for the LCF Material Movement Gala. Photographs by Richard Eaton.

to move away from and a physical ergonomic building block to adapt. The mannequin or shoe lasts remain as an imprint in the final object, offering the viewer a visual reference point.

In 2012, I was commissioned by Hugo Worthy, curator at New Walk Gallery and Museum in Leicester, to create a fashion installation to stand alongside the Crafts Council touring exhibition *Block Party*, whose curator was Lucy Orta. The *Block Party* show looked at contemporary craft inspired by the art of the tailor. In response, I created a conceptual fashion triptych titled "Dress Block" (Figure 3.5), an interpretation of three separate but interrelated fashion elements: form, pattern, and copy. The first piece was a human-scale wooden body block referencing the three-dimensional making methods used to create shoes and millinery. The body block functioned as a working tool to directly mold replica felt forms; Piece 2 illustrated this material duplication. In Piece 3, a duplicate felt form was placed back onto a standard mannequin to illustrate fashion's more recognizable appearance. The making process required me to straddle the block; my body working its body in a form of hypnotic physical enmeshment, creating a more heightened experience than one only involving the hands on a standard mannequin.

In "Twisted Stiletto" (2016) (Figure 3.6), part of the collection "The Language of Feet in the Walk of Life," a standard shoe last was distorted. I wanted to capture past and future contexts through and relating to one footwear object. The role of "Twisted Stiletto" was to act as a piece of design fiction, illustrating an alternative reality to the perfectly desirable, superficial illusion that fashion can help to create. It is in part an observational commentary on the potential disparity between mental and physical states when presenting one's self to others. I am using the idea of the "fashioned self" as a means of misrepresentation in the encounter of others to influence the final object's aesthetics. I am creating links between the stilettos' connections to the sexualized self. In *Shoes: An Illustrated History* (2014), Rebecca Shawcross discusses the potential origin of the stiletto, starting with prostitutes in Venice. "Twisted Stiletto" is a twenty-first-century commentary on online dating such as Tinder which relies on split-second aesthetic judgments. The making methodology started and ended with a wooden last and was assisted by new tech processes including laser scanners and CAD. The final last was milled from wood at Spring Line in Northampton, the last remaining last-making company in the UK. The making of this historically related wooden object, even if somewhat mutated, allowed the shoe to be constructed in leather using traditional shoemaking techniques. The use of the traditional last, even when distorted, aids the stiletto in being a visually relatable

Figure 3.5 Jo Cope, "Dress Block" triptych (2012), exhibited at New Walk Museum and Gallery, Leicester. Photograph by Stephen Lynch.

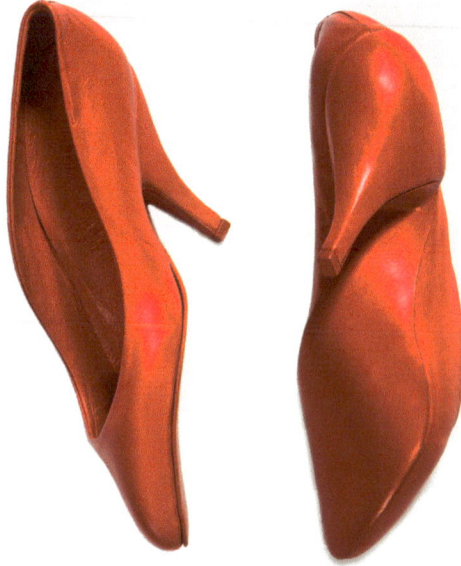

Figure 3.6 Jo Cope, "Twisted Stiletto" (2016). Photograph by Nigel Essex.

object, allowing other more psychological messages to be read. When exhibited at YKK in 2018 as part of an installation titled "Lessons in Love," one of the visitors looked down at the "Twisted Stiletto" saying "That is me, that is exactly how I feel." I am promoting the value of a fashion artefact as a tool for deeper self-connection. I use mannequins and lasts as representations of my physical self, modifying them to express emotional states on the outside to provoke thought and discussion. The generic body form invites the viewer to make connections between the work and themselves.

You also mentioned about working directly with the human body as part of your creative process, which is interesting, as most fashion designers' starting point is often the mannequin and prototypes and finished garments are later tested on human bodies. It also seems that the body for you is more than just a form to work around but also a metaphor and a source of inspiration, and your practice addresses not just the physical needs of the body but the mental as well. Is this true?

The human form itself is a metaphor for the "standard," the mass-market in fashion and the average person. At the root of my work, I am trying to make sense of being outside of the average template in society, and yes, the body is a constant source of inspiration. Theorist Merleau-Ponty talks about the human body itself as a subject. I often use my own body as a starting point to act out ideas about the self that manifest in the mind's eye. The mannequin is sometimes used to explore current social matters that relate to concepts of being a human. In "Your Only Obstacle" (2018) (Figure 3.7), I created a mannequin with a carved-out center to provoke thought around an idea that I was thinking about, in which the only obstacle in life is a person's own mental limitations. I use the open space in the center of body to symbolize that we can move through and past ourselves "the obstacle." One of the ways that I process information when reading or listening to podcasts for example is to transform aspects of the information that resonate into three-dimensional fashion-based metaphors in my mind. I feel that materializing this type of symbolism can also be helpful to a more visually motivated audience and which can also represent a social trend alongside the progressive form and voice of fashion in an art context.

During and since my formal fashion education, I have explored ways to expand the traditional practice of making and continue to question the purpose of fashion. I use the mannequin as a human framework to build around, more in line with the French method of *moulage*, where fabric is constructed directly on the tailor's dummy. At times, I've wanted to challenge the static upright position of the mannequin by starting to cut around a jointed mannequin in multiple positions. I have also explored cutting around the live body. I did this most recently with "The Death of Love" dress (2017) (Figure 3.8), which was built around the body of a recently widowed family member. The introduction of the secondary person's body unintentionally created alternative narratives and interpretations, which could appear to relate more literally to concepts of love and loss, but which also had many of its own more complex meanings. The subtext that can be accidentally created from using a live person is a reminder that the body can have a mind of its own. In 1971, Diane Arbus talked about the photograph as a secret about a secret; in the same way, my work is often a meaning within a meaning.

I sometimes work around multiple mannequins or bodies to represent a situation with more than one person or to talk about a concept that relates to the singular self. The implications of gender are created through the use of classic shoes or garments which are purposely non-descriptive as if to create anonymity for the real people they represent. Proximity and body language are used to aid the narration of human relationships, as people are both external and internal entities. I am using fashion to encompass ideas relating to mental and physical states. Commercial fashion is like a superficial bodily covering, yet fashion psychology research continues to show the deeper psychological impact that

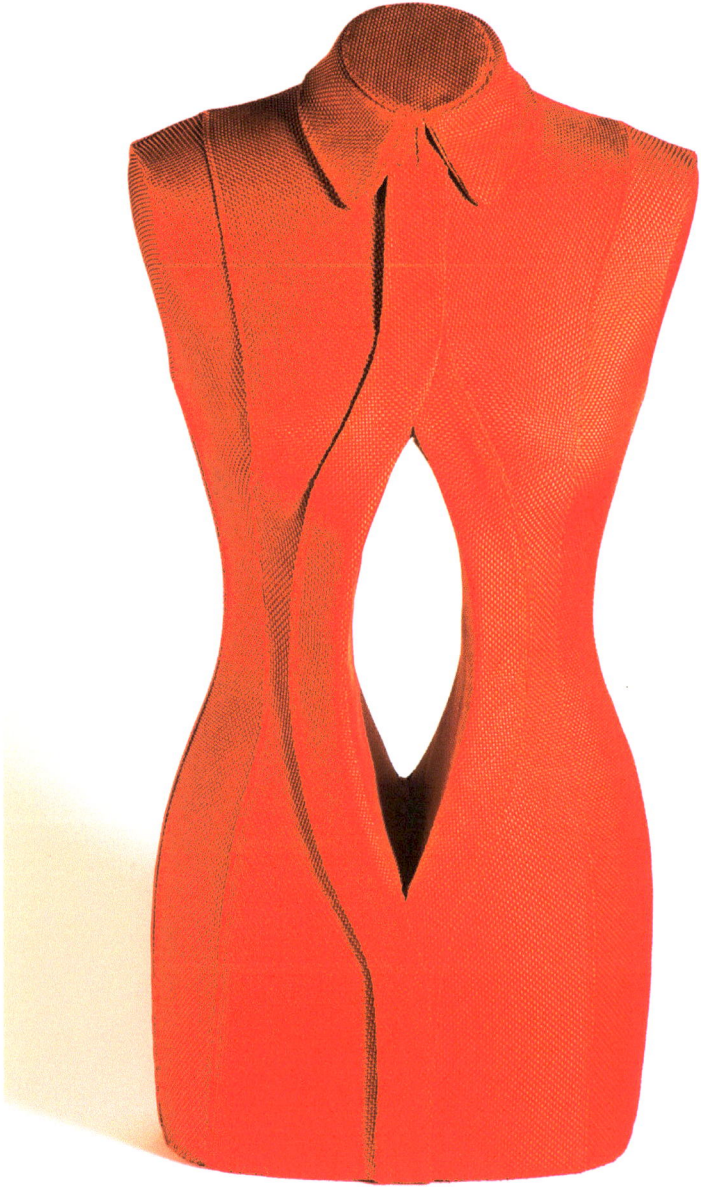

Figure 3.7　Jo Cope, "Your Only Obstacle" (2018). Photograph by Nigel Essex.

Figure 3.8 Jo Cope, "Death of Love" dress (2017). Photograph by Nigel Essex.

clothing has on the wearer and the people they encounter. I am interested in the role that metaphors can play in fashion in creating a more powerful dialogue between itself and the audience. Grieder (1990) reminds us that art is an expressive means of communicating with the world, and the metaphor is a way of connecting with an audience in a non-literal way.

"Walking in Circles" (2017) (Figure 3.9) transforms the visual language of the shoe by capturing its essence conceptually "when the shoe becomes its action." The circle of shoes materializes the negative space between the foot and ground in the swing stage of the walking gait, a metaphor for inability to move forward in life. The objective of the piece is as a form of material exorcism. I have more recently been looking at the similarities between my work and a method used in

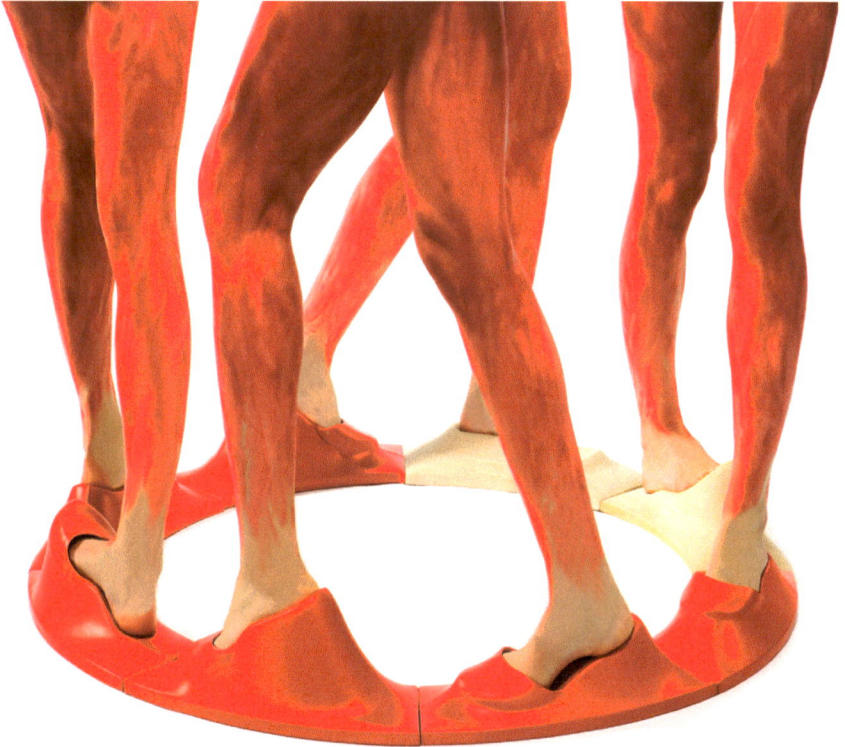

Figure 3.9 Jo Cope, "Walking in Circles" (2017). Photograph by Nigel Essex.

therapy called "Symbolic Modelling" where therapists use "Clean Language" to develop a series of symbols and metaphors in order for people to see more clearly and achieve a better sense of well-being. Freud believed that the key to curing issues in the self was in making unconscious thoughts conscious. My work looks at how in physically manifesting unconscious thoughts and emotions, self-therapy can be achieved from these insights and analysis.

The role of design has always been to propose solutions in a commercial framework. Matt Malpass (2017) articulates "critical design" as something that is more about asking questions. According to him, critical design practice rejects the "role of industrial design that is limited to the production of objects conceived solely for fiscal gain" and instead it is used to "mobilize debate" and to "avoid conventional production and consumption" (1). It seems to me that you are working in this very same framework. Your work is situated in fashion that is all about commerce and creating desire but you are challenging the very notion of it through your practice.

Fashion as commercial consumable has to stop at being comfortable and practical—this idea that things have a preconceived template that makes everything start and end at a similar place. If we take these away, I believe that never-ending possibilities exist not only in reimagining form and function, but in the future relationship of fashion to human beings in both a physical and mental sense. I think my work is critical in mobilizing debate and challenging others to see things differently.

I have used my practice to find an alternative place away from commercial constraints, while also using this as a subject. The first work I created after graduating from my fashion degree in 2006 was a self-funded 250-piece bag installation called "Clearly a Bag." It was my first serious opportunity to explore fashion's alter ego, an exercise to answer the question: What is a bag? I wanted to rethink design codes and environments, challenging and questioning prescriptive lazy design. I used the bag's relationship to the body to break down its fundamental functions. When constructed as a large repeat, its final minimalist acrylic block shape became an overpowering sculptural structure. The installation was placed back into the fashion context as well as gallery spaces, asking the audience to look beyond what they already knew in order to see differently. My objective was not to alienate the viewer but to challenge and encourage their own conceptual thinking and design ability.

Each bag created for this installation was designed around mathematical references to the body, the opposite of designing from frivolous trends. I took my own body as the generic reference, the "handle" becoming a continuous line, with measurements taken from the grip width of the hand in the most natural holding position. The "bag" width was taken from the distance between the arm and body in the most natural carry position. It was an exercise in minimalist ergonomic construction, driven by anti-fashion consumerism subtext. Desire itself is a perpetuating trap within fashion, a cycle that encourages us to consume and discard frivolously. I once heard fashion psychologist Dr. Carolyn Mair talking about this as a cycle in which once the desire has been fulfilled though purchase, the serotonin levels that have built up in the brain drop significantly, which drives us toward the next purchase, much like in an addiction.

Your work is very contemporary in its appearance and present in its aura. There is a history of practitioners taking a similar approach to thinking and making as you, but also there is a sense of the archived body and histories that manifest in molds and lasts that you are working with. What's your relationship between the past and your work?

In relation to the mind and the body, the present, future, and past coexist in our understanding of the self at any given moment in life. Each helps build mental pictures and landmarks that aid the understanding of our own momentary realities and the wider journey of life. The reference to my own past is through a family history rooted in shoemaking that goes back eight generations. My engagement with old historical wood lasts has led me to think about past lives and the footwear industry, the people who in the past gave their lives to the making of boots and shoes. These past histories allow me to question ideas about an object's deeper value as well as the human's value as maker while also questioning the future purpose of my own work as potential fashion archive.

I was commissioned to celebrate the history of the boot and shoe industry in Northamptonshire in a project called Global Footprint by the Northampton Shoe Museum in 2012. This was part of the Cultural Olympiad that coincided with the London Olympics. As part of this commission, I visited Edward Greens, one of the oldest shoe manufacturers still in existence, where I observed over 300 singular repetitive craft processes in the making of one pair of shoes. In the final commissioned piece, I wanted to pay homage to the people who most often gave their lives to a single repetitive action in this process, an action both essential to the shoe's creation and often to the workers' own financial survival. This repetitive investment related to the life of my own grandmother, who was a heel coverer and mother of seven, which often saw her working repetitively and relentlessly from 7 a.m. to 10 p.m., six days a week. The final piece titled "Sold" (Figure 3.10) was a large solid leather block made up of layers of 5 mm soling leather which could exist as one unit or component parts. The negative space of the foot was milled out of the block forming the inside space of the shoes, and the outside of the shoes was milled from the block to form the space to embed the shoes to fit perfectly into the block. The shoes' surface was completely flat and challenged the aesthetics, role, and construction of footwear. I was talking about the spirit of the maker being deeply embedded as a footprint in footwear's history through their blood, sweat, and tears. When the piece was exhibited, I was informed by the curator of an elderly man who had shed a tear in reading the meaning behind the piece. I was grateful that this futuristic form was able to touch a life in the way that it respected and commemorated the past.

Figure 3.10 Jo Cope, "Sold" (2012). Boot and Shoe Museum, Global Footprint project, Northampton. Photographs by Jo Cope.

References

Grieder, T. (1990) *Artist and Audience*, Fort Worth, TX: Holt, Rinehart, and Winston.

Horn, R. (2004) *Body Landscapes: Drawings, Sculptures, Installations, 1964–2004*, London: Hatje Cantz.

Malpass, M. (2017) *Critical Design in Context: History, Theory and Practices*, London: Bloomsbury.

Shawcross, R. (2014) *Shoes: An Illustrated History*, London: Bloomsbury.

Trimingham, M. (2011) *The Theatre of the Bauhaus: The Modern and Postmodern Stage of Oskar Schlemmer*, New York: Routledge.

4

Pioneering, Nonconforming, and Rematerializing

Crafting Understanding of Older Men's Experiences of Fashion Through Their Personal Archives

Ania Sadkowska

Introduction

When talking about fashion as a social phenomenon, we cannot escape the complexity of the relationships between many intertwined fields and concepts. Style, apparel, psychological attitudes, subcultures, clothes and the body, are just a few of many elements defining fashion and influencing its dynamics (e.g. Kaiser, 2012; Entwistle, 2015). But often when speak of fashion we tend to automatically default to womenswear and youth (e.g. Twigg, 2013), somewhat overlooking the involvement of mature men and the importance of sartorial self-expression (e.g. McCauley Bowstead, 2018). Therefore, in establishing this research project it was important to consider how to capture the different values encompassed within older men's experience of aging through fashion. In particular, this project's aim was to develop an in-depth understanding of contemporary older British men's experiences of aging and the associated changes to the body through the lens of fashion and clothing (Sadkowska, 2016).

By virtue of the project's focus on male aging and fashion, exploration of issues such as masculinity, embodiment and identity emerged as significant. Furthermore, as a fashion and textile designer, seeking novel ways of extending standard interpretative research processes was equally important. This method of enquiry enabled experimental design responses, linked to personal artistic skills, expertise and sensitivities. These approaches were key to analysing the study participants' experiences, while discovering and responding to their personal fashion and clothing archives. This chapter explains stages of the research process in regards to three emergent themes and corresponding artefacts; Pioneering, Non-Conforming and Re-Materialising.

Methods of inquiry

To enable understanding and further the field of practice-based research on older men and fashion, a novel methodology was required. This was achieved through creating a fusion of the qualitative processes of interpretative phenomenological analysis (IPA; Smith 1996; Smith, Flowers, and Larkin 2009) with the practice-based procedures of arts-informed research (Cole and Knowles 2008; Butler-Kisber 2010). This novel fusion elicited a rigorous and integrative research and included methods of semi-structured interviews (captured via a series of audio recordings), personal inventories of the participants' private fashion and clothing archives (evidenced via a series of field notes and photographs), and the intertwined practices of interpretative writing and making, i.e., practical explorations to gain further insights into their thoughts. The "writing practices" were stimulated through immersion in the data and personal reflexivity (Etherington 2004), while the "making" contained elements of creative techniques and artful material explorations, in this case, located within the field of fashion and clothing design.

Inquiry in action

In his seminal text Steinar Kvale (1996: 125) offers a useful definition of a research interview: "[it] is an interpersonal situation, a conversation between two partners about a theme of mutual interest. It is a specific form of human interaction in which knowledge evolves through a dialogue."

In his later text (Kvale 2006: 480), he supplemented this definition by describing dialogical interviewing as potentially sensitive, powerful, and "a democratic emancipating form of social research." While this highlights the unique role of the interviewees as experts in their experiences, it also acknowledges the important role of the interviewer in the process of listening and reacting to given accounts.

As described elsewhere (e.g., Sadkowska, Wilde, and Fisher 2015; Sadkowska et al. 2017) for the purpose of this project, five men were interviewed (Table 4.1). The interviewees' main characteristics were deliberately consistent: they were British, white, heterosexual, middle-class, professionally active, appearance-

Table 4.1 Sample characteristics

Name[a]	Age	Occupation	County of Residence
Eric	60	Artist	Nottinghamshire
Grahame	61	Social care worker	Derbyshire
Henry	54	Academic	Leicestershire
Ian	58	Company director	Nottinghamshire
Kevin	63	Lecturer	Nottinghamshire

Note:
[a] Pseudonyms are used to preserve participants' anonymity.

conscious men located in, or strongly connected to, Nottingham, UK, which made the sample homogenous.

Each interview lasted between 90 and 120 minutes and was recorded with consent from each participant. The interview schedule consisted of eight open-ended questions about the different aspects of their experiences of fashion and clothing, including questions about the participants' personal definition of the term "fashion." This included their past and present fashion practices, such as purchasing, wearing, storing, or styling their clothes, and future expectations. They were also asked about their current relationship with fashion and clothing and how this has changed over time, encouraging them to describe occasions when they felt really good/bad about the way they looked, their perfect fashion item, and fashion artifacts that were personally meaningful for them. The interviews were conversational in style and prompts and probes were used to encourage the participants to elaborate further when unexpected, but potentially interesting, areas of discussion arose, and to clarify ambiguities and avoid misunderstandings; these included a variety of standard interviewing phrases such as: Can you give me an example of this? Can you tell me more about that? How do/did you feel about that? It looks like you are saying . . . / I just would like to make sure that I got it right.

Personal fashion and clothing archives

While the in-depth interviews allowed for the generation of research material that revealed both the richness and complexity of the participants' experiences, "interviews can be made more productive when based around artifacts" (Martin and Hanington 2012: 102). Csikszentmihalyi and Rochberg-Halton (1981: 1) comment that in order "[t]o understand what people are and what they might become, one must understand what goes on between people and things." Since the aim of the research was to explore the variety and complexity of the types of relationships that participants have developed with fashion and clothing as they matured and grew older, gaining access to, and the use of objects that were personally meaningful to the participants as the stimuli for conversation was pertinent for it. This led to employing the method of personal inventories which in turn allowed for the uncovering of the participants' private fashion and clothing archives. These archives took different forms, from carefully stored and preserved objects (garments, accessories, textiles, etc.) and photographs, to vivid and fond memories of no-longer-existing items and experiences linked to them.

With the intention of conducting personal inventories, prior to the interview each participant was emailed with the brief instruction to bring along three or four fashion-related objects (e.g., pieces of clothing, accessories, textiles, photographs, or other relevant artifacts). This was addressed as the final part of the interview in which the participants were invited to speak about these objects. It is important to highlight that one of the themes was to explore the participants' "meaning making" of their experiences, and so it was critical to allow them not only to freely choose the artifacts they wanted to bring to, and discuss during, their interview, but also to be open as to what kind of artifacts they were to be.

As a consequence of the limited instructions, the personal inventories conducted differed significantly from case to case; the participants presented a variety of different types of artifacts from accessories such as rings and ties, to garments such as shirts and jackets, but also different amounts of them. Three of the participants presented the researcher with the photos of their favorite items, two of the participants wore their "favorite" outfit/garment to the interview, and four participants showed their "special" garments, of whom two extended an opportunity for a viewing of their entire wardrobes. Arguably, such diversity of the types of artifacts and the ways in which they were presented in an otherwise small sample accentuates the diversity of the participants' experiences. But it also highlights the need for a more holistic approach to understanding individuals' unique lived experiences, and acknowledging the role of the past episodes and artifacts in their present experiences.

While personal inventories as a research method might give an impression of being rather straightforward to implement, allowing the participants to have an entirely autonomous selection of the objects proved to be problematic when it came to their documentation. The challenge rested precisely in how to capture the richness and diversity of the presented material. There was a significant discrepancy between the numbers of objects brought by each of them; one participant, Eric, presented as many as twenty-two objects (eight clothing pieces and fourteen photos), while Kevin did not bring any artifacts at all. Only two participants followed the given parameters and brought four items each (Table 4.2).

Such discrepancy can be interpreted in a twofold way; first, the two participants who were interviewed in their own homes, Eric and Grahame, presented more artifacts than the three participants who were interviewed within the university settings. This could easily be explained by the fact that these two participants simply did not need to carry these objects with them to the interview, and in a sense they did not even need to plan in advance showing them. Such an explanation would be in line also with the fact that, in general, the three interviews conducted at the university were shorter, suggesting that perhaps home settings did influence how relaxed the participants felt and potentially influenced the depth of the interview. On the other hand, however, to create distance from any such theories, it is important to highlight that all the participants in this study, while having certain characteristics in common, varied

Table 4.2 Personal inventories

Pseudonym	"Special" Outfit Worn (Y/N)	Artifacts Demonstrated	Photos
Eric	N	8 (4 Paul Smith suit jackets, 1 tie, 1 hat, 2 silver rings)	14 (collection of images from his childhood to the present time)
Grahame	Y (favorite shirt)	13 (2 rain jackets, 1 suit jacket, 1 Levi's denim jacket, 1 denim shirt, 2 tops, 2 hoodies, 1 scarf, 1 hat, 2 bags)	0
Henry	Y (suit and shirt by Gresham Blake)	3 (2 Vivienne Westwood suits, 1 tie by Barbara Hulanicki)	1 (Henry aged 18 in his first suit)
Ian	N	3 (G-Force cardigan, Paul Smith shirt, Nick Coleman jacket)	1 (image of the Johnson's shirt; emailed to the researcher after the interview)
Kevin	N	0	0

significantly in the way they explained their experiences and offered their interpretations.

In this sense, an interpretation is that it may well be that Kevin, who was the only participant who did not bring any artifacts with him, although admitting to having a rather large private fashion archive at home, simply did not feel the need to do so, which would be consistent with his interview's narrative, where he often compared his past and present experiences of fashion. This comparison was based on highlighting the difference between his active participation in various male-dominated youth subcultures where having certain clothes allowed him to simply "fit within" a group's standards, and the current time when he valued originality and being "a little bit different" more. Overall, in his

Figure 4.1 The artifacts and photos the participants presented during their interviews. Top, left to right: Ian's leather jacket; Graham's hooded jacket; Henry's Biba tie. Bottom left to right: Eric's Paul Smith suit jacket; Eric modeling *c.* 1981, photo P. Edmondson, image courtesy of T. Brack for Olto Ltd.; Henry in 1978, photo courtesy of the owner. Artifacts photographed by Ania Sadkowska.

interview, on multiple occasions he expressed his confidence in his individual style and displayed a strong, rebellious disconnection from any forms of social participation.

Additionally, it is also worth noting that on many occasions this potential research data was presented in a rather chaotic manner; for example, in the case of two interviews conducted in the participants' homes, the interviewed men tried on some of their garments, changing them quickly and often providing little verbal commentary about them, even when prompted. This indeed posed certain challenges of how to record this potentially rich research data. Consequently, adopting photography as a means of documentation enabled the sensory richness of these material objects to be captured. This generated a series of photographs capturing the participants themselves wearing their artifacts, as well as the photos shown by the participants (Figure 4.1). However, while such a variety of the generated images accurately reflected the diversity of the participants' personal archives and the richness of their experiences, it required being selective when it came to the analyzed material.

Crafting understanding

As a result of implementing the hybrid methodology of Arts-Informed Interpretative Phenomenological Analysis (Sadkowska 2016), the analysis of the data had three interconnected stages. At the first stage the interview recordings and transcriptions were analyzed using techniques standard to IPA (e.g., Smith, Flowers, and Larkin 2009; Finlay 2011). At the second stage a series of photographs of the participants' outfits was analyzed. Both these stages were completed in a close relation to the participants' fashion and clothing archives revealed via a series of personal inventories. The final stage of the data analysis was based on a series of practical explorations.

Stage 1: Interview coding

IPA as a methodology deals nearly exclusively with text; the analyzed text comes usually from interview transcriptions, which can be supplemented by the researcher's comments, reflections, field notes, photographs, etc. (Smith, Flowers, and Larkin 2009). Consequently, conducting an IPA analysis is based mainly on the activity of reflexive writing. In this vein, the first stage of data analysis was devoted exclusively to written coding of the five interview transcriptions and included the following steps: reading and rereading of the interview transcripts; initial note-taking; developing emergent themes; searching for connections across emergent themes; moving to the next case; and, finally, looking for patterns across cases (ibid). This stage of IPA textual analysis concluded in identifying a set of emergent themes.

Stage 2: Image analysis

However fruitful, the stage of interview coding opened up the important question of how to code the visual material gathered via the participants' personal inventories and how to even begin understanding their unique fashion archives. Moreover, it was crucial to facilitate the analysis conditions to enable the moving back and forth between the images and the participants' verbal accounts, so one informed the other in a form of interpretative dialogue. The extremely diverse empirical material was challenging to analyze in a systematic and a unified way. For this reason a decision was made to analyze the common factor for all the participants which was a photograph of what they were wearing on the day of the interview, would be the most stable factor (Figure 4.2). This was

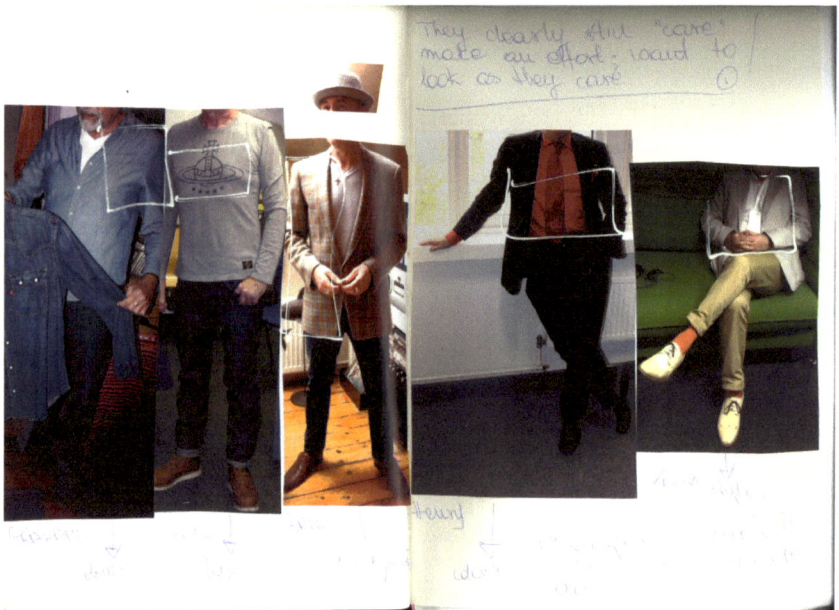

Figure 4.2 The participants on the day of their interviews; left to right: Grahame (61), Ian (58), Eric (60), Henry (54), and Kevin (63). Photographs by Ania Sadkowska.

significant because all of the interviewed men admitted during their interview that they very carefully crafted their attire on the day for the purpose of projecting themselves as stylish individuals.

Drawing on the framework developed by Boden and Eatough (2014), in which the researchers proposed to interpret an image on three interconnected levels, namely, how it was made, how it was composed, and its potential meanings, first, the stage of visual data analysis was devoted to a detailed description of each outfit. Subsequently, it was modified to this study's conditions by extending it to take into account the relationship between clothing and the body. The visual data was then analyzed and interpreted alongside the data from the interview transcripts following a similar procedure: describing in detail the image (through the framework), followed by its interpretation in relation to the commentary provided by the participants during their interviews as well as field notes. This was done separately for the image of each participant of the study on the day of the interview and resulted in five cases of "outfit analysis" which influenced the emergent themes and allowed for the creation of a final table of three superordinate (master) themes with three subordinate themes each (Table 4.3). When labeling each theme the intention was to directly reflect the participants' words and thoughts but also develop interpretations. This enabled responding to the gathered data by creating a series of initial interpretive accounts based on the co-construction of meanings and understandings between each participant and the researcher (Sadkowska 2018).

Stage 3: Practical explorations

Finally, the stage of practical explorations was when the processes of final shaping and crafting an understanding of older men's experience took place by re-approaching each of the nine subordinate themes. For this, engaging with

Table 4.3 Final superordinate and subordinate themes in the study

SUPERORDINATE THEMES		
Learning Fashion	**Defining the Fashion-Self**	**Fashion-Age(ing) Performance**
SUBORDINATE THEMES		
Mirroring	Pioneering	Presenting
Discomforting	Nonconforming	(Un-)fashioning
Peacocking	Distancing	Rematerializing

various artful creative practices as a way to stimulate and enhance thinking about the data and initial findings (Table 4.3; subordinate themes) was used. It was at this stage that the unique embodied processes and creative responses really came to the fore. The process of adopting practical explorations as an analytical and interpretative tool is explained below in regards to three selected subordinate themes: Pioneering, Non-Conforming, and Re-Materialising.

Pioneering

Pioneering emerged as a strong and relatively straightforward theme, touching upon the participants' past connections with the various subcultures, which resulted in their current attitudes toward aging stylishly (Sadkowska, Wilde, and Fisher 2015). All five participants expressed their beliefs that, in the past, they pioneered certain youth movements and related menswear styles, as explained by Henry (54): "Having grown up in the '60s and '70s I have probably lived through [...] some of the most exciting changes and developments in male clothing."

While all of the participants felt very strongly about their pioneering past, they also felt that currently their generation of men is actively influencing and redefining what it means to grow older. Bovone (2012: 67) comment that the dressed body is "a basic element of our identity"; in this vein, throughout history it played a central role in how men age and how they enact what it means to be a man. Inspired by this, a process of practical explorations was initiated by looking into the relevant historical aspects, including the history of menswear from the 1950s to 1980s. This was a significant first step toward developing a deeper understanding of the theme, because it allowed a better appreciation of the social aspects of the youth fashion, which started in the 1950s. Admittedly this is how we understand fashion to be today; however, for the participants in this study, youth-oriented fashion was something that was associated with cultural change or, for some, even a kind of rebellion or revolt (Hebdige 1979; Hall and Jefferson 1976; Polhemus 2010). Furthermore, it was interesting to note how, for some participants, pioneering became so deeply engraved in who they have become that it is an inherent part of their everyday practices and behaviors, as discussed by Grahame (61): "I never needed anybody to tell me that a new band's in fashion, you know, music. Because I am already there. I know it's in fashion because I bought it last week."

To deepen this primary understanding of the theme, firstly a mind map exercise was completed and, secondly, all relevant passages from the interviews and the images from the participants' past were revisited. Especially useful here were images provided by Eric (Figure 4.3), who presented a collection of fourteen photos starting from his early childhood; his attire in each of these photos was a direct representation of the contemporary fashion trends forming an interesting form of visual fashion archives. These photos revealed something of value and worth exploring further and were used to create a short fashion film illustrating how his clothing style has changed over the years and exploring how this might relate to the pioneering theme.

However, before being able to truly embrace the interpretative potential of the practical explorations within the Pioneering theme, it required further understanding from a sociological point of view. For this reason, embarking upon reading various sources related to subcultures and their theories, two books, *Subculture: The Meaning of Style* by Hebdige (1979) and *Resistance Through Rituals: Youth Subcultures in Post-War Britain* (1976) edited by Hall and Jefferson, were especially relevant. It is from reading this literature that came the realization of the importance of the various contexts surrounding these

Figure 4.3 Eric's old photos (visual archives; selection of). Photo credits: P. Edmonson and D. Sedgwick.

subcultural movements, and the key elements of attire adopted by them as a form of identification and affiliation. Especially influential was this quote from Clarke (1976: 178): "[w]hat happens is not the creation of objects and meanings from nothing, but rather the *transformation* and *rearrangement* of what is given (and 'borrowed') into a pattern which carries a new meaning, its *translation* to a new context, and its *adaption*" [emphasis in original].

This quote resonated strongly with the Pioneering theme: (new) context(s) influencing (fresh) meaning(s). Inspired by this, and the review of historical accounts and images (both from Eric's archives and books) of menswear from the period of the1950s onwards, enabled identification of the various elements typical to different groups; the focus of the analysis lay primarily on men's suits. These were, for example, velvet collars for Teddy Boys, narrow lapels and the use of the Union Jack for Mods, or safety pins and raw edges for Punks. Here, the aim was to enable an understanding of the context in which these elements are normally used in order to give them new meanings; this appeared to draw a direct parallel to the current generation of the third-age men (including the participants) actively influencing new meanings of male aging.

At this stage, the purchase of a second-hand men's jacket took place which was selected because of its black-and-white dogtooth pattern wool alluding to the Mod aesthetics. Once the jacket was photographed a series of collages were completed in a sketchbook; these collages become a method of visual exploration for how to incorporate the identified "typical" elements of different subcultures within the jacket. Also, in parallel to this activity, through noting conceptual ideas regarding the theme, writing was stimulating making and vice versa. With especially strong convictions about the idea of creating new concepts, finally the jacket was deconstructed;[1] this was achieved by removing the sleeves and the collar. These were then reapplied as well as other elements in different forms, shapes, and positions; a sleeve hole became a neck hole, the collar was changed to a black velvet collar (Teddy Boys and Mods) and the safety pins (Punks) were used as a method of joining the elements superseding standard stitching, as well as the black and white safety pins that were used to emphasize the dogtooth pattern, and to imitate the tartan pattern (Punks). Throughout this process, it was important to use a sketchbook to visually document and continuously reflect on how applying these elements differently was influencing the unfolding interpretation. Consequently, completing the Pioneering jacket (Figure 4.4) enabled the verbalizing and interpretation of how the participants and their contemporaries are influencing our fresh perceptions of mature men, how they view their fashion-oriented masculinities, and how this affects their interpretation of their bodies.

Figure 4.4 Ania Sadkowska, "Pioneering"; sketchbook pages—deconstructing and reconstructing a second-hand jacket; the Pioneering jacket; front and back. Photographs by Fraser West.

Nonconforming

The Nonconforming theme, similarly to the Pioneering one, emerged as a theme linking the participants' past affiliations with various youth subcultures to their current attitudes and values. However, in contrast to the Pioneering theme, the connection was less direct and overt; instead, it was more of a general and settled tendency to go against the flow of mainstream trends and behaviors. In some sense, the Nonconforming theme was also linked to the rupture of these past subcultural connections; it emerged as a theme that was especially complex, multifaceted, and open to various creative interpretations.

Before starting practical explorations of it, it became important to reread all the relevant passages, including the results of the outfit analysis. This was especially important because the participants often talked about the objects from their pasts that allowed them to actively rebel against the existing clothing norms and expectations. In the following extract, Henry describes his current feelings toward such a clothing piece. Interestingly, in his utterance, he displays a certain level of regret, indicating a peculiar sense of loss or even grief caused by this artifact's absence in his life:

> There is only one thing that I really regret uhm… getting rid of. I would never wear them now. But they were fabulous at the time. Fabulously disgraceful I'm sure. Early '80s post new romantic uhm… trousers that were, sort of, khaki green. But streaked almost like they were tie-dyed. They had darker streaks through them. Which had uhm… brass zips from the ankle to the thigh. Uhm… on the front. And you could wear them zipped up and they were quite narrow trousers. But you could undo the zips and they ballooned out into baggie, sort of, new romantic-y type of trousers, which were fabulous. But people must have thought that they were horrible bottoms I was wearing. But I loved them. And I wish I had kept them. But I wore them out! You know, I couldn't afford many clothes.

Special attention was given to a particular section from Henry's interview where he commented on the various color associations linked with the male and female genders. In the passage he openly discussed his liking of the color pink, and how, through wearing pink clothes, he felt he was "going against" the dominant male clothing standards:

> [As a young boy] I wore colours that boys wouldn't wear. But boys… I mean Hippies would wear the colours I wore. But no ordinary schoolboys in the northeast of England would wear pink. And I still find men still comment on me wearing pink.… I wear a lot of pink. And a lot of men still have difficulty with that. And still mention it. And they come to me and say: "I wish I dared to wear it." And I think: "Well, why daren't you?" Yeah, it is a lovely colour. And there is nothing wrong with it.

Significantly, this sentiment was further reflected via his personal archive:

> **So can you tell me about a time that you felt really good about the way you looked? About your best fashion experience?**
> This is the suit I brought in, I will show you. This is the one that I had the most fun and wonderful times I had that involve clothing. I will show you. It is not just my clothing. You can see it is a Vivienne Westwood suit from about uhm… five years I think, five years. Again I would call that a sort of squashed raspberry colour… it's pink.

Coincidentally, at the same time, a JOOP aftershave advert was released in which a young and muscular male model commented that "Real men wear pink."[2] This was especially intriguing, particularly the disconnection between what Henry reported and the alleged new norms of masculinity, as presented in the aforementioned advert. With this in mind, and having purchased a black plain corduroy jacket, this led to the instinctive exploration of the process of change from what Henry as a young man viewed as the norms of masculinity and what contemporary young men might view as such; the progress from dark, sober masculinity to the "pink" image, as presented in the advert.

A series of practical experimentations was begun in which the aim was to attach to the purchased jacket a row of parallel panels that were black on one side, and pink on the reverse. Perhaps such a "device" would enable the quick change of the color of the garment from one to another; just as the social norms of masculinity and male attire are in constant flux. Importantly, the aim was not to mimic the fashion trends, but, instead, an attempt to understand the changing social norms regarding masculinity (indeed, arguably the pink color on the menswear catwalks might be just a reflection of quickly changing trends[3]).

Through metaphorically exploring the coloring processes more generally, the underlying question to answer was: If and how was it possible that a black garment could become a pink garment? This corresponded to how it evolved that the "old" masculinity became the "new" one. As an integral part of this process the question being explored was: Is it possible that the limitations of the social norms that the participants experienced in the past might in fact have changed with younger generations of men being no longer restricted by them? And, in turn, how might this relate to the various nonconforming attitudes clearly so important to these participants? Furthermore, how were these concepts, even in their past state, influencing their current experiences of aging? It was at this stage that the ideas evolved and moved from using this panel device; instead, starting a series of experimentations in which a bleached black cotton corduroy was dyed pink (Figure 4.5). The resultant shade of pink, which was intense and deep (closely resonating with "shocking pink" used often by Elsa Schiaparelli), was particularly interesting and relevant to what could be described as the "contemporary shade of masculinity." This was indeed an intriguing idea of an interplay between the old-black and new-pink masculinities, one that would not be able to be explicated in any other way but via these practical experimentations.

Having returned to the purchased corduroy jacket and unpicking all its elements; was significant because it appeared that the Pioneering and the Nonconforming themes had a lot in common and, for these reasons, some steps

Figure 4.5 Ania Sadkowska, "Nonconforming"; sketchbook pages—bleaching and dyeing experimentations; the Nonconforming jacket; front and back. Photographs by Fraser West.

of the practical analysis should also correspond, i.e., deconstruction processes. This was followed by bleaching all the elements, which were then dyed pink and restitched together. What was interesting in this process was that, while the black jacket was indeed transformed from black to pink, the old threads stayed black in spite of the intense bleaching and dyeing processes. This contributed to the verbalizing of the interpretation of the Nonconforming theme focusing on newly established understanding, while the various social norms regarding masculinity and masculine attire might have changed in the last few decades significantly, in this study, participants might still relate to the norms present when they were younger and ones that they once rebelled against.

Rematerializing

Finally, the Rematerializing theme emerged as a relatively straightforward theme based on a series of accounts in which participants referred to particular garments from their past toward which they had a strong sentimental connection. Importantly, most of these objects no longer existed and, therefore, were not available to the participants, offering a peculiar form of intangible and very emotional personal archives. But while this aspect of the theme was rather straightforward, it was the way in which the participants reported the desire of having these garments back nowadays that brought a certain level of complexity into the potential understanding of it, as explained for example by Kevin (63): "I've had a thing about three-quarter-length coats ever since the '60s when I came into possession of a three-quarter-length green leather coat, which was just the bee's knees. You know... and I never wore anything else.... I lost it and I really wish I'd still got it. I'd probably have it framed."

First, some participants reported their willingness to wear these garments again in the present. This suggests that the desire to rematerialize the idealized artifact can often be interpreted as their hidden wish to relive the joy they experienced while wearing those items.

Second, others reflected that, due to the changed trends in fashion, as well as their altered physicality, they would no longer wish nor be able to wear them. These participants still, however, had a strong desire to have them back, to look at them, and still be able to engage with them on a tactile level. It is in the situation of a material contact with the garment, and embodied and haptic experiences of it, that this desire to repossess the garment from the participants' past came to function so distinctively.

This was an interesting idea and one which, to a designer, is especially intriguing. Taking this as a first step in the practical exploration of this theme, and returning to the relevant images and passages, a note was taken of all these sentimental garments as their owners explained them. The objects described by the participants were as follows: a green leather three-quarter-length coat (Kevin), Jonson's *Clash of the Titans* shirt (Ian), and khaki green trousers, with zips from the ankle to the thigh so they could be worn in a tight or loose style (Henry). Design interpretation led to attempts to find a way to combine all these garments into one jacket, to create a form of a "fashion collage" using the key elements from each of these significant garments.

Next a second-hand jacket was purchased, which had both red and green stripes within its pattern. The significance of this garment was within retaining the colors that the participants mentioned as part of their "special" garments. Simultaneously, a mind-mapping exercise was completed, through which the various possibilities of creating such a "collage" artifact were explored and

Figure 4.6 Ania Sadkowska, "Rematerializing"; sketchbook pages—"special" artifacts collages; the Rematerializing jacket; front and back. Photographs by
Fraser West.

visualised. Consequently, the jacket was produced with poppers on the bottom that could be used to elongate it to a three-quarter-length coat[4] with inserted circular green leather collar.

At this stage, experimentation with different kinds of leather, as well as dyeing, printing, and embellishing was explored. However, none of these practices provided any stimuli or enhancement for understanding of the theme, which triggered the process of questioning this through reflective writing. It was important for the understanding of the theme more generally, that somehow this struggle as a maker to utilize these elements was significant to the way the participants were able or not to wear these garments. Something really important was there; however, it evaded being verbalized, even to the researcher herself. Having looked through all the photos from the participants' pasts again, however this time looking not only at the garments but at the participants wearing them was particularly interesting in regards to the interplay between the garment and the body. In other words, gaining an understanding of the essence of the embodied experience of a fashion garment was important.

This triggered a second series of experimentations, this time questioning not the intended garment itself but to create the experience it could bring to its potential wearer. It was at this point when it was realized that, in fact, what these participants had shared and revealed about themselves was not only the importance of these objects, but even more significantly the memories of how they *felt* when wearing them. They all had very positive embodied experiences while wearing them and this realization informed the researcher that the aims for this garment was to create something contemporary and wearable, yet something that would encompass those identified elements.

Having completed another series of drawings and collages (Figure 4.6), it was chosen to produce the design in which the original jacket collar was replaced by a circular green leather collar. This was a highly tactile experience of engaging with various materials and tools that, in turn, allowed for the exploration and expression of ideas via stimulating embodied responses. It was a simple, wearable, and contemporary solution suitable for the participants which would also be appropriate for them to wear; furthermore, each of them would connect to those elements relevant to them while wearing it.

Summary

The approach outlined brings together a focused multimodal methodology using a novel method and is further exploited by the inclusion of a series of practical creative experimentations involving various tools, materials, and artifacts. The objects revealed as part of the participants' personal archives were unique for each participant and included garments, accessories, and photos. All of the study participants clearly expressed the importance of maintaining and preserving their personal archives; various past garments functioned as reminders of their past fashion selves. In many instances the men reflected upon how they thought that their past bodies and experiences were imprinted on those garments which were often discussed with a tone of nostalgia over the elapsed time. At the same time these men presented themselves as forward-thinking fashion individuals, sensitive and responsive (yet selective) to quickly changing fashion trends and their aging physicality. In this sense these past objects were significant for the research process at the stage of data gathering because they worked as a stimulus for the conversation; and, while the body was not addressed explicitly by the interviewer, through describing and reflecting on these past objects, all of the participants discussed the body and bodily changes at great length.

Second, these past objects were important also at the stage of data analysis due to being able to experience them in a haptic way, that is to touch and feel the quality and texture of the fabric, see the colors, and inspect the details; such an embodied engagement was enabling to the creative practitioner. It was this series of embodied practical explorations that stimulated interpretation of the phenomenon under study; inevitably, some elements and details of these artifacts are represented in the garments produced. It could be argued that such complex data analysis was enhanced by the embodied, visual, and tactile interrogation of the participants' fashion and clothing archives, and thus permitted a stronger appreciation of the research material, which in turn enabled the production of highly interpretative written accounts and corresponding fashion artifacts. The process of interpreting through "making" facilitated development of alternative insights into the participants' lived experiences that could only be achieved through creative artful practices. The unique composition of the textual and visual research outcomes more fully represents the complexity of mature men's relationships with fashion and clothing as they grow older, and their bodies and outlooks change.

Notes

1 Here, informative and inspirational were designers such as Martin Margiela, Vivienne Westwood, Helmut Lang, and Rei Kawakubo whose works often allude to "the philosophical projects of deconstruction, to rethink the formal logic of dress itself" (Evans 2003: 250).

2 JOOP! Homme.

3 See, for example, catwalk collections from Christopher Raeburn S/S 2014, Sibling F/W 2015/16, or Moschino S/S 2016.

4 A three-quarter-length coat aesthetically alludes to a drape coat popular among the Teddy Boys and Mods in the 1950s and 1960s, once again highlighting the significance of the participants' past experiences of fashion and clothing and their individual histories.

References

Boden, Z. and Eatough, V. (2014) "Understanding More Fully: A Multimodal Hermeneutic-Phenomenological Approach," *Qualitative Research in Psychology*, 11(2): 160–77.

Bovone, L. (2012) "Fashion, Identity and Social Actors," in A. González and L. Bovone (eds.), *Identities Through Fashion: A Multidisciplinary Approach*, 67–93, London: Bloomsbury.

Butler-Kisber, L. (2010) *Qualitative Inquiry: Thematic, Narrative and Arts-Informed Perspectives*, London: Sage.

Clarke, J. (1976) "Style," in S. Hall and T. Jefferson (eds.), *Resistance Through Rituals: Youth Subcultures in Post-War Britain*, 175–91, Birmingham: The Centre for Contemporary Cultural Studies.

Cole, A. L. and Knowles, J. G. (2008) "Arts-Informed Research," in J. G. Knowles and A. L. Cole (eds.), *Handbook of the Arts in Qualitative Research*, 55–70, London: Sage.

Csikszentmihalyi, M. and Rochberg-Halton, E. (1981) *The Meaning of Things: Domestic Symbols and the Self*, Cambridge: Cambridge University Press.

Entwistle, J. (2015) *The Fashioned Body*. 2nd ed. Cambridge: Polity Press.

Etherington, K. (2004) *Becoming a Reflexive Researcher: Using Our Selves in Research*, London: Jessica Kingsley.

Evans, C. (2003) *Fashion at the Edge*, London: Yale University Press.

Finlay, L. (2011) *Phenomenology for Therapists: Researching the Lived World*, Oxford: Wiley-Blackwell.

Hall, S. and Jefferson, T., eds. (1976) *Resistance Through Rituals: Youth Subcultures in Post-War Britain*, Birmingham: The Centre for Contemporary Cultural Studies.

Hebdige, D. (1979) *Subculture: The Meaning of Style*, London: Methuen.

Kaiser, S. (2012) *Fashion and Cultural Studies*. London: Berg.

Kvale, S. (1996) *Interviews: An Introduction to Qualitative Research Interviewing*, London: Sage.

Kvale, S. (2006) "Dominance Through Interviews and Dialogues," *Qualitative Inquiry*, 12(3): 480–500.

Martin, B. and Hanington, B. (2012) *Universal Methods of Design*, Beverly, MA: Rockport.

McCauley Bowstead, J. (2018) *Menswear Revolution*. London: Bloomsbury.

Polhemus, T. (2010) *Street Style*, 2nd edn, London: PYMCA.

Sadkowska, A. (2016) "Arts-Informed Interpretative Phenomenological Analysis: Understanding Older Men's Experiences of Ageing Through the Lens of Fashion and Clothing," PhD thesis, Nottingham Trent University.

Sadkowska, A. (2018) "Arts-Informed Interpretative Phenomenological Analysis: '*Making*,' as a Means of Embodied Fashion Enquiry into Older Men's Lived Experiences," *Fashion Practice*, 10(3): 405–32.

Sadkowska, A., Wilde, D., and Fisher, T. (2015) "Third Age Men's Experience of Fashion and Clothing: An Interpretative Phenomenological Analysis," *Age, Culture, Humanities: An Interdisciplinary Journal*, 2: 35–70.

Sadkowska, A., Townsend, K., Fisher, T., and Wilde, D. (2017) "(Dis-)engaged Older Men? Hegemonic Masculinity, Fashion and Ageing," *Clothing Cultures*, 4(3): 185–201.

Smith, J. A. (1996) "Beyond the Divide Between Cognition and Discourse: Using Interpretative Phenomenological Analysis in Health Psychology," *Psychology and Health*, 11(2): 261–71.

Smith, J. A., Flowers, P., and Larkin, M. (2009) *Interpretative Phenomenological Analysis: Theory, Method and Research*, London: Sage.

Twigg, J. (2013) Age Ordering in Dress: Fashion, the Body and Age. In: Black, S., De La Haye, A., Entwistle, J., Rocamora, A., Root, R., and Thomas, H. (eds.) *The Handbook of Fashion Studies*. London: Bloomsbury, pp. 78–94.

5

"The Electric Corset and Other Future Histories"

Katherine Townsend, Sarah Kettley, and Sarah Walker

Introduction: "The Electric Corset"

"The Electric Corset" is a speculative "archives to wearables" practice-based research project and methodology with potential applications for fashion, e-textile, and hybrid designers working across disciplines and boundaries. Established by the authors in 2014, this creative inquiry was initiated in collaboration with the Lace, Costume and Textiles Collection, held by Nottingham City Museums and Galleries for the exhibition *Crafting Anatomies* (Bonington Gallery 2015). The aim of the project is to demonstrate the wealth of archival references available to designers of smart and electronic textiles (e-textiles) by considering the anatomy and modularity of historical dress as a catalyst for future wearable technology platforms (wearables). The chapter discusses some of the different theoretical and philosophical perspectives informing this interdisciplinary creative research; merging historical, contemporary, and critical approaches to fashion/textile design and conservation, in and beyond the archive (Vänskä and Clark 2017). The first half covers our rationale for accessing the archive, responding to the materials within it, and how evidence of past wearers is provided by traces on artifacts, or "imprints" (Freud in Derrida 1996). The second part discusses how we reconceptualized items selected from the archive through the development of the "remake–remodel" methodology and a series of speculative[1] prototypes incorporating e-textiles to visualize and actuate past and future networks on and between bodies.

The project title was inspired by a Victorian advertisement for one of Dr. Scott's electric corsets from 1883 (Art and Picture Collection 2014), designed using "medical and scientific principles"[2] and powered electromagnetically to enhance the health and well-being of the wearer. Based on the style and

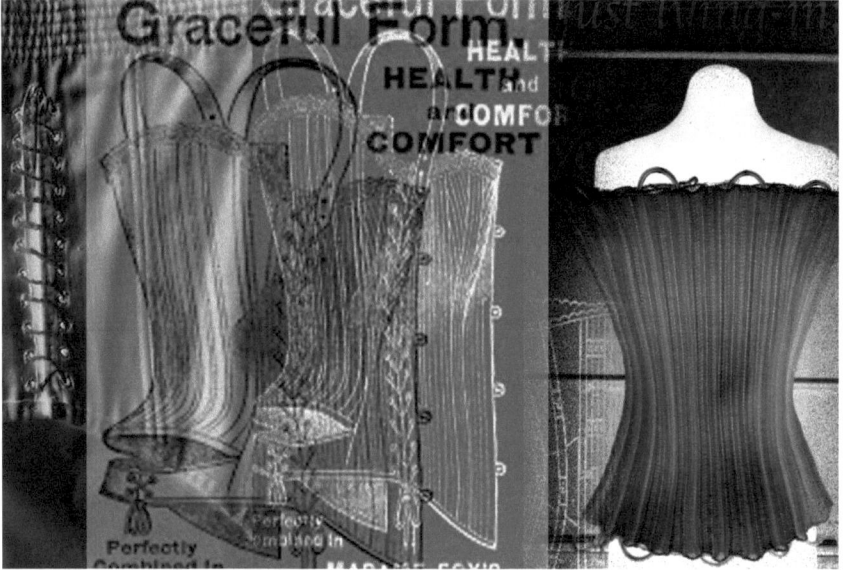

Figure 5.1 Composite image (left to right): lacing detail of corset, *c.* 1880 from the Lace, Costume and Textiles Collection archive; Parisienne-style corset advertisement *c.* 1880s; e-textile corset made by the authors. Photograph and image credits: Katherine Townsend and Sarah Walker.

construction of Parisian corsets for women, with elaborate belt designs for men; the devices were marketed to cure all manner of female ailments or enhance male sexual performance (Marvin 1988). Other examples of electronic textiles being used at this time include illuminated headbands worn by ballet dancers in *La Farandole* in 1883 (Guler, Gannon, and Sicchio 2016: 3). However, it is the enthusiasm of manufacturers to integrate new technology with fashion that makes the electric corset, a wearable device from the past, such an appropriate metaphor for future design speculation.

Archives to wearables rationale

In "The Emotional Wardrobe," Stead (2005) identified the need for further research to be undertaken from a "fashion perspective," by integrating smart materials and electronics with the contemporary body. In the last decade digital tools have made a significant impact on the fashion system, with advances in wearable technologies being "the result of a new systemic interaction among diverse approaches belonging to different sectors" (Tenuta and Testa 2018: 35).

The scientific and the creative processes associated with "electronic" and "textile" design are essentially different, but it is possible to identify their intersection through experiential practice that balances "objective testing with inductive reasoning based on emotional responses" (ibid.: 37). Consequently, this research responds to the need for the development of experiential methodological approaches to fashion wearables that blur scientific and creative methods, and textile and product aesthetics with e-textile functionality (Starner 2001; Tenuta and Testa 2018).

To date, "wearable technology" (WT) has not been adopted as quickly as predicted with healthcare, fitness, and entertainment being the most significant applications (Page 2015). The field of fashionable technology (Seymour 2008) includes various WT product categories, including one-off pieces for the catwalk, exhibition, stage, screen, or red carpet, often incorporating phone-based apps with textile sensing and display on the body (Berzowska 2013: 456; Farrington 2017). Angel Chang's electronically enabled collections were a notable exception and grew out of a vision to offer women versatile wardrobe solutions that could actually "do things"—beyond just looking good.[3] However, despite recent growth in the WT sector, this leaves ongoing ambitions for it to be a more natural part of daily life (DeVaul, Schwartz, and Pentland 2001; WEAR Sustain 2018). To date, wearables have been typically approached as a complete "input–processing–output" system within a single garment, in line with a "seamless" vision of utility and comfort (Guler, Gannon, and Sicchio 2016; Kettley 2016). In contrast, we believe that this implicit focus on the single garment as whole system has contributed to the lower than hoped for take up of WT in everyday life, creating barriers to integration in dynamic practices of dress (Entwistle 2015), durability, and safe disposal at end of product lifetime (McLaren, Hardy, and Hughes-Riley 2017).

While e-textile components are shrinking and becoming more flexible, they continue to present constraints in relation to their integration into fashion and textile design processes[4] (Veja 2015). E-textiles also necessitate a step-change in established production processes, dependent on whether they are first (components applied onto textile surfaces), second (components integrated into textile structures, typically woven or knitted), or third generation (microcomponents integrated into yarn structures)[5] in approach (Davies 2016; Myers et al. 2017; Hughes-Riley, Dias, and Cork 2018). Innovative on-demand and limited-edition processes offer one way of dealing with the "wicked" nature of the wearable production process (Kobakant 2018; Raeburn 2018), but the wider practical turn in fashionable clothing, the rise of gender neutral, "classless" styles (Laver 1995) and fluid fabrics and silhouettes present limited scope for discreet technical interventions, whatever the e-textile generation level. While modularity through layering and bespoke pattern cutting, as found in historical tailoring, is still present in haute couture and high-end designer labels, details such as pockets, buttons, and collars (with stands) and cuffs (and their associated functionality) are increasingly omitted from ready-to-wear and particularly fast fashion, due to cost implications.

It is for these reasons that we looked to past categories of dress and practices of wear, to help us reconceptualize the wardrobe, and individual garment, as a contemporary "system of [dress] objects"[6] (Baudrillard 2005). Following an initial literature review, the concept of the accessory within historical clothing, particularly up to the Edwardian period, became instrumental to the study, by representing a removable detail that was cared for differently and could be reattached as necessary to host garments. The flexibility of this partial garment provided a potential model for working with e-textiles in contemporary fashion practice (Møller and Kettley 2017). Based on this premise, the researchers studied fashion artifacts from various archives, including: The Lace Archive, Nottingham Trent University; The Clothworkers' Centre at the Victoria and Albert (V&A) Museum, London; and particularly the Lace, Costume and Textiles Collection (LCTC)[7] housed at Newstead Abbey, Nottinghamshire. The aim was to explore how accessorizing e-textile elements via fashion details (or fragments) could be a method of heterogeneous integration, as a way of developing the fit/non-fit of the science/textiles model.

Accessing the archive: Responding to the materials

According to curators at the V&A, museums are now trying to put human intent back into the making process rather than preserving the "natural order" of things in glass cases; by focusing on dress as an enacted practice instead of exquisite examples of technique in collections of random objects.[8] The opening up of the archive to wider access and interpretation follows the "material turn" in fashion conservation (Scaturro 2017), presenting researcher/practitioners with new opportunities to investigate how isolated artifacts might be better understood and interpreted, in terms of their ecologies of production and consumption (Clarke 2011; Entwistle 2015). The empirically focused "Electric Corset" project therefore contributes to a developing body of research into the impact of the archive on creative practice by designers, artists, and curators who are catalyzing innovative ways of responding to collections (e.g., Maier 2014; Clark and Phillips 2010; Pierce 2017). This work echoes an approach established in the twentieth century by visual artists who questioned and exploited the concept of "what constitutes an archive and what authority it holds in relation to its subject" (Merewether 2006: 10).

Traditionally, fashion and textile practitioners have sought inspiration from museum repositories to inform new designs, or to rework historical styles. While this form of scholarship is still valid, changing views on textile and fashion conservation have influenced practices both within and in response to the archive, leading to more critical and creative engagement in design and cultural production (Brooks and Eastop 2016). Mode Museum, Antwerp and The Museum at the Fashion Institute of Technology, New York are notable for developing "new concepts of museology and museography, linking art and life in an essential, critical and innovative way" (Calefato 2019: 39).

The readable nature of textiles and dress enables them to act as conduits into design and production techniques and related theories and practices of crafting, wearing, and re/presenting "dress" (Fletcher 2016; Entwistle 2015; Clark and Phillips 2010). Of particular importance to the "Electric Corset" "archives to wearables" methodology, is how outcomes are influenced by first-hand observations of the visible and tangible evidence of distributed cognition and memory, found within selected, material artifacts (Merleau-Ponty 1969; Sutton 2008; Malafouris 2013). This style of "idiosyncratic probing" is still relatively new for textile practitioners (Pierce 2017) but can be increasingly identified in exhibitions using archival materials to highlight lost craft skills by catalyzing contemporary practice, for example in *Closely Held Secrets* (Townsend 2016) and *Bummock: The Lace Archive* (Bracey and Maier 2018).

The processes of selecting, recording, responding to, and reinterpreting archival sources have instigated a series of creative approaches and experimental prototypes, employing "craft" as a methodology. By describing and analyzing various stages of the "Electric Corset" project (from 2014 to 2017), the following sections present different conceptual and physical methods for "unmaking and [re]making" the archive (Olowu, Buenfeld, and Globus 2016). By recording and animating objects within and outside of the repository, new assemblages of historical and imagined "wearables" have been originated that diverge from the aesthetic limitations and ethical implications of copying (Pierce 2017). This open-ended engagement refutes the idea of the archive as a receptacle of preserved (hidden) things by reinforcing the idea of the "lab" where experimentation may lead to new concepts informed by the past.

Tracing the archived body: Absence as presence

Our interest as archival researchers lies in identifying the formal, aesthetic design and biographical (or social) clues held within an object (Brooks and Eastop 2016) to inform our own ideas of what might constitute a contemporary object of use. This draws on the "absence of (human) presence", by acknowledging Burgin's (1969) philosophical ideas, and in turn the multidisciplinary approaches required in e-textile and wearables design. We also consider Merleau-Ponty's (1969) intertwining of the "visible and invisible," objective and subjective nature of our embodied cognition through engagement with material things. For example, having assessed the style and specification of a historical garment, one intuitively considers the conceptual dimensions of the item in relation to how it has been worn (or effectively used) as evidenced through "traces [and] residual marks" left by the body (Merewether 2006: 10). This anthropological and ontological focus on the "material and immaterial qualities" of dress (Scaturro 2017) by the team is supported by previous research into narratives of making and wearing textiles (Townsend 2011). By exploring values associated with the "material agency" (Malafouris 2013: 119) of conserved artifacts, the perception of the archive as the place where things are ordered chronologically and legally (Derrida 1996) is questioned. Instead, this closer reading of textile things correlates with the Freudian, impressionistic power of collections to reveal bodily "imprints" (ibid.).

When considering the absence of the physical body in archives, an analogy we found helpful was to imagine the historical items we were viewing as ghosts of the original wearer's intimate relationship with a garment. Geczy and Karaminas (2019: 21) discuss how contemporary fashion's ontology is based on its haunting capacity and that, as Derrida states: "no one can be sure if by returning [the spectre] testifies to a past or living future."[9] The notion of *dure* or history has famously been incorporated into clothing via the simulation of patina and abrasion by designers such as Vivienne Westwood (and Malcolm McLaren), Rei Kawakubo, Martin Margiela, and Hussein Chalayan (Geczy and Karaminas 2019; Townsend 2011; Verhelst and Debo 2008). "The recycled garment, or the new garment that replicates signs of wear, is from the start a provisional entity in which the present state of wear is haunted by implications of a better past" (Geczy and Karaminas 2019: 28). Margiela's deconstructed approach to the repurposing of vintage fashion/accessories into alternative wearable configurations and conception of "relics" as classic wardrobe staples, correlates with our own aims to view archived objects beyond the confines of their "museumization" (Calefato 2019: 38).

Figure 5.2 Artifacts selected from The Lace, Costume and Textile Archive, including a footman's livery coat (1890–1910); a twill ("jean") woman's corset (1800–10); a woman's dress collar, embellished with shells and glass beads (1920–30) and three detachable men's starched linen shirt collars (1850–1952). Property of Nottingham City Museums and Galleries. Photographs and image credits: Katherine Townsend and Sarah Walker.

In the following section, we discuss the selection of dress artifacts from the LCTC based on their facility to provide a "way in" to the (past) body and potential to be reimagined and remade as contemporary "dress objects" (Skjold 2016: 140). In this way, the historical items were released from their suspension in time, and recontextualized as dynamic objects to inform experimental creative practice.

Developing the remake–remodel methodology

The core aim of the "Electric Corset" inquiry was to develop a practice research methodology by utilizing historical dress objects to inform the design of future wearables, as finally disseminated at *Research Through Design 2017* (Kettley et al. 2017).

The first phase of the project (April 2014–January 2015) involved various visits to view, select, and study items from the LCTC, under the guidance of the Curator of Costume and Dress, Judith Edgar. As researchers in an unfamiliar archive, we approached the task of identifying items with an open mind, requesting "corsets, undergarments and items of dress that interfaced directly with the body and/or had decorative/functional details with the potential to be reinterpreted artistically as wearable design ideas." We were naturally drawn to fashion accessories and garment details, which have primacy within the "bodyscape" by marking its edges and demarcating potential access points (Vainshtein 2012).

A small collection of items was chosen to work with for the exhibition *Crafting Anatomies* (2015) where we installed an annotated physical anthology of historical artifacts augmented by a film featuring a sequence of speculations on e-textiles and wearables. The pieces included a twill ("jean") woman's corset (or jumps) (1800–10), a woman's dress collar, embellished with shells and glass beads (1920–30), and three detachable men's starched linen shirt collars (1850–1952). Edgar also showed us a footman's livery coat (1890–1910) incorporating the tailoring and trims (e.g., frogging, crested buttons, epaulettes) found in formal uniforms (Figure 5.2), offering considerable potential for e-textile reinterpretations. By engaging with these archival materials and photographing other related pieces that "spoke" to us, such as lace collars and a poacher's jacket with expansive pockets, themes began to emerge, which we believed could inform the design of future wearables, based on functionality, care and maintenance, modularity, and layering (Kettley, Townsend, and Walker 2015).

Having identified workable objects, we progressed the creative experimental inquiry by developing a methodology for working between the archive, fashion, e-textile, and wearables design. The methods applied in this first phase of the study acknowledge fashion and scientific design models of practice through four iterative stages: 1. Object research, 2. Ideation through craft, 3. Presentation, and 4. Evaluation.

Stage 1: Object research—consisted of using the LCTC database and other historical costume sources followed by active research to identify artifacts in the archive and record them using photography, notes, and sketching. As described above, the selection criteria for objects was based on the curator's expert knowledge of the collection, the object's aesthetic and technical, visual and tactile qualities, and its fragmentary status as part of a larger system of dress. This directed approach was supplemented by further "controlled rummaging" (Bracey and Maier 2018: 4) under the guidance of the curator, during which we allowed our selections to be influenced by what spoke to us (e.g., the potential to be refashioned, and future wear-ability) referred to by Barthes as the "punctum" of an object (cited in Roberts 2018: 66). The primary recording stage was crucial, as the objects could only be viewed through the gloved hands of the curator (and occasionally our own) but not removed from the archive at this point.

Stage 2: Ideation through craft—this work was undertaken outside the archive in the design studio[10] incorporating diverse design developments using photographs from Stage 1, along with drawings and photocopies to represent the original historical source while allowing for reinterpretation. The boning and ten-hole lacing of the corset, the buttons, fastenings, pockets, and decorative cording (frogging) of the footman's jacket, and the varied collar shapes inspired 2D drawings, collages, and material sketches and assemblages. Following this, 3D partial garments were "moulaged" (Duburg and van der Tol 2008) by working on half and full-size mannequins using cloth manipulation, stitching, and the placement of electronic components such as LilyPad (Arduino) and SMAs (shape memory alloys). As illustrated in Figure 5.3, this crafts-driven creative prototyping was used to extend the material available to develop a novel visual language (Kettley 2012), prioritizing hand making as a "way in" to the programming and use of digital tools (Taylor and Townsend 2014).

Stage 3: Presentation—the artifacts selected from the LCTC (e.g., footman's jacket, corset, collars) formed the basis of "The Electric Corset and Other Future Histories" installation in the *Crafting Anatomies* exhibition (Bonington Gallery 2015). An especially made-to-measure wall-mounted vitrine was made to house the jacket, and the corset and collars were placed in two glass cases. The artifacts

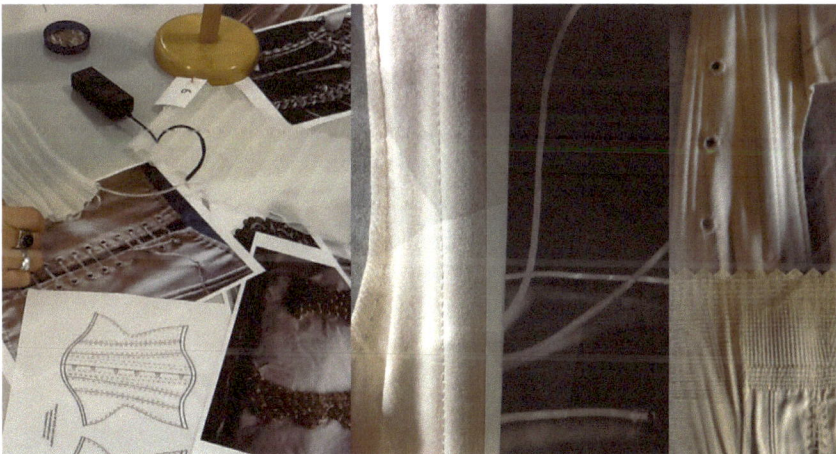

Figure 5.3 Examples of wearable ideation by "remaking" and "remodeling" artifacts from the archive. Photographs and image credit: Katherine Townsend and Sarah Walker.

were presented together with a film, communicating the research methodology through a series of short video clips and images, overlaid with historical quotations (Figures 5.1 and 5.4). The content included photographs of the original garments and accessories (taken in the archive) and documentation of the process of experimental ideation, or "play" (Glazzard et al. 2014). The slides also incorporated historical fashion plates (e.g., from copies of the *Ladies Tailor*, 1880s) and texts such as: "It was not until the tailor learnt to cut that the designer could 'compose' a costume" (Cunnington 1949: 57) to create a visual and textual anthology—a "dictionary" of sorts (Clark and Phillips 2010).

Stage 4: Evaluation—the montages featured in the stills comprising historical inspiration, sketches, designs, and fragments reinforced a "seemingly handmade" (Ligon in Olowu, Buenfeld, and Globus 2016: 9) approach, incorporating pattern cutting, machine and hand sewing, and traditional making skills (perhaps surprisingly) crucial to e-textile development (Guler, Gannon, and Sicchio 2016). The use of hand and digital making and collaging techniques was particularly effective in terms of informing and communicating the developing methodology. Having to visually communicate the different but overlapping stages of the research journey to make it tangible to ourselves and others required reflection on the deconstruction/reconstruction process to understand how historical things were made while "figuring out"[11] new electronically enabled material forms.

These reflections, together with audience feedback on the prototypes visualized in "The Electric Corset and Other Future Histories" film, in relation to

Figure 5.4 Stills from "The Electric Corset and Other Future Histories" film 2015. Photographs and image credits: Sarah Walker and Katherine Townsend.

how we might fabricate these 2D designs as 3D material artifacts, informed our heuristic research approach in the next stage of the project.

From accessories to ontological objects

In the second phase of the "Electric Corset" (February–July 2015) we recreated items found in the LCTC archive, including spats, collar stands, a flat lace collar, cuffs, and pockets as "sacrificial"[12] calico toiles (Figure 5.5). By drafting patterns of these fragments of larger systems of dress, we were able to make representations of them to act as tools that could then be experienced bodily through narrative

Figure 5.5 Fragment Toiles, 2015. Calico copies of original items found in the Lace, Costume and Textile Archive, including men's detachable shirt collar, bib (or dickie) and spats, and women's detachable half-sleeve (for a blouse), and pocket. Toiles made by Karen Harrigan. Photographs and image credits: Martha Glazzard and Katherine Townsend.

play and phenomenological material encounters (Kettley et al. 2017). Multiples could be made, and versions of them iterated to explore constraints and opportunities for the placement of electronic circuitry (which may be "soft," composed of conductive yarns), and of hardware components (such as batteries and microprocessors).

In the development of fashion "wearables" it is important to include human–garment interaction as part of the design space or problematization. That is, the wearable, by definition, includes computational functionality, and so the experience of interaction, its expressive nature, and its use-value and function all need to be considered as part of an extended design process, beyond the object itself. Historical references to connecting technologies in dress and haberdashery were introduced into the process, such as Rudofsky's (1947) account (and map) of buttons and pockets on men's suits in the 1940s and the historical embodied language of dress was referred to as a reminder of Malafouris's concept of material agency across time (2013). We wanted the form (of the simulated artifact) to suggest user-defined functionality rather than beginning with a utilitarian "need" as is more usual in human–computer interaction (HCI) (Berzowska 2013). We have already noted that the extremities and details of garments serve to mark the territories of the body (Vainshtein 2012). Other accounts of the edges of dress illustrate their transition to the status of accessory; consider the lace cuffs, lappets, and collars of seventeenth-century Netherlands (du Mortier and Bloemberg 2009: 227–31). The idea of the "accessory" is therefore important to our work on various levels. The term today suggests a small thing, often decorative, unnecessary but signifying taste or social commentary, attached to a larger central, functional garment (Møller and Kettley 2017). However, accessories once included starched bibs ("dickeys"), collars, and cuffs in functional wardrobes (Roche, cited in Jones 2013: 125); items that would now be integrated into a shirt or jacket or even erased through fast fashion processes, as discussed at the beginning of this chapter. As researcher/practitioners we are concerned with the development of the "archives to wearable" methodology as a way of enhancing an individual's management of the dynamic expression and functionality of clothing. However, this aim is challenged by the constraints of the contemporary imaginary of the wearable, as noted by both Georg Simmel and Ferdinand Tönnies, who understood fragments of fashion as "instantaneous reflections of social status" at the turn of the last century (Lehmann 2000: 141). Thus "the fragment" may offer a more appropriate term than "accessory," allowing us to more fully explore the analogous architectures and topologies of the fashion wearable and networked computing. The fragment is also relevant for WT from a pragmatic perspective, as hard electronic components in wearables are fragile and expensive. There is an analogy here with costly fabrics such as silk or lace, and with labor-intensive surface embellishments such as hand embroidery. The care practices of such ostentatious materials have always been necessarily different from those of more utilitarian or frequently worn garment parts like the body of a shirt; precious pieces such as detachable trims were removed before potentially harsh treatments could harm them or shorten their lifespan. Jacquard by Google suggest their Levi's Commuter Trucker (marketed as a cycling jacket) can be washed up to ten times, but if the cuff that contains the electronic yarns could be removed, this could extend garment laundering and longevity. The aftercare requirements of the Levi's jacket and other wearable products (Guler, Gannon, and Sicchio 2016; Hughes-Riley, Dias, and Cork 2018) highlight the need for a wider ecology of materials and practices to be developed to support their development within the context of everyday life. If the design of a new detergent entails the redesign of a washing machine, and domestic laundry practices (Domen 2013), then how complex is the relational material world we must bring forth for textile-based wearable systems to fully emerge? We propose that this way of imagining care goes well beyond the standard washability tests of current innovative products.

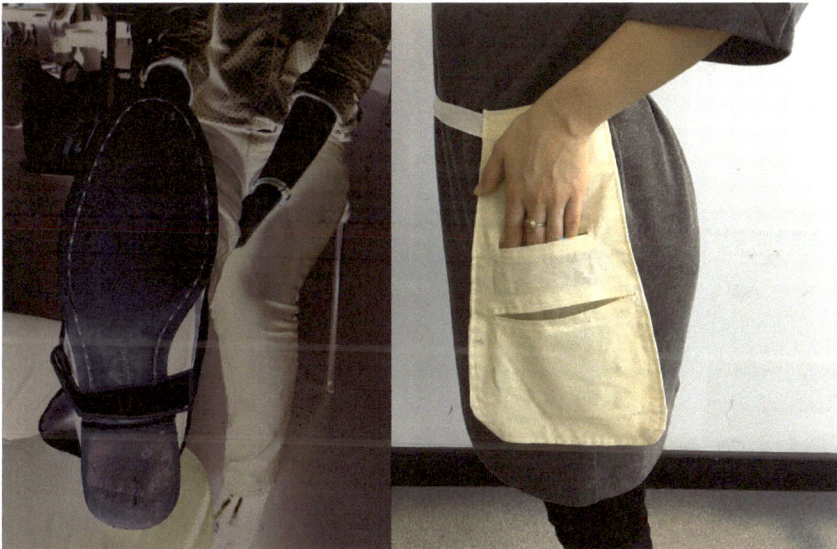

Figure 5.6 User (playful) interaction with Fragment Toiles (made by Karen Harrigan). Photographs and image credits: Martha Glazzard, Sarah Walker, and Katherine Townsend.

Toward experiential networks on and between bodies

Our practice-based research into the creative development of an ontology of e-textile/dress objects has been pursued through the lens of the material turn, by "privileging the agency of objects [in fashion archives] within a broader contextual framework" (Scaturro 2017: 22). However, we have also been working through the lens of the ontological arrangements of code and hardware found in computer systems. Lindley, Coulton, and Cooper (2017) recently expanded on object-oriented ontology (both a speculative-realist philosophical view of the world, and an approach to programming) as a way of conceptualizing, and therefore designing effectively for the Internet of Things (IoT), which WT will necessarily be a part of.

Our efforts to deconstruct the normative imaginary of the wearable as a single garment might be understood as a direct engagement with ontology as a material in itself. Such "design and crafting of a material world" is made manifest in video games (Bogost cited in Lindley, Coulton, and Cooper 2017: S2489), while for us the manifestation takes the form of related fragments of garments and dress systems. Therefore, we do not so much aim to design one reactive or interactive wearable concept but demonstrate the potential of the deconstructed garment system as a way of conceptualizing a platform for the development of multiple future wearable designs and products. We also envisage the relationship between garments and their individual components as a way of posing questions about the configuration of the ontology of wearables as one category of an entangled network or "constellation"[13] that comprises an IoT.

If this is an attempt to open up our own understanding of the wearable as an assemblage of entangled fragments, then we also have the ambition to offer the wearer a space for creativity in the dynamic manipulation of their wardrobe, and its potential functionalities. In the "Electric Corset," the opportunity for wearer interaction and intervention is facilitated by making experimental garment prototypes in the form of playful "tools" to elicit spontaneous and embodied responses from participants. This draws directly on actor-network-theory, particularly the uncertainty and agency of objects within the social space (Latour 2005). We therefore hope that through playful dress-acts (after the linguistic "speech act") and performative, phenomenological wearing practices, wearers are also able to engage with the relationships and ontologies of their worlds.

The approach and experience of creating the initial prototypes led us to develop a series of three shirtdresses, or Networked Toiles[14] in the third phase of the project (September 2016–January 2017). The three shirtdresses were

Figure 5.7 Networked Toiles exhibited at *Research Through Design 2017*, National Museum of Scotland. Shirtdresses configured with multiple, detachable fragments incorporating e-textile functionality. Photographs and image credits: Sarah Kettley and Katherine Townsend.

configurable using multiple cuffs, collars and bibs, and pockets, based on those identified in the LCTC archive. Consequently, each shirtdress body comprised a platform for multiple possible circuits, created by attaching garment fragments with snap fasteners (Figure 5.7). In this respect we took a deconstructed approach by revealing the e-textiles and their fastenings. As Cunnington (1949: 124) states: "There are three kinds: the concealed, the visible, and the conspicuous .... A visible fastening device shall have an aesthetic as well as a merely practical function."

As a result, the circuit remained formally (as well as ontologically) flexible on the textile base through the application of a silver/bamboo fabric cut into strips to create visible conductive wires with an aesthetic reference to the military inspired livery garments we had seen in the LCTC at Newstead (Figure 5.2) and deconstructed fashion, where the making of the garment is visually referenced. The bibs (or "dickies") most successfully visualized the potential for engagement with varying levels of LED display (ostentation) and functionality, while interchangeable pockets manifested different interaction behaviors through diverse electronic switch mechanisms (for example, magnetic switches in combination with cuffs). Such two-part switches, of course, also offer the potential for circuit completion (and therefore display and functionality) between bodies and environments, not just within one garment.

The next stage of the inquiry would be to develop an attendant ontological approach to data, as a further material and actant to be engaged with in the design of such constellations (e.g. Hardy et al 2019). Options for this further phase could include the use of "design fictions," including branding and marketing materials, as in Lindley, Coulton, and Cooper's work (2017), Service Design approaches to "product-service-systems" (PSSs) (ten Bhömer et al. 2013), and Speed and Oberlander's (2016) framework for design from, with, and by data, which looks forward to a world in which data learns from itself to become the designer.

Other future histories

"The Electric Corset" is a metaphor for speculative wearables design based on archival research. Dr. Scott's and others' "electric" accessories were a pragmatic and imaginative response to advances in technology at the end of the nineteenth century. Our own interest in third generation e-textiles (Hughes-Riley, Dias, and Cork 2018) in relation to their improved flexibility and potential seamless connections to cloth and bodily performance, is to consider them as actuators within a reimagined system of dress objects. Our approach has been facilitated by adopting a craft methodology for developing wearables as a natural extension of the contemporary wardrobe. The methodology has been informed by engaging with different archived dress objects, which bear testament to their interactions with bodies of the past that adapted to them, often through regular patterns of use. While the lives and actions of these ghosts can only be imagined their legacies should not be static.

As Valerie Steele observed at the End of Fashion conference in 2016 (see Geczy and Karaminas 2019), she has an issue with the term "costume," which seems to negate that a garment was once fashionable and new. Her work as Director and Chief Curator of The Museum of the Fashion Institute of Technology has been influential in the shift away from fashion's death drive to museumization, toward a more innovative (and sustainable) form of conservation that synthesizes design practice with cultural analysis and intervention (Calefato 2019). By learning from the valuable, but often overlooked, object biographies of artifacts crafted by previous generations of makers and wearers, we can speculate upon how the body might electronically augment its own interactions within contemporary culture. In this way, we may also be able to create new, longer lasting things that are "wearable" on an aesthetic, functional, and technological level.

Notes

1   "Speculative" in this sense is intended to provoke praxis, and ecologies of production, rather than the more usual use of the term "speculative design," which seeks to provoke questions in the viewer around familiar patterns of meaning and consumption.

2   See: https://www.theatlantic.com/technology/archive/2016/11/electric-corsets-the-original-wearable-devices/507230/ (accessed August 13, 2019).

3   Chang's 2006 collection, which incorporated the use of innovative materials, including color-changing prints, light-up fabrics, and self-heating linings, was a first for the American designer market. Her work also focuses on the conservation of indigenous textile crafts and sustainable fashion production. See: http://angelchang.com/blog/angel-chang/ (accessed August 13, 2019).

4   The Advanced Textile Research Group (ATRG) and members of the Fashion, Textiles and Knitwear (FTK) department at Nottingham Trent University, including Townsend, have developed knitted, woven, and embroidered prototypes incorporating e-textiles.

5   The Levi's® Commuter™ Trucker jacket achieves this to some degree, but with reliance on a smart phone to support product functionality.

6   Else Skjold (2016) uses the term "dress object" to define it as a physical item of clothing, as opposed to its signifier, as referred to in *The Fashion System* (Barthes 2010).

7   The LCTC is owned and managed by Nottingham City Museums and Galleries.

8   Comments made by the curator as part of the State of Early Modern Undress course, Victoria & Albert Museum, London, January–March 2017. See: https://www.vam.ac.uk/info/learning-academy (accessed August 13, 2019).

9   Geczy and Karaminas's discussion of fashion's capacity to haunt itself builds on Jacques Derrida's concept hauntology (a composite of haunting and ontology) explored in his 1993 book, *Specters of Marx*. See Derrida (1998: 143).

10 The MA Fashion, Textiles and Knitwear design studio, School of Art and Design, Nottingham Trent University.

11 Cocker, Gansterer, and Greil (2015: 54) use the term "figuring" to describe "the small yet transformative energies, emergences and experiential shifts which operate before, between and beneath the more readable gestures of artistic practice."

12 Glazzard coined the phrase "sacrificial" to describe the "throwaway" nature of the toile compared to the preciousness of the original artifact as discussed in Kettley et al. (2017: 493–5).

13 Constellations are linked to Gilles Deleuze and Felix Guattari's ontological framework "Assemblage Theory" (2013 [1980]).

14 A collection of three Networked Toiles was developed by the authors with pattern cutter Karen Harrigan and shown in the exhibition at the National Galleries of Scotland as part of the team's submission for *RTD2017* (Kettley et al. 2017).

References

Art and Picture Collection (2014) The New York Public Library. "Dr. Scott's Electric Corset." New York Public Library Digital Collections. Available online: http://digitalcollections.nypl.org/items/510d47e0-fcc0-a3d9-e040-e00a18064a99 (accessed April 27, 2014).

Barthes, R. (2010) *The Fashion System*, London: Vintage Classics.

Baudrillard, J. (2005) *The System of Objects*, London: Verso.

Berzowska, J. (2013) "XS Labs: Electronic Textiles and Reactive Garments as Sociocultural Interventions," in S. Black, A. de la Haye, J. Entwistle, A. Rocamora, R. A. Root, and H. Thomas (eds.), *The Handbook of Fashion Studies*, 456–75, London: Bloomsbury.

Bonington Gallery (2015) *Crafting Anatomies: Materials, Performance, Identity*, Exhibition: January 7–February 4; Symposium: January 30, Nottingham Trent University. Available online: http://www.boningtongallery.co.uk/exhibitions/crafting-anatomies (accessed January 8, 2017).

Bracey, A. and Maier, D., eds. (2018) *Bummock: The Lace Archive*, Waddington: Flipping the Bummock Press.

Brooks, M. and Eastop, D. (2016) *Refashioning and Redress: Conserving and Displaying Dress*, Los Angeles, CA: Getty Conservation Press.

Burgin, V. (1969) "The Absence of Presence." Available online: http://theoria.art-zoo.com/the-absence-of-presence-victor-burgin/ (accessed February 25, 2019).

Calefato, P. (2019) "Fashionscapes," in A. Geczy and V. Karaminas (eds.), *The End of Fashion: Clothing and Dress in the Age of Globalization*, 31–47, London: Bloomsbury.

Clark, J. and Phillips, A. (2010) *The Concise Dictionary of Dress*, London: Violette Editions.

Clarke, A. J. (2011) "The Anthropological Object in Design: From Victor Papanek to Superstudio," in A. J. Clarke (ed.), *Design Anthropology: Object Culture in the 21st Century*, 74–87, New York: Springer.

Cocker, E., Gansterer, N., and Greil, M. (2015) "Notion of Notation," *Performance Research: A Journal of the Performing Arts*, 20(6): 53–7.

Cunnington, C. W. (1949) *The Art of English Costume*, London: Collins.

Davies, D. (2016) "Case study," in S. Kettley, *Designing with Smart Textiles*, 224–5, London: Bloomsbury.

Deleuze, G. and Guattari, F. (2013 [1980]) *A Thousand Plateaus*, London: Bloomsbury Academic.

Derrida, J. (1996) *Archive Fever: A Freudian Impression*, trans. E. Prenowitz, Chicago, IL: University of Chicago Press.

Derrida, J. (1998) "From Specters of Marx," in *The Derrida Reader: Writing Performances*, Omaha, NE: University of Nebraska Press.

DeVaul, R. W., Schwartz, S. J., and Pentland, A. (2001) MIThril: Context-Aware Computing for Daily Life. Whitepaper, MIT Media Lab. Available online: https://www.media.mit.edu/wearables/mithril/MIThril.pdf (accessed August 8, 2019).

Domen, T. (2013) "Scenario Thinking: An Ambitious Roadmap for Transformative Change," talk given as part of the Horizon Scanning lecture series, Nottingham Trent University, October 25, 2013.

du Mortier, B. and Bloemberg, N. (2009) *Accessorize! 250 Objects of Fashion and Desire*, Amsterdam: Rijksmuseum.

Duburg, A. and van der Tol, R. (2008) *Draping: Art and Craftsmanship in Fashion Design*, The Hague: De Jonge Hond.

Entwistle, J. (2015) *The Fashioned Body: Fashion, Dress and Modern Social Theory*, 2nd edn, Cambridge: Polity Press.

Farrington, C. (2017) "Wearable Technology as Personalised Fashion: Empowering or Oppressive?," in I. Kuksa and T. Fisher (eds.), *Design for Personalisation*, 51–70, Abingdon: Routledge.

Fletcher, K. (2016) *Craft of Use: Post-Growth Fashion*, Abingdon: Routledge.

Geczy, A. and Karaminas, V., eds. (2019) *The End of Fashion: Clothing and Dress in the Age of Globalization*, London: Bloomsbury.

Glazzard, M., Kettley, S., Acti, T. M., and Harrigan, K. (2014) "Experiential Collaborations from Garment to Costume: Play and the Thing as Design Outcome," *Craft + Design Enquiry*, 6: 137–57.

Guler, S. D., Gannon, M., and Sicchio, K. (2016) *Crafting Wearables: Blending Technology with Fashion*, New York: Apress.

Hardy, D., Townsend, K., Kgatuke, M., Salter, E., Downes, T., Harrigan, K., Allcock, S. and Dias, T. (2019): Light my elbows: a cycling jacket incorporating electronic yarn, Conference contribution in *Textile Intersections 2019*, Loughborough University, London 12–14 September, pp. 1–10. Available online: https://doi.org/10.17028/rd. lboro.9741278.v1.

Hughes-Riley, T., Dias, T., and Cork, C. R. (2018) "A Historical Review of the Development of Electronic Textiles," *Fibers*, 6(2): art. 34. Available online: https:// www.mdpi.com/2079-6439/6/2/34 (accessed August 8, 2019).

Jones, J. (2013) "Gender and Eighteenth-Century Fashion," in S. Black, A. de la Haye, J. Entwistle, A. Rocamora, R. A. Root, and H. Thomas (eds.), *The Handbook of Fashion Studies*, 121–36, London: Bloomsbury.

Kettley, S. (2012) "The Foundations of Craft: A Suggested Protocol for Introducing Craft to Other Disciplines," *The Journal of Craft Research*, 3(1): 33–51.

Kettley, S. (2016) "End-User Development: E-Textiles and the Wearable IoT," *In This Place: Cumulus 2016*, Nottingham Trent University, April 27–May 1, 2016.

Kettley, S., Townsend, K., and Walker, S. (2015) "Evidencing Embodied Participatory Design," *Proceedings of Critical Alternatives* 5th Decennial Aarhus Conference, August 17–21, Aarhus.

Kettley, S., Townsend, K., Walker, S., and Glazzard, M. (2017) "Electric Corset: An Approach to Wearables Innovation," in *RTD2017: Proceedings of 3rd Biennial Research Through Design Conference*, Edinburgh, 22–24 March, 486–500, Research Through Design.

Kobakant (2018) "Wicked Tailoring." Available online: https://www.kobakant.at/KOBA/koba-school-of-wickedfabrics/ (accessed February 25, 2019).

Latour, B. (2005) *Reassembling the Social: An Introduction to Actor-Network-Theory*, Oxford: Oxford University Press.

Laver, J. (1995) *Costume and Fashion: A Concise History*, 4th edn, London: Thames & Hudson.

Lehmann, U. (2000) *Tigersprung: Fashion in Modernity*, Cambridge, MA: MIT Press.

Lindley, J., Coulton, P., and Cooper, R. (2017) "Why the Internet of Things Needs Object Orientated Ontology," *The Design Journal*, 20(suppl. 1): S2846–S2857.

Maier, D. (2014) *Stitch and Peacock*, The Collection Museum and Usher Gallery, Lincoln, September 26, 2014–January 11, 2015.

Malafouris, L. (2013) *How Things Shape the Mind: A Theory of Material Engagement*, Cambridge, MA: MIT Press.

Marvin, C. (1988) *When Old Technologies Were New: Thinking About Electric Communication in the Late 19th Century*, Oxford: Oxford University Press.

McLaren, A., Hardy, D. A., and Hughes-Riley, T. (2017) "Electronic Textiles and Product Lifetimes," in C. Bakker and R. Mugge (eds.), *PLATE: Product Lifetimes And The Environment: Conference Proceedings of PLATE 2017,* Delft, the Netherlands, 8–10 November 2017, Research in Design series, 9. Amsterdam: IOS Press, 473–6.

Merewether, C. (2006) *The Archive: Documents of Contemporary Art*, London: Whitechapel Gallery.

Merleau-Ponty, M. (1969) *The Essential Writings of Maurice Merleau-Ponty*, trans. A. L. Fisher, New York: Harcourt, Brace and World.

Møller, T. and Kettley, S. (2017) "Wearable Health Technology Design: A Humanist Accessory Approach," *International Journal of Design*, 11(3): 35–49.

Myers, A., Bowles, A., Shahariar, H., Bhakta, R., and Jur, J. S. (2017) "Wearable Electronics," *Textile World*, March 21. Available online: https://www.textileworld.com/textile-world/features/2017/03/wearable-electronics/ (accessed October 15, 2018).

Olowu, D., Buenfeld, G., and Globus, D., eds. (2016) *Duro Olowu Making and Unmaking*, London: Ridinghouse.

Page, T. (2015) "A Forecast of the Adoption of Wearable Technology," *International Journal of Technology Diffusion*, 6(2): 12–29.

Pierce, G. (2017) "The Fabric of the City: Archive Textiles Inspire a Collaborative Project in Contemporary Design and Innovation," in *Proceedings of Intersections: Collaborations in Textile Design Research Conference*, September 13, Loughborough University London.

Raeburn, G. (2018) "Local Eco-systems and Dynamic Supply Chains," Burberry Material Futures Research Centre launch, September 21, Royal College of Art, London.

Roberts, D. (2018) "The Rustle of Taffeta: The Value of Hapticity in Research and Reconstruction of an Eighteenth-Century Sack-Back Dress," in L. Millar and A. Kettle (eds.), *The Erotic Cloth: Seduction and Fetishism in Textiles*, 60–72, London: Bloomsbury.

Rudofsky, B. (1947) *Are Clothes Modern? An Essay on Contemporary Apparel*, Chicago, IL: Paul Theobald.

Scaturro, S. (2017) "Confronting Fashion's Death Drive: Conservation, Ghost Labor and the Material Turn Within Fashion Curation," in A. Vänskä and H. Clark (eds.), *Fashion Curating: Critical Practice in the Museum and Beyond*, 21–38, London: Bloomsbury.

Seymour, S. (2008) *Fashionable Technology: The Intersection of Design, Fashion, Science, and Technology*, Vienna: Springer.

Skjold, E. (2016) "Biographical Wardrobes—A Temporal View on Dress Practice," *Fashion Practice*, 8(1): 135–48.

Speed, C. and Oberlander, J. (2016) "Designing From, With and By Data: Introducing the Ablative Framework," *Proceedings of DRS 2016, Design Research Society 50th Anniversary Conference*, June 27–30, Brighton.

Starner, T. (2001) "The Challenges of Wearable Computing: Part 2," *IEEE Micro*, 21(4): 54–67.

Stead, L. J. (2005) "The Emotional Wardrobe: A Fashion Perspective on the Integration of Technology and Clothing," PhD thesis, London: University of the Arts.

Sutton, J. (2008) "Material Agency, Skills and History: Distributed Cognition and the Archaeology of Memory," in C. Knappett and L. Malafouris (eds.), *Material Agency*, 37–55, Boston, MA: Springer.

Taylor, J. and Townsend, K. (2014) "Reprogramming the Hand: Bridging the Craft Skills Gap in 3D/Digital Fashion Knitwear Design," *Craft Research*, 5(2): 155–74.

ten Bhömer, M., Brouwer, C. E., Tomico, O., and Wensveen, S. A. G. (2013) "Interactive Prototypes in the Participatory Development of Product-Service Systems," in H. Melkas and J. Buur (eds.), *Proceedings of the 3rd Participatory Innovation Conference* (PINC 2013), June 18–20, 36–42, Lahti, Finland.

Tenuta, L. and Testa, S. (2018) "Scientific Method and Creative Process for Wearable Technologies from Invention to Innovation," *Airea: Arts and Interdisciplinary Research*, 1: 35–46.

Townsend, K. (2011) "The Denim Garment as Canvas: Exploring the Notion of Wear as a Fashion and Textile Narrative," *Textile: The Journal of Cloth and Culture*, Special Denim Issue, 9(1): 90–107.

Townsend, K. (2016) "*Closely Held Secrets*: Embodied Knowledge in Digitally Crafted Textiles," in N. Nimkulrat, F. Kane, and K. Walton (eds.), *Crafting Textiles in the Digital Age*, 189–205, London: Bloomsbury Academic.

Vainshtein, O. (2012) " 'I Have a Suitcase Just Full of Legs Because I Need Options for Different Clothing': Accessorizing Bodyscapes," *Fashion Theory*, 16(2): 139–69.

Valle-Noronha, J. (2019) Becoming with Clothes: Activating Weaer-Worn Engagements Through Design, PhD Thesis, Finland, Helsinki: Aalto University.

Vänskä, A. and Clark, H., eds. (2017) *Fashion Curating: Critical Practice in the Museum and Beyond*, London: Bloomsbury.

Veja, P. (2015) "An Investigation of Integrated Woven Electronic Textiles (e-Textiles) via Design Led Processes," doctoral thesis, Brunel University, London.

Verhelst, B. and Debo, K. (2008) *Maison Martin Margiela "20" The Exhibition*, Antwerp: MoMu.
WEAR Sustain (2018) Final event and symposium, November 21, Bozar, Brussels. Available online: https://legacy.wearsustain.eu/event/wear-sustain-final-event-symposium/ (accessed August 9, 2019).

Part Two

The Body in Dialogue

Edited by Rhian Solomon

6

Fashion and Participation in Hands of X

Andrew Cook and Graham Pullin

Hands of X is a project about prosthetic hands, identity, fashion, and ownership. This chapter will explore tensions between participatory design and creative direction, and design for disability and fashion design.

A fashion-led approach to designing prosthetic hands

Hands of X is a service, encompassing retail, co-design, and manufacturing, developed and prototyped in Dundee, Glasgow, and London. The project is fashion-led in that, at the very least, it holds that prosthetic hands are accessories that are worn as much as used, and so need to make aesthetic sense in the context of the wearer's identity, sense of style, and wider wardrobe. In prosthetics this is still a radical stance.

The service is designed as a consultation and retail environment, to be set up in shops, makespaces, or even limb-fitting centers, temporarily or permanently. It allows wearers to try different material combinations, at first as swatches, then as hand prototypes, before making a specification for their own hand, which is then made to order.

We prototyped the point of sale service as a mode of inquiry; to explore subtle issues of ownership, understatement, and material nuance with wearers and with other participants from the worlds of fashion and prosthetics.

Hands of whom?

As Frances Corner writes in *Why Fashion Matters*, "faster than anything else, what we wear tells the story of who we are—or who we want to be. Fashion is the most immediate and intimate form of self-expression" (Corner 2014: 4–5).

Just about every object that we might wear or carry on a day-to-day basis comes in a diversity of styles, materials, and finishes, which goes some way toward acknowledging the diversity of the people who might wear them. There is a never-ending choice of stories that we can tell and from coats and bags to umbrellas, phone cases—even key fobs—most of us can find an object that we feel tells part of the story of who we are, or who we want to be. If only to ourselves.

A prosthetic hand is a visible object, both worn and carried intimately on a daily basis. And yet the commercially available range of prosthetic hands offers a choice—broadly—of two stories via two aesthetic languages.

The first, and most common, is the language of imitation; supposedly skin-colored silicone or PVC, in a form imitating a natural hand. The aim is sometimes expressed in terms of not wishing to draw attention to a prosthesis, which is a priority for some—albeit a decreasing number of—people with limb difference. Yet a degree of camouflage can be implied that many disabled people do not feel the need for—and may even be uncomfortable with the deception of "passing" in this way.

The second, and more recent, is the language of the post-human; bionic, visibly high-tech, with exposed engineering, featuring obviously "high-performance" materials like titanium and carbon fiber.

Those whose identities and fashion sense don't square with either of these aesthetic languages have little to no choice of nuanced design languages between these extremes. It's very difficult to think of fashion that's even slightly analogous to either of these design languages.

Design for disability more generally tends to embody either a simplistic notion of "fashion"—bright red hearing aids "to make a fashion statement" for example—or else reject or resent the very notion of fashion for being arbitrary and short-lived, and therefore somehow extravagant and useless.

Of course, fashion *is* socially constructed and transient, and that is part of its joy and attraction. Tony Gross, recently departed founder of eyewear pioneers Cutler and Gross said he had "once shared all the typical accusations that the world of fashion was 'superficial, ephemeral and lightweight,' but came to realise that it's 'exactly these traits that make it so exciting'" (*The Telegraph* 2018).

Cutler and Gross could be said to have revolutionized the eyewear industry by connecting it to the culture of the fashion industry. "It was as if you visited a chiropodist and when he had finished treating your feet, he expected to help you choose a fashionable pair of shoes. Yet that was the service that opticians were offering and that many still are" (Pullin 2009: 237).

So, with prosthetic hands: we are not attempting to challenge the professional role of prosthetists and technicians in limb-fitting centers but, like eyewear, we do see another part of the process that needs to be approached as an experience in itself.

Wearers, not users

The dominant culture in the prosthetics industry casts the people who use prosthetic services and products as *patients* and *users*. Clinical concerns and practical function understandably (if somewhat narrowly) dominate the development and delivery of prosthetics. But we are interested in prosthetic hands as objects that are as much worn or carried as "used"; we believe that people should be thought of as *wearers* as much as *patients* or *users*.

This shift in perception elicits a very different design response. *Wearing*, whether talking about prosthetic hands or clothes, implies a certain synergy between the body and the item being worn. The two together are indivisible, perceived as a whole. *Wearing* also implies choice and intent on the part of the wearer, with a heavy subtext of *intentional* visibility. *Patient* and *user* don't, to our ears, imply any of this.

Service prototypes

In mid-2017, we prototyped the Hands of X service in London, at eyewear retailer Cubitts (Figure 6.1), and in a dedicated shop in Glasgow's East End.

A window display is intended to be the first point of contact between customer and service, with a white neon sign atop a set of pigeonholes. Each hole is sized to hold a black Hands of X box. These are much like shoeboxes, but smaller with hand-sized rather than foot-sized proportions. The lid is branded with a foil-stamped Hands of X, with three round holes below.

Some of the boxes in the pigeonholes display material swatches through the holes. Each of these represents a material specification for a previous client's hand. So from the very start, before even entering the shop, these materials, set against black, form a defining part of the visual experience of the service.

On entering, the customer is invited to browse a full palette of one-inch-square materials swatches, and to try combining them. These are organized in a comb on a large cabinet top, alongside some examples of finished hands in different materials, with plenty of room to play and experiment.

Figure 6.1 Hands of X window display at Cubitts eyewear shop, London (2017). Photograph by Andrew Cook and Graham Pullin.

A materials-focused brand

At its heart, our brand is characterized by the unremarkable and everyday, yet it is as considered and resolved—we hope—as one would expect from any nascent fashion brand. Here, *no-big-deal* is the maxim and this spirit is embodied in every element of the service; signage, furniture, printed material, product, service script, and so on.

Most deeply of all this is manifested in the palette of materials at the heart of Hands of X: not any material at all but a carefully curated palette of everyday materials with deep associations.

The first material collection (Spring–Summer 18) featured various woods (beech, cedar, walnut) in oiled, waxed, and soaped finishes, cellulose acetates ("tortoiseshell" and translucent), leathers, woolen felts, and steels.

Avoiding the "hipster hand"

We recognized that the materials palette, with its air of "heritage," would be all too easily read as a clichéd hipster vernacular—we regularly expressed our horror at the prospect of being referred to as the "hipster hand project." And in this sense we are keen to avoid a short-lived brand language. The visual language was intended to help offset this.

As communication theorist Paul Watzlawick wrote, "one cannot not communicate" (Watzlawick, Bavelas, and Jackson 1968). Visual communication, brand, and signage was a way of setting expectations and encouraging a mode of engagement. Visual identity—logotypes, typography, paper stock, signage—was one of the first things that we developed, and in many ways led the design language of the whole service.

Browsing

Given that each hand is manufactured to order, and likely to be worn for a long time, it feels important that the client is able to explore, to take their time and familiarize themselves with their choices before committing. After all, isn't that exactly what we all do when we browse for any new piece of high-value fashion?

There's a quandary when having something bespoke made, though. How is it possible to browse when the piece you'll eventually choose doesn't exist yet *by definition*. If we look at the world of bespoke suits—and eyewear—there are some clues. In many tailors, the very first step is that the customer is left alone in the front of shop with sets of sample books, to browse the available materials choices. Indeed, Cubitts themselves have a wall of dozens of eyewear acetate swatches to browse, pick up, combine, and compare above their consultation table. The first part of our service is the same; to explore, play, and combine the materials on offer in the form of swatches.

The reveal

Next, we open a drawer in the plan chest to reveal "jigsaw" parts in all of the same materials as the swatches. Each drawer contains every part in every applicable material. Using these parts, customers can make abstracted 2.5-dimensional hand prototypes in any possible material combination.

Opening the drawer as a shop assistant, one feels like something of a magician: it's a big reveal (Figure 6.2). Something about the plethora of materials in recognizable shapes gives a sense of abundance.

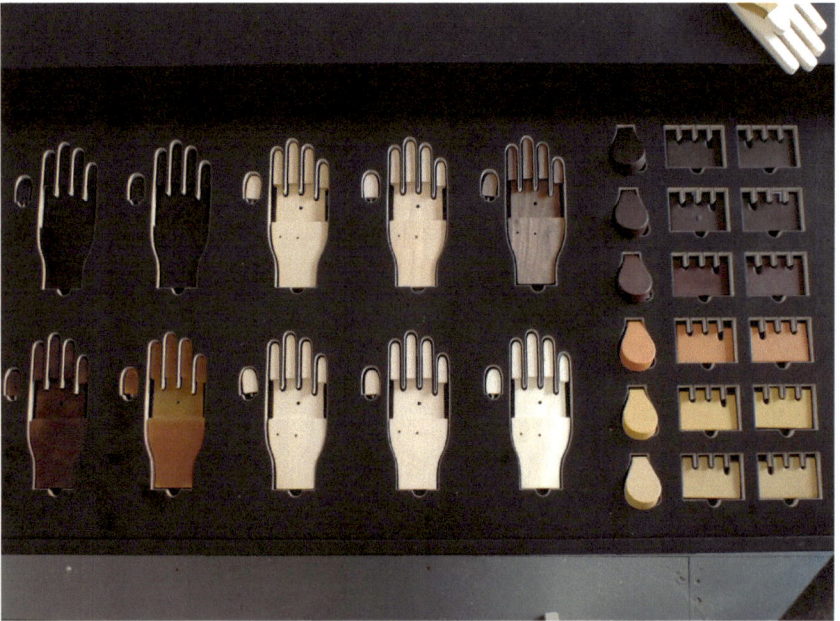

Figure 6.2 A cabinet drawer opens to reveal "jigsaw" hand parts in an array of materials (2017). Photograph by Andrew Cook and Graham Pullin.

Swapping

We begin by pulling out jigsaw parts in all of the client's chosen materials, using their swatches as a reference. Then they put these together into hands, using their swatch combinations as a reference. These are designed to be easily constructed using one hand.

Then, we discuss what's working, what's not, and if there are any alternatives that they might want to try. A lot of swapping tends to take place. A promising combination in swatch form can suddenly feel not-quite-right when seen in full-hand proportions. We swap between hands, pull alternative parts from the drawers, swap them back again for a last look before declining them . . .

Living with it

Once the client has decided on a final material combination for their hand, they are given an empty black box from the display cabinet in the window. We put the swatches for their chosen combination in the front, and fill out a form on the back. The box itself becomes the specification for their hand, and they can use it to take the jigsaw prototype hand home, to live with for a while. The hand would be fitted with a connector compatible with their own socket so that they could try it on, with different outfits and in different moods. They can see if it really does feel like *their* hand before committing.

Through this process, a dialogue takes place between the wearer, the hand, and their wardrobe. And most likely also with family, friends, and trusted style advisers.

Participatory design within Hands of X

The service we have described was the culmination of a process of co-design. We worked with wearers (and non-wearers) in conceiving and defining Hands of X; the designs of the hands, the materials palette, the fundamental nature of the project. In this section we'd like to offer our experience of, and reflections on, the practicalities of designing with wearers.

We worked hard to take control of the tone of the dialogue

Our first substantive contact with participants, in the first months of the project, was a series of events at Dundee Design Festival, The Institute of Making at UCL, and MAKlab Glasgow, a public access makespace. A mix of prosthetics wearers, prosthetics professionals, designers, makers, artists, and materials experts attended.

Each of these workshops culminated in participants making a specification for a hand in two materials, which we intended would directly inform the development of the hand designs, materials palette, and service.

At these events, we sought to set the spirit of engagement through every available means. Copywriting, graphic design, exhibition design, tone of voice of presentations—every element of an experience helps to guide the spirit in which people engage with it. Those who work in branding are well aware of this. But these opportunities are taken advantage of much less both in research- and development-based activities. In this sense the participation was, as we shall see and discuss further, a hybrid of open-minded, open-ended participatory design and vision-led, fashion-led design.

The events consisted of three activities, and the first two can be viewed as another means of framing engagement and setting the scene for the final, pivotal task.

Task 1—Materials speed dating

The first, straight after introductions, was a "materials speed dating" exercise, where participants were paired with three material samples from the Institute of Making's materials library, and asked to reflect upon their qualities in a one-minute stream-of-consciousness.

This exercise was crucial in setting a tone of reflective—yet instinctual—engagement with, and dialogue around, the qualities of materials, a tone that we hoped would make its way into the more obviously hand-related tasks.

Task 2—Badge making

The second exercise again involved direct engagement with materials, but this time narrowed the palette to much more everyday materials, an important aspect of the spirit of the project. We provided a selection of circular materials swatches, the participants chose two, and made a wearable badge from them. One material faces out to the world, the other faces inward, toward the wearer, not visible to the world.

This exercise introduces several important considerations. The idea of combining materials swatches, and that combinations of materials can be more (or less) than the sum of their parts; of choosing materials, based on a sense of personal style, to be worn with the rest of one's outfit (and perhaps even whole wardrobe); and of how materials might express something of one's identity to the world at large or, like the silk lining of a suit, exist almost entirely for the wearer.

Task 3—Hand specification

Our final task was to design a two-material hand. Participants specified the materials used, then photocopied material samples and collaged a design showing how the hand would be partitioned between these materials. They made this specification on a specially designed hand specification sheet.

Probes

The specification sheet is an example of what we've come to refer to broadly as a probe. For our purposes, we may define a probe as a design research tool designed to provoke and capture insights, where the design values of the tool itself aim to set an appropriate tone for engagement.

The basis of the concept—and the term probe—has its roots in the design research method of "cultural probes" (Gaver, Dunne, and Pacenti 1999). These were developed as tools for gathering insights, using novel, sometimes even irreverent, means; one classic example is a disposable camera and list of carefully crafted instructions of subjects for photographs. Where this exercise has since often become formulaic, the fundamental strength of the original work, from our point of view, was that the materials were so thoughtfully considered. The design values were high and consistent, and set the bar at a level of care and imaginativeness that the designers hoped for in the participants' responses.

It's not just quality, either, but tone of voice. The irreverence and lightness of touch of the original cultural probes, both conceptually and visually, makes it implicitly clear that the designers are expecting some irreverence and creativity in return.

Design values can set the agenda on a more nuanced level too. In our case, we tried to set the agenda of the everyday through a workaday design language, and through the thumbnail images of objects and hands that pepper the probe. But there's gentle humor there, too. One thumbnail image of a paint-spattered hand holds a cigarette, a minor act of rebellion against the overwhelming formality and wholesomeness of spirit that defines so much design for disability.

Printing and paper quality is important too; we printed using spot inks rather than process, and ordered specific GF Smith paper stock. We wanted it to feel a little like those paper placemats, familiar from UK mid-market chain restaurants like Wagamama or Pizza Express, disposable enough that people aren't precious about them, but still obviously considered, and a defining part of the whole experience. All of this is intended to frame the terms of the ensuing dialogue—dialogue between the participants and the sheet, between their bodies, clothing, and the available materials, and between all of the people in the room.

Specifications

The hand specifications that went on to be most influential as the project progressed came from C and E (Figure 6.3).

C is a businesswoman, charity founder, and ex-Glasgow pub landlady. She lost both hands and feet through illness a few years ago. She is unapologetic about her lack of hands, and has a hi-tech bionic hand that she rarely chooses to wear. She spoke of her desire for prostheses to be "interesting"—even for them to provide a talking point.[1]

E is a sweet-natured writer and lecturer who was born in the early 1950s with one hand. He wears a simple mechanical hand in an oxblood leather glove. In contrast to C, he talked about wearing a hand to avoid making other people feel uncomfortable. He doesn't really use his hand for any practical purposes, apart from occasional incidental uses, such as knocking in nails or cleaning mud off his golf clubs.

C's and E's specifications reflect their different attitudes. E uses materials that are resolutely everyday: beech and steel. C's material choices, while far from being ostentatious, are more striking and literally remarkable: yew wood, with its undulating grain and red color, tortoiseshell cellulose acetate, and imperfect, burnished leather.

The partitioning of these specifications became pivotal; their essence went on to define the final hand designs and materials palette. E specified a steel section in the outer heel of the palm, originally intended for knocking in nails, while C used leather on the fingertips and knuckles, specified to give grip when picking up and leaning on the hand.

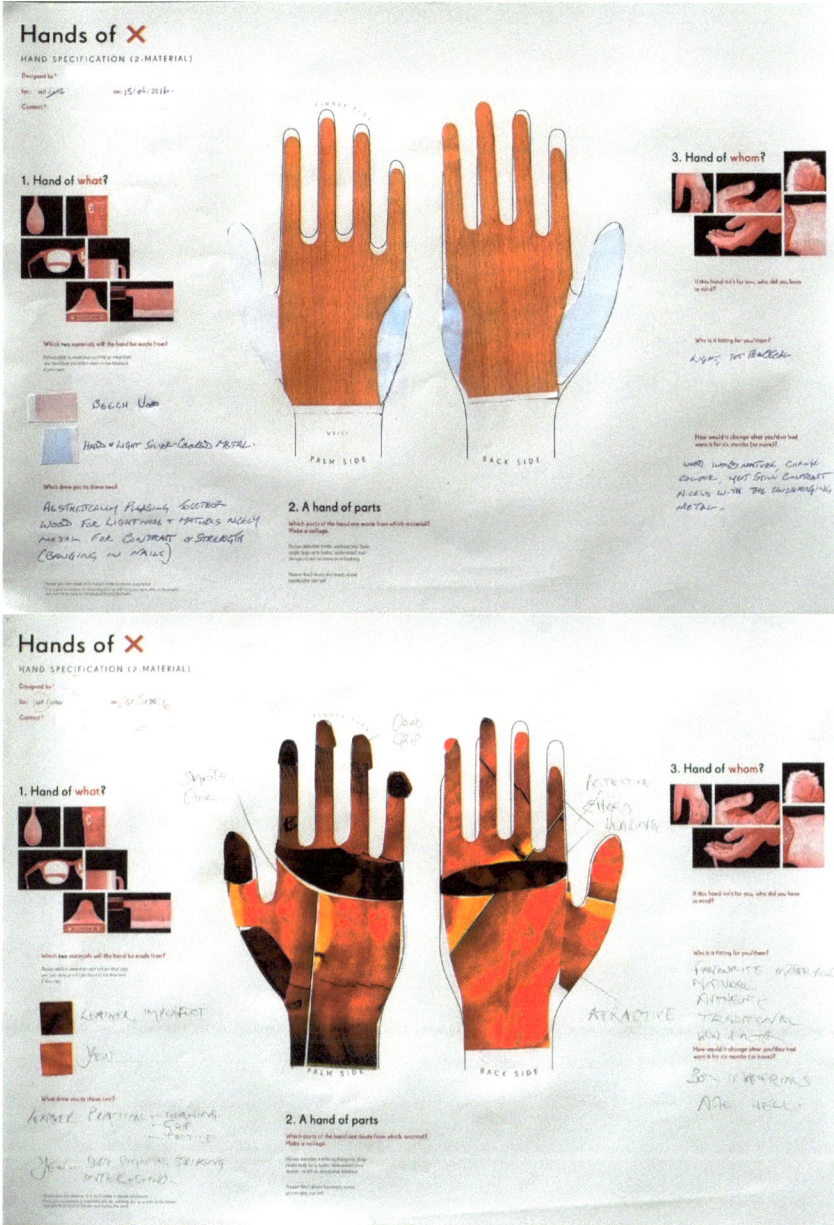

Figure 6.3 Completed hand specification sheets by C and E (2016). Photograph by Andrew Cook and Graham Pullin.

Two-material hand prototypes

In all, we received more than sixty hand specification sheets from the three workshops. We mapped these specifications using various axes as a means of selecting twelve that embodied a diversity of approaches, while still fitting with the ethos of the project. We adapted some of them, making changes to materials and partitioning, while respecting the original intent of the hand authors.

We prototyped these in what we referred to as 2.5 dimensions. These were a simplified two-dimensional hand outline, made in the actual specified materials, extended to a thickness of 18 mm to give a sense of materiality, weight, and object-ness (albeit abstracted) (Figure 6.4). This is very much in the lineage of the single-material hands, the first set of abstracted prototypes that we made, which deliberately set aside much of the complexity of wearable prosthetics.

These twelve hands were intended to form the basis of conversations—internally between the team, but also with wearers, to provoke discussion about the relative merits of the twelve approaches illustrated. The physical objects facilitated discussions with a depth that couldn't have been achieved without

Figure 6.4 C discusses her impressions of a 2.5-dimensional prototype in tortoiseshell acetate and leather (2016). Photograph by Andrew Cook and Graham Pullin.

them. Deep conversations around materials and design, but also surprisingly emotional and touching conversations around taste, fashion, and personality; around what we wear, including prostheses, and what that means to us, and says to the world.

C and E, while reflecting deeply on the qualities of the other hands, ultimately each returned to "their" hands—the ones based on their original specifications—as their favorites.

Two hand models

The final Hands of X service offered two hand models, one mechanical and one motor-powered myoelectric (Figure 6.5).

They were designed by the team, product designer Joshua James and glovemaker Riina Õun. Even after many iterations considering form, materials partitioning, and manufacturability, the essence of those original specifications from C and E still define these hands.

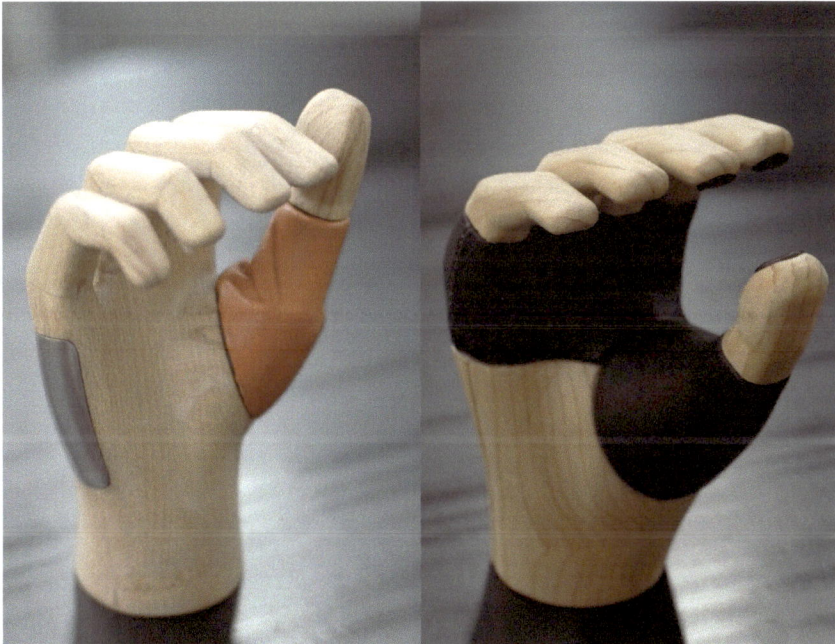

Figure 6.5 Hand prototypes. Mechanical hand (left) in beech, tan aniline leather, and carbon steel. Myoelectric hand (right) in cedar and gris fumé aniline leather (2017). Photograph by Andrew Cook and Graham Pullin.

In *Hertzian Tales*, Tony Dunne characterized early prototypes that—despite being rough, unformed, or unrealistic—go on to define an object as it develops as genotypes. "From a product design point of view these models lack industrial realism . . . [we] might regard it as embodying the essence of the design idea, a 'genotype' rather than a prototype . . . The object's 'content' or 'genes' are important, not its appearance" (Dunne 2008 [1999]: 90).

The early specifications from C and E shown in Figure 6.3 can be considered genotypes for the two final models. Their genes are still defining, even as the objects and service were iterated and developed into something more concrete.

Mechanical / Hand of E / Hand No. 1

This is a simple mechanical hand with the thumb as the only moving part. This acts as a simple clip, and can be used to hold small objects by manually pulling the sprung thumb open using the other hand.

The design of the Mechanical Hand of X is partitioned into three materials. The main body of the hand, made from a rigid material, a leather gaiter covering the moving thumb, and a panel in the outer heel, made from either a metal or a felt.

It's easy to see how E's original specification, with its metal section to allow the hammering in of nails, has informed this design. This detail may have started as a slightly jokey one-liner, but through the 2.5-dimensional prototypes, it became apparent that this could be a beautiful, defining detail; a section that the hand rests on when the wearer is sitting at a table, in hard-wearing metal, or in soft, quiet felt.

This particular prototype is made in E's original material choice of beech and steel. Throughout our co-design with E, through every prototype iteration and opportunity to reconsider, E stuck with these materials, speaking of a sense of ownership over this hand, even before it existed in any physical form. This was a decision, taken relatively quickly, that was nonetheless informed by decades of experience and E's own sense of fashion.

Myoelectric / Hand of C / Hand No. 2

This is a two-material hand model, with an opposed, gripping first two fingers and thumb, operated by a muscle sensor in the forearm. It has a rigid body with leather gaiters covering the moving parts, and three leather fingertips on the gripping fingers.

Again, it's easy to see how C's original hand specification sheets have informed this design. The partitioning of the leather parts remains almost unchanged from those collages. They were originally intended for grip, which still stands, but they have also become a flexible cover for mechanical parts. Perhaps more importantly, aesthetically they define how the hand reads, breaking up the composition, adding to its artificiality, but, we feel, reducing its uncanniness.

Like E, C stuck very close to her original decisions throughout the process.

Ownership

This sticking with decisions, from the first to the last opportunity, feels to be a true indicator of ownership, whether this ownership comes from the rightness and longevity of the decision, or through the very act of taking (and remembering) the decision. When the project started, we thought that it was mostly about fashion, materials, and prosthetic hands. Yet as it progressed, we realized that the overarching theme of the project was in fact ownership. Our co-designers talked consistently about "their" hands. Some even pinpointed, unprompted, the moment in the service when the hand prototype felt like "theirs."

Controversies arise around declining ideas

Yet to present this journey from ideas to designs as a clean, linear journey would be to oversimplify it, as would to gloss over the complexities of the ownership shared between designers and wearers. Our position as designers with an acknowledged agenda meant that we were at liberty to decline ideas that didn't fit with the project as we defined it. For example, at the London workshop, participant Y rejected choice of materials in favor of applied decoration, and rejected an abstracted hand in favor of redefining a three-digit gripper.

We declined to take these ideas forward on the project. While (of course) a wholly valid personal wish, it represented a negation of our ethos and starting point (importantly, in a context where many more wearers embraced it and appropriated it). There was little productive that we could do with it, except to acknowledge that Hands of X was not all things to all people, which we were clear about from the start.

This approach can be criticized as simply ignoring inconvenient contributions, and indeed caused some tension between team members with design backgrounds, and those with anthropological backgrounds. One could even question whether to decline some contributions but not others is unethical.

Our co-investigators at UCL, Sarah Wilkes and Mark Miodownik, have written that "the fundamental differences in what different members of the team perceived co-design to be only became apparent later in the project. The materials researchers understood this to mean a participatory approach where users inform and become part of the creative process from start to finish" (Wilkes and Miodownik 2018: 17). Where we thought that this was exactly what our co-design process was doing, Wilkes and Miodownik felt that 'users' should be more involved in specifying requirements.

In traditional anthropological, data-gathering, and analyzing activities, our approach may well be ethically ambiguous. But as designers—whether commercial or researchers—it's routine to work this way. Extensive design ethnography will often gather just one or two unexpected and inspiring insights that go on to define the rest of the project (Suri and Howard 2006). The rest of the ethnographic investigation isn't lost, but rather becomes context, influencing design activity in less explicit ways.

How our fashion brand is disability-led after all

As we have seen in detail in the section "Participatory design within Hands of X," designing with wearers and prosthetics professionals was pivotal in creating the service that we've described.

In fact, it's the *only* way that we could approach this design process. Not only is the value added to the project by participants immeasurable, but to design any sort of prosthetic product or service without the involvement of wearers would be indefensible. However, we also had an unashamed design agenda, and a vision of our own.

Squaring a strong agenda with input from co-designers is something that any designer working with these methods has to address. This section contains our reflections on why resolving the tension between these two is possible, and indeed necessary—for fashion-led design for disability, perhaps even more than for other domains.

Nothing about us without us

"Nothing about us without us" has become a mantra for the disability rights movement. As James I. Charlton explains in his text of the same name, the phrase "expresses the conviction of people with disabilities that they know what is best for them" (Charlton 1998).

Even in design fields not explicitly related to disability, the process of involving the people that you are designing for—and involving them in ways that go way beyond lip service to fundamentally guide the design process and outcome—is increasingly considered not just good practice, but vital practice.

This project involves very complex issues. It needs the input of potential wearers. It needs their deep and personal understanding of these issues, informed by lived experience, to have any chance of a compelling, sensitive, and successful outcome, by whatever terms success is measured.

And yet . . .

Compelling fashion design, from couture to streetwear, typically relies on a singular vision informed by a strong ethos and brand. For all the people that it takes to bring a fashion brand's collection together, the creative director's vision sets the agenda. The value of an agenda that displays a point of difference from what-everyone-else-is-doing, and exhibits genuine personality and idiosyncrasy cannot be overstated.

To take one recent critically lauded, and much talked about, example: Alessandro Michele's AW18 collection at Gucci was inspired by Donna Haraway's text *A Cyborg Manifesto*, well known in academic circles but rather unexpected as the key inspiration for one of the world's biggest fashion houses. Michele's collection presented a purposeful, yet wryly critical, post-human narrative that saw boundaries between human, animal, and machine blurred, including models apparently carrying their own severed heads as clutch bags (Marriot 2018). It's safe to say that Michele's agenda was not set through an extensive co-design process with his brand's wearers, nor through consultation with trend-forecasting agencies.

Even in less high-concept circles, successful fashion brands are almost always sprung from a clear vision and ethos; they are unashamed about having a personality. One of our own biggest inspirations for Hands of X, Universal Works, rubbed gently against the grain when it was conceived, with collections inspired by super-functional twentieth-century workwear at a time when that was still an unexpected source of inspiration. The label was, arguably, instrumental in setting a fashion agenda that has since been picked up (and upended by) Vetements at their peak of influence, among others. Faux "heritage" workwear is now very common in mainstream circles—among people who probably couldn't have imagined themselves wearing a farm laborer's jacket a few years ago.

So a successful fashion brand, by definition, isn't for everyone. It has a strong and individual ethos and personality, which may even seem odd or counterintuitive when it first appears, only to subsequently inform the mainstream.

It was our intention that this project be led by a strong design ethos from the start, informed by the 'super normal' (Fukasawa and Morrison 2008) and the everyday.

Reconciling a strong design stance with being disability-led (and vice versa)

There is tension here, two agendas that at first glance aren't that obviously compatible; a clear stance and design ethos, and the necessity (and desire) to be fundamentally guided by wearers throughout the design process. And this is compounded in disability-related design by our own involvement as non-disabled designers.

How do we square a strong stance and ethos as designers with meaningful co-design? In this case the reconciliation comes from the fact that our stance echoed that which many disabled people have toward their own disability. A stance that is not reflected in current alternatives in prosthetics hands.

No triumph, no tragedy as a stance on disability

Those two aesthetic stories that prosthetic hands currently tell reflect the two narratives that our culture habitually tells around disability—tragedy and triumph, or more usually triumph *over* tragedy.

The realistic, skin-colored hand can be seen to reflect a perceived "tragedy" of impairment. It is an attempt to replace something that is missing, and doing so with ultimate discretion is its overriding aim. This aim of discretion is telling in itself, perhaps suggestive of a perceived shame. The design language of bionic hands shouts of the triumph of engineering over impairment; the ability of these extraordinary objects to restore function via technology and engineering, writ large in its form and materiality.

Peter White's radio program *No Triumph, No Tragedy*, in which he interviewed people with disabilities, sought to reposition the narrative of disability neither as a tragedy nor something to triumph over, but as something important yet everyday, one aspect of a personal story as complex as any other (BBC 1994–2017).

Disability objects can imply a transformative arc of triumph over tragedy. That this narrative is all too dominant is reflected in the title and stance of Peter White's program. Many other disabled people resent an expectation that they feel is imposed upon them by others, that design will transform their lives. "We would like to evolve unremarkably" says Liz Jackson, Founder of the "Inclusive Fashion & Design Collective," rebranded as "The Disabled List" (Pullin 2018: 176).

No-big-deal as a design stance

From the start of the project, Hands of X too took a stance that challenged these narratives, with aspirations toward designs that were not seeking to "pass" as a natural hand, but neither to be extraordinary. "No-big-deal" was a project mantra from the start. Not that we were presuming that limb difference be perceived in this way, just that these hands, as objects, be positioned so.

A radical juxtaposition of the binary choice between anatomical realism and bionic technophilia can be found in Sophie de Oliveira Barata's Alternative Limb Project. While we are great admirers of the ethos and imagination of this project, and the opportunity for self-expression that this affords through prosthetic limbs conceived as "highly stylised wearable art pieces" (The Alternative Limb Project 2018), it does not aspire to subtlety and understatement. The intent of Barata's extraordinary work is—deliberately—*not* no-big-deal. Being clear that in this way Hands of X is fundamentally different to the Alternative Limb Project was another key part of defining the project's identity.

Post-it and big-ego design

So Hands of X had a strong point of view on its identity and ethos, on its aesthetic language and tone of voice from the earliest days. We knew what we were *not* as well as what we were. We were also clear that the design process had to be fundamentally participatory. We had to find an approach that squared the two.

This dilemma has been reflected upon by design academic Ezio Manzini, who makes a distinction between "big-ego design" and "post-it design" (Manzini 2015). In post-it design, the designer becomes primarily a facilitator of ideas expressed by stakeholders during participatory design exercises, usually on the ubiquitous Post-It™.

The post-it itself is emblematic of the problems with this approach in a couple of ways; no matter how well thought through the exercise might be, providing a group with post-its and a pack of pens to record their responses doesn't exactly speak of care or designerly spirit. And deep thinking can be difficult to express on a few square inches, so instead it's tempting to fill hundreds of post-its with more shallow thoughts. At its most extreme conclusion, this approach means that the designer becomes a mere "process facilitator"—a scribe of participants' one-line ideas, synthesizing and embodying them (Manzini 2015).

Conversely, big-ego design represents a dominant model of twentieth-century design, a "demiurgic vision, in which design is the act of particularly gifted individuals capable of imprinting their personal stamp on artifacts and environments" (Manzini 2015: 66). And this approach is undeniably still relevant in certain types of design, not least those fashion houses mentioned earlier. But in any area where the designer is addressing complex social, personal, or behavioral issues, it reads less as being visionary, rather more so as being willfully ignorant.

By being conscious of making our participatory methods as engaging, visually driven, materials-focused, and designerly as possible, we set the spirit of engagement as visual, materials-focused, and designerly. As a result, the responses had a depth, unexpectedness, and richness that transcended "post-it design." And yet, not least because it was impossible not to be influenced and inspired by the responses, the process was genuinely wearer-led.

Inspiration vs. requirements

Both post-it and big-ego approaches can have their merits, but the balance between the two can be difficult to strike. Go through too much of a "post-it"–driven process, and it's easy to capitulate to your subjects, with little critical thought or editing, ending up with a *flying submarine*; something that does too many things, and none of it particularly well, ultimately appealing to nobody.

There is always a danger that the outcomes of participatory design become a list of requirements to be beholden to. This is to miss the true value of the insights from this process. The insights of participants, when the exercise is appropriately framed, is a source of incredible insight and inspiration, and treating them as such is an unending supply of fuel to drive the design process. And just to be clear, we are talking about *design* inspiration here, not the connotations of patronization that Harilyn Rousso's consummately written *Don't Call Me Inspirational* denounces (Rousso 2013).

We argue for undertaking co-design methods while:

- being unashamed about having an agenda
- being unashamed about declining ideas
- being unashamed about being designerly, and aesthetically focused
- being unashamed about taking a promising kernel of an idea and adapting it so that it fits with the agenda.

We felt justified in adopting those wearer-led ideas that we felt embodied the values and vision of Hands of X (not exactly those ideas "that we liked" since the lens they were viewed through was that of a highly considered brand, and so more objective). And we naturally went on to co-design in more detail with wearers whose perspectives complemented our own, without fundamentally contradicting them.

The flip side of this is that the depth of influence of the individual can go way beyond more traditional academic approaches. In our case, the individual participants acted as the seed of everything. As ideas develop around (and sometimes away from) their initial response, the original *genotype*, the "genes" of their idea, still defines the direction that we take (Dunne 2008 [1999]). As designers, it's impossible to forget where these ideas came from.

A last word

"It's nice if glasses can be sexy and mysterious. People who need glasses don't have to feel separated from glamour"

Tony Gross[2]

"My idea of design is a bit old-fashioned. It should be practical, functional and then look good—in that order"

Graham Cutler[3]

Tony Gross embraced the "superficial, ephemeral and lightweight" culture of fashion, whereas his partner Graham Cutler values practicality above all things. Perhaps this tension is what made Cutler and Gross so successful and influential a brand. So perhaps it is less important that fashion-led and co-design principles are completely reconciled than that they merely coexist—as we hope that they do in Hands of X. Our further hope is that this approach becomes more influential, and that as a result disability-led design can become more nuanced.

Disclosure statement

Hands of X was initially a partnership between DJCAD University of Dundee and the Institute of Making UCL, with MAKlab as supporting partners, funded by the EPSRC.

Notes

1 Since the time of writing, C has undergone a successful double hand transplant.
2 See: https://www.fashioneyewear.co.uk/designer-glasses/cutler-and-gross/frame_colour/green.html (accessed September 6, 2019).
3 Ibid.

References

BBC (1994–2017) *No Triumph, No Tragedy*, radio program, BBC Radio 4.

Charlton, J. I. (1998) *Nothing About Us Without Us: Disability, Oppression, and Empowerment*, Berkeley, CA: University of California Press.

Corner, F. (2014) *Why Fashion Matters*, London: Thames & Hudson.

Dunne, A. (2008 [1999]) *Hertzian Tales: Electronic Products, Aesthetic Experience, and Critical Design*, Cambridge, MA: The MIT Press.

Fukasawa, N. and Morrison, J. (2008) *Super Normal: Sensations of the Ordinary*, Baden: Lars Müller.

Gaver, W., Dunne, A., and Pacenti, E. (1999) "Design: Cultural Probes," *Interactions*, 6(1): 21–9.

Manzini, E. (2015) *Design, When Everybody Designs: An Introduction to Design for Social Innovation*, trans. R. Coad, Cambridge, MA: The MIT Press.

Marriot, H. (2018) "Gucci Shuns Glamour and Sex for Philosophy and Severed Heads," *The Guardian*, February 21. Available online: https://www.theguardian.com/fashion/2018/feb/21/gucci-moves-from-glamour-and-sex-to-philosophy-and-severed-heads-milan-fashion-week (accessed August 11, 2019).

Pullin, G. (2009) *Design Meets Disability*, Cambridge, MA: The MIT Press.

Pullin, G. (2018) "Super Normal Design for Extraordinary Bodies: A Design Manifesto," in K. Ellis, R. Garland-Thomson, M. Kent, and R. Robertson (eds.), *Manifestos for the Future of Critical Disability Studies, Volume 1*, 166–76, Abingdon: Routledge.

Rousso, H. (2013) *Don't Call Me Inspirational: A Disabled Feminist Talks Back*, Philadelphia, PA: Temple University Press.

Suri, J. F. and Howard, S. G. (2006) "Going Deeper, Seeing Further: Enhancing Ethnographic Interpretations to Reveal More Meaningful Opportunities for Design," *Journal of Advertising Research*, 46(3): 246–50.

The Alternative Limb Project (2018) "About." Available online: http://www.thealternativelimbproject.com/about/the-alternative-limb-project/ (accessed March 26, 2018).

The Telegraph (2018) "Tony Gross, Designer of Fashionable Glasses—Obituary," March 11. Available online: https://www.telegraph.co.uk/obituaries/2018/03/11/tony-gross-designer-fashionable-glasses-obituary/ (accessed August 11, 2019).

Watzlawick, P., Bavelas, J. B., and Jackson, D. D. (1968) *Pragmatics of Human Communication: A Study of Interactional Patterns, Pathologies, and Paradoxes*, London: Faber and Faber.

Wilkes, S. E. and Miodownik, M. A. (2018) "Materials Library Collections as Tools for Interdisciplinary Research," *Interdisciplinary Science Reviews*, 43(1): 3–23.

7

Tissue Engineered Textiles

Craft's Place in the Laboratory

Amy Congdon, Lucy Di Silvio, and Carole Collet

Introduction by Professor Carole Collet

What can a textile designer learn from tissue engineering? What knowledge can a biologist gain from textile research? The conversation in this chapter is both a testimony and a tribute to the relevance of design–science collaborations. When a true interdisciplinary journey evolves, it is for the benefit of both the design and science fields.

Amy Congdon, a textile designer and embroidery specialist by training, has a long-term interest in tissue engineering, "an interdisciplinary field that applies the principles of engineering and life sciences toward the development of biological substitutes that restore, maintain or improve tissue function or a whole organ" (Langer and Vacanti 1993: 920). She has explored textile craft techniques as well as design fictions to challenge and inform the field. As a PhD candidate at Central Saint Martins, University of the Arts London (UAL), she is working in collaboration with Professor of Tissue Engineering Lucy Di Silvio at King's College London to explore the role of design and textile craft in the tissue engineering lab.

By developing a novel material archive and a range of bespoke embroidered interfaces, Congdon has developed a new approach to tissue engineering practice, where the selection of textile fibers combined with a tailored textile matrix can control the level of cell attachment and alignment required for tissue repairs.

By learning the scientific protocols of working in a lab, and by incorporating textile knowledge in the microfabrication of body compatible textile interfaces, Congdon has orchestrated a new hybrid practice. There is no recipe for such a design journey, and it is very much the interactions between the design expert and the tissue engineering specialist that have led to this successful and groundbreaking project.

Hence, we have chosen to share a somewhat typical interaction between the designer and scientist, to decode their levels of understanding and communicate how they share and learn from each other.

This interview took place at Central Saint Martins in January 2018, and was designed to facilitate discussion and review what was learned and achieved in this project. We hope this will inspire other interdisciplinary exchanges across design and science.[1]

Origins of the collaboration

Carole   **Amy, how did the collaboration come about? And Lucy, what drew a professor in tissue engineering to allow a textile designer access to their lab?**

Amy   I really wanted to find an interdisciplinary laboratory that was looking at a range of techniques and approaches.

Lucy   There's a big drive for an interdisciplinary approach within the sciences now.

Carole   That's true, collaborations.

Lucy   Collaboration, exactly, you've got to demonstrate that you're reaching out across different disciplines. Science and art are interlinked. Both are creative; science allows the acquisition of knowledge in a more objective manner, whereas art expresses knowledge in a more subjective way. Art creates in one way, science creates in another, and they meet somewhere in the middle. One should embrace the other. I've learned from Amy, and I hope that Amy has learned from me.

Amy   Absolutely—I was so fortunate to find Lucy's lab and that she agreed to let me in! Even though I think it was a little left of center as a request!

Lucy   I think initially I was a little skeptical and it wasn't until Amy almost forcefully said, "Oh can I just come and have a chat with you," that seriously, suddenly my whole attitude changed, and I started to realize that there is a whole new world out there, that as scientists we live in quite a blinkered world...

Carole   **What were those initial conversations and how did these change your perspectives?**

Amy   When I first met with Lucy I took a range of my previous work to show her. Both from an earlier residency I had completed at SymbioticA,[2] where I first learned how to tissue culture, and some of my speculative work exploring the future of haute couture. The Biological Atelier[3] work (Figure 7.1), which I

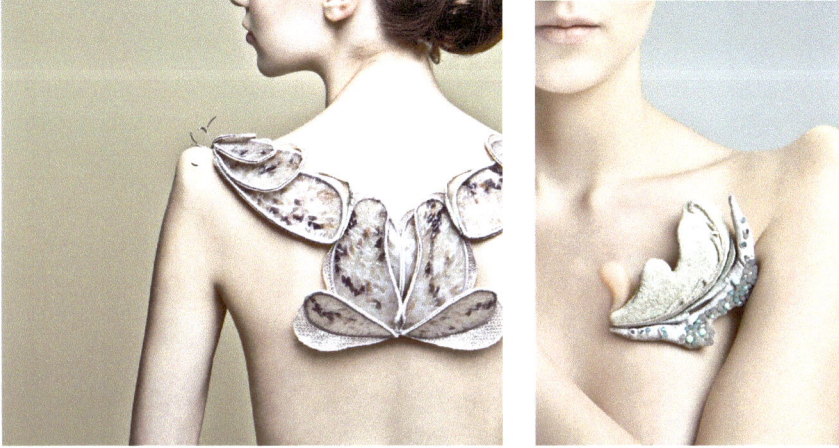

Figure 7.1 Amy Congdon, Biological Atelier SS 2082: Extinct Collection (2011). Photo credit: www.lornajanenewman.com.

had come to a point with where I wanted to move away from speculation into practical exploration, was actually useful as a conversation starter. I already knew from this early stage that the technology was a long way off realizing those speculative prototypes[4] and that the research would focus much more on the fundamentals of what a design-based approach could bring to the lab.

Crafting the body: Initial experiments and material exploration

Carole   **A key parallel that I think is interesting is the link between textile craft and the repair of the body.**

Amy   There is a really close relationship between textiles and the body, and we've been "crafting" our bodies, both for repair and aesthetically, for millennia. I think the earliest examples that I found when researching this were in India around the sixth century BCE (Saraf and Parihar 2006).

Additionally, there are obviously strong links between current surgery methods and centuries-old textile techniques—for example, in the stitches used to suture. You can look in any standard medical or textile textbook and you'll find a blanket stitch, although it may not be called that in surgical terminology (Figure 7.2).

Lucy   Absolutely, I mean that's where it was taken from. If we look back in ancient cultures, natural materials were used for suturing wounds, treating diseases, and as implants in the body.

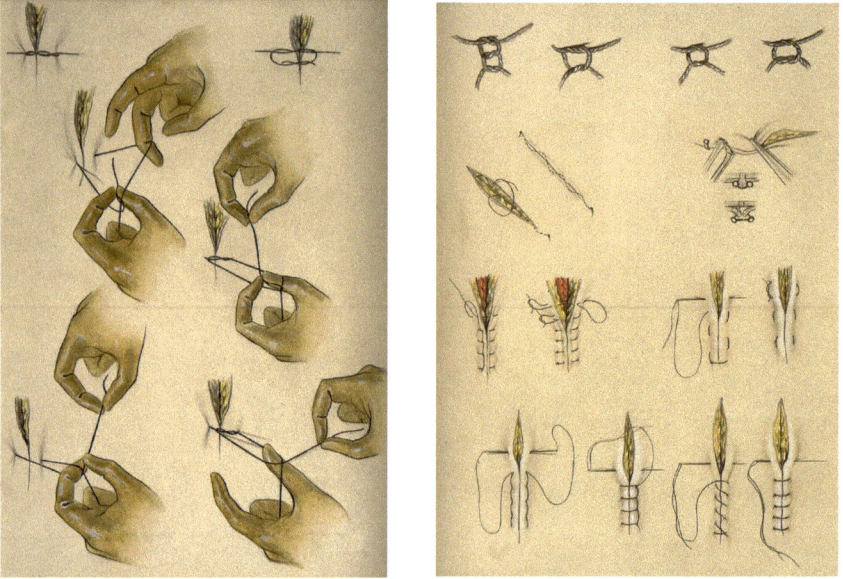

Figure 7.2 (left) "Surgical stitches. Coloured pencil drawing." Credit: Wellcome Collection CC BY (https://wellcomecollection.org/works/wevr3dun); (right) "Surgical stitches and knots. Coloured pencil drawing." Credit: Wellcome Collection. CC BY (https://wellcomecollection.org/works/xn6wtqvp).

Amy   It's that crossover that started my fascination in this area—I saw an embroidered medical implant[5] and became obsessed with how my skillset as a textile designer could be used in different disciplines—for example, traditional stitches being used to mimic natural structures found within the body. This was the approach we took in the initial work together—we were looking at the anterior cruciate ligament (found in the knee) and I was using digital embroidery techniques to mimic the structure of that part of the body (Figure 7.3).

Carole   **So what is it that you got out of it, in design terms, that you would not have acquired otherwise?**

Amy   I think anyone who goes into a lab without a scientific background, at some point will feel the temptation to try to become a tissue engineer, or to become more and more scientific, because you know that your skillset is different, and you're in this very new environment.

However, it was the most important process to go through and realize you need to approach things the same way that you would outside of the lab, but with the skills you've learned working in the lab. So rather than trying to fit myself into what I thought I "should" be doing in the lab, I learned to say "Okay, let's go back to that craft way of working—approach this as a maker." And that's when interesting things really started to happen.

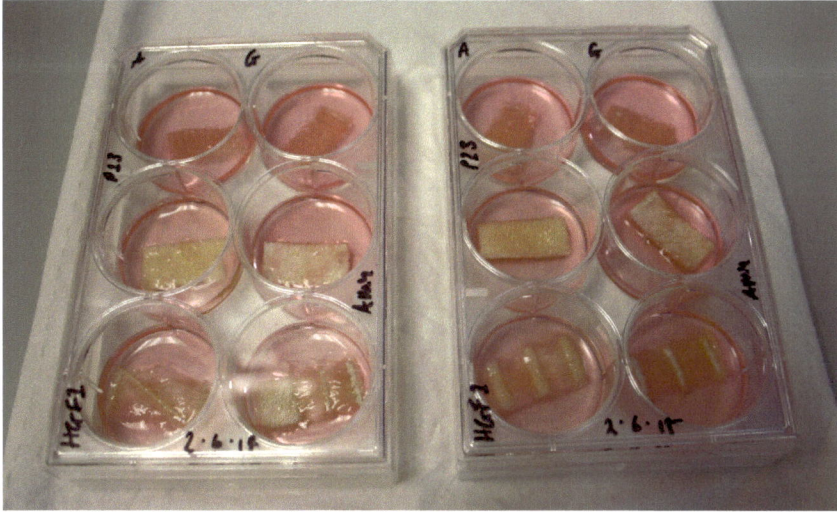

Figure 7.3 Amy Congdon, Tissue Engineered Textiles (2014–16). Digitally embroidered scaffolds designed and constructed to mimic the structure of the anterior cruciate ligament. Photograph by Amy Congdon.

Lucy Tissue engineering is transforming the way we look at tissues and repair. At its core, it is about designing and constructing physical objects like hearts, lungs, livers, etc. This requires biological "building skills"; essentially scientists need to be trained to be craftsmen.

Amy And I think I came to realize that the rigor you learn from the process of structuring experiments isn't uncreative, but it actually helps you be creative faster.

Development of the research: Textile craft techniques

Carole **How did you approach the work in the laboratory differently after the initial experiments?**

Amy I took it right back to basics—what materials will cells grow on and which won't they? This simple question led to the creation of a "materials archive" with different materials all seeded with the same cells, in the same way. There were ten different fiber types tested from across the textile spectrum. But in many ways it's a small snapshot, a start of what could be a much larger, ongoing research project.

Interestingly however, one of the key learnings in this part of the research was the importance of the size of structures seeded and how that affects cell orientation and growth. It was one of the things I found most fascinating—understanding the relationship and impact of scale.

Lucy   Scale is so important. Cells in their natural microenvironment respond to a multitude of signals, such as biophysical cues in the form of change in topography or stiffness of a scaffold. It can almost be a selective mechanism, whereby you choose a specific topography to bring about a specific cell response to that scale.

Microscale topographies[6] can change the way a cell adheres and migrates across its surface. Different cell types will respond differently to these cues, and the cellular cytoskeleton[7] can reorganize itself depending on the feature size.

One of the problems we have when we make porous materials is that we need to make sure that we've got micro and macro porosity and that these pores are interconnected to ensure cells can migrate down the material. Also different sized cells have to migrate such as osteoblasts (bone cells) and endothelial cells, as well as the responsible vasculature.[8]

Amy   Cell migration is really interesting, and I know that when talking to different researchers in the lab, that each cell type behaves differently. This made me want to keep screening because you might find that one material works on a particular cell type and not on the other!

Lucy   This is another key area, which is "bio-selectivity" and all materials will have different characteristics to which the cells will selectively respond.

Amy   And that's really intriguing. Because it brought up ideas of concepts like textile resist[9]—and the understanding of what scale the cells that you're working with are at, the scale of the thread, and then what they will and won't attach to allows you to start constructing a scaffold, which not only helps the cells to align, but also controls patterns of cell attachment and alignment.

This all relates to the traditional process of textile resist—when you're dyeing, you want to have dye go in one area and not in the other (Figure 7.4, top). It's really interesting to have those very traditional craft skills, and ways of thinking, be applied in something like tissue engineering that seems on the surface so radically different (Figure 7.4, bottom).

Amy   What's also an interesting problem to consider is how to represent and communicate work that often cannot be seen by the naked eye (Figure 7.4). The success of most of the scaffolds created, using techniques such as braiding and French knots, was assessed by looking down a microscope. And because you're working at such a minute scale, it's hard to communicate the ideas visually to people. It's something I'm working on developing—how best to articulate the results and implications of the work.

Lucy   But Amy, you're not really at an end point yet, if anything you're just at the beginning!

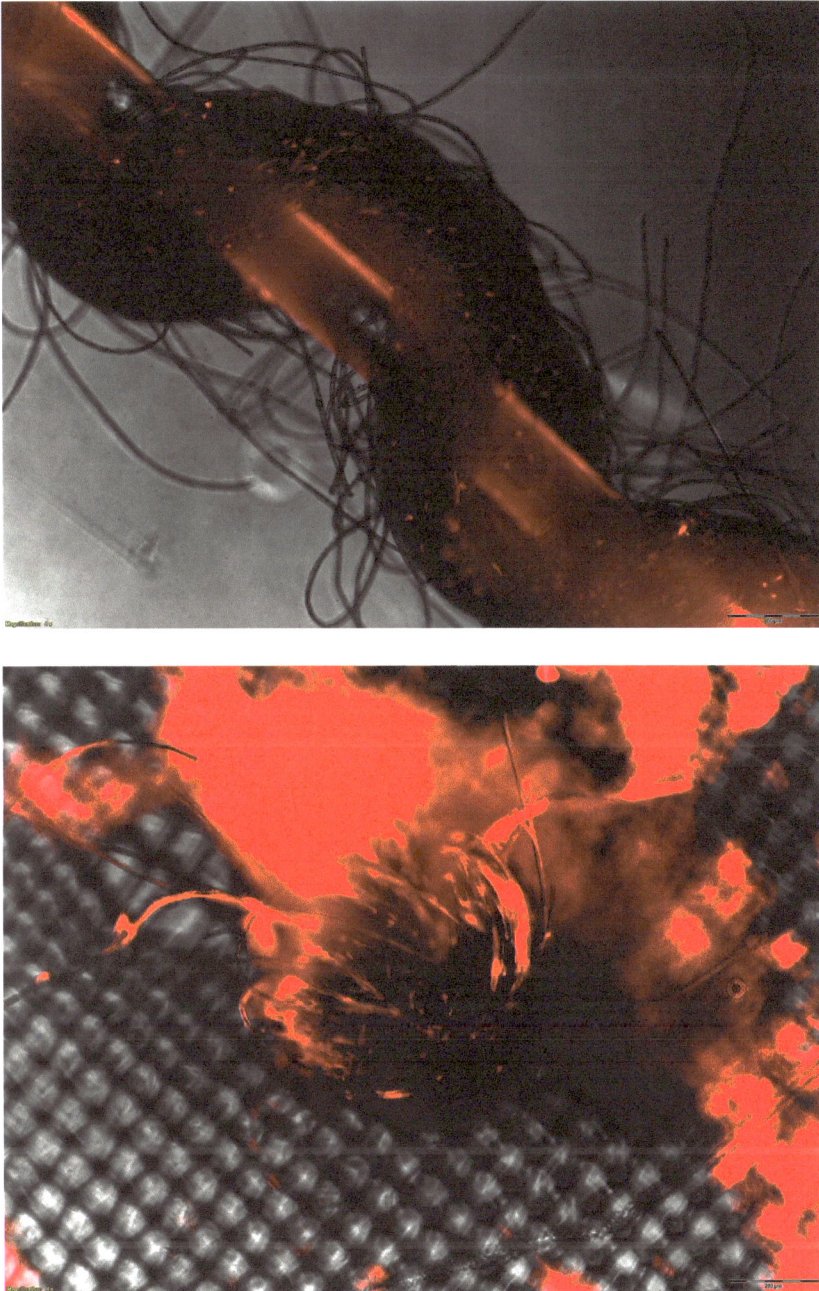

Figure 7.4 Amy Congdon, Tissue Engineered Textiles (2016): (top) A three-strand braid whereby one yarn prevents cell attachment, the scaffold is designed based on the textile technique of "resist"; (bottom) French knot made from cellulose yarns. Seeded with C2C12 (muscle) cells (red shapes) that follow the direction of the structure. Photographs by Amy Congdon.

Amy   Definitely, but it's still important to think about how to communicate the work and its outcomes to those outside of the lab.

Carole   The products you're creating, I call them "silent interfaces." Because they're silent in the body, they're not active, but they are supporting the activity of the cells growing in alignment.

Lucy   Well, in scientific terms we talk about tissue interfaces. Tissues exist as multiple types and are assembled in a complex organ system. Tissues interface with a seamless integration, with the tissue-to-tissue interfaces exhibiting a gradient of structures and properties that serve a number of functions. Successful tissue engineering requires a direct structural interface with the host tissue (Atala, Kasper, and Mikos 2012; Mikos et al. 2006).

Amy   I think that's one of the things I remember from early on, going back to how this all began, when I came into your office and you talked of nothing in the body growing in isolation—everything is interfacing or integrating with something else. And when you work in a lab there's sometimes that danger that you end up working with one cell type on its own, and it's never that way in the body.

Lucy   That's a really important point that you bring up. Because even scientists are specialized in their area "I'm a soft tissue biologist," "I'm a hard tissue biologist," etc. But no tissues exist in isolation. So, when you are developing your tissue engineered bone for example, you've got to think of what tissue it's going to interface with.

Amy   I think that links back in some way to textiles. When you're working with materials, many times you're trying to make something whereby you're not just working with one type of material. You're trying to construct something with materials of different characteristics and working with how those substrates want to behave.

Lucy   The aim of tissue engineering is the desire to regenerate tissues that mimic nature, which does it very well. Scientists are inspired by natural structures— we have this desire to create tissues that look like, and behave like, natural tissues … and I'm a biologist, so my main interest is that it's got to be biologically responsive. However, if you speak to an engineer, or a material scientist, they'll say, "Oh no, strength is the most important thing, it's got to be strong!" And we're coming at it from quite opposing ends.

Lucy   Amy, did you also look at some morphology changes in cells?

Amy   I did, and I was able to observe some structural change in the shape of the cells.

Lucy   Because I thought I saw some pictures where cells were different shapes.

Amy   They were. And they were different shapes depending on the diameter of the thread that they were seeded onto—it would affect whether they would elongate or not.

Lucy   Whether they would spread out or get long?

Amy   A number of papers I've read support these findings—how scaffold scale and thread diameter affect the alignment of cells. I found that my experiments matched up with what this research found, but I have not yet discovered anyone who's taken it any further. Because for me as a textile designer, if I know what scale of the thread causes alignment, I can then start to design structures that use that knowledge.

For example, if I want a cell to grow in one direction versus another, I can manipulate the outcome. And that's where I think that making knowledge comes into play of knowing how to structure a textile.

Lucy   See, that kind of information would be of extreme importance to us as scientists trying to design scaffolds.

Carole   It's actually creatively reconsidering how you can rethink the basics of tissue engineering with cell attachment, using in-depth textile knowledge to generate a set of research tools. The material archive you created by testing a range of natural and artificial fibers has not been done before. Your PhD project is not a science communication project, it's a real design project, that is actually pushing both the design and the tissue engineering fields.

The importance of multidisciplinarity and creative freedom

Carole   **What would you say is one of the key learnings of this collaboration for your lab?**

Lucy   I think for us, it will be that we want to get as close as we can to nature by trying to understand normal repair mechanisms using normal materials. Everything is about biomimetic materials, bio-mimicking nature (Fernandez-Yague et al. 2015; Patterson, Martino, and Hubbell 2010; Shin, Jo, and Mikos 2003). And so, I think we look to quite a few natural materials such as silk because we want to move toward them

More importantly, Amy demonstrated, where she worked with different threads and different structures, a concept that we know but we don't really understand—which is that you can actually tailor make a patch, a pad, an implant, to make your cells go where you want them to. For example, nerve cells have to go in a specific direction or you won't get regeneration. Other cells you know you can randomly put them there and they will organize themselves into a structure.

Carole   I think in terms of design methodology,[10] that's a contribution to knowledge as well—establishing how you do that without compromising on the rigor of the scientific protocols but managing to open up new ways to think about experimentation.

Lucy   I think you're also making us look at our science with different eyes. I mean now it is very empirical data, graphs, results, asking "what have I discovered?" But you've given us the freedom almost. And you're really genuinely interested. And because you're passionate about what you're doing, I think it gives a scientist that freedom of expression, too.

Amy   The notion of "freedom" is an interesting one and is something that's come up with numerous scientists I've spoken to.[11] Most noticeably the lack of freedom in current research—which seems to come as a result of a department's research focus and ultimately funding. It was incredible to be able to experiment without having a prescribed end goal.

Lucy   And I think the other thing is, it was an evolving thing, wasn't it? So that pressure being removed, there's suddenly this freedom of, "wow, that's interesting, let's look at that. Or maybe we should try that." Whereas you can only do that to a certain extent when you have a defined project. You've got a limited amount of money to do a limited project, you've got to come out with something at the end. And this freedom of being innovative and thinking outside the box, it is a luxury, as far as I was concerned, to be able to think that way.

Amy   One of the other things that has emerged from doing the research, and this is a generalization but relates to end goals, is the idea of top-down versus bottom-up. And I think a lot of science (and research) is driven by something that's top-down. Because of funding, because of the research remits and the stress researchers are under. There are specific issues you're trying to address— so it's about knowing you're trying to fix "x," and then asking the subsequent question "so how do we get there?"

 Whereas I came in going, "I want to start from the opposite end of the spectrum. I'm not saying I'm going to try and do 'x' or fix this problem, I'm going to explore, which is very much a design 'sampling'[12] approach. And then through that understand what this knowledge could be applied to."

Lucy   Normally in science we create and design an experiment to answer a specific question, for example, one of the things we're working on at the moment is a 3D-printed scaffold that mimics a natural structure and we are trying to functionalize it, i.e., make it biologically more responsive so that it behaves like natural tissue. We do the experiments knowing what we want to achieve at the end, and if we don't achieve our goal we're going to be grossly disappointed, as will our funders. So, that's a pressure if you've got to get to that finite point.

Carole   **So, finally touching again on the legacy of this project, would you consider employing a textile designer in your lab?**

Lucy   Absolutely!

Amy   Well, I can't ask for any more than that! I hope from my side that the legacy of the project is that more of this type of work is carried out. There's so much potential opened up by these types of collaborations and by a multidisciplinary approach to all aspects of the scientific and creative fields.

Notes

1   Although there are many speculative design projects that explore the potential of new technologies, from outside of the laboratory, there are fewer where a designer has worked directly with scientists on a project. Some of these notable exceptions include the Biojewellery project (http://www.materialbeliefs.co.uk/biojewellery/project.html), the Synthetic Aesthetics Project (http://www.syntheticaesthetics.org), and Natsai Audrey Chieza's work (https://faberfutures.com).

2   SymbioticA is the first research laboratory of its kind, enabling artists and researchers to engage in wet biology practices in a biological science department. It also hosts residents, workshops, exhibitions, and symposia (SymbioticA 2018).

3   The Biological Atelier projects (SS 2082 and AW 2082) are speculative design projects that seek to explore what the materials and tools of tissue engineering will mean for design; "from the re-appropriation of textile skills such as embroidery, through to the new technologies that may facilitate the production. The project considers the changing and blurring roles of the designer, the craftsman and the scientist in the biotechnological future—through the imagined fashion Atelier of 2080" (Congdon 2016).

4   Pieces from the Biological Atelier project were designed to look like products, even though they were not grown in the laboratory. Through using design prototyping skills they are intended to make real the potential of tissue engineering and how it could be utilized in future product applications.

5   Embroidered medical implants by Julian Ellis of Ellis Developments Ltd.

6   The structure of a surface at the micro scale.

7   The cytoskeleton is a structure that helps cells maintain their shape and internal organization, and it also provides mechanical support that enables cells to carry out essential functions like division and movement (Nature.com 2014).

8   Vasculature is "the arrangement of blood vessels in the body or a part of the body" (Collinsdictionary.com 2019).

9   Resist-dyeing is a widely used method of applying colors or patterns to fabric. A substance that is impervious to the dye blocks its access to certain areas of the fabric, while other parts are free to take up the dye color (V&A n.d.).

10 The methodology of the work described in this interview can be classified as research through design, defined by Christopher Frayling as "materials research," "development work—for example, customising a piece of technology to do something no one had considered before," and "action research" based. It is where the knowledge is created through design practice (Frayling 1993: 5).

11 The notion of "creative freedom" also noted by other designers who have engaged in the sciences, such as Calvert and Schyfter (2016).

12 Congdon uses the term "sampling" to mean an iterative process of creating small prototypes designed to test techniques, materials, and ideas.

References

Atala, A., Kasper, F. K., and Mikos, A. G. (2012) "Engineering Complex Tissues," *Science Translational Medicine*, 4(160): art. 160rv12. Available online: http://stm.sciencemag. org/content/4/160/160rv12 (accessed September 29, 2018).

Calvert, J. and Schyfter, P. (2016) "What Can Science and Technology Studies Learn from Art and Design? Reflections on 'Synthetic Aesthetics,'" *Social Studies of Science*, 47(2): 195–215.

Congdon, A. (2016) "Biological Atelier: SS 2082 'Extinct,'" *Amy Congdon*. Available online: http://www.amycongdon.com/biological-atelier-ss-2082-extinct/ (accessed September 29, 2018).

Fernandez-Yague, M., Abbah, S., McNamara, L., Zeugolis, D., Pandit, A., and Biggs, M. (2015) "Biomimetic Approaches in Bone Tissue Engineering: Integrating Biological and Physicomechanical Strategies," *Advanced Drug Delivery Reviews*, 84: 1–29.

Frayling, C. (1993) *Research in Art and Design*, research paper 1(1), London: Royal College of Art. Available online: http://researchonline.rca.ac.uk/384/3/frayling_ research_in_art_and_design_1993.pdf (accessed September 29, 2018).

Langer, R. and Vacanti, J. P. (1993) "Tissue Engineering," *Science*, 260(5110): 920–6.

Mikos, A. G., Herring, S. W., Ochareon, P., Elisseeff, J., Lu, H. H., Kandel, R., Schoen, F. J., Toner, M., Mooney, D., Atala, A., van Dyke, M. E., Kaplan, D., and Vunjak-Novakovic, G. (2006) "Engineering Complex Tissues," *Tissue Engineering*, 12(12): 3307–39.

Nature.com (2014) "Concept: Microtubules and Filaments," *Scitable*. Available online: https://www.nature.com/scitable/topicpage/microtubules-and-filaments-14052932 (accessed September 29, 2018).

Patterson, J., Martino, M. M., and Hubbell, J. A. (2010) "Biomimetic Materials in Tissue Engineering," *Materials Today*, 13(1/2): 14–22.

Saraf, S. and Parihar, R. (2006) "Sushruta: The First Plastic Surgeon in 600 BC," *The Internet Journal of Plastic Surgery*, 4(2): art. 4. Available online: http://ispub.com/ IJPS/4/2/8232 (accessed July 10, 2016).

Shin, H., Jo, S., and Mikos, A. G. (2003) "Biomimetic Materials for Tissue Engineering," *Biomaterials*, 24(24): 4353–64.

SymbioticA (2018) *SymbioticA*, Perth: The University of Western Australia. Available online: http://www.symbiotica.uwa.edu.au/ (accessed September 29, 2018).

V&A (n.d.) "Resist-dyed textiles," London: Victoria and Albert Museum. Available online: http://www.vam.ac.uk/content/articles/r/resist-dyed-textiles/ (accessed September 29, 2018).

8

Mind–Body–Garment–Cloth

Holly McQuillan and Timo Rissanen

Introduction

As our understanding of fashion and sustainability broadens beyond quantified accounts of supply chains and material use, the fashion system requires an expanded, holistic understanding of how we clothe the body and through it the mind, and how design may contribute to this understanding. Here we ask questions about the presence and absence of mind–body dialogues in contemporary fashion design practice, and the roles of technology, weaving, and cutting in facilitating these dialogues.

In this chapter mind refers to that of designer, maker, and wearer of clothing. Body is explored through discussion of the labor of both craftsman and factory worker, and the role of the wearer's body in the design of, and lived experience in, garments. Cloth is explored in relation to the reduction of waste and the simultaneous design and production of cloth. Garment behaves like a vehicle, facilitator, and communicator of these interactions.

The themes of mind, body, garment, and cloth are expanded through a series of case studies to provide multiple perspectives on the potential models and approaches possible as we seek to transform the fashion industry. The practitioners discussed in this chapter diverge significantly from each other, in terms of the contexts in which they practice, their methods of practice, and in their relationships to materials. We nonetheless speculate on a connecting thread that creates a common ground for all of them—all of us, in fact, since we count ourselves in this group. The common thread is a pursuit of wholeness or completeness in the practice—not only relating to designer, maker, and cloth but also industry and wearer.

How a sense of wholeness manifests in the practice and its outcomes of each practitioner varies broadly, yet it provides a robust and useful lens with which to examine these divergent practices. It is necessary at this point for us to define holism as both a process of expanding out to see and act on a range of problems, issues, and perspectives while pulling and holding together these divergences in order to ameliorate the industry we are actors within. We do not believe there can ever be a single solution to our complex industry. This is the spirit in which these case studies are explored.

Having an holistic respect for cloth and body in garment design is not a new proposition: in *Cut My Cote*, Dorothy Burnham (1973) presented her thesis that the loom type of a particular culture was directly connected with the widths of the cloth that that loom produced, and the width, in turn, informed the cuts of the garments made from the cloth. Historically most garments were produced with careful consideration for the cloth they were cut from. The quality of the cloth in many garments was directly impacted by the body of the maker—such as in the case of back strap looms where tension is provided by the body of the weaver, while in Japanese Kimono the form of the garment is an interaction between the width of the cloth produced, the maker, and the body of the intended wearer—a relationship that changed over the garment and wearer's lifetime.

Additionally, designers such as Yeohlee Teng have used the dimensions of the cloth as both a limit and instigator in her design practice. This is a type of completeness that we investigate in contemporary practice, including our own practices; however, we do not limit our investigation to it. Wholeness or completeness can have multiple meanings that are not necessarily mutually exclusive but, rather, complementary. In much of contemporary fashion, the body is subservient to industry, serving to either produce (as makers) or buy (as consumers) the garments the industry produces. The experience of being and living in garments is often underexplored by designers, and the experience of making garments either by the skilled home sewer or the factory machinist is almost entirely ignored. It is a one-sided dialogue where the garment is primarily valued as a unit of sale, while other inputs such as material and time, and outputs such as waste and physical or social impacts, are secondary.

In this chapter we will explore holistic conversations between body, mind, cloth, and garment, first in the context of McQuillan's practice within the existing fashion industry, providing a counterpart for the more avant-garde practices explored later.

The belly of the beast: Industry context

It often feels that the fashion industry—as an emblem of capitalism and Fordism[1]—is the antithesis of the holistic: originally it was a cottage industry where growers, weavers, makers, and wearers were known to each other. When the goal became to produce as many units in as short a time frame as possible this craft-centric structure began to change. Division of labor, a key tenet of Fordism (Forty 1986: 122–3), is unmistakably in action within the conventional fashion factory and clothing production, as far from a cottage industry or the notion of craft as we can imagine. At times it seems utterly removed from the human scale, yet abusive toward the bodies who produce it. The sprawling, globalized, and disjointed supply chain of the fashion industry is difficult to discern due to its goliath size, and its opaqueness makes a holistic approach difficult to realize at large scale. Achieving holism is difficult for a range of reasons: trade agreements restricting materials you can source, inconsistent or underutilized machinery and technology, along with more obvious obstructions such as geography and language. However, one of the biggest barriers to holistic change in the fashion industry is the ingrained hierarchical systems caused by the need to control this beast of an industry.

Many attempts to wrangle the ills of the industry have been made at the atomic level, for example, through organic fibers and non-toxic dyes. These changes are important and necessary because of the high ecological and human impacts that they will have, if left unchanged. Tackling ingrained systemic issues about consumption, labor, design systems, and economic models are even more difficult due to the multiple stakeholders and complex interdependencies involved. One explanation for why most of the attempts to change these systems have been on a small scale is that holistically implementing a design and production system that benefits all involved becomes exponentially more complex the larger the supply chain and company.

Industry in pursuit of zero waste

Pursuing a radical reduction in waste in a large garment company requires a holistic, multifaceted approach, but it is only through attempting this that the complexities of achieving holism are revealed. McQuillan collaborated with an outerwear brand that carries iconic pieces through decades with minimal changes, meaning successful change can last for many years. This company dedicates time to developing materials and testing garments in the elements for which they are made before approving them for production. Wearers of their garments are supported to repair instead of replace, and they were pioneers in the movement toward reducing the use of toxic chemicals in their materials. Despite these advancements, the brand still adheres to many of the conventional systems that make the transformation to a holistic approach, such as zero-waste design,[2] difficult.

In preparation for a workshop with the company, McQuillan was asked to redesign a mid-layer fleece jacket using zero-waste design principles, demonstrating to the team what may be possible when applying these methods. Working from the current pattern, measurement chart, and sketches, McQuillan was able to design a fleece jacket with different seam lines, which maintained the same fit as the current fleece jacket, and created almost zero waste. A physical sample was never created in her design process due to the tight time frame but the 3D software McQuillan used reduced the need for this. Team members constructed garments in the company's R&D center during her visit, and the garment was presented to all designers at the end of the week with the following feedback provided: the sleeve seams were determined to deviate too strongly from the original, a center back seam was not a viable option for aesthetic reasons, and cutting on the cross grainline was considered infeasible. Changes to seam placement—such as moving a seam 0.5–1 inches for reasons of function, taste, or aesthetics—were suggested by the wider design team; however, when making these changes, both large and small, efficiency and yield returned close to the original. McQuillan and the product teams both learned together many valuable insights through this process.

It became clear that no steps can be skipped, and cross-departmental teams must be involved in all parts of the early phases of the design process. Importantly design language must be confirmed and articulated—such as what aspects of the design are negotiable, and what are not. Ultimately a holistic overview of the entire garment design, construction, and production is needed, from customer expectations to the machinery used to construct it, to the size of the cutting table used in its production. Zero waste is not merely a design or pattern-cutting technique: it *enforces* a holistic way of working.

This approach is in contrast to other collaborations undertaken with similarly sized brands where McQuillan would be asked to work with a specific section of a company in isolation. Often the interactions would be with the marker-makers,[3] who have little to no authority to change the design, and no ability to impact on fabric suppliers, or with junior designers, who would then be expected to argue for holistic change with their superiors. In these projects, the siloed, hierarchical structure of the fashion industry would reveal itself to be a key player preventing meaningful change.

"High efficiency"

Building on McQuillan's workshop and initial case study, the company continued work on developing low-waste styles, making small improvements to high volume styles and, eventually, the team decided to embark on another case study with McQuillan—this time redesigning a technical fleece mid-layer. The goal was set at reaching "high efficiency" of 92 percent efficiency, rather than 100 percent. This is still a lofty goal, as the average garment in all the fashion industry is only 75–85 percent efficient (Rissanen 2013; Runnel et al. 2017)—it is complicated to achieve this because there is a minimum of five different sizes that need to be cut all with the same or very similar design lines, with all the same construction methods and relative fit. Overall, however, the development progressed in a method more closely aligned with their usual way of working, with many months of collaboration, where the team attempted to uncover together with all stakeholders—such as technical designer, designer, line manager, factory management, factory marker-makers, and sewers on the factory floor (Figure 8.1)—what is needed to be known.

Figure 8.1 The manufacturing context of the industry project discussed here, Colombia (2017). Photograph by Holly McQuillan.

Questions arose during the process, including:

- How does the width of the cloth impact on outcome (fit/aesthetic/finish/ grading) and how much can/should we control this?
- How do we ensure factories are engaged in these radically different ways of working?
- What does a reduction in cloth consumption mean for the business model of the company and suppliers?

In some cases these questions addressed and pointed toward the deeper dialogue between McQuillan and staff at the company, as well as internally within the company, about the relationship between the mind of the person wearing the garment, the bodies that make and wear it, the cloth required to produce it, and the industry context in which these interactions are situated.

Overall, these projects demonstrate this company's ongoing commitment to critically evaluating their processes and systems, and a long-term commitment to changing the way they do business—far removed from the tokenistic approach often seen in the fashion industry. Most importantly for the authors, it reveals that at its core, zero-waste fashion design cannot be reduced to an exercise in efficient marker-making, garment design, or pattern cutting. Instead, it demonstrates that any attempt to radically reduce the textile waste produced in garment production needs to be undertaken as a holistic redesign of the system itself and a mindful renegotiation of value with the stakeholders involved.

ThreeASFOUR

ThreeASFOUR[4] is an avant-garde New York-based brand founded by three designers, Angela Donhauser, Adi Gil, and Gabi Asfour. During a studio visit in 2016, Asfour described a one-piece t-shirt to Rissanen that they had refined for several years, a process that still continues (Figure 8.2). The t-shirt is composed of one piece of cloth that travels asymmetrically around the body through curvilinear cutting, as distinct from the vertical and horizontal seaming of a conventional t-shirt.

On initial inspection the t-shirt seems wasteful: its cutting and making result in relatively large off-cuts of fabric. Asfour himself acknowledged this as an issue. Two counterpoints, however, ought to be acknowledged in relation to the t-shirt. First, its evolution over many years jars with the capitalist relationship fashion has to time, of focusing on novelty at a high speed. Over a span of years, Asfour returns to the t-shirt, tweaking it, proposing it again, tweaking it once more. Asfour is not alone: Rissanen (2011: 136) has examined other designers' relationships to time,

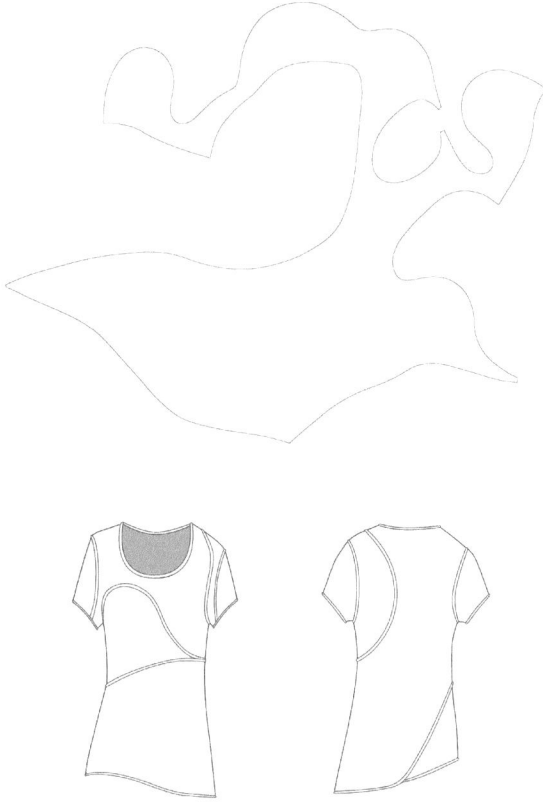

Figure 8.2 This one-piece t-shirt by ThreeASFOUR has been through many iterations in its design journey. Photo credit: ThreeASFOUR.

and several agree that good ideas in fashion design do not follow the industry's traditional six-month schedule, or the accelerated schedule of recent years.

The artificial pace of fashion change is required by the economic system in which fashion operates, not by fashion users. We, the authors, are not in any way against fashion change; rather, we invite the reader to notice that different speeds of fashion production can and should be encouraged to coexist in the fashion system. We invite the reader to notice that very fast speeds now dominate, and we call for a balance of speeds. Second, the ThreeASFOUR studio keeps all fabric off-cuts, including those created by this t-shirt. They are carefully sorted and stored by type and color, always ready to be used as an embellishment or as a contrast fabric. ThreeASFOUR have a deep respect for the materials they work with, be they traditional silks or 3D-printed polymers. This is not unlike the companies Yeohlee, Alabama Chanin, and Dosa Inc., led by Yeohlee Teng, Natalie

Chanin, and Christina Kim, who also show reverence to the materials they use, by wasting as little as possible through holistic, systemic thinking that permeates each respective company. Scraps become amulets, filling for cushions, appliqué, and so forth. The material is valued in and of itself, as well as for what can be created from it. ThreeASFOUR, Yeohlee, Alabama Chanin, and Dosa model a form of materialism that the fashion business more broadly could learn from. Although ThreeASFOUR's approach differs from those presented by Dorothy Burnham, the deep respect for the material is a shared pillar of both. The cloth is viewed and treated as an inherent part of a larger whole.

Rickard Lindqvist: Designing for a body in motion

Rickard Lindqvist is a Swedish designer and co-founder[5] of experimental fashion brand Atacac. In 2015 Lindqvist completed his PhD titled "Kinetic Garment Construction: Remarks on the Foundation of Pattern Cutting," and subsequently set up Atacac as a way to apply his research. A key facet of Lindqvist's research is situated in his disregard of the static tailor's matrix, which he criticizes as not responding adequately to the actual moving human body. Instead, Lindqvist's design and pattern-cutting approach hinges on the biomechanical points of the body that pivot and move, allowing the cloth, body, and garment to interact in a harmonious manner.

Lindqvist's seam lines flow around the human form similar to the work of French costume designer Geneviève Sevin-Doering, and like Sevin-Doering, the resulting garment patterns (Figure 8.3) are almost unrecognizable as patterns; however, they come together into forms we do recognize: shirts, coats, pants (trousers), and suits. Lindqvist's consideration for the moving body as a tool for design enables a different kind of relationship to develop between garment and wearer, and the garment moves with the body in ways that are unexpected. A seemingly conventional casual suit is revealed, by lifting the arms, to offer a full range of motion, through its unconventional pattern construction.

Umberto Eco (1986) wrote of the relationship between dress and thought in his essay "Lumbar Thought." He describes the way in which the physical body impacts the mental. He wrote of how garments impose on behavior: "As a rule I am boisterous, I sprawl in a chair, I slump wherever I please, with no claim to elegance: my blue jeans checked these actions, made me more polite and mature" (Eco 1986: 192).

Moreover Eco felt that the restrictive nature of jeans (and armor, corsets, bras, high heels, suits, etc.) changed not only the wearers' behavior but also restricted their thoughts: that "thought abhors tights" (Eco 1986: 194). Lindqvist seems to

Figure 8.3 Rickard Lindqvist's Kinetic garment construction matrix, applied to an outdoor jacket style. Red lines indicate Lindqvist's body-centric pattern-cutting matrix (2015). Photograph by Rickard Lindqvist.

understand this and has dismantled the rigid tailor's matrix to facilitate the full expression of the body by designing garments patterns in response to free movement, not in spite of it. Lindqvist's work requires a deep understanding of the behavior of cloth and body, and his work developing Atacac explores the multifaceted dialogues these can have with the mind of the wearer through garments. By allowing the wearer's body to move freely, he allows their mind to also.

By utilizing digital design tools Atacac does away with the need to sketch a design. The CLO 3D program enables the design of the garment's aesthetic and pattern form simultaneously on a digital avatar, a process which also provides a digital fit prototype the company uses to promote the garments for sale through their website. This design model flows through into a pricing and production model in which the prices behave more like airline tickets, becoming more expensive the closer they are ordered to the production date, while their "micro-factory" only produces what is ordered by their clients.

Atacac experiments with the use of holograms in order to "show" customers garments without having to materialize them. While producing waste, the notion of wholeness in the Atacac brand encompasses a holistic understanding of the body as a medium and tool for garment design as well as a design process, production model, and pricing structure that carefully address one of the key issues the fashion industry faces—overproduction—while embracing technology to deliver a contemporary design and retail experience.

friends of light

Considerations of wholeness can inform the design of a supply chain as much as that of a garment. It can also be the basis for both. Thinking about human-scale supply chains, it helps to regard the body, both of the maker and the wearer. friends of light[6] is a weaving cooperative based in the Hudson Valley, New York state, that demonstrates such an approach. friends of light work with wool grown in the Hudson Valley; knowing the origin of materials is important to the cooperative. Working directly with the fiber producer facilitates direct conversations about the quality of the yarn.

Stewart Brand's (1999: 35–6) six layers of speeds of activity in a resilient civilization is a holistic view of time: the wholeness of time. Nature is the slowest layer, with the layers of culture, governance, infrastructure, and commerce leading to the fastest layer, fashion. The faster layers innovate while the slower layers stabilize.

The work of friends of light builds connections between the fast speeds of fashion and commerce and the slow speeds of nature and culture. It is important to note that Brand does not make a value judgment about the different speeds—that "slow" is better—but rather, he reinforces the point that in a resilient system the different layers of civilization are in balance with one another.

friends of light provide one example of bringing balance to the fashion system, which, like the capitalist system, focused on limitless economic growth, is disproportionately slanted toward the faster layers. Kate Fletcher, a scholar of fashion and sustainability, states: "Nature's power is in us understanding that it has value that goes beyond its usefulness to us. The literacy this gives us—the knowledge this gives designers—is deeply held and has the potential to shape all our ideas and actions" (St. Pierre 2015). friends of light demonstrate this literacy: the jackets are literally born of the Hudson River valley, both in fiber and labor. Place—a particular ecosystem and its human and non-human actors—is woven into each jacket.

friends of light weave each jacket to shape, to the specific measurements of their clients. Rissanen (2013: 33–4) has referred to this approach as "fully-fashioned weaving,"[7] following from the widely used method of fully fashioned knitting, of knitting garments to shape. This approach eliminates the off-cut waste created during the cut-and-sew method of clothing manufacture. Each component of the jacket—fronts, backs, and sleeves—are woven to shape on looms that the members of friends of light construct for themselves. Each jacket component has its own loom, which is a wooden board with nails hammered into it in the shape of the component. The warp is then laid between the nails, and the weft woven in with a needle. The weft ends are spliced into each other so that no knots or visible joins exist in the cloth.

In this the friends of light's approach resonates with the four-selvedged cloths of ancient Peruvian weavers. Elena Phipps (2013), a textile scholar, has investigated the Peruvian textiles in the collection of the Fowler Museum at UCLA extensively. Peruvian four-selvedged cloths have all four edges finished with a clean selvedge. They are whole and complete through weaving and sometimes joining, instead of through cutting and sewing. This approach came to the collective from an innate desire; they later found the work of Phipps, remarking how "it was beautiful to feel such kinship with weavers that preceded us by several centuries" (Gatzen et al. 2016). At a presentation about the jackets in 2016, Pascale Gatzen said: "I don't want to cut into the cloth. For me the beauty [is] the endlessness; there's no cutting" (ibid.). The jackets by friends of light produce no warp waste: the warps are continuous and loop back into the cloth. Often, the question of scaling such an approach is raised: there is a tendency to want to commercialize or industrialize great waste-saving ideas for clothing. If successful, however, this would mean plugging a waste-less idea into an inherently wasteful industry, negating the positive effects over time through growth and overproduction. Perhaps instead we need to work in reverse and deindustrialize parts of the system? It is easy to dismiss craft-based approaches in relation to the global industrial behemoth that fashion has become, however as Max-Neef (1992) has pointed out, creation is one of the nine fundamental human needs. We ought to make space and opportunities for creation, at a diversity of scales and speeds.

The friends of light cooperative functions akin to an haute couture business in that each jacket is woven and constructed once a client has placed an order for it. An individually fitted pattern is developed for the client and the toile is fitted until both the client and the weaver are satisfied. The jackets are extraordinary examples of workmanship and technical ingenuity: precisely curved armholes and set-in sleeves are woven to exact shapes, while simultaneously warps are woven back into the cloth. Once the pieces are complete, they are woven and hand-sewn together into a jacket for the client. Each jacket takes approximately 150 hours to finish. Mae Colburn says of the process: "That is where the relationships happen" (Gatzen et al. 2016). With friends of light, the notion of wholeness extends into the maker–client relationship. The contact is direct and due to the intensely personal process, intimate.

As well as Peruvian weaving, the work of friends of light can be likened to the work of French couturier Gabrielle Chanel. Ease of movement in the sleeves was a signature of Chanel's; friends of light ensure that the jackets are comfortable and accommodate movement. They are to be worn, not to be worn by.

Like Chanel, friends of light include fully working pockets in their jackets. The pockets are woven in rather than sewn in as separate pieces of fabric. While this technique is somewhat common in knitted garments, it is rarely applied in weaving. Even if a woven-in pocket was desired for a cut-and-sew garment, the overall dimensions of the garment would need to be known before weaving the long lengths of cloth. The dominant industry schedule and dynamics do not support such an approach; industrial weaving is not human scale. Fabrics are woven mostly before it is known what will be designed and made from them. To rephrase the proverb that gave Burnham's book its title, "I cut my cote according to my cloth," the friends of light weave their cloth according to their cote. The work of friends of light elevates Dorothy Burnham's ideas in that they are weaving tailored garments to shape. The work is human-scale weaving: weaving that responds to the human body, weaving pieces and shapes to fit the body, and responding to individual desire as opposed to a somewhat abstract market demand.

The supply chain is also human scale: it is fathomable by a single person. One of the challenges for sustainability in fashion systems is the incomprehensible scale of supply chains: entire teams are needed to retroactively map supply chains before any sustainability work can take place. We are not naively suggesting that brands need to know every individual person in their supply chain; however, we do advocate for human-scale systems in fashion and textiles,: systems that can be understood and analyzed by a single individual. The efficiencies achieved by scale should not mask issues such as a structurally unsound garment factory, as was the case with the Rana Plaza building collapse in 2013. The tragedy seemingly came as a surprise for several brands whose clothes were being manufactured in the building, including Benetton, JC Penney, and Primark. Surely we ought to strive for systems that do not leave room for such deadly surprises, by affording us a view of the whole system.

Manonik

Yoshiyuki Minami of Manonik[8] is a creator who values nature in his work. Minami is a Japanese artist and designer based in Brooklyn, New York. Unlike friends of light, Minami weaves shaped volumes that compose garments, for example, cylindrical tailored sleeves with a sleeve cap and voluminous torsos with shaped armholes, on a traditional four-harness floor loom. Minami has honed fully fashioned woven coats, pants, and shirts. Due to the loom type with its continuous warp, each garment results in some warp waste, which Minami collects. Often he will use waste from one garment as an embellishment on a later garment (Figure 8.4); there is barely any yarn waste going to landfill from

Figure 8.4 Coat by Manonik with "waste" thread from a past project as surface embellishment (2017). Photograph by Yoshiyuki Minami.

the Manonik studio. Time begins to overlap in his work: the surplus from past work becomes material for new work. Through its layering, time is both linear and cyclical in Minami's work.

Knowing where things come from—for example, the organic cotton farmer—imbues value into the material. Minami works with fiber producers within the United States. Organically grown cotton is a major fiber in his work, and Minami acknowledges the history of "blood, sweat, and tears" within the history of cotton production in the US: the country's economy was built on slavery. Minami knows the entire supply chain for every garment he designs and makes. From fiber to yarn, to dye plants, to metal hardware, everything is documented on the brand website. Everything and everyone is given value.

Anni Albers (2000: 7) wrote that "we use materials to satisfy our practical needs and our spiritual ones as well." Echoing Albers, knowing the locality and the humanity of the fibers he works with is non-negotiable for Minami.

MakeUse: How does knowing how garments are made transform our relationship to them?

Zero-waste fashion design—as distinct from efficient marker-making—and any design practice fully engaged with the pursuit of wholeness, demands a holistic approach and broad understanding of the multiple stakeholders involved. Designing within the concept of wholeness is, at its core, a process of "critical making."

Critical making, as explored by Ratto (2011) and Hertz (2012), challenges us to understand—through making—the cultural, historical, and social context, and implications of the solutions and technologies we use and master. It asks: Once we know how to use Arduino (or make a zero-waste garment), what then? How do we ensure we use this understanding to make a positive change?

Many fashion wearers lack a full understanding of the "work" required to both design and produce the garments that they wear every day. Historically, garment production occurred close to those who wore it, with garments frequently being made at home. This close relationship meant there was a tacit understanding of the time, resources, and work (of the body and mind) needed in garment creation. In recent history, changing time pressures and rising clothing affordability has buried this knowledge. MakeUse is a project that employs critical making to excavate a richer understanding of garment making for the wearer.

MakeUse[9] (McQuillan et al. 2018) is a collaborative, open source system, which aims to provide "scaffolding" (Sanders and Stappers 2008) for making user-modifiable, zero-waste garments, its overarching goal being to assist in the realization of an active user of clothing from a passive purchaser—a "maker-user." MakeUse provides a user-centered toolset that helps consumers gain agency in the making and ongoing use of the clothing that they wear.

The system was provided at a range of cost points, speeds, locations, and modes of access[10] to cater for as wide a range of people as possible. This multimodal approach followed the work of Dr. Kate Fletcher as discussed in her book *Craft of Use* (2016) and catered to the wide range of ways in which fashion participants engage with their clothing, striving to amplify some of their existing practices while satisfying some expected modes of engagement (such as retail).

In addition to the multimodal access approach, the design of the range was driven largely by the underlying geometry of a garment pattern that is thought, by Burnham, to be at least Danish Bronze age in origin (1973: 20). Used extensively by many designers throughout history, including Cristóbal Balenciaga and Yeohlee Teng, it was from this ancient anchor that the entire collection was derived (McQuillan et al. 2018). Commonly called the "bog coat," in its simplest iteration it is a one-piece pattern (Figure 8.5) where all the sections of the garment are connected to each other, and form is created through two or three simple cuts that enable the cloth to wrap the body in straight tubes. This approach is very different to the front/back and side/shoulder seams division of form that occurs most commonly in contemporary garment design, and questions the flatness of a fashion design process that favors croquis and specification drawings for their speed, over working with cloth on a body.[11] The bog coat and its iterations were from a time before the industrialization of the garment industry, where having a separated front, back, and sleeve enabled the division of labor through the division of the garment. The use of the "whole" pattern of the bog coat enables makers to critically question the conventions of how contemporary garments are made.

The workshops have been the most enduring aspect of MakeUse, and have been taught so far in New Zealand, Australia, California, New York, Sweden, Denmark, Spain, and the UK. In delivering them McQuillan has gained insight into the kind of thinking required for participants to successfully engage with making a zero-waste garment. The scale of the cloth, body/garment dimensional relationship—or "fit"—cutting plan and sewing methods, all need to be considered in a holistic manner to achieve the overall desired design outcomes. Participants who were home-sewers or garment professionals

Figure 8.5 MakeUse Tube Dress pattern and garment. Garment design by Holly McQuillan, textile design by Greta Menzies (2015). Photograph by Bonny Beattie.

Figure 8.6 MakeUse workshop participants developing their work—Objectspace, Auckland, New Zealand (2015). Photograph by Bonny Beattie.

used to working with cloth often felt at an advantage but the way of working introduced through the MakeUse workshops differed, particularly in terms of the sequence that information or decisions were required. Seam allowances, for example, need to be considered very early on in the design process as they are incorporated into the cloth and pattern itself, and not added after the garment pattern is determined. The relationship between cloth width and body circumference needs to be considered when selecting the fabric from which to make the garment.

The proverb loved by Burnham, "I cut my cote according to my cloth," rings true here. In these workshops, thinking this way is a fundamental requirement—choosing the cloth for its width and not just for its handle or color, becomes extremely important. The relationship between body and cloth needs to be considered at the same time as fabric selection and resulting fabric width, as they are tied to each other in a flexible matrix.

The most successful outcomes of the MakeUse activities resulted when a holistic approach was taken by the participant, careful consideration of fabric weight and width relative to the body, garment proportions, and desired garment type, allowing for a more equal interplay between mind, body, cloth, and garment.

Importantly, MakeUse advocates for a conversation between maker-user and the cloth itself; the dialogue is not one-sided and is not dictated by industry. Instead, it is in the hands—literally and figuratively—of the maker-user. Through this dialogue, a broader understanding of the value of our garments and those making them for us may be achieved.

Conclusions

In this chapter, we have contrasted our shared research interest and practice in zero-waste fashion design with fashion designers and fashion practitioners, whose approaches diverge from ours and yet are connected through ideas of

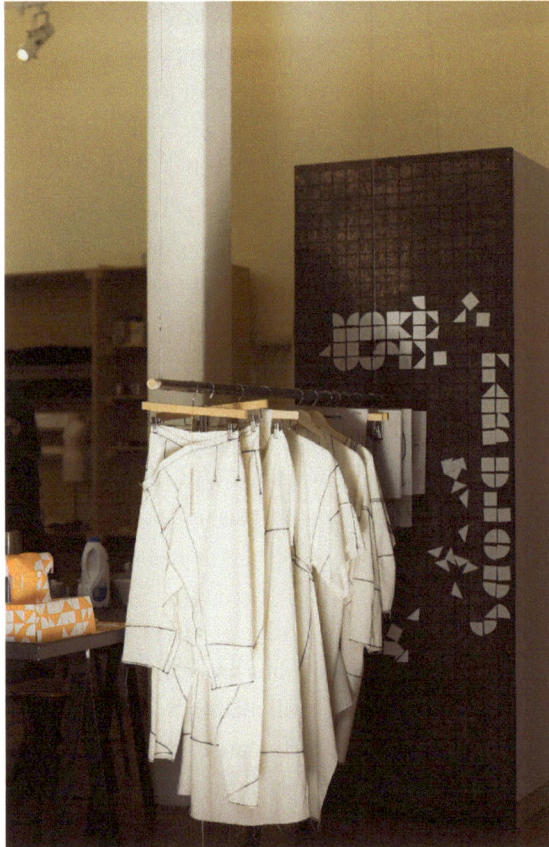

Figure 8.7 MakeUse workshop demonstration garments as used in the gallery / public workshop space and design residency—Objectspace, Auckland, New Zealand (2015). Photograph by Bonny Beattie.

wholeness and completeness. These connections are not formulaic; rather, our intention is to invite the reader to explore questions of wholeness in different systems, at different scales, and in their own practice. In much of our contemporary fashion industry, the body—subservient—has entered into a one-sided dialogue where the garment is primarily valued as a unit of sale, while other inputs such as fiber and labor, and outputs such as waste and the many physical or social impacts, are secondary. In this chapter we have explored some of these ideas, demonstrating attempts at holistic conversations between body, mind, garment, and cloth, first in the context of the existing fashion industry in the case study with a large sustainable outdoor brand, then in the context of craft practitioners such as Manonik, or the avant-garde approach of ThreeASFOUR. We call for more research on different models of different scales: Diversities in scale and approach are essential to the resilience of the fashion system as a whole.

The relationships possible between mind, body, garment, and cloth are many and varied; however, the fashion industry is focused on only a few narrow interactions. Garment aesthetics and cost are usually prioritized over the mind, body, and cloth, and diversity is sacrificed for speed and profit. Cutting holistically can enforce a different way of thinking, allowing different questions to be asked. We note that many companies aim to maintain current design and production systems while asking designers to perform some kind of apparel alchemy to turn a wasteful design into an efficient marker.[12] If the relationships between the mind of the consumer and designer, and the interaction of body and cloth through garment are reduced to units of sale, it can still be possible to generate more efficient designs—but is higher efficiency enough and does the industry actually want this? If you reduce waste and thus increase yield, then less fabric is required and purchased, unless end-user consumption is increased. Reducing overproduction by companies and overconsumption by purchasers has a similar outcome. So, while many in the fashion and textile industry lament the existence of waste and wring their hands over what to do with it, waste remains an inherent component of their business model.[13] The tendency to want to scale good waste reduction ideas may serve only to increase efficiency—the so-called "rebound effect" (Ghisellini, Cialani, and Ulgiati 2016: 24)—therefore increasing profit and growing production. This does little to tackle the vast overproduction that occurs in the fashion industry.

Throughout the development of the fashion industry, we have sought to diminish complexity by dividing up the actions required to make a garment so that each person only needed to deal with their own discrete unit. However, it seems we have merely spread the complexity out—making it harder to see, harder to wrangle, and far more inflexible. And now, when we need to change it, we say we can't because the system is too complex. The hierarchies and systems in the fashion industry make holistic approaches and comprehensive changes difficult to implement, but these fundamental shifts in focus, toward a human scale, are drastically needed. Kate Fletcher has mused that the gains we have made in improving the sustainability of fashion, have likely been absorbed and overtaken by corresponding increases in production (Fletcher 2016: 21–2). Again, we suggest that we need to deindustrialize parts of the garment industry. We do not say this from an anti-technology perspective; instead, we encourage readers to consider how and why innovation and technology are used, in what context, and how, if, and when we scale innovative ideas. By taking a human and local approach to fashion design and production, we can critically address the systems, forge ahead with a different and, at times, difficult conversation, and in doing so transform the industry.

Notes

1 Fordism is "a technological system that seeks to increase production efficiency primarily through carefully engineered breakdown and interlocking of production operations and that depends for its success on mass production by assembly-line methods" (Merriam Webster Dictionary). In the fashion industry, this presents as the dissection of the act of making a garment into many different steps performed by different people, sometimes in different parts of the world.

2 Zero-waste fashion design, as defined by the authors in their book of the same name (Rissanen and McQuillan 2016), refers to designing and making clothes without creating fabric waste in the process.

3 A marker-maker takes the provided garment pattern and works with specialized marker-making software to achieve the most efficient layout of the pattern of fabric for production.

4 See: https://www.threeasfour.com.

5 With Jimmy Herdberg.

6 The cooperative's four founding members are: Pascale Gatzen, Mae Colburn, Jessi Highet, and Nadia Yaron.

7 Fully fashioned refers to an approach of making in which the garment pieces are created individually through knitting or weaving to their exact shapes and then joined to create the garment. This is distinct from the more common cut-and-sew

approach, in which the garment pieces are cut from fabric and then joined together to create the garment.

8 See: http://www.manonik.com. Minami received his BA in Economic Sociology from the University of Michigan in 2005 and founded Manonik in 2015 following an artist residency at the Textile Arts Center in New York.

9 See www.makeuse.nz for further detail.

10 In August of 2015 MakeUse was simultaneously presented at Objectspace Gallery in Auckland, New Zealand, its development visible through the "designer in residence" program at the gallery, learnable via a series of workshops, downloadable for free from the MakeUse website, and available for purchase as finished fashion product at the boutique fashion store The Keep.

11 See also Rick Owens AW2016 collection which he draped entirely himself (Lau 2016).

12 Indeed, the authors propose that much of this kind of work should be performed by software making small insignificant changes to the design to improve efficiency.

13 The authors propose that this paradox is why circular strategies are favored by industry because it does not seem to require a reduction in the production of waste or use of material inputs. However, with the increase in production that a growth model demands, continued virgin inputs will be required unless we limit the pursuit of growth.

References

Albers, A. (2000) *Selected Writings on Design*, Middletown, CT: Wesleyan University Press.

Brand, S. (1999) *The Clock of the Long Now: Time and Responsibility*, New York: Basic Books.

Burnham, D. K. (1973) *Cut My Cote*, Toronto: Royal Ontario Museum.

Eco, U. (1986) "Lumbar Thought," in U. Eco (ed.), *Travels in Hyperreality: Essays*, trans. W. Weaver, 191–5, San Diego, CA: Harcourt Brace Jovanovich.

Fletcher, K. (2016) *Craft of Use: Post-Growth Fashion*, Abingdon: Routledge.

Forty, A. (1986) *Objects of Desire: Design and Society Since 1750*, London: Thames & Hudson.

Gatzen, P., Colburn, M., Highet, J., Yaron, N., and Phipps, E. (2016) " 'friends of light' in Conversation with Elena Phipps," public talk, September 8, New York.

Ghisellini, P., Cialani, C., and Ulgiati, S. (2016) "A Review on Circular Economy: The Expected Transition to a Balanced Interplay of Environmental and Economic Systems," *Journal of Cleaner Production*, 114: 11–32.

Hertz, G., ed. (2012) *Critical Making*, Hollywood, CA: Telharmonium Press.

Lau, S. (2016) "Why Rick Owens Hand-Draped Every Garment Himself This Season," *Dazed Digital*, March 4. Available online: http://www.dazeddigital.com/fashion/article/30201/1/rick-owens-isn-t-afraid-of-fashion-s-impending-breakdown (accessed August 15, 2019).

Lindqvist, R. (2015) "Kinetic Garment Construction: Remarks on the Foundations of Pattern Cutting," PhD thesis, University of Borås, Sweden.

Max-Neef, M. (1992) "Development and Human Needs," in P. Ekins and M. Max-Neef (eds.), *Real-Life Economics: Understanding Wealth Creation*, 197–213, London: Routledge.

McQuillan, H., Archer-Martin, J., Menzies, G., Bailey, J., Kane, K., and Fox Derwin, E. (2018) "Make/Use: A System for Open Source, User-Modifiable, Zero Waste Fashion Practice," *Fashion Practice*, 10(1): 7–33.

Phipps, E. (2013) *The Peruvian Four-Selvaged Cloth: Ancient Threads, New Directions*, Los Angeles, CA: The Fowler Museum at UCLA.

Ratto, M. (2011) "Critical Making," in B. Van Abel, L. Evers, R. Klaassen, and P. Troxler (eds.), *Open Design Now: Why Design Cannot Remain Exclusive*, 202–9, Amsterdam: BIS Publishers.

Rissanen, T. (2011) "Designing Endurance," in A. Gwilt and T. Rissanen (eds.), *Shaping Sustainable Fashion: Changing the Way We Make and Use Clothes*, 127–38, London: Earthscan.

Rissanen, T. (2013) "Zero Waste Fashion Design: A Study at the Intersection of Cloth, Fashion Design and Pattern Cutting," PhD thesis, University of Technology Sydney, Sydney.

Rissanen, T. and McQuillan, H. (2016) *Zero Waste Fashion Design*, London: Bloomsbury.

Runnel, A., Raihan, K., Castle, N., Oja, D., and Bhuiya, H. (2017) "White Paper: The Undiscovered Business Potential of Production Leftovers Within Global Fashion Supply Chains: Creating a Digitally Enhanced Circular Economy—Insight from Research Among Fabric and Garment Factories of China and Bangladesh," *Reverse Resources*, Tallinn. Available online: http://www.reverseresources.net/about/white-paper (accessed August 17, 2018).

Sanders, E. B.-N. and Stappers, P. J. (2008) "Co-creation and the New Landscapes of Design," *Co-design*, 4(1): 5–18.

St. Pierre, L. (2015) "An Interview with Kate Fletcher," *Current*, November 26. Available online: http://current.ecuad.ca/an-interview-with-kate-fletcher (accessed August 17, 2018).

9

Empowerment and Self-Care*

Designing for the Female Body

Giulia Tomasello and Teresa Almeida

Introduction

This chapter discusses how design, at the intersection of science and technology, is uniquely situated to address women's intimate care and contribute to revolutionize practices within the female body. Everyday practices that are conducive to mitigating health disparities and promote well-being throughout the life course are needed, as much as advancements in the design of tools and services that highlight our relationship to the body are crucial to shape our place in society. Knowledge that was once inaccessible and technologies that were institutionally bound are today being challenged by the rise of citizen science, do-it-yourself (DIY), and open source approaches. These are community-oriented viewpoints that emphasize active participation as possibility to gathering and generating data, e.g., about ourselves, our bodies, or the environment. These data have the potential to disrupt, e.g., institutional care, and to promote self-care, which in turn creates opportunities for change.

Knowledge available about women's and men's bodies is disproportionate, and that knowledge, or lack thereof, is actively produced. In building on this, we argue that knowledge available *to* women is lacking. It is therefore urgent to challenge traditional forms of engaging women in understanding their bodies. New methods are required that value self-care.

We start by reviewing feminist theories that underpin our woman-centred approaches to designing materials that promote bodily awareness, inviting women to become embodied knowers. In addition, we discuss the design of a series of toolkits as mediums to engender conversations and break taboos. Our exemplars include DIY alternative biological practices that embrace domestic remedies through playful hands-on interventions with electronic textiles and digital applications. This is a suite that aligns with design inquiries concerned with addressing the body as a lens for innovating in intimate technologies. They configure woman as an active participant, and her (taking) action is at the fore of our quest to design systems that promote agency, autonomy, and knowledge.

Bodies of knowledge

The bodies through which we produce knowledge matter (Haraway 1988; Harding 1991), and how we know what we know is shaped by patterns of inclusion and exclusion from the communities who configure those scientific, social, and political systems (Schiebinger 1993). Traditionally, women have been a group of people ignored in the production of knowledge (Tuana 2006), even when knowledge is directly related to them and their own bodies. It was with the age of Enlightenment in the 1700s that the professionalization and medicalization of women's health surfaced, in detriment of women's traditional knowledge, which was instrumental in establishing "women as objects of knowledge not as authorized knowers" (ibid.: 9). Whereas the politics of participation at the time determined that women were excluded from molding scientific knowledge, notions of gender dictated ideals that put things defined as feminine, including women, aside (Schiebinger 1993). While the neglect of research that could potentially be beneficial to women has been wrought in institutions dominated by men (ibid.), more open and inclusive approaches, e.g., DIY biology or citizen science, use research methods that traverse institutions and put tools in the hands of disparate communities of people. At a time when such approaches proliferate and are recognized as powerful to improve quality of life among many, and digital technologies become accessible, we strive to demystify the existing status quo.

The science of the female body, but whose science is it anyway?

The science of the female body remains a contested topic (Stockly 2011). The existence of gender bias and disparities in women's health and care was constructed on the fact that biomedical research had been based on male subjects and later generalized to women (Munch 2006). This has given rise to stereotypes based on assumptions that are then sustained through cultural biases. In addition, history also shows us that scientists have always sought to distance themselves from any association with things female (Schiebinger 1993). Surely, the question of the bodies of women in history is well documented within social theory and feminist critique of science? While the concept of the female body might be "underpinned by a core of identification" of experiences associated with women (Riley 1999: 220), such as pregnancy or menstruation, woman as a category continues to evolve. Women are far from being one homogeneous group. Regardless, what counts as scientific knowledge, as the "facts," depends on who counts it as such and in what context (Birke 1999). An understanding of how gender influences the result of science is therefore crucial. Science is not a neutral culture when it comes to women (Schiebinger 1993). Historically, the ways that institutions mediated knowledge was highly gendered, underlined by the lack of women's access to higher education. Is this politics of participation perpetual or has it changed throughout time? If knowledge grows out of who is doing the studying, and for what ends, and knowing that women continue to be underrepresented, then it is critical to partake in engendering and shaping these agendas. Surely, the female body will remain a contested topic. Moreover, what we attempt to do in this chapter is to explore notions of the scientific body in its relation to biology and entanglements with technology.

The body in bio(techno)logy

"What are our bodies? First, they are us. We don't inhabit them, we are them."
The Boston Women's Health Book Collective 1971: 4

As noted by feminist philosopher Iris M. Young, "the lived body is particular in its morphology, material similarities, and differences from other bodies" (2005: 25). It is also built for care, visible in daily rituals such as grooming, washing, and eating (Hamington 2004). Evidently, a lack of everyday knowledge and misconceptions about the female body still abound (Braun and Wilkinson 2001). The female body has been a subject of taboo, limiting the development of women's health and care in general (Rossmann 2008). In spite of this, routines and behaviors we adopt as part of our everyday have an impact on our lives over time. Experiences that are traditionally considered female have a meaning of their own and depend upon the subjective experiences each woman might have.

Considering women as both oppressed and free, Simone de Beauvoir, in her book *The Second Sex* (1949), made a clear separation of the social and emotional gender between the physical and natural body. A woman's relationship with her body is the most direct relationship she has with the earth itself. It depends upon the extent to which a woman sees herself as a free subject rather than as the object of society's gaze. Birke (1986) argues that claiming that body gender is socially constructed is emphasized by ideas that society holds about women's biology, that gender is reflected by their social subordination; further, biology cannot be understood outside of its social, economic, and psychological context, and that biology alone is insufficient to explain why women are constituted as the Other; and, finally, she suggests that biological experiences do contribute to the way we experience indirectly our lives as women. "One is not born, but rather becomes, woman" (de Beauvoir 1949: 14).

The female body has been considered a societal taboo all through the early 1970s, when women activists from Boston, USA, calling themselves Women's Doctors, decided to publish a radical and pedagogical magazine to explain women's healthcare in a unique political and social context, accessible and understandable to everyone. Their knowledge became an extraordinary piece of writing, easily available to be shared as a model, for women who wanted to learn about themselves, communicate their fears with doctors, and challenge the medical establishment to change and improve the care that women should receive. Within just a few days of publication, the magazine *Our Bodies, Ourselves* became an underground success that sold 250,000 copies, a liberal and public format to educate women in the knowledge and care of their own body and well-being. The magazine, now book, introduced stories of women who experienced illegal and often fatal abortions, domestic violence, precarious pregnancies, at the same time including natural remedies to treat vaginal infections, menstrual and ovulation pain, and educating women on the different types of contraceptives. A book was written by women, for women.

The meaning of the body changes dramatically over time. Therefore, the questions we should ask about the female body should be set within the context and concerns of particular historical moments (Shildrick and Price 1999). Similarly, technologies *of convenience* need to be reimagined in relation to the body. One example is that of the vaginal speculum: a medical gynecological device used to perform the pelvic exam and cervical smear test (Figure 9.1).

Historically, the vaginal speculum is the first in a line of "spectacular" instruments used in the care of women (Sandelowski 2000: 73). It was developed during the nineteenth century, a controversial invention of a male doctor and an

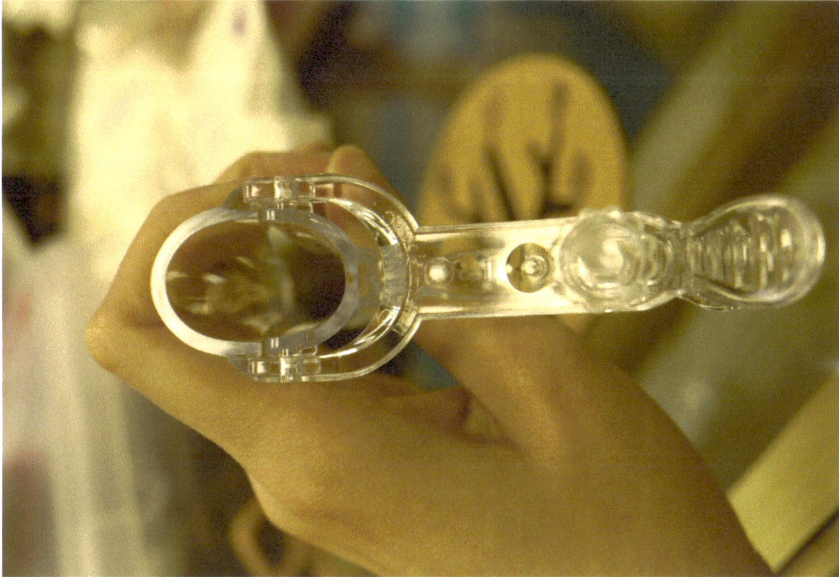

Figure 9.1 Vaginal speculum (2015). Photograph by Ko-Le Chen.

instrument of a "contested technology" within a somewhat contested history (ibid.). Its "purpose is to retract the vaginal walls to allow a clinician to visually examine the cervix and obtain culture specimens for tests, such as the Pap smear" (Rossmann 2008: 47). In spite of advancements in technology and in the understanding of the (scientific) body, it has seen little improvement in design since its invention. It is an example of a technology that "gets its job done," its design taking little or no account for the intimate needs, values, and experiences associated with such exam—that it may be unpleasant, even causing fearfulness, and impacting on whether most women decide to do it or not. To this day, health and care of intimate parts such as the vagina have not only seen little technological breakthrough in its (clinical) interventions, they also persist as an "uncomfortable". social, even personal, topic, which in turn perpetuates a culture of shame, secrecy, and lack of awareness that can be (broadly) damaging to genital integrity.

We live in a culture of silence that distorts reality, by emphasizing the gender construction of women's body (Gopal and Gopal 2010). The female apparatus is perceived as a mystical taboo, a site of struggle for definition and control (Braun and Wilkinson 2001) and because it is often reduced to isolated parts in the women's body, is therefore most popular for pleasure yet fears based in myth make it a target for violent abuse and adverse moral judgment (Brownmiller 1984). From social sciences to popular literature, academic texts, theatre, television, newspaper articles, and fiction, there is a lack of attention to the vagina as a topic. The mythology pictures the vagina as dentata, altering inevitably the symbol of reproduction and central to womanhood, as well as the menstrual uncleanliness myth, the cunt connotation, and so forth. Women are taught that the vagina is vulgar and socially inappropriate to mention.

Today's society is calling women to talk about it, women who recently turned to the internet for answers instead of keeping doubts inside. The need to speak about their own bodies and intimate health is becoming urgent, in addition to engendering a sense of belonging and sisterhood. The challenge is in having a conversation with your body and understanding its silent language.

By declaring that the vagina has its own consciousness, Naomi Wolf (2012) explores the secret language of the vagina's anatomy as the coexistence of the female soul and brain, understood also as medium of self-knowledge and freedom.

Dr. Alfred Kinsey in 1953 interviewed 6,000 American women, reporting that the cervix "is the most completely insensitive part of the female genitalia anatomy" and has no nerve endings, so any discomfort will feel more like pressure and cramping (Region of Peel; see Kinsey et al. 1953: 584). Considered the pioneer in human sexuality, Kinsey was completely wrong. Studies proved against the myth and his report, that the cervix is the only organ that receives a sensory impulse from three different pairs of nerves: the pelvic, hypogastric, and vague (Wise, Frangos, and Komisaruk 2017). In mammals there are two brains, the cranial and the abdominal, of almost equal importance to the individual and also to the species. The first is the instrument of physical protection and the second of visceral rhythm and nutrition. In the abdomen, the female uterus area, exists a brain of wonderful powers that controls, initiates, sustains, prohibits, receives, and transmits—an automatic nervous center, a physiological and anatomical brain (Robinson 1907). Today, doctors from San Diego Sexual Medicine confirm that "there is an assault of women's genitals going on now in medicine" (Goldstein, quoted in Lane 2018).

A call for the development of new health technologies, designed with, by, and for women has started. Design through technology becomes the tool to explore social needs and empower citizens from healthcare and well-being perspectives.

Designing technologies for intimate care in women

In tying together our practices, we advance woman-centred approaches that inquire into knowledge practices in health and (self-)care. In this section, we

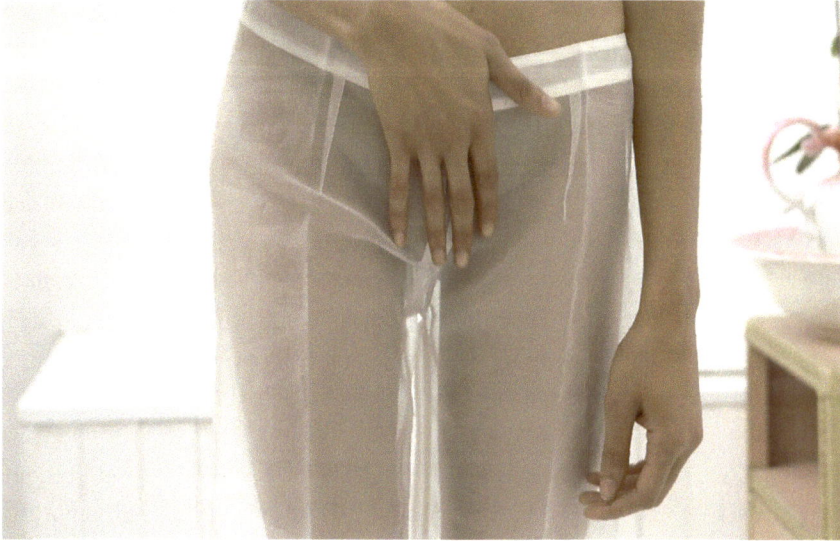

Figure 9.2 Future Flora addresses women who are taking control of their own bodies as a precious and intimate practice of self-care (Giulia Tomasello 2016). Photograph by Jan Vrhovnik.

introduce four novel design concepts and devices that tackle bodily taboos and awkwardness, and offer insights on how designing for intimate care is entwined in woman-centred design (Almeida 2017)—an ongoing methodology that highlights the distinct attributes and experiences in, on, and within the female body. These include Future Flora (Figure 9.2), a kit designed to prevent vaginal infections, in which we discuss the delicate interaction of nurturing microorganisms at home, as an intimate practice of self-care, whereby women become participants in the culture and knowledge of science; *TNUC*, a magazine that frames the meaning lost behind the word *cunt*, by researching the etymology and sociocultural understandings of the word; the design of an *eTextile Toolkit* that explores textile materials with electronics as interaction materials for (intimate) health literacy and as a method for engaging women in self-care; and *Labella*, a system that exploits nontraditional embodied interactions to promote pelvic health in women.

Female biophilia: Crossing boundaries

We aren't just single individuals walking the planet: we are walking ecosystems made of microbes. Microbes are in the soil, in the water, and even in our bodies.

We coexist with them. The human body is 50 percent composed of different microorganisms, most of which are beneficial to their host. Microbes such as bacteria, fungi, and viruses are part of our skin microflora, covering both the inside and the outer surface of the body. Even though invisible to our eyes, our microflora has a symbiotic relationship with the interface between our body and the environment, our skin. The Human Microbiome Project, designed to identify the core human microbiome and to determine whatever changes can be correlated in human health, in 2010 developed research based on vaginal microbiome and genetic diseases.[1] The vagina communicates through an invisible and interactive interface with the environment, covered by a protective epithelial surface, colonized by millions of microorganisms that protect the host from pathogens. What changes in the vaginal microbiome are associated with relevant infectious diseases and conditions (Fettweis et al. 2010)? Research was conducted to identify the role of the vaginal microbiota in the urogenital tract health of females and to evaluate the factors that lead to important therapies or intervention strategies.

Women's bodies are considered sacred in society. Female sexual pleasure and fertility are the only issues that matter. If design could become the tool to empower women and their health care, would women be ready to wear bacteria in their underwear to prevent vaginal infections (Figure 9.3)?

Future Flora is a harvesting kit designed for women to treat and prevent vaginal infections (Figure 9.4). For women who are taking control of their bodies as a new precious and intimate practice of self-care. The kit is composed of an inoculation loop, a spreader, a pipette with freeze-dried bacterial compound and the nutrient agar-agar recipe, plus an instruction leaflet providing the necessary steps to grow and harvest your own pad at home. The included tools are now considered basic laboratory equipment. In this context, the user is a woman who wants to embrace biotechnology in her home, allowing science to show alternatives to traditional medicines and probiotics.

How can design challenge our perception to celebrate the relationship between the human body and its microbiome? Future Flora aims to incentivize the symbiotic relationship between the beneficial presence of microbes in the skin and to suggest alternatives on wearing probiotics to keep the body healthy. The bacterial pad positioned inside the underwear grows the necessary strings of *Lactobacillus* bacteria[2] to create a hostile environment for the further development of *Candida albicans*,[3] acting as living culture of probiotics. By placing the pad in contact with the female genitalia, the healthy bacteria grow on the surface of the infected area, reconstructing the microflora missing in the

Figure 9.3 Future Flora aims to celebrate a Female Biophilia approach, by women wearing bacteria in their knickers (Giulia Tomasello 2016). Photograph by Tom Mannion.

Figure 9.4 Future Flora is a kit designed for women to prevent vaginal infections (Giulia Tomasello 2016). Photograph by Giulia Tomasello.

vagina epithelium. Considering that 75 percent of women worldwide suffer from a candida infection every year, Future Flora explores women's approaches in the context of personal self-care and body awareness, generating an intimate and delicate interaction between nurturing bacteria while they grow, and wearing them as a second layer within your knickers.

Celebrating a female biophilia, Tomasello opens the possibility of wearing microorganisms in the future, embracing them as part of our natural well-being. Following Biohacking[4] and DIY procedures, merging biology with health-tech, the female becomes a citizen scientist. By taking care of her own health, she establishes a first relation between her body and what is part of her living surroundings. Clothes and accessories become the ecosystem that balance the entire body skin microflora. Future Flora proposes alternatives to embrace biological remedies in our daily life, by questioning the materialistic behavior embedded in society, aiming to challenge new propositions for the future of women's healthcare.

Figure 9.5 *TNUC* zine—reclaiming the term "cunt" in society (Giulia Tomasello 2017). Photograph by Giulia Tomasello.

TNUC is a zine that describes the meaning behind being female in contemporary society (Figure 9.5). Currently the term "cunt" is undergoing a period of transition. Its meaning has become the most profane and offensive swear word, and as a result society is taught to refrain from discussing it. Feminists are attempting to reappropriate it, having so far achieved only limited success, and liberal attempts to integrate it into popular culture. This fear attached to the word "cunt" is developed in the publication, as a historical exploration to frame and research its cultural and scientific perspectives, to highlight its power and significance as a word both socially and individually. The aim of the zine is to open a new dialogue between us (women) celebrating cunts every day and in everything related with them. To educate about subjects such as fertility and infertility, mental health and gynecology enabling women to feel comfortable to conquer taboos. The real question is whether or not cunt is going to ever lose its taboo (Goldman 1999).

Engendering conversations in health

Electronics for Women was a project exploring traditional handicrafts and soft electronics. It consisted of a series of workshops that took place at the Thai–Myanmar border town of Mae Sot. It investigated how hands-on activities could inspire and contribute to promoting positive well-being.

When living and working in Southeast Asia (2007–11), Almeida became inspired by the richness of local textiles and interested in the potential of handicrafts as critical power tools in contemporary culture. One instance included spending a period of three months working with a group of Myanmar women to weave stretch sensors and create light-emitting textiles while learning from their traditional handicrafts (Figure 9.6). This was a practice-led inquiry into the making of craft technology in an unexpected context: that of a rural environment and displaced people, with a distinguished and rich textile tradition.

At the time, it was through volunteer activities and workshops that Almeida promoted e-textiles (textile crafts and electronics) as materials innovation and inventive methods to interact within cultures characterized by extreme disparities in access and mobility. At the core, questions explored how traditional practices, such as weaving and stitching, each with a history that is devoid of electronic artifacts, intersect with today's technology and, importantly, how could this approach support capacity building for women who use their skill to earn an income. This exploration interwove traditional craft and digital practice, which later would inform the design and development of a set of interventions— the eTextile Toolkit and Labella (2013–16).

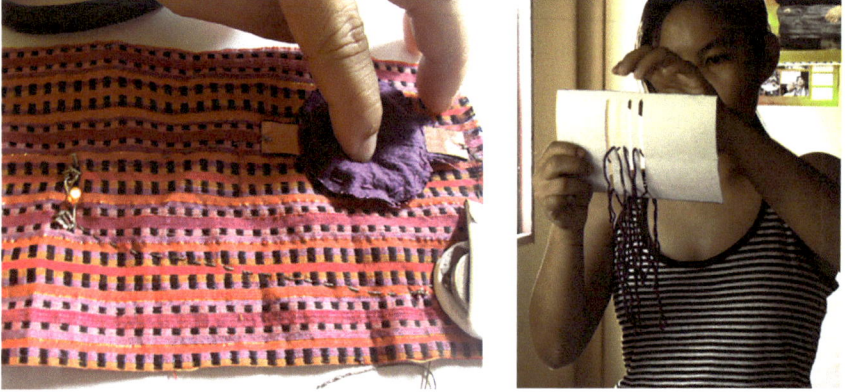

Figure 9.6 Electronics for Women: Weaving stretch sensors and creating light-emitting textiles while learning from traditional handicrafts; the intersection of soft technology with traditional handwork in rural Southeast Asia. Women weavers at the Thailand–Myanmar border (2011). Photographs by Teresa Almeida.

In designing systems and interactions that tackle bodily functions and body organs that are intimate, the cases of the eTextile Toolkit and Labella serve to bring to the foreground research in sensitive topics and challenge lines of inquiry that continue to be absent. These attempts aim to enable a woman's knowledge, i.e., for her to engage in her own development (Young 1990) through empowering her to look and know more about her intimate body. The eTextile Toolkit by Almeida combines technologies that explore novel ways to promote bodily awareness around pelvic health. Body mapping and wearable e-textile materials are the chosen methods to tackle issues of intimate health and well-being. The toolkit is an open invitation for people in a workshop to recall existing body knowledge, and to expand on that same knowledge through a hands-on process of DIY discovery "of" and "on" the body.

These activities put a focus on interweaving aesthetics with the material landscape of electronic textiles and the body. This situatedness enables participative development in understandings of the biology of the body, biology which, to quote Lynda Birke, "is crucial—and a vital ally—in terms of how we understand both embodiment (our own and others) and the subtly sociopolitical dimensions of scientific knowledge production" (Åsberg and Birke 2010: 416). Biology is also what includes bodily functions, and this study was aimed at using novel interactive materials as tools to open the dialogue within communities of women in understanding biological processes such as those involved in pelvic care.

Similarly, Labella is an augmented system that invites the woman to be an active participant in looking through an interactive surface (a mirror) to the body

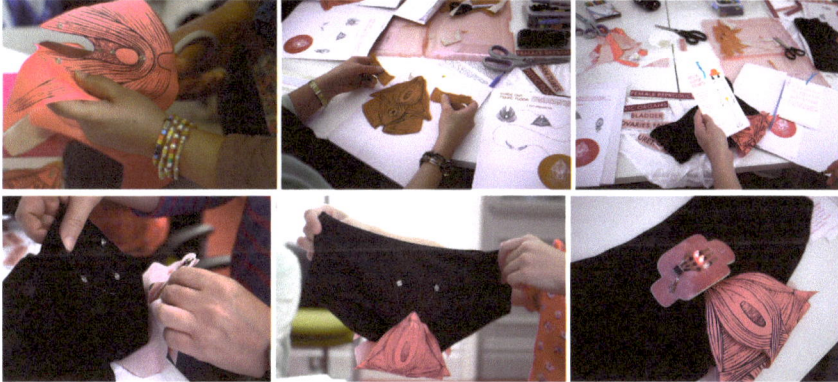

Figure 9.7 DIY wearable e-textiles, assembling pelvic floor muscles: From screen print to knickers (Teresa Almeida 2014). Photographs by Ko-Le Chen.

(the vulva). It combines a piece of underwear for embodied intimate interaction, and a mobile phone as a tool for embodied discovery (Almeida et al. 2016). It is an unconventional tool that works in the interest of generating knowledge that is actively produced, in this case by considering biological embodiment as part and parcel of what makes bodies and what they are, to draw attention to the "scientific" intimate body and pelvic fitness in women. Conceptually, Labella is inspired by the Women's Health Movement, as introduced before, a time in which women used a mirror as a technology of choice to not only highlight health rights (or lack thereof) but foremost to reclaiming control over their bodies. Women "located power in the mirror and in genital self-visualization, and they reclaimed both as productive tools with which to confront the male-dominated institution of gynaecological medicine" (Labuski 2008: 13).

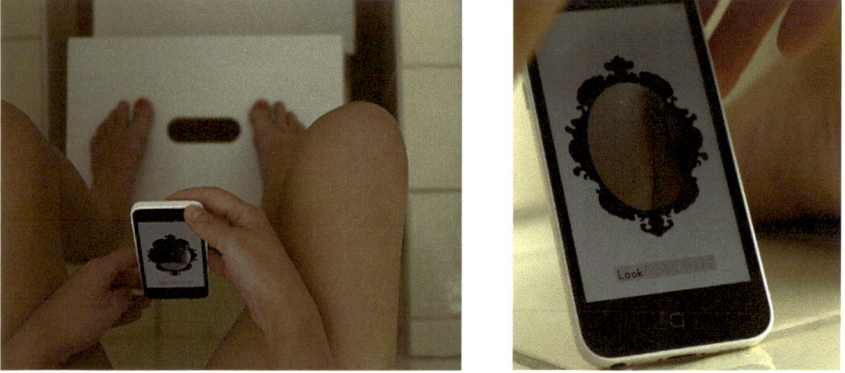

Figure 9.8 Labella, using a bespoke piece of underwear and a mobile app to "Look Down There" (Teresa Almeida 2016). Photographs by Ko-Le Chen.

A mirror is a technology for surveillance (Twigg 2004), a tool to support control by display, and the cultural context in which women live with their reflected image highlights "exteriority." "The mirror," after all, "almost always serves to reduce us to a pure exteriority. . . . We look at ourselves to *please someone*, rarely to interrogate the state of our body or our spirit, rarely for ourselves and in search of our own becoming. . . . [T]he mirror is a frozen—and polemical— weapon to keep as apart" (Irigaray quoted in Labuski 2008: 13, original emphasis).

The primary emphasis is on the visual sense that the mirror provides to us, as a means of outer representation. Alternatively, in her book *This Sex Which Is Not One*, Luce Irigaray (1985) introduces Alice, who "exists behind the screen of representation." It is so to describe "the necessity for going through the mirror in order to free oneself from a traditional sort of representation(s)" (Irigaray 2008: 162). In this sense, Almeida's interest in using a mirror was in extending "genital integration beyond the visual" while engendering an "articulation between the visual and the tactile" (Labuski 2008: 14). Looking at oneself, as requested by the experience with Labella, allows for creating a deeper bodily integration. While exploring external and internal organs, it is sensible that these organs are integral to bodily functions, critical to reproductive health and sexual well-being.

In "going through the mirror," the woman is invited to explore her body in a nontraditional way, one in which the body space merges with a sort of representation(s) on the screen (Irigaray 2008). By doing this, Almeida aims to explore technology as an extension of the body, one that invites the senses of (visual and tactile) representation to operate in tandem with the physicality inherent to the interaction.

Since their initial conceptualization, the eTextile Toolkit and Labella have been reintroduced as The Bitness Project, a creative DIY toolkit for women and girls to learn about their intimate health. Almeida has presented the project at a women's summit in the African country of Cabo Verde (2017), where there is an growing interest in technologies that support sociocultural change and break taboos. In aiming to tailor this interactive toolkit to the contemporaneity of this African country, Almeida is currently devising strategies to bring the toolkit to all ten islands of the Cabo Verde archipelago, reaching over 50 percent of the country's population (youth under twenty-four years of age).

On becoming embodied knowers

Similarly to the radical intent put forward by the Women's Health Movement, that of involving *women* in understandings of their bodies, we strive to carry on this legacy of empowerment through innovating design in self-knowledge. Our work aims to encourage women to turn to their bodies and become "embodied knowers" (Tuana 2006: 8). That is, other than simply consult medical textbooks to obtain information and understand the intimate body (ibid.), our desire is to explore ways for technology-enabled materials to contribute to creating bodily awareness around intimate health and shape and strengthen knowledge of processes within and between bodies.

The potential of crafting technology to tackle taboos and stigma that continue to be associated with intimate care, e.g., in gynecological health, opens new directions in the production of (self-) knowledge. This approach to craft as a practice to both embody and discover in intimate health goes hand in hand with the most recent democratization of science-oriented practices. If access to expert tools and materials was once contained within the (medical) institution, now they become more readily available; new information becomes devised and shared through creative and nontraditional approaches. Moreover, this entails varied levels of engagement and a set of skills that emphasize craft and making-as-enquiry to explore bodily materiality itself. All in all, this suggests a radical shift that has just started to enable us to tailor personal experiences with customized products rather than standardized ones and to speculate on the future directions of intimate self-care practices.

The toolkits described in this chapter aim to educate and enable women to take up a more active role in their health and care. Future Flora examines the possibility of using scientific tools as part of everyday life, one that provides the experience of growing and wearing live bacteria cultures as a second skin, and Labella extends the body as unclothed in digital technology; an eTextile Toolkit that draws from a feminist biology approach to assimilate notions of embodiment and bodily functions in ways that are conducive to knowledge production, and *TNUC* that reframes and embraces the character of a misunderstood and misused word as a celebration. These are a series of design interventions that act as prompts, first to break the barriers of silence and taboo associated with intimate care and urogynecological health, and then to inspire a much-needed active role in self-care. For a woman to become a participant in the culture and the science of her body we suggest that knowledge turns to self-awareness and renewed practices of care. With the dissolution of boundaries between the body and technologies that are, e.g., biologically enhanced or contraceptive, we see how culture and subjectivity are embedded in these practices. Nevertheless, it is at such intersections that design in its multiple forms, e.g., toolkits, systems, products, becomes personal. This marks a shift in understandings of health and care that is crucial and (re)defines female empowerment, one that encourages an increasing and well-informed dialogue with our bodies.

Notes

*   We use the gendered term woman to refer to anyone who has a vagina. However, we acknowledge not all people who have a vagina identify as women, and people who identify as women do not always have a vagina.

1   The Human Microbiome Project, a research initiative by the US National Institutes of Health (2008–17), investigated the role of microbial flora in human health and disease. Information adapted from: https://en.wikipedia.org/wiki/Human_Microbiome_Project (accessed August 15, 2019).

2   The genus *Lactobacillus* is taxonomically complex and is composed of over 170 species that cannot be easily differentiated phenotypically and often require molecular identification. Although they are part of the normal human gastrointestinal and vaginal flora, they can also be occasional human pathogens. They are extensively used in a variety of commercial products including probiotics. See: https://academic.oup.com/cid/article/60/suppl_2/S98/379146 (accessed August 15, 2019).

3   The polymorphic fungus *Candida albicans* is a member of the normal human microbiome. In most individuals, *C. albicans* resides as a lifelong, harmless commensal. Under certain circumstances, however, *C. albicans* can cause infections that range from superficial infections of the skin to life-threatening systemic infections. See: https://www.ncbi.nlm.nih.gov/pmc/articles/PMC3654610/ (accessed August 15, 2019).

4 The hacker culture is a subculture of individuals who enjoy the intellectual challenge of creatively overcoming limitations of software systems to achieve novel and clever outcomes. The act of engaging in activities in a spirit of playfulness and exploration is termed hacking. See: https://en.wikipedia.org/wiki/Hacker_culture#cite_note-Gehring_2004_43-1 (accessed August 15, 2019).

References

Almeida, T. (2017) "Designing Technologies for Intimate Care in Women," PhD thesis, Newcastle University, UK. Available online: http://hdl.handle.net/10443/3868 (accessed August 15, 2019).

Almeida, T., Comber, R., Wood, G., Saraf, D., and Balaam, M. (2016) "On Looking at the Vagina Through Labella," in *Proceedings of the 2016 CHI Conference on Human Factors in Computing Systems*, San Jose, California, May 7–12, 2016, 1810–21, ACM. Available online: https://dl.acm.org/citation.cfm?doid=2858036.2858119 (accessed August 15, 2019).

Åsberg, C. and Birke, L. (2010) "Biology Is a Feminist Issue: Interview with Lynda Birke," *European Journal of Women's Studies*, 17(4): 413–23.

Birke, L. (1986) *Women, Feminism and Biology: The Feminist Challenge*, Brighton: Harvester.

Birke, L. (1999) *Feminism and the Biological Body*, Edinburgh: Edinburgh University Press.

The Boston Women's Health Book Collective (1971) *Our Bodies, Ourselves: A Book by and for Women*, Boston, MA: Boston Women's Health Book Collective and New England Free Press.

Braun, V. and Wilkinson, S. (2001) "Socio-cultural Representations of the Vagina," *Journal of Reproductive and Infant Psychology*, 19(1): 17–32.

Brownmiller, S. (1984) *Femininity*, London: Hamish Hamilton.

De Beauvoir, S. (1949) *The Second Sex*, New York: Oxford University Press.

Fettweis, J., Alves, J., Borzelleca, J., Brooks, J., Friedline, C., Gao, Y., Gao, X., Girerd, P., Harwich, M., Hendricks, S., Jefferson, K., Lee, V., Mo, H., Neale, M., Puma, F., Reimers, M., Rivera, M., Roberts, S., Serrano, M., Sheth, N., Silbert, J., Voegtly, L., Prom-Wormley, E., Xie, B., York, T., Cornelissen, C., Strauss, J., Eaves, L., and Buck, G. (2010) "The Vaginal Microbiome: Disease, Genetics and the Environment," *Nature Precedings*. Available online: http://precedings.nature.com/documents/5150/version/1 (accessed September 5, 2019).

Goldman, A. (1999) *Knowledge in a Social World*, New York: Oxford University Press.

Gopal, S. and Gopal, M. (2010) "Body, Gender and Sexuality: Politics of Being and Belonging," *Economic and Political Weekly*, 47(17): 43–51.

Hamington, M. (2004) *Embodied Care: Jane Addams, Maurice Merleau-Ponty, and Feminist Ethics*, Urbana, IL: University of Illinois Press.

Haraway, D. (1988) "Situated Knowledges: The Science Question in Feminism and the Privilege of Partial Perspective," *Feminist Studies*, 14(3): 575–99.

Harding, S. (1991) *Whose Science? Whose Knowledge? Thinking from Women's Lives*, Ithaca, NY: Cornell University Press.

Irigaray, L. (1985) *This Sex Which Is Not One*, trans. C. Porter and C. Burke, Ithaca, NY: Cornell University Press.

Irigaray, L. (2008) *Conversations*, London: Continuum.

Kinsey, A. C., Pomeroy, W. B., Martin, C. E., and Gebhard, P. H. (1953) *Sexual Behaviour in the Human Female*, Bloomington, IN: Indiana University Press.

Labuski, C. (2008) "Virginal Thresholds," in L. Irigaray and M. Green (eds.), *Luce Irigaray: Teaching*, 13–23, New York: Continuum.

Lane, S. N. (2018) "This Cervical Procedure to Prevent Cancer Is Causing Complications," *Healthline*, April 25. Available at: https://www.healthline.com/health-news/cervical-procedure-to-prevent-cancer-causing-complications#1 (accessed October 5, 2018).

Munch, S. (2006) "The Women's Health Movement: Making Policy, 1970–1995," *Social Work in Health Care*, 43(1): 17–32.

Riley, D. (1999) "Bodies, Identities, Feminisms," in J. Price and M. Shildrick (eds.), *Feminist Theory and the Body: A Reader*, 220–6, Edinburgh: Edinburgh University Press.

Rossmann, J. S. (2008) " 'Built to Spec'? The Vaginal Speculum as a Case Study of Inadequate Design," *Ambidextrous*, Fall: 47–9. Available online: https://dspace.lafayette.edu/handle/10385/589 (accessed August 15, 2019).

Sandelowski, M. (2000) " 'This Most Dangerous Instrument': Propriety, Power, and the Vaginal Speculum," *Journal of Obstetric, Gynecologic & Neonatal Nursing*, 29(1): 73–82.

Schiebinger, L. (1993) *Nature's Body: Gender in the Making of Modern Science*, Boston, MA: Beacon Press.

Shildrick, M. and Price, J. (1999) "Openings on the Body: A Critical Introduction," in J. Price and M. Shildrick (eds.), *Feminist Theory and the Body: A Reader*, 1–14, Edinburgh: Edinburgh University Press.

Stockly, O. D. T. (2011) "The Epistemology of Ignorance," *Anthós*, 3(1): art. 5. Available online: https://core.ac.uk/download/pdf/37768007.pdf (accessed August 15, 2019).

Tuana, N. (2006) "The Speculum of Ignorance: The Women's Health Movement and Epistemologies of Ignorance," *Hypatia*, 21(3): 1–19.

Twigg, J. (2004) "The Body, Gender, and Age: Feminist Insights in Social Gerontology," *Journal of Aging Studies*, 18(1): 59–73.

Wise, N. J., Frangos, E., and Komisaruk, B. (2017) "Brain Activity Unique to Orgasm in Women: An fMRI Analysis," *Journal of Sexual Medicine*, 14(11): 1380–91.

Wolf, N. (2012) *Vagina: A New Biography*, London: Virago

Young, I. M. (1990) *Justice and the Politics of Difference*, Princeton, NJ: Princeton University Press.

Young, I. M. (2005) *On Female Body Experience: "Throwing Like a Girl" and Other Essays*, Studies in Feminist Philosophy, New York: Oxford University Press.

Part Three

The Fabricated Body

Edited by Katherine Townsend

10

OurOwnsKIN

The Development of 3D-Printed Footwear Inspired by Human Skin

Manolis Papastavrou, Liz Ciokajlo, and Rhian Solomon

Introduction

OurOwnsKIN[1] is a research project exploring the interplay between man, material, and machine to create innovative footwear design constructions inspired by human skin. The aim is to harness the capabilities of 3D printing in preparation for future biotechnologies.

Could a deeper understanding of how our skin behaves as a material inform the design of 3D-printed shoes?

Today's digital technologies and tomorrow's biomaterials present vast opportunities but also challenges to the way footwear is designed, urging designers to define systems of making that emerge directly from radical changes in material and process.

Manufacturing is moving toward new territories whereby 3D printing is allowing us to construct exceptionally fine and intricate features with high accuracy "enabling design to take place concurrently at scales ranging from the micrometre to the metre" (Beckett and Babu 2014: 113). Properties of materials are effectively becoming defined through the design of their inherent microstructure. In parallel, biotechnology is also providing sustainable materials that are cultured in a laboratory, posing very real alternatives to polymer synthetics and leathers in the fashion industry.

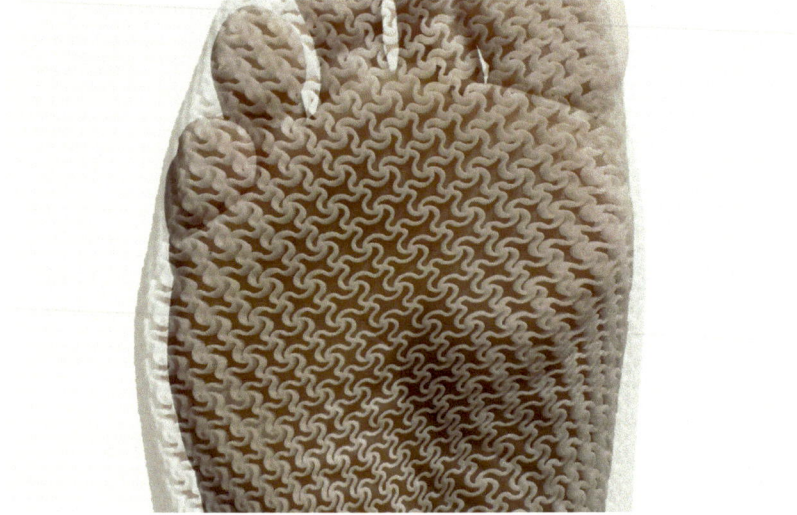

Figure 10.1 OurOwnsKIN 3D-printed shoe inspired by human foot skin (2017). Film by Craig Gambell and George Ellsworth; OurOwnsKIN directed by Liz Ciokajlo and Rhian Solomon.

While inspiration for future footwear will undoubtedly be informed by new materials and technologies, in order to make designs more relevant to our anatomy and more relatable to humans, the OurOwnsKIN project argues that influence must also come from ourselves, the materiality of our own bodies (Figure 10.1) ... Our skin.

By studying the interface that connects us most intimately with our world, can we perhaps propose new design approaches that inform materials, machine, and resultant products?

Man–matter–machine

Our skin has arguably been evolving for the last 300,000 years (Hublin et al. 2017). Paleoanthropologist Erik Trinkaus (based on his studies into the evolution of human toe bones) proposes that humans have been wearing footwear for roughly 40,000 years (Trinkaus 2005); appropriating the skin of another animal to produce footwear for around 5,500 years, as evidenced by the oldest found leather shoe (Pinhasi et al. 2010).

Leather (and a detailed knowledge of its structure) has had a formidable influence on the way that we manipulate sheet materials in shoe constructions, evolving systems of footwear production as we know them today.

The pattern cutting of leather for shoes, for example, is a sophisticated process that exploits the properties of skin in its application. Cobblers will map lines of minimal and maximal stretch on leather hides to inform how they are cut and reassembled to make shoes; poetic designs such as the welted brogue[2] comprise of multiple sections of the hide, arranged in a way that reflects the different performative parts of the shoe.

When a footwear designer develops a design, he or she is working within a well-established system of making that considers numerous parameters associated with the shape of the shoe; the last,[3] fit points on the foot,[4] pattern cutting, the selection of material, employment of machines, and, finally, the entire assembly process.

Each established system determines an archetypal design; the brogue, stiletto, and wellington boot have all been informed by the leading available materials and processes of their time, in turn creating an entirely new category of footwear.

A detailed knowledge of leather and its intrinsic material properties has driven hand-production processes to create these designs. It is the archetypal designs themselves, however, that have shaped the automation of footwear production (and resultant machinery) during the industrial age.

Twentieth-century machines vs twenty-first-century technologies

The Industrial Revolution was driven by the need to mechanize industry, in order to automate repetitive hand-making processes (Shawcross 2014). This resulted in footwear design constructions made by hand significantly influencing the design of the machines used in their production.

Manufacturing techniques became responsible for driving the performance specifications and aesthetics of a shoe, locking designers into regimented ways of making as too much time, skill, and finance became invested by industry.

Despite the introduction of "new" materials, such as polymers during the Plastics Age of the mid-twentieth century, standardized footwear production techniques prevailed. As the century progressed, digital machines began to be introduced, making it more efficient for goods to be produced within the factory and for designers to instruct from their desk.

The development of computer-aided design (CAD) software tools, such as Adobe[5] and SolidWorks[6] suites for 2D and 3D technical drawings also gave designers the freedom to send design instructions to factories across the world, without ever having to be there in person. Efficiency became the catalyst for producing faster machines, motivating designers to adopt rapid digital design methods as a result.

Form driven by machine, material . . . or body?

Materials anthropologist Susanne Küchler describes how the manufacturing and commoditization of products in the Industrial Revolution occurred in parallel to the commoditization of the materials supplied to such factories (Drazin and Küchler 2015). A system to manufacture materials was effectively shaped by a system that manufactured machines.

Just as hand-made shoe processes informed the design of machines that automated hand tasks, there needed to be direction as to what form materials would take in order to be supplied to factories. An interplay between machine and material factors started to define the parameters from which a designer made construction design choices.

Materials were (and still are) largely supplied in the form of sheets, ready to be cut and constructed, molded polymers also tending to have one consistent property, a given stiffness and density. Late twentieth-century footwear designers would work with the properties inherent in the extended range of materials on offer, to command shoe functions, joining a variety of materials together when a change of performance was required. The dominant construction technique that persisted (even to today) was the connection of an upper,[7] or top part of the shoe, to its outsole.[8]

In the evolution of footwear manufacturing, machines and matter became the defining industry systems in the hierarchy of how things were made. Form and finer details of construction were the only possible variables for altering the property of a given material, in turn defining the overall aesthetic of a design.

The promise of Additive Manufacturing

Since the dawn of the twenty-first century, new manufacturing technologies and design tools have been introduced, namely Additive Manufacturing[9] (AM) and advanced computational design, allowing the designer to specify the behavior of a material in ways never achieved before.

Opportunities afforded by this technology have led to a rapid transformation in manufacturing, as products and components are redesigned to capitalize on its unique advantages, which include the light weighting of parts, enhanced customization, and the production of highly complex forms.

Global performance sportswear companies currently adopting AM techniques in the production of components for commercial footwear include Adidas for 3D-printing parametrically designed midsoles (Futurecraft); Nike for developing a 3D-printed upper (Flyprint); and New Balance, in collaboration with Nervous System, who have used pressure data taken from runners to construct 3D-printed midsoles to a shoe (data-driven midsoles).

The footwear industry is yet to embrace the full capabilities of 3D printing, however, as it continues to apply conventional multipart assembly systems, overlooking the opportunity to specify the material density and performance features across a shoe comprising a single part—the influence of the laced brogue construction prevails. It is also not uncommon in footwear innovation departments for managers to ask for laces to be added to radical designs, in order to make them more "shoe-like."

Computer-aided design

To fully capitalize on the design freedom available through AM advanced digital design tools are required. Conventional approaches to CAD are limited in terms of the complexity of forms and features that they can produce. Computational or parametric design[10] remains one of the only methods capable of generating highly complex forms in 3D space.

In Grasshopper[11] for Rhinoceros[12] the designer can define the form of an object by linking different elements of a digital model together using parametric relationships. When applied to 3D printing, this allows for the precise control of different processing and material parameters during the fabrication of a part, as the object is built layer by layer.

AM and its associated CAD tools (in addition to opportunities provided by biotechnologies) are undoubtedly revolutionizing the way that we design and fabricate products in the twenty-first century—marking a shift from a "structure-driven" to a "material-driven" approach to design (Oxman 2010).

Küchler suggests that the real innovation of 3D printing is not the objects that we produce using this technology or how we revolutionize manufacturing, it is the way that 3D printing changes a designer's mindset on how objects can be constructed; "how the mind will inhabit this material technology that calls for and creates structures of internally held, manifold relations" (Küchler 2014: abstract).

Archetypal designs in 3D-printed footwear

Deyan Sudjic, design writer and Director of the Design Museum in London, has described archetypal designs as designs so unique that they define their own category (Sudjic 2009). As this chapter has demonstrated, archetypal designs of the past, such as the brogue, have been greatly informed by the properties of materials available to designers (namely leather), and by the techniques and technologies developed for their manipulation and mass manufacture.

Currently, however, there exists no established system for evolving 3D-printed shoes. Designers must therefore generate new reference points to inform future footwear constructions when using this technology.

Can human skin act as inspiration for archetypal 3D-printed shoes—whereby design is not determined by a machine, or conventional forms of matter, but by an inherent understanding of our bodies?

The OurOwnsKIN project set out to disrupt current approaches to 3D-printed footwear by employing the knowledge of the anatomy of human skin to create 360° responsive shoes.

Collaborate

Rethinking the process of designing and manufacturing 3D-printed shoes is a highly complex problem that requires the employment of interdisciplinary teams. The OurOwnsKIN team consisted of a design researcher and visual artist (Rhian Solomon), a materials specialist with a background in chemical engineering and industrial design (Manolis Papastavrou), and a concept development footwear designer (Liz Ciokajlo)—each with a unique knowledge of the human body, materials, manufacturing, and form.

Rhian Solomon brought to the team insights into how skin behaves from the people who work with skin as a material—reconstructive plastic surgeons. This was drawn from previous innovation projects that she had facilitated across design and medical sectors—sKINship[13] (Ravetz, Kettle, and Felcey 2013; Solomon 2013) (Figure 10.2). Whilst disciplines have traditionally been divided and defined by the formation of practices associated with the body (Blackman 2008), Solomon considers "our body as the meeting place"; an opportunity to open dialogue between diverse communities. (Solomon 2018) (Figure 10.2).

Manolis Papastavrou offered specialist technical knowledge in AM, as well as methods for extracting principles from biological systems, translating them into design solutions. This was based on recent research in which he developed

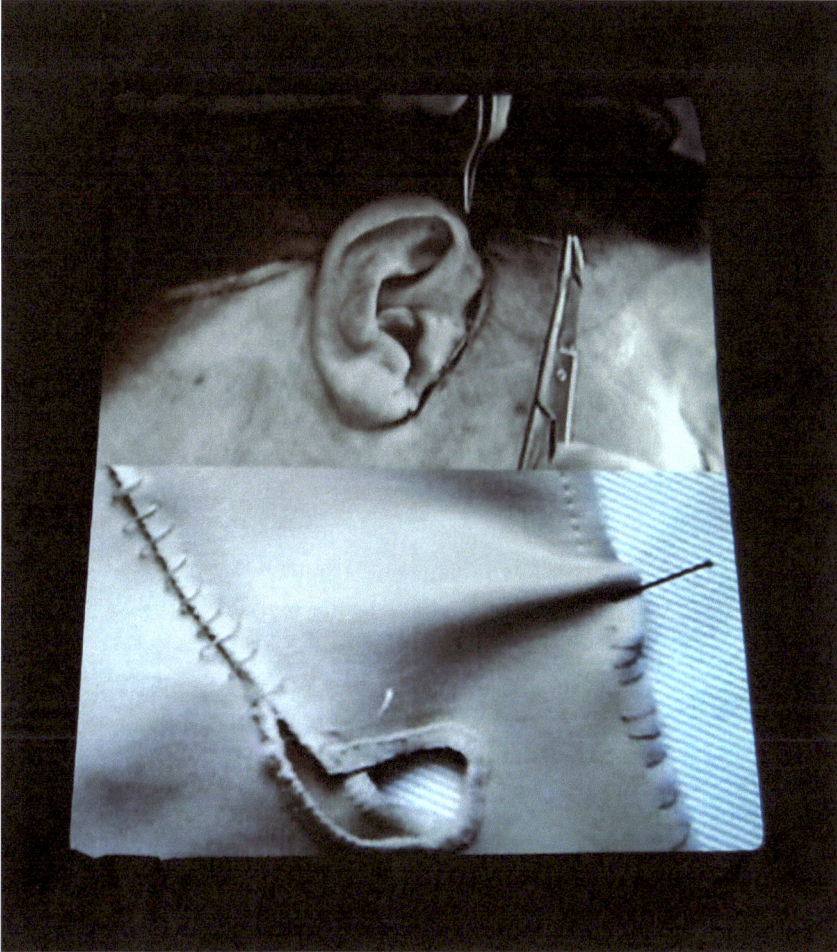

Figure 10.2 Skin or Cloth? A film comparing plastic surgery and pattern-cutting techniques (2012) by Rhian Solomon.

novel AM techniques to create synthetic bone substitutes (Papastavrou 2016) (Figure 10.3).

Liz Ciokajlo provided an understanding of how footwear construction has evolved in relation to materials and fabrication processes, being interested in the changing role of the designer in specifying material properties that could inform future design archetypes.

Previous projects had included working with non-woven materials, as in the GreyFeltShoes (Figure 10.4, left) and biomaterials in projects such as the Mars Boot (Figure 10.5).

Figure 10.3 Bio-ceramic lattice structures fabricated using an extrusion based AM technique (2016) by Manolis Papastavrou.

Her collaboration on the BioCouture "Grown Shoe" (Figure 10.4, right) was also one of the catalysts for the OurOwnsKIN project as it questioned how our desire to recreate the familiar might impact on design innovation. The piece purposefully employed iconic brogue patterning in a bid to make bacterial cellulose more accepted and relatable as a leather alternative.

If we are working with radically new technologies and materials, what should inform resultant designs? Does a completely new production process require a completely new point of reference?

Figure 10.4 (left) GreyFeltShoes with additive binders, creating three levels of density over a continuous surface (2013) by Liz Ciokajlo. Photograph by Stephanie Potter Corwin; (right) the BioCouture "Grown Shoe" made from bacterial cellulose, Liz Ciokajlo (footwear designer) in collaboration with Suzanne Lee (art director) (2013). Photograph by Bill Waters.

Figure 10.5 Mars Boot—Mycelium variants and 3D-printed auxetic sole, Liz Ciokajlo in collaboration with Maurizio Montalti, Manolis Papastavrou, and Rhian Solomon (2017). Photograph by George Ellsworth.

Body matter—material properties of skin

Exploring skin as a source of inspiration, the team first needed to understand its behavior and the principles associated with its function.

Skin protects the underlying tissue structures of the foot by enveloping or wrapping around its complex contours; conforming to its ever-changing shape as it flexes and rotates (Langer 1978). It continuously remodels and adapts to the environmental conditions it is subjected to—a common strategy among tissues, including bone (Thompson and Bonner 1992).

Consisting primarily of two materials—collagen (dermis) and keratin (epidermis)—skin is arranged in a multitude of ways at different scales. Its mechanical properties and thickness transition gradually from elastic to rigid and from thick to thin across the human body in its entirety. Despite being localized, these properties do not appear as distinct zones but rather as gradients (Humbert et al. 2017).

Skin has a grain, just as cloth has a grain, which is dictated by how collagen fibers align themselves. In 1861, Austrian anatomist Karl Langer demonstrated this principle using a round-tipped instrument to make perforations on the skin of hundreds of cadavers. The skin's intrinsic tension would transform the wounds from round to elliptical, with their principal axis revealing each time the orientation of collagen fibers across the entire body (Humbert et al. 2017) (Figure 10.6).

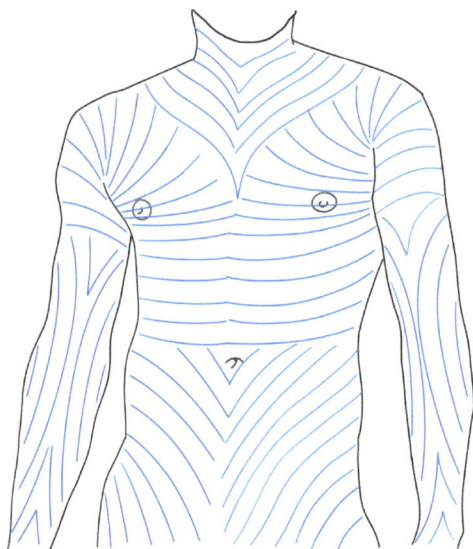

Figure 10.6 Illustration showing Langer's Lines mapped across the human body (2018) by Manolis Papastavrou.

Bioinspired design

Mimicking rather than copying (or growing) human skin was deemed the most viable route toward a functional footwear product for the OurOwnsKIN project, as shoe construction requires materials with reproducible properties that can be retained at conditions of high pressure or temperature.

Grown materials are not yet resilient enough for use in this particular context (Viney and Bell 2004). Typical problems such as the complexity and duration of their production also persist due to the high levels of investment that are required to convert traditional manufacturing into systems of biofabrication.

We are, however, on the cusp of a biomaterial revolution that is being driven by an evolving community of designers, scientists, and visionaries who are advancing sustainable biomaterials and production processes.

A future strand to the OurOwnsKIN project will seek to harness the capabilities of this technology, combining it with 3D printing; however, it was decided that the current project would take inspiration from the design principles of skin as a material, instead of replicating the biological process of its growth and regeneration.

Design development

The first developmental stage of the project was to establish a computational framework, inspired by human skin, that was both responsive and dynamic.

The mechanical behavior of skin has been described by Ridge and Wright using a simple orthogonal mesh positioned diagonally in relation to Langer's Lines (Ridge and Wright 1966) (Figure 10.7, top). The mesh is stretched more in one direction than the other, causing its cell units to deform into rhombi (diagrid). This could be visualized by a continuous braided structure, wrapped around the human body, that is not static, but constantly changes with body movement as it gets pulled in different directions.

Using Grasshopper for Rhino, the OurOwnsKIN team generated a diagrid lattice on a surface obtained from a foot scan (Figure 10.7, bottom right). Each member (or strut) of the lattice behaved like a spring under tension or compression—an approach which has the advantage of manipulating a "digital skin," by assigning different values of elasticity (stretching force) in each section of the foot, and making possible the complete customization of fit.

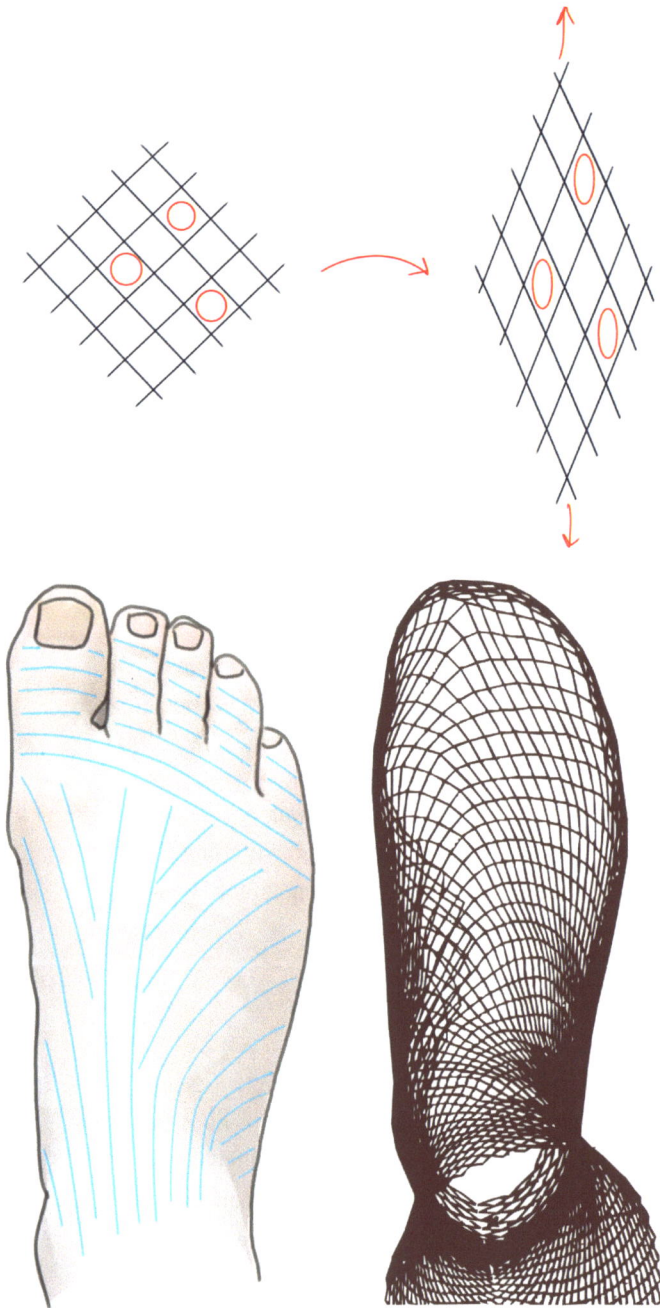

Figure 10.7 (top) Simplified model of the mechanical behavior of skin under tension proposed by Ridge and Wright, illustration by Manolis Papastavrou (2019); (bottom left) Directional grain of Langer's Lines as positioned on the human foot skin, illustration by Manolis Papastavrou (2019); (bottom right) OurOwnsKIN diagrid framework generated over scanned surface of the foot using Grasshopper for Rhino by Manolis Papastavrou (2017).

Auxetic lattices and footwear prototypes

In order to vary the stiffness in structures consisting of single materials, the team experimented with using lattices called auxetics. Auxetics are a family of lattices with a unique mechanical behavior; when stretched, they become thicker. Similarly, when compressed, they shrink and become stiffer.

The project employed two of the most popular types:

- the "bow tie" lattice—consisting of bow tie shaped cell units
- the "chiral" lattice—consisting of chiral shaped cell units

Each type of auxetic cell unit was inserted into the diagrid mesh framework in order to design and fabricate, what is called in the footwear industry a series of "socks."[14] This framework allowed for the variation of scale and the distortion of cell units, adapting to the contours of the foot in different areas while following the skin's tension lines.

Samples using these structures were initially 3D printed in a low-cost nylon 12 material, using selective laser sintering[15] (SLS). This was found, however, to be too rigid (Figure 10.8). The team decided to pursue using thermoplastic polyurethane (TPU) for further printouts, which offered an alternative material that was both durable and flexible.

These samples fully exploited the capabilities of 3D printing by rejecting a conventional upper and outsole footwear construction system. Printed in one

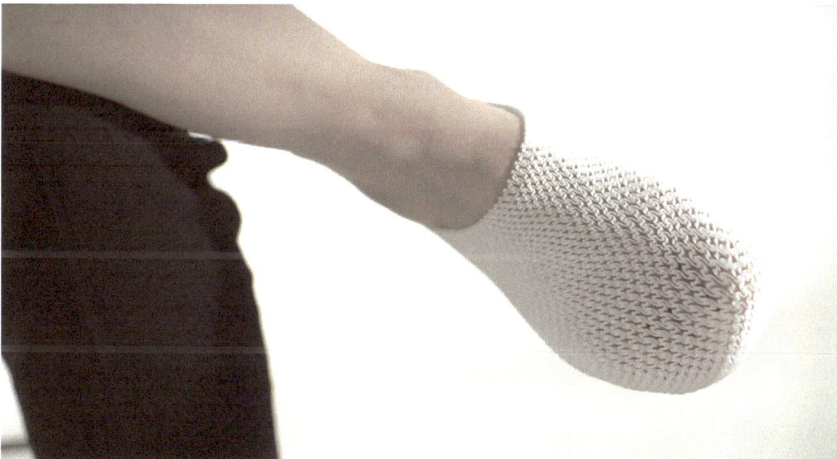

Figure 10.8 OurOwnsKIN 3D-printed "sock" using chiral auxetic pattern. Film by Craig Gambell and George Ellsworth (2017); OurOwnsKIN directed by Liz Ciokajlo and Rhian Solomon.

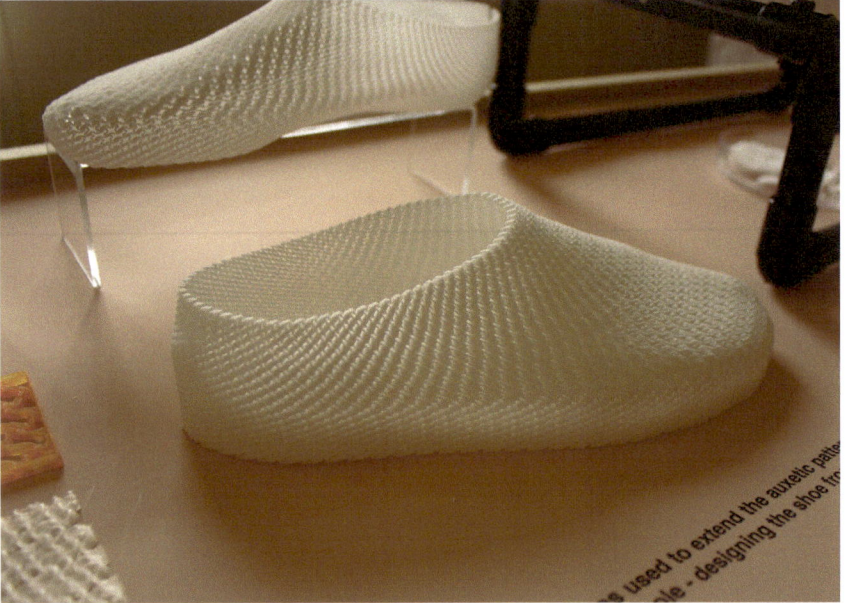

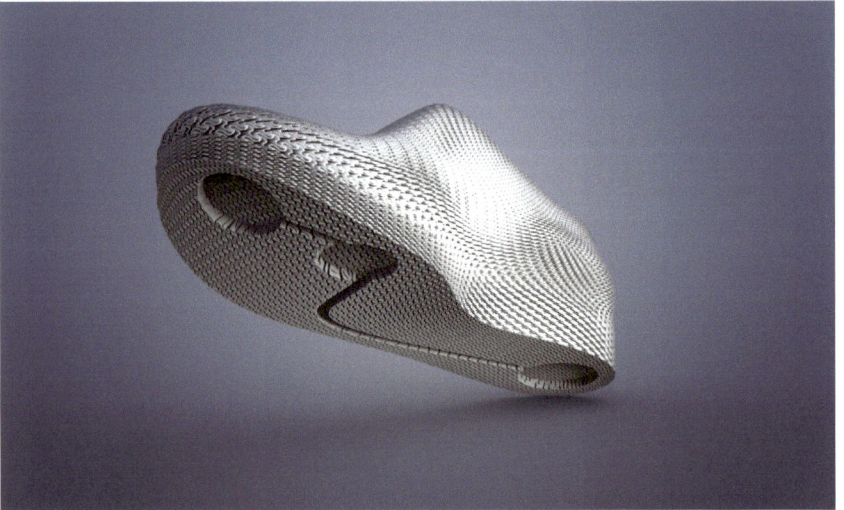

Figure 10.9 (top) OurOwnsKIN 3D-printed shoe featuring generated outsole (2016). Photograph by Manolis Papastavrou; (bottom) Evolving the aesthetic of the OurOwnsKIN 3D-printed shoe (2016). CAD file produced by Jason Taylor; OurOwnsKIN directed by Liz Ciokajlo and Rhian Solomon.

part, from a continuous mono material, they enveloped the foot in its entirety, creating a structure that was not only responsive to both movement and pressure but also integrated a closure system, requiring no need for traditional laces. The use of auxetic cells and personalized production processes (working from scans of the foot), also provided a bespoke fit and enhanced comfort for the wearer.

Subsequent stages of the project looked to generate an outsole to the shoe by extending the auxetic framework from its base, while at the same time maintaining a purity of form (Figure 10.9, top). The skills of additional CAD designers were also drawn upon to explore further variations of mesh.

Jason Taylor, of make X design,[16] coded the design structure onto a last, resulting in an evolved aesthetic for the shoe (Figure 10.9, bottom). The rationale for this exploration was to investigate manufacturing opportunities that might encompass the standardization of production.

Tom Mallinson, of Digits2Widgets,[17] developed a series of prototypes that added complexity to the structure by using 3D auxetic lattices, the aim being to enhance the performance of the shoe in areas under step impact.

Electrospinning

Each of the shoe samples required waterproofing or covering in some way. Reluctant to fill the structures using infill materials (which might have impacted on the stretch and responsiveness of the auxetic framework) the pieces were electrospun, creating a non-woven coating to the shoe. This process was also carefully selected so as to maintain the project's principle of rejecting conventional footwear manufacturing processes; moving away from sheet-formed material.

Electrospinning is a method that uses electrostatic forces to draw charged threads of polymers onto an oppositely charged surface. A thin coating of an highly elastic co-polymer PLA + polycaprolactone (PCL) formulation was applied to the shoe as it rotated on a lathe to create a fine non-woven scaffold (Figure 10.10). The thickness of the material can easily be tuned through altering the duration of this process.

Used frequently in medical applications in the production of wound-care products, implant coatings, and drug delivery systems, electrospun fibers hold incredible material properties as they support the growth of biological materials and can also be sustainable. The introduction of these fibers has opened opportunities to the OurOwnsKIN project to combine digital and biotechnological approaches to production. The next phase of the venture will aim to grow materials into the micro structures of electrospun, 3D-printed shoes.

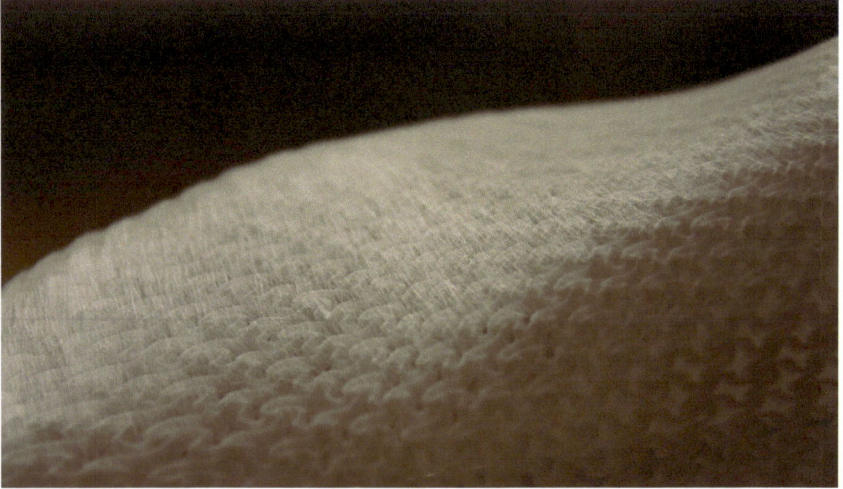

Figure 10.10 Electrospun fibers applied to the OurOwnsKIN 3D-printed shoe (2016). Photograph by Manolis Papastavrou; OurOwnsKIN directed by Liz Ciokajlo and Rhian Solomon.

Future manufacturing opportunities

The OurOwnsKIN project has attracted interest from international research groups and major footwear companies through its bid to subvert current industry practices.

Benefits of methods such as this include shorter production timescales, by significantly reducing the number of processes, tools, and machines required; in turn lowering financial investment.

Parametric design also enables the industry to make changes more easily and cheaply during the early design phases of a shoe, allowing for mass customization and tailored fit. When coupled with AM this means that products can be produced for specific user groups, in small runs of production.

The OurOwnsKIN project in particular allows for the customization of fit to be distributed across different elements of a shoe (contour, material, and structure) resulting in a design that fits a wider population for mass production scenarios.

A final word . . .

OurOwnsKIN is a speculative project that positions the human body as the blueprint to instruct future design form and digital making processes. It is an approach that flies in the face of traditional sheet production techniques; one that is not driven by conventional materials, machines, or established design forms, but is driven by our own anatomical makeup.

As this chapter has identified, 3D printing (and biotechnologies) are today allowing us to subvert thousands of years of hand and machine-based construction knowledge—enabling a migration toward a future whereby form may be driven by algorithms, or choreographed by cell growth.

This raises questions, however, around the potential of these technologies to disrupt our emotional connections to the items that we choose to consume and wear. Whereby once humans appropriated the skin of another animal, now there is opportunity to wear our own skin, or "cloth" inspired by its materiality. What happens, therefore, when our relationship with commercial products is derived from the emotional connections that we hold with ourselves and our bodies? Will this enhance our intimacy with things—building resilience into associations between people and products. Or will this purely repulse us?

The OurOwnsKIN project additionally challenges our current relationship with the natural world from which we have become both separate and superior, following gross exploitation of the agricultural and industrial ages (Morton 2016). Perhaps a technique such as this, in which the materiality of the human body is reconsidered to produce commercial goods, can somehow integrate us back into nature, enhancing our empathy for the ecosystems in which we currently coexist?

If leather and its associated processes have been the driving force behind footwear manufacturing to date, can our own skin become the material that drives 3D-printed design form constructions of the future?

Acknowledgments

OurOwnsKIN has been kindly supported by Makerversity (MV Works), Arts Council England, Knowledge Transfer Network, Ravensbourne University London, and Innovate UK.

Notes

1 OurOwnsKIN is both a research project and innovation design consultancy directed by Liz Ciokajlo and Rhian Solomon. See http://www.ourownskin.co.uk, http://www.lizciokajlo.co.uk, and http://www.rhiansolomon.co.uk.

2 The brogue is a style of low-heeled shoe or boot traditionally characterized by multiple-piece, sturdy leather uppers with decorative perforations and serration along visible edges.

3 A last is the hard form that represents the foot used in footwear construction. Depending on the manufacturing process to make the shoes, a last will be made from wood, aluminum, or, most commonly, plastic.

4 Fit points are key measurement points on a foot that are used to ensure the best fit and wearing of a shoe.

5 Adobe Suite is a suite of computer drawing software (including Illustrator and Photoshop) used by footwear designers to draw and specify designs.

6 SolidWorks is a CAD program commonly used by footwear designers to design the outer sole units of polymer shoes.

7 An upper is the part of the shoe that covers the top part of the foot from heel to toe and does not include the sole.

8 The outsole is the bottom most part of the shoe that comes into contact with the ground.

9 AM encompasses a great number of manufacturing techniques that share a common approach: the object is built layer by layer, allowing for the precise control of its internal architecture and composition (Campbell et al. 2012).

10 Parametric design is a process based on algorithmic thinking that enables the expression of parameters and rules. Together these define, encode, and clarify the relationship between design intent and design response.

11 Grasshopper is a visual programming language and environment that runs within the Rhinoceros CAD application.

12 Rhinoceros is a commercial 3D computer graphics and CAD application program developed by Robert McNeel & Associates.

13 sKINship is a collaborative network promoting cross-disciplinary interactions between visual arts and science-based practitioners—namely reconstructive plastic surgeons and designers who create and make for the body. See: http://www.skinship.co.uk.

14 A "sock" in the footwear industry is a thin piece of material that lies inside the shoe and surrounds the foot. A footwear "sock" is part of the shoe.

15 Selective laser sintering is an AM technique in which tiny particles of plastic, ceramic, or glass are fused together by heat from a high-power laser to form a solid, three-dimensional object.

16 make X design is a multidisciplinary consultancy designing digitally manufactured prostheses. See: http://www.makexdesign.com.

17 Digits2Widgets is a London-based consultancy specializing in 3D print, CAD, and scanning technologies. See: https://www.digits2widgets.com/.

References

Beckett, R. and Babu, S. (2014) "To the Micron: A New Architecture Through High-Resolution Multi-Scalar Design and Manufacturing," *Architectural Design*, 84(1): 112–15.

Blackman, L. (2008) *The Body: The Key Concepts*, London: Berg.

Campbell, I., Bourell, D., and Gibson, I. (2012) "Additive Manufacturing: Rapid Prototyping Comes of Age," *Rapid Prototyping Journal*, 18(4): 255–8.

Drazin, A. and Küchler, S. (2015) *The Social Life of Materials: Studies in Materials and Society*, London: Bloomsbury.

Hublin, J.-J., Ben-Ncer, A., Bailey, S. E., Freidline, S. E., Neubauer, S., Skinner, M. M., Bergmann, I., Le Cabec, A., Benazzi, S., Harvati, K., and Gunz, P. (2017) "New Fossils from Jebel Irhoud, Morocco and the Pan-African Origin of *Homo sapiens*," *Nature*, 546: 289–92.

Humbert, P., Fanian, F., Maibach, H. I., and Agache, P. (2017) *Agache's Measuring the Skin: Non-invasive Investigations, Physiology, Normal Constants*, 2nd edn., Cham: Springer.

Küchler, S. (2014) "Additive Technology and Material Cognition: A View from Anthropology," *Journal of Cognition and Culture*, 14(5): 385–99.

Langer, K. (1978) "On the Anatomy and Physiology of the Skin: I. The Cleavability of the Cutis," *British Journal of Plastic Surgery*, 31(1): 3–8.

Morton, T. (2016) *Dark Ecology: For a Logic of Future Coexistence*, New York: Columbia University Press.

Oxman, N. (2010) "Structuring Materiality: Design Fabrication of Heterogeneous Materials," *Architectural Design*, 80(4): 78–85.

Papastavrou, E. (2016) "Incorporating Self-Assembly into Robocasting for Applications in Hard Tissue Engineering," PhD thesis, Nottingham Trent University.

Pinhasi, R., Gasparian, B., Areshian, G., Zardaryan, D., Smith, A., Bar-Oz, G., and Higham, T. (2010) "First Direct Evidence of Chalcolithic Footwear from the Near Eastern Highlands," *PLoS ONE*, 5(6): e10984. Available online: https://doi.org/10.1371/journal.pone.0010984 (accessed August 20, 2019).

Ravetz, A., Kettle, A., and Felcey, H. (2013) *Collaboration Through Craft*, London: Bloomsbury.

Ridge, M. D. and Wright, V. (1966) "The Directional Effects of Skin: A Bio-engineering Study of Skin with Particular Reference to Langer's Lines," *The Journal of Investigative Dermatology*, 46(4): 341–6.

Shawcross, R. (2014) *Shoes: An Illustrated History*, London: Bloomsbury.

Solomon, R. (2013) "sKINship: An Exchange of Material Understanding Between Plastic Surgery and Pattern Cutting for Fashion," in A. Ravetz, A. Kettle, and H. Felcey (eds.), *Collaboration Through Craft*, 114–24, London: Bloomsbury.

Solomon, R. (2018) "Our Body as the Meeting Place . . .," *Rhian Solomon*. Available online: https://www.rhiansolomon.co.uk/phd/ (accessed April 24, 2018).

Sudjic, D. (2009) *The Language of Things: Understanding the World of Desirable Objects*, New York: W. W. Norton.

Thompson, D. W. and Bonner, J. T. (1992) *On Growth and Form*, Cambridge: Cambridge University Press.

Trinkaus, E. (2005) "Anatomical Evidence for the Antiquity of Human Footwear Use," *Journal of Archaeological Science*, 32(10): 1515–26.

Viney, C. and Bell, F. I. (2004) "Inspiration Versus Duplication with Biomolecular Fibrous Materials: Learning Nature's Lessons Without Copying Nature's Limitations," *Current Opinion in Solid State and Materials Science*, 8(2): 165–71.

11

Material Robotics

Shaping the Sensitive Interface

Amy Winters

Introduction

The human body is soft. Even the spine is conceived from fluid-filled joints generating a bendable structure. Bodily fluids cause us to be supple while acting as carriers of both nutrients and disease.

Moreover, bile, blood, mucus, saliva, sweat, and tears hold sensory capabilities. Saliva, for example, enhances taste,[1] sweat can act as a thermoregulator,[2] and tears can be triggered by emotional states such as sorrow and joy. Vomiting, for its part, is the great "liquid carrier," effectively expelling toxins from the body.

Bioinspired technologies acting at the interface of the human body offer an opportunity to extend, explore, and enable new experiences for the wearer. The growth and development of "soft machines" propose enhanced, nuanced, and multimodal forms of expressions—these can be visual, proprioceptive, auditory, olfactory, and tactile. It is at this newly defined junction that we now examine the potential of soft robotics and interaction paradigms through a frame of embodied imagination and making.

Until now, wearable soft robotic applications have, for the most part, been generated through specific frameworks—with a technological, functional, or user-led design approach.[3] However, what these particular methods overlook is what can be the more compelling, multisensory capabilities of "artificial muscles."

This chapter begins with "The Sensitive Interface," which offers an alternative interpretation of human-centered interaction, responsive, for example, through verbal, nonverbal, and environmental inputs. This concept is emphasized by observing the rhythm and the sensual qualities of elemental materials such as wind and water in "Liquid Rhythm."

How, therefore, can we design processes to facilitate these multisensory fabrications? A post-Cartesian[4] positioning structures our exploration by actively using the body, and then responding to what we see, hear, feel, touch, and smell. "Alchemical Prototyping" thus offers an experiential method of working with soft robotic technologies.

Next, we explore "Hacking—Bricolage—Alchemy" to reframe the skill set of the modern textile designer. We build on how these characteristics operate in this newly defined design space through "Material Cooking: Lab as Kitchen." Here, the human body is employed as an active part of the living design process that can facilitate the link between imagination, material, and the hand; a method of acknowledging the human value and potential of the tactile and kinaesthetic mind. Thus, by directly establishing an intimate and procreative relationship with and through material, the designer can intuitively follow the rhythm of the numerous substances with which they work. This challenges the dominance of Aristotle's "hylomorphic model of creation" (Ingold 2010) whereby a predefined mental artifact breaks down the design process into objectified components. Moreover, the potential for experimental "material robotics" can be situated in standard textile processes: mold-making, seaming, and couching, for example, are encountered within the tacit "know-how"[5] of the textile designer rather than via established scientific laboratories.

"Soft Bioinspired Skins" surveys how biomimetic materials shape natural and synthetic material developments, followed by a hands-on prototyping example of liquid materials in "Unconventional Microfluidics."

The chapter closes with reflections on how such an approach can create a multifaceted skill set for a new studio practice. And to conclude, a four-stage methodology for the post-digital design practitioner is defined: "The Soft Programmable Material Toolbox": Experiential Understanding, De/Construction, Re/Construction, and Definition.

The sensitive interface

Technology-driven experiences developed by the consumer electronics industry have reduced our physicality to "body real estate"[6] (Dvorak 2010: 107), as described through the self-quantification movement, by exploiting smartwatches, wristbands, and headgear embedded with sensing capabilities (Winters 2016). The body, however, does encompass more than this rather reductive, commodified landscape. Rooted within the skin and musculature are somatosensory systems delivering multisensory feedback—both tactile (temperature, vibrations, and texture) and kinesthetic (inertia, shape, weight, and deformation).

Further evaluation of this limitation, leading to "experience prototypes" rather than "usability prototypes" could open up new, alternative modes of human-centered interaction. To illustrate, Vigneshwara's (2018) light-powered musical instrument, "The Screaming Sun: Choreographing Synesthesia," invites the user to explore the artifact through playing with light and shadow, which results in sound frequency fluctuations. This contrasts to merely switching it on using standard buttons or switches, lending agency to an instrument, which is depicted by Vigneshwara as "much like a living being" (562). In this sense, the interaction shifts from one-sided use into collaborative play.

Another example, "MetaSolid" (Winkler, Steimle, and Maes 2013) holds programmable phase-change abilities. This speculative "imaginary material" morphs between the hard and soft thus suggesting fresh user interactions such as "crumbling" or "tickling" rather than purely traditional handling interactions such as "folding."

This emerging material turn in human–computer interaction (HCI), as highlighted by Robles and Wiberg (2010), has spawned a series of physical-digital prototypes, which offer novel and sensory forms of interactive responses. As these examples illustrate, textile designers can now use their unique proficiencies to experiment in the design space of tangible user interfaces (TUI).

Soft interfaces can exploit intrinsic textile properties such as colors, surfaces, textures, patterns, and structures, which move beyond merely crafting aesthetics by developing affordances and interactive possibilities.

Fernaeus et al. (2012), for example, assert that soft hardware establishes the facility to shape new forms of interaction due to the articulation of their direct material affordances. Accordingly, textiles present a range of properties, tools, and techniques, which can be synthesized by integrating multisensory points of reference into an embodied design process of technology development. Consequently, "soft robotic" actuators[7] can offer unprecedented opportunities for interactive surfaces through displacement, deformation, and strain. Examples of soft actuators include: pneumatic elastomers (air activated) (Holland et al. 2013)[8] shown in Figure 11.1; electroactive polymers [9] (high-voltage); shape memory polymers[10] (temperature); microfluidics[11] (liquids); and nylon coils[12] (temperature).

Organisms devoid of rigid skeletal structures such as octopus tentacles, lizard tongues, and elephant trunks provide the foundation for soft robotic constructions (Rus and Tolley 2015). While "soft robotic skins" certainly work in harmony with

Figure 11.1 Amy Winters, Actuators in the form of pneumatic inflatable air chambers, made using the soft robotics toolkit (Holland et al. 2013). Image © Amy Winters 2016.

the flexible and adaptable nature of textiles, offering a compliant means to interface with the human body, what is perhaps more notable is that these are also actuators—which are key among the post-digital practitioner's newfound tools for developing expressive design possibilities.

Materials are moving from a position of static to temporal expressions, and as we begin to analyze these new actuators, a distinctive vocabulary will begin to emerge. We can start by drawing on Robles and Wiberg's (2010) novel interaction approaches, such as "elements scale, datum, rhythm, transformation, circulation, approach and entrance" into the context of the human body to imagine amplified "experiences" (139).

Liquid rhythm

"Rhythm" is central to this story and can be located in both the slower, deeper, and seasonal paces of the natural world and the corporeal pulse of our bodies. As Dewey suggests in *Art as Experience*, "day and night, rain and sunshine, are in their alternation, factors that directly concern human beings" (Dewey 2005: 153). The body's sensual and multisensory interactions with the elements such as rain, snow, wind, frost, fog, and sunshine are recognized through our perceptions of thirst, color, taste, smell, temperature, and even pain (Winters 2017).

Human–environment interactions are a form of immersive and nonverbal communication. For example, Bachelard's statement (1983: 6) that "water is truly the transitory element" identifies its transformational capabilities and our subconscious affinity with water as the result of its "viscosity" and "organic associations" (1983: 105).

The ephemeral user interfaces (EUI) (Döring, Sylvester, and Schmidt 2013) focus on the inherent materiality of translating transient phenomena found in nature, such as ice, bubbles, water, fog, air, earth, and fire, into a user interface. Elemental materials offer playful and haptic characteristics with multisensory feedback of "interesting and diverse textures, liquids, fragile structures and temperature" (Döring, Sylvester, and Schmidt 2013: 77).

Similarly, "Fluids," Rudomin et al.'s interactive and immersive mixed-reality art installation demonstrates a concept of programmable water and air, suggesting that this type of "tactile reference expands the imagination of the user" (Rudomin et al. 2005: 156). Thus, liquids can be seen as expressive "substances" which embody temporal qualities such as rhythm and texture, as revealed in Figure 11.2, "Liquid Rhythm," where water is filmed as a type of "visual, time-based bricolage." The character and expression of water are composed of several different properties, namely: "Rhythm, movement, brilliance, reflexion, colour, sound, and transparency" (Snell 2013: 264). These multifaceted visual and tactile assets are explored through our prototyping experiments later in the chapter.

Alchemical prototyping

Alchemical prototyping is fundamentally a focus on praxis through the lens of the body. The action of experiential learning, or "thinking *through* making" (Ingold 2013: xi, emphasis added), establishes an alternative type of knowledge which is not necessarily problem-driven. This could be a complementary strand

Figure 11.2 Amy Winters, "Liquid Rhythm," Neuhausen am Rheinfall, Switzerland. Image © Amy Winters 2014.

of R&D strategy, the establishment of which could deliver the next disruptive technology.

With the growth and democratization of physical computing and digital fabrication, it is now possible for designers to process, or even invent and composite new programmable materials, merging both their physical and digital capabilities.[13] Within this cultural shift, designers can integrate tools that are usually found in the context of product design and design engineering, such as 3D printers, laser cutters, CNC routers, and mechatronics technology, into their practice.

Designers working in the field of wearable technology and interactive textiles have been able to employ an array of sensors from sound, movement, and light yet, to date, the creative output has largely been restricted to using color-changing inks, LEDs, or cumbersome motors (vibrating or rotating) within their designs. Wearable technology and "smart textiles," closely aligned to the consumer electronics industry, have largely inherited the "binary" constraints of software engineering. This focus on predominately digital rather than interactive physical qualities cultivates a "preprogrammed" order of expression, often resulting in predictable and prescriptive outcomes.

By way of contrast, the textile designer expresses a particular sensitivity to the experience of materials (Igoe 2010, 2013), which can be characterized as "delicacy," "subtlety," "intuition," "feeling," "responsiveness," and "perceptiveness," and cannot necessarily be quantified or measured. This sensory fluency is embedded within specific and personal tacit, unarticulated knowledge (Polanyi 2009).

Vallgårda and Redström (2007) assert that for a designer to grasp and master the technical possibilities of material it is essential for its working language to acclimatize to the sensibilities of the designer. Given the differences identified, could the material-led disciplines devise a language that would stimulate the imaginative and evocative facets of technological tools? Can we imagine, even speculatively, that textile designers could invent their own type of soft robotic "maker" kits using their specific tacit knowledge and tinkering with the machines they already have a physical connection with? This could, for example, take the form of "embodied speculation" workshops, as devised by industrial designers Rozendaal, Heidingsfelder, and Kupper (2016), in which participants imagine and critically reflect on the implications of emerging technologies by conceiving and constructing hands-on artifacts.

Hacking—bricolage—alchemy

Here we can break down this emerging skill set into three characters: that of the hacker, bricoleur, and alchemist. All three share the same assets of being guided by their senses, rather than relying on scientific verification, and an ability to communicate to a wider audience through these sensory translations. This conceptualization of a "materials designer" raises parallels with Ingold's (2010: 94) analogy of working with materials as a form of "cooking"; that is, blending substances through "an endless process of transformation" (ibid.). As trained sensory specialists, textile designers not only use their visual sense but also develop tacit knowledge through the use of touch, sound, smell, space, and weight. To illustrate: in printed textiles, there are the particular characteristics of blending various pigments during a color-mixing experiment, or the texture and scent of a substance such as expanding puff-binder applied to leather—all appeal directly to the senses.

This hands-on approach is more akin to creating a recipe, whereby tacit knowledge, visual memory, and fine motor skills are employed. Within the expanding agency of materials, this imaginative "play" can be seen as a reenactment of various material experiences that have a sensory quality and can demonstrate a new level of expression through engagement with the body. Familiar textures, for example, bring a sense of comfort while nostalgia triggers our senses, and these tacit connections subjectively affect the methods informing how we design.

This reciprocal approach draws on "reflective practice" (Schön 1983: 79). The designer becomes increasingly aware of the knowledge they possess, the knowledge they are absorbing, and the knowledge they still need, thus enabling reflection and learning based on experience during practice (reflection-in-action) and after practice (reflection-on-action). Interaction researchers Klemmer, Hartmann, and Takayama (2006: 142) highlight that artifact-centric prototyping provides a "concrete manifestation" of ideas and one in which reflective practice can uncover problems that would otherwise have stayed hidden while at the same time generating new concepts and ideas to support knowledge-sharing. The author can, therefore, be placed as a researcher and participant in a method that includes human experience, materials experience, and problem-solving.

As well as being a reflective practitioner, the designer-researcher may take on many different but related roles in the creation of new expressive materials:

A hacker

The role of material hacker can be manifest in the design process both on a practical and systemic level. First, the skill of the hacker within this context lies in the construction of new material systems through a reinterpretation of tools and processes. The hacker could adapt a standard hardware component for an alternative purpose; hack an open-source commercial 3D printer to enable the fabrication of specific mixtures of multi-matter materials; subvert and tinker with the traditional machines they tacitly understand, and employ them within their own practice (knit, weave, print, and embroider) to generate explorative material possibilities—potentially enabling newfound commercial markets which may not otherwise materialize by employing traditional user-led design processes.

An alchemist

The skills of the alchemist are particularly relevant to the development of biosynthetic materials, stimuli-responsive ink, dyes, pigments, and surface phenomena, and by deploying processes such as fermentation, filtration, sublimation, and calcination. An alchemist may be theatrical in nature, utilizing a type of spontaneous craft, inventing new recipes, and discovering fresh substances. Alchemists, alongside their knowledge of, for example, printed textiles, painting, or printmaking, might collaborate with color chemistry departments, or synthetic biologists, thus incorporating their own tacit knowledge of pigments, dyes, and additives to a variety of experimental substrates.

A bricoleur

A key player in "accidental innovation," a bricoleur improvises a material innovation through transforming preexisting developments and "leftover" components into new systems. Interpreted through Lévi-Strauss's (1962: 11) concept of bricolage, the bricoleur's skill set appropriates technological mediums in a hands-on manner within an iterative cycle of making. The textile designer draws on their personal inventory of skills and "know-how" developed through knitting, printing, weaving, or mixed media.

Material cooking: Lab as kitchen

As explored earlier in the chapter, through our cooking analogy, the designer as "cook" requires multiple skills and sensitivities which, in turn, make her/him adept at inventing and amalgamating with multiple material properties.

The commonality between disparate tactile practitioners is notable; as Ingold (2010: 94) states: "As practitioners, the builder, the gardener, the cook, the alchemist and the painter are not so much imposing form on matter as bringing together diverse materials and combining or redirecting their flow in anticipation of what might emerge." Thus, the textile designer's multifaceted skill set shares a common understanding with the painter, alchemist, and cook, a type of creative invention process undertaken through an embodied mixture of "substances" or even flavor-pairing possibilities. These "substances" can be multilayered as fibers, yarns, gels, films, and coatings. An example of such an approach is the patented *International Klein Blue*, invented by painter Yves Klein through experimenting with a polymer binder and unstable ultramarine pigment.[14]

Within this chapter, microfluidics, traditionally a medical diagnostic application will be transported into the experimental contexts of textiles and wearable technology. Illustrated through a series of small-scale material explorations, the author devises and categorizes a set of fresh interactions. These experiments are powered by channels, micropumps, microcontrollers, and soft reservoirs (Figure 11.3). The process of lending computational abilities to liquids and air becomes the catalyst to reimagine interactive surfaces through the manipulation of colors, iridescence, contrast, opacity, rhythm, shape, and texture.

Figure 11.3 Amy Winters, "Lab as Kitchen," a selection of ingredients and utensils for the creation of Material Robotics. Silicon (Ecoflex-30), Tygon tubing, silicone pigments, colored flocking fibers, soft reservoirs, mixing/measuring jug, 3D printed scaffolds, flow controlled micropumps, sensor, laser-cut Perspex molds, weighing scale. Image © Amy Winters 2017.

Sourcing ingredients

Our form of exploratory research encompasses a series of open-ended material experiments and development processes as a way of generating new knowledge. The act of making here becomes a catalyst to manifest technical knowledge (Toomey and Kapsali 2014). In this context, the designer needs a good understanding of all the ingredients of the recipe to be in a position to select which individual ingredients will be brought together, successfully.

Once the designer gains an experiential understanding of the substances, machines, and tools they are working with, tacit knowledge can be documented by reflection through journals, filming, and sketches as a form of visual time-based bricolage. This contextual inquiry encompassed short films and vignettes of bioinspired structures. For example, observing carnivorous plants such as the venus flytrap as a sensing and actuating model or examining the various features of animal skin. The poison dart frog exhibits a colorful, glistening, and clammy skin texture—sweating poison through a toxic slime. Figure 11.4 demonstrates this visual and tactual reference to the wet skin of an amphibian.

As Igoe (2013: 82) notes, textile designers manipulate, play, and recontextualize when designing and experimenting through "stuff, trappings, bits and pieces,

Figure 11.4 Poison dart frog, amphibian skin patterning, Zurich Zoo. Experiments with silicone texture—simulating the look and feel of moist skin. Images © Amy Winters 2015.

accoutrements, paraphernalia." This specific method employs contextual and first-hand tactile references, which lie in contrast to the ocular-centric methods found in traditional user experience (UX) practices such as wireframes[15] or personas.[16] Rather, these tactile references can be synthesized into a more complex multisensory and contextually rich programmable system.

Soft bioinspired skins

As explored at the start of this chapter, soft robotics are often biologically inspired. Similarly, some textiles have the unique ability to mimic surfaces, drawing inspiration from biosystems such as the fibrous structures made from pineapples (Piñatex), seaweed (SeaCell), and cork (Pelcor).

Another development, "Structural Colour", the stretchable "Polymer Opal" color-change Lycra simulates a type of color found in beetle wings, morpho butterflies, and peacock feathers. As displayed in the garment (Figure 11.5) developed by the NanoPhotonics Group at Cambridge University and Rainbow Winters. Here, a scalable, manufacturing method used a roll-to-roll process where stacked nanoparticles are fabricated onto thin transfer films (Zhao et al. 2016). The film can be either laser or vinyl cut into custom shapes, logos, and patterns and heat pressed onto a stretchable substrate such as Lycra.[17]

Our skin is an organ made up of tiny pores, which open and close, absorbing and excreting a wide variety of substances such as oil and sweat. Historically, the "pore" has been echoed in soft material form in the form of the ubiquitous sponge. For example, the Ancient Greeks conceived the use of sea sponges for domestic, medical, and artistic applications.[18] Moreover, Hippocrates notes a parallel to the human anatomy whereby the lungs, spleen, and breast are associated with the distinctive texture of the sponge (Voultsiadou 2007). A more recent material science invention, the "Oleo" sponge (Barry et al. 2017), holds a power to both absorb and release mass quantities of liquids for final applications such as large-scale oil spills.

Thus, the characteristics of the skin's surface provide the building blocks for this series of material probes. The "Skin Series" experiments (Figure 11.6) further explore silicon as tactile skin structures through embedding yarns, casting textures, and encapsulating fibers. Rather than a direct mental conversion of a finalized "wearable technology" artifact into a physical form, this hands-on engagement with silicon began as a series of experimental iterations. The material probes served as "hosts for thought," as part of the "Re/Construction: Embodied Making" stage outlined at the end of this chapter in "The Soft Programmable Material Toolbox." Here, the basic recipe is the same, and compares, for example,

Figure 11.5 "The Awakening of Insects Collection," Polymer Opal stretch-reactive material. Rainbow Winters in collaboration with NanoPhotonics Centre, Cambridge University. Exhibited at National Museum of Taiwan, 2017. Photo credit: Cereinyn Ord, 2013.

to a classic sponge cake made of flour, sugar, eggs, and butter—or in our case silicon, molds, flock, and tubing. Yet it is only through working *through* material— unsuccessful recipes, adaptations, and reappropriating ingredients—that the design process can evolve to create more complex concepts.

Reflecting on the activity of making, the encapsulated fleshy flock fibers (Figure 11.6) felt warm, grainy, and lifelike to touch. The cast proximity-sensitive[19] pneumatic surface texture also invited touch, thus provoking speculation on potential tactile communication abilities.

In our experiments, the ingredients exhibited in Figure 11.4 such as silicon (Ecoflex-30)[20] begin as a demi-fluid in mucilaginous or gooey form acting as a "carrier"—suspending solid particle matter (Figure 11.7) and absorbing pigments which, in turn, can manipulate the physical properties. As the silicon

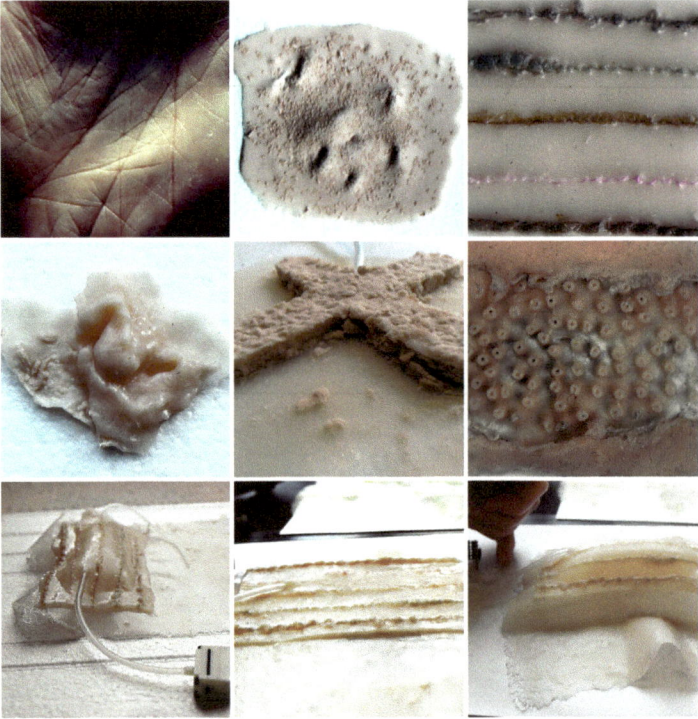

Figure 11.6 Amy Winters, "Skin Series": (top left to right) author's palm; tactile "flock" surface; yarn embedded silicon; (middle) dripped silicon texture and fiber encapsulation; pneumatic actuator; cast texture; (bottom) 3V DC mini air pump and lithium battery test; proximity-sensitive pneumatic surface texture (before activation); proximity-sensitive pneumatic surface texture. Image © Amy Winters 2016.

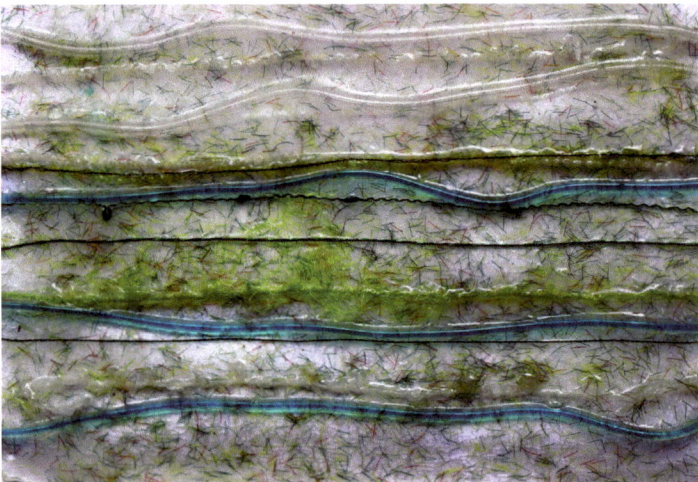

Figure 11.7 Amy Winters, "Material Fluidics," translocation of fluids through soft materials. Final sample encapsulating flock, yarns, and silicon tubing suspended in silicon. Image © Amy Winters 2016.

begins to air cure at a room temperature of 23°C, it solidifies into a stretchable material, yet it can still soak up fiber deposits rendering the surface as textured (Figure 11.7). In addition, soft silicon tubing 2 mm outside diameter (Figure 11.7) can be encapsulated and layered onto the silicon composite alongside textured yarns, creating slight imperfections giving the resulting substrate an organic quality.

Reminiscent of lichen, moss, or algae on a waterbed, the fabric starts to convey a narrative as the translocation of liquids engages with several of our senses. The silicon composite material appears moist and slippery and as the sound-activated,[21] blue-tinted water drizzles through the surface, this feeling of tactility is stimulated through our visual sense. Tactile feedback could be further enhanced through the water temperature feedback—cool (icy and frozen) or warm (saturated and humid).

Unconventional microfluidics

"Unconventional" microfluidics (Nawaz et al. 2013) locates microfluidics into new contexts, such as robotics and electronics. Our design method is adapted from a microfluidics production process by biochemists Saggiomo and Velders (2015).[22] Designers may find this approach particularly suits their requirements as prototypes can be built quickly through Makerspace DIY facilities which are both low cost and cleanroom free (Winters 2017).

Aligned with the initial principle of the "actuated elastomer channels and chambers," shown in Figure 11.1, the stretchable microfluidics developed through this research are reflective of the human circulatory system. These microstructures are inherently transparent, and fluids can be directed and manipulated inside the material.

In Figure 11.8, the 3D-printed ABS[23] pattern is placed inside a 90 mm petri dish, a smidge of 0.5 mm nylon flesh-colored flock (usually used in prosthetic makeup) is folded into the soft silicon mixture (Ecoflex 00-30) and poured into the petri dish. Once aired cured at 23°C for four hours, the ABS scaffold is dissolved in an acetone bath for twenty-four hours to reveal a hollow scaffold encapsulated within the silicon.

Adapting the ABS scaffold design produces various morphologies. A standard off-the-shelf 3D printer, for instance, can fabricate a microfluidic scaffold in any shape or pattern required. Therefore, in addition to flat and soft moldable surfaces (Figure 11.8), it is also possible to build 3D microfluidic structures (Figure 11.9) presenting further opportunities to develop microfluidic yarns,

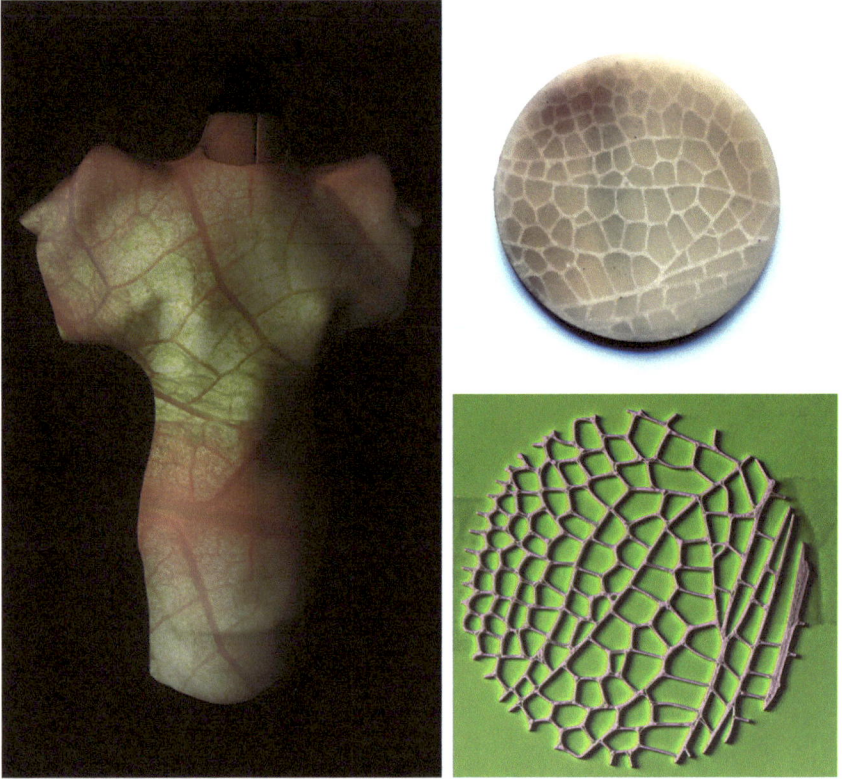

Figure 11.8 Amy Winters, "Stretchable Microfluidic Vein Pattern Sample."
Microfluidic dress visualization, stretchable microfluidic vein sample, and 3D-printed
scaffold. © Amy Winters 2017.

knots, or even more complex knitted and woven constructions. Textile methods
may lead, therefore, toward "wearable robotics" that move beyond the function-
led exoskeletons and both challenge and offer a broader understanding of what
a robot may be. The prototypes shown in Figures 11.8 and 11.9 propose an
unsettling aesthetic, located between human and machine, suggesting an idea of
how the body could transcend its biological constraints.

Moreover, stretchable microfluidic structures have the potential to facilitate a
whole repertoire of interactive and expressive interactions. Six programmable
"liquid" categories are identified: currents,[24] opacity,[25] viscosity,[26] separation,[27]
color change,[28] and iridescence.[29] These features could, in turn, create visual and
tactile opportunities for aesthetic (fashion), functional (intelligent mobility),
and communicative (virtual reality) purposes. Color change and opacity could,
for example, craft dramatic optical effects such as bleeding, dripping, melting,

Figure 11.9 Amy Winters, "Microfluidic Patterning": (clockwise from left) Wearable microfluidic shoulder-piece 3D stretchable microfluidic, tangerine pigment, and surface structure in silicon. © Amy Winters 2017.

and dissolving a dress to externalize or amplify self-expression by, for example, releasing "tears." Viscosity, currents, and separation might be turned into alternative tactile expressions such as breathing, shivering, and cracking, thereby potentially communicating or translating subjective user sensations.

Applications may include intelligent mobility from the functional; body "posture-responsive" actuating car seats to the more speculative, such as environmentally sensitive "mobility skins" where the transport mechanism shell transforms in shape triggered by temperature, moisture, light, or wind-speed pressure. Moreover, could these rich material possibilities be harnessed toward the future of virtual reality (VR)? The body is driving a new wave of artificial reality, VR experiences, tapping into the body's own movements to make immersive experiences feel more natural. Drawing on Lanier's concept of "post-symbolic" communication (Lanier 2011: 190) wearable, programmable microfluidics have the potential to facilitate new languages via nonverbal communication—one example is through the simulation of "synthetic sensations" that enhance the physical experience of the body.

Further, linking back to our discussion on "Liquid Rhythm" earlier, Häkkilä and Colley (2016) have conceptualized a tactile interaction experience suggesting that viscosity can manipulate how a liquid "feels" (34:3). In this manner, "friction or slowness in the interaction" can be choreographed, creating novel associations such as "difficulty or resistance" (ibid.). The prototypes shown in Figure 11.9 interface directly with the body. The movements of the fluid through the channels can activate thermal and physical stimulation on the skin. When cold liquids are introduced, for example, the body evaporates heat to create a "wet" sensation.

Thus, as Rubio-Tamayo, Barrio, and García (2017) suggest, the next stage of VR may include how we can experience the sensations and subjective perceptions of both humans and animals.

The soft programmable material toolbox

This research aims to understand the concrete, felt, and interpretative experience of a creative textile design researcher who is working within the domain of Material Robotics, traditionally led by scientific expertise. However, these tools are also transferable, to a broader range of hybrid collaborations, for example, synthetic biology and additive printing.

Based on the research undertaken and examples discussed above, the research methods, or "tools", can be distilled into four stages—a methodology for other researchers to follow: Experiential Understanding, De/Construction, Re/Construction, and Definition.

- **Experiential Understanding: Learning through experience**—At this stage, mood boards and sketchbooks offer a fluid approach to start devising material concepts, employing a subjective design process of contextual and first-hand references—an observation of direct experience that keeps the designer embodied; thereby enhancing a phenomenological approach to the development of technology. Additionally, time-based bricolage methods can assist at this stage as a form of visual and tactile prototyping. These can materialize as color palettes, textures, storyboards, and short films to capture interactions and narratives.
- **De/Construction: Reverse engineering**—The next step is characterized by a close analysis and deconstruction of a soft material development. This approach of reverse engineering considers analytically the procedures of how a "technology case study" is assembled, initially working backward to

discover how the underlying technology is constructed. To demonstrate this, earlier in the chapter we followed a fabrication process toward devising a microfluidic system (Saggiomo and Velders 2015). This particular approach was chosen because it could be built relatively cheaply and without laboratory facilities. Once the basic recipe is understood in an accessible language, the ingredients can be exchanged.

- **Re/Construction: Embodied making**—The next stage following the technical analysis is the designer's interpretation of that innovation, which is the manifestation of "embodied material thinking," a direct, personal, and visceral experience with material during hands-on experiments underpinned by a synthesis of technical knowledge. Once the designer holds an elementary understanding of how their chosen "material system" could be constructed, they are in a position to adapt their recipe working directly through the material, immersing concepts from the mood board into their practice. The basic recipe can be reinterpreted with the addition and substitution of ingredients from a bank of tacit knowledge. These may include numerous subjective translations of the recipe for either applicative or speculative interpretations.

- **Definition: Explicitly outline the new outcome**—The final stage is to outline the newfound outcome into an explicit and reproducible format. Once this tacit knowledge is documented through reflective practice, the recipe can be rewritten using exact specifications, thus recognized as a form of codified knowledge.[30]

While it may be suggested that DIY maker-culture (Dougherty 2012) can be seen as the pursuit of the dilettante, it could also be more strongly argued that this culture and method of learning can form part of an iterative design model for professional and commercial practice—releasing a prototype range of abilities within the designer. Further, the form of "material hacking" applied in this experimental research is one in which, by grasping the medium of technology through experiential knowledge, we can allow a more formal understanding of the decoding of scientific papers and principles.

As designers build composites in the resin studio, reformulate dyes, and grow their own synthetic biomaterials, insights are facilitated which would usually remain tacit. Moreover, how can these new hybrid processes in the creation of innovative textiles affect not only the aesthetic properties of the final product, this being in fashion, interiors, or future mobility but its functionality and distinctive interactive qualities? In this way, this chapter has advocated that a proficiency to amalgamate and design with multiple material properties, both active and passive, can offer a unique contribution to the development of novel, soft computational interfaces.

In fashioning the future body, material-driven interactions may be the creative catalyst to push beyond utilitarian dimensions into new categories of immersive experiences in virtual reality, intelligent mobility, and fashion.

Notes

1 Chemicals in food need to be transported in a liquid medium to be detected by taste receptors.

2 When the body is heated, but also triggered via emotions in the palms, soles, and armpits.

3 This study is positioned within the context of "design thinking" as an explorative approach that serves as a point of departure to the user-led design methodologies of industrial design engineering.

4 The philosopher Maurice Merleau-Ponty's (1962) embodiment theories offer an alternative to René Descartes' dualistic division between mind and body.

5 Polanyi's (2009) premise of tacit knowledge offers informed "hunches" as specific and embodied ways of knowing. Tacit knowledge is interpreted through reflection and analysis whereby the maker's subjectivity became an essential component of this research.

6 CES is a global consumer electronics show that typically displays new electronic products and the latest developments in technology. The author showcased wearable technology under "Rainbow Winters" at CES 2014. At the trade show, the human body was often referred to by the press, exhibitors, and industry insiders as "body real estate."

7 Actuators are mechanisms that convert stored energy into motion through a control signal. Traditional mechanical actuators are, for example, driven by wheels, pulleys, and chains. Soft actuators include pneumatic and hydraulic structures, electroactive polymers (EAPs), and stimuli-responsive polymers (SRPs) such as shape memory polymers and pH/thermally responsive hydrogels.

8 Air is pumped through the inner channels and chambers to bend and twist the soft bodies. The microcontroller and sensors can further control and program this air through inflation and deflation. This development is part of the Soft Robotics Toolkit, an open-source platform for expanding soft robotics (Holland et al. 2014).

9 Polymers that change dimensions, shapes, or volumes triggered by a strong electric field.

10 Shape memory polymers, stimulated by external activators such as heat, can return to a preprogrammed shape.

11 The manipulation and control of fluids through networks of channels.

12 Nylon coil actuators are thermally/electrically activated and change shape in response to temperature (Haines et al. 2014).

13 An example of "digital crafting" by textile designer-researchers is illustrated by Taylor and Robertson (2014). Their "Digital Lace" project combined their respective expertise in constructive (fiber-optics) and printed textiles (thermochromic inks) to develop a digitally controllable material and visual outcome.

14 Klein collaborated with chemical manufacturer Rhône-Poulenc to source a particular polymer binder; this "carrier" could hold the intensity of an unstable ultramarine pigment.

15 A visual representation of a user interface.

16 A fictional character created to epitomize a specific end-user type.

17 The film can be applied to a flexible substrate using a bonding layer such as thermoplastic polyurethane (TPU) with a standard heat-press.

18 As documented through records in their medical works.

19 Gesture sensor APDS-9960.

20 Ecoflex is a platinum-catalyzed extremely soft silicone rubber.

21 Sound sensor, electret microphone BOB-09964.

22 The expanded fabrication process is outlined in the "Water Dress" prototype, Winters (2017).

23 Acrylonitrile Butadiene Styrene (ABS) See: https://www.sculpteo.com/en/glossary/abs-definition/.

24 Currents refer to the directed movement of liquids. These could be generated and programmed by specific pump pressure and the direction of channels.

25 Opacity relates to how translucent or transparent the fluidic display or surface might be. Inks and dyes here might allow light to pass through.

26 Viscosity is understood as the "thickness" of a liquid. Honey is more viscous than water, for instance, because it has a high flow resistance.

27 Separation is used here to define immiscible liquids. These liquids are incapable of being mixed, one such example being oil and water.

28 Rapid or slow color changes could be formed by using two separate colors of ink and dyes in the microfluidic system.

29 Iridescence describes a surface which gradually changes color created by diffraction of light. Examples could include oil slicks and soap bubbles. In the context of programmable fluidics, this could be iridescent ink or dye.

30 Patents are a form of propositional and codified knowledge (Lee 2012), and "know-how" is not currently patentable, yet patents often need the know-how of the inventor to become operational.

References

Bachelard, G. (1983) *Water and Dreams: An Essay on the Imagination of Matter*, Dallas, TX: Pegasus Foundation.

Barry, E., Mane, A. U., Libera, J. A., Elam, J. W., and Darling, S. B. (2017) "Advanced Oil Sorbents Using Sequential Infiltration Synthesis," *Journal of Materials Chemistry A*, 5(6): 2929–35.

Dewey, J. (2005) *Art as Experience*, New York: Penguin.

Döring, T., Sylvester, A., and Schmidt, A. (2013) "A Design Space for Ephemeral User Interfaces," *Proceedings of the 7th International Conference on Tangible, Embedded and Embodied Interaction—TEI '13*, 75–82, New York: ACM.

Dougherty, D. (2012) "The Maker Movement," *Innovations: Technology, Governance, Globalization*, 7(3): 11–14.

Dvorak, J. L. (2008) *Moving Wearables into the Mainstream: Taming the Borg*, New York: Springer.

Fernaeus, Y., Vallgårda, A., Tharakan, M. J., and Lundström, A. (2012) "Touch and Feel Soft Hardware," *Proceedings of the Sixth International Conference on Tangible, Embedded and Embodied Interaction—TEI '12*, 359–62, New York: ACM.

Ftc.com.tw (2018) *FTC-SeaCell Yarn*. Available online: https://web.archive.org/web/20180901100741/http://www.ftc.com.tw/prod_bodytek_seacell01e.htm (accessed August 21, 2019).

Haines, C. S., Lima, M. D., Li, N., Spinks, G. M., Foroughi, J., Madden, J. D. W., Kim, S. H., Fang, S., Jung de Andrade, M. J., Göktepe, F., Göktepe, O., Mirvakili, S. M., Naficy, S., Lepró, X., Oh, J., Kozlov, M. E., Kim, S. J., Xu, X., Swedlove, B. J., Wallace, G. G., and Baughman, R. H. (2014) "Artificial Muscles from Fishing Line and Sewing Thread," *Science*, 343(6173): 868–72.

Häkkilä, J. and Colley, A. (2016) "Towards a Design Space for Liquid User Interfaces," *Proceedings of the 9th Nordic Conference on Human–Computer Interaction—NordiCHI '16*, art. 34, New York: ACM.

Holland, D., Park, E. J., Polygerinos, P., Bennett, G. J., and Walsh, C. J. (2014) "The Soft Robotics Toolkit: Shared Resources for Research and Design," *Soft Robotics*, 1(3): 224–30.

Igoe, E. (2010) "The Tacit-Turn: Textile Design in Design Research," *Duck Journal for Research in Textiles and Textile Design*, 1: 1–11.

Igoe, E. (2013) "In Textasis: Matrixial Narratives of Textile Design," unpublished doctoral thesis, Royal College of Art, London, UK.

Ingold, T. (2010) "The Textility of Making," *Cambridge Journal of Economics*, 34(1): 91–102.

Ingold, T. (2013) *Making: Anthropology, Archaeology, Art and Architecture*, Abingdon: Routledge.

Klemmer, S. R., Hartmann, B., and Takayama, L. (2006) "How Bodies Matter: Five Themes for Interaction Design," *Proceedings of the 6th ACM Conference on Designing Interactive systems—DIS '06*, 140–9, New York: ACM.

Lanier, J. (2011) *You Are Not a Gadget*, London: Penguin Books.

Lee, P. (2012) "Transcending the Tacit Dimension: Patents, Relationships, and Organizational Integration in Technology Transfer," *California Law Review*, 100(6): 1503–72.

Lévi-Strauss, C. (1962) *The Savage Mind*, Chicago, IL: University of Chicago Press.

Merleau-Ponty, M. (1962) *The Phenomenology of Perception*, trans. C. Smith, London: Routledge.

Nawaz, A. A., Mao, X., Stratton, Z. S., and Huang, T. J. (2013) "Unconventional Microfluidics: Expanding the Discipline," *Lab on a Chip*, 13(8): 1457–63.

Pelcor Store (2018) "PELCOR—The Genuine Cork Skin." Available online: https://www.pelcor.pt (accessed September 20, 2018).

Piñatex (2018) "Piñatex." Available online: https://www.ananas-anam.com (accessed September 20, 2018).

Polanyi, M. (2009) *The Tacit Dimension*, Chicago, IL: University of Chicago Press.

Robles, E. and Wiberg, M. (2010) "Texturing the 'Material Turn' in Interaction Design," *Proceedings of the Fourth International Conference on Tangible, Embedded, and Embodied Interaction—TEI '10*, 137–44, New York: ACM.

Rozendaal, M. C., Heidingsfelder, M. L., and Kupper, F. (2016) "Exploring Embodied Speculation in Participatory Design and Innovation," *Proceedings of the 14th Participatory Design Conference on Short Papers, Interactive Exhibitions, Workshops—PDC '16*, 100–2, New York: ACM.

Rubio-Tamayo, J., Barrio, M. G., and García, F. G. (2017) "Immersive Environments and Virtual Reality: Systematic Review and Advances in Communication, Interaction and Simulation," *Multimodal Technologies and Interaction*, 1(4): 21.

Rudomin, I., Diaz, M., Hernández, B., and Rivera, D. (2005) "Water, Temperature and Proximity Sensing for a Mixed Reality Art Installation," *Lecture Notes in Computer Science*, 3814: 155–63.

Rus, D. and Tolley, M. T. (2015) "Design, Fabrication and Control of Soft Robots," *Nature*, 521: 467–75.

Saggiomo, V. and Velders, A. H. (2015) "Simple 3D Printed Scaffold-Removal Method for the Fabrication of Intricate Microfluidic Devices," *Advanced Science*, 2(9): 1500125.

Schön, D. A. (1983) *The Reflective Practitioner: How Professionals Think in Action*, New York: Basic Books.

Snell, H. (2013) "Water," in A. Müller-Schöll and R. Baur (eds.), *Manuscript*, Basel: Birkhäuser.

Taylor, S. and Robertson, S. (2014) "Digital Lace: A Collision of Responsive Technologies," in *Proceedings of the 18th International Symposium on Wearable Computers—ISWC 14*, 93–7, New York: ACM.

Toomey, A. and Kapsali, V. (2014) "D-STEM: A Design Led Approach to STEM Innovation," *A Matter of Design: Making Society through Science and Technology: Proceedings of the 5th STS Italia Conference*, 425–38, Milan: STS Italia Publishing.

Vallgårda, A. and Redström, J. (2007) "Computational Composites," *Proceedings of the SIGCHI Conference on Human Factors in Computing Systems—CHI '07*, 513–22, New York: ACM.

Vigneshwara, M. (2018) "The Screaming Sun: Choreographing Synesthesia," *Proceedings of the Twelfth International Conference on Tangible, Embedded, and Embodied Interaction—TEI '18*, 562–6, New York: ACM.

Voultsiadou, E. (2007) "Sponges: An Historical Survey of Their Knowledge in Greek Antiquity," *Journal of the Marine Biological Association of the United Kingdom*, 87(6): 1757–63.

Winkler, C., Steimle, J., and Maes, P. (2013) "MetaSolid: On Flexibility and Rigidity in Future User Interfaces," *CHI '13 Extended Abstracts on Human Factors in Computing Systems—CHI EA '13*, 2885–6, New York: ACM.

Winters, A. (2016) "Building a Soft Machine: New Modes of Expressive Surfaces," *Design, User Experience, and Usability: Technological Contexts, DUXU 2016—Lecture Notes in Computer Science, Vol. 9748*, 401–13, Cham: Springer.

Winters, A. (2017) "Wearable Rhythms: Materials in Play," *Design, User Experience, and Usability: Designing Pleasurable Experiences, DUXU 2017—Lecture Notes in Computer Science, Vol. 10289*, 737–46, Cham: Springer.

Zhao, Q., Finlayson, C. E., Snoswell, D. R. E., Haines, A., Schäfer, C., Spahn, P., Hellmann, G. P., Petukhov, A. V., Herrmann, L., Burdet, P., Midgley, P. A., Butler, S., Mackley, M., Guo, Q., and Baumberg, J. J. (2016) "Large-Scale Ordering of Nanoparticles Using Viscoelastic Shear Processing," *Nature Communications*, 7: art. 11661.

12

The Genetics Gym

Adam Peacock

Introduction: Speculating on the design of the future body

In this chapter, I will discuss my research practice as a commercial-academic design practitioner, through my studio's experimental lens, The Validation Junky and its most recent creative output, The Genetics Gym. I established The Validation Junky in 2013 while studying MA Design Interactions at the Royal College of Art (RCA) under Anthony Dunne and Fiona Raby, widely acknowledged as the founders of Speculative Design (Dunne and Raby 2013). Speculative Design (SD) is a response to the effects of computational design, or of applied technology within society. Most traditional design methodologies might ask, "What can we do with technology?," SD reframes designed problems with greater philosophical emphasis on, "What do we want (or need) from technology?" in order to ask the questions necessary to help uncover and understand the future needs of society. As Dunne and Raby (2013: 2) state, "We need to dream new dreams for the twenty-first century as those of the twentieth century rapidly fade."

Within the practice of SD, the output of a project is not necessarily something that fits within a commercial context. The strength of SD is to develop creative strategies that leverage emotive responses to help reframe contemporary design problems. Based on this premise, I believe that the role of art and design holds within it a responsibility to not only talk about the type of future we want to live in, but to guide discussions on the boundary between utopia and dystopia. This is increasingly important as we encounter the positives and negatives arising from the application of technologies such as the internet, synthetic biology, genetic engineering, and Artificial Intelligence (AI). Designers have a critical, responsible role to play in developing the creative potential of new technology, while considering its effect through everyday use and impact on society through commodification by multinational corporations.

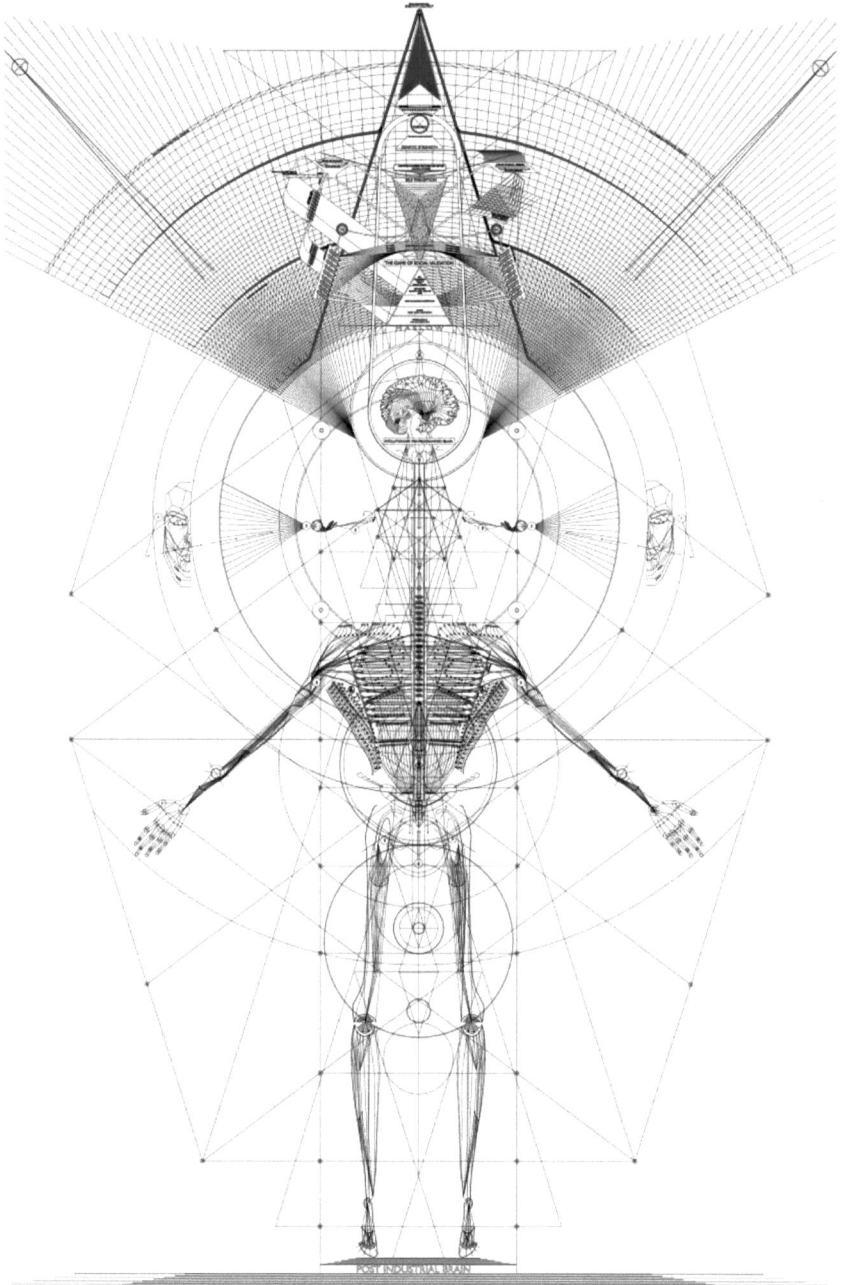

Figure 12.1 Adam Peacock, "Brain–Body–Society," The Validation Junky. Image © Adam Peacock 2014.

We believe that by speculating more, at all levels of society, and exploring alternative scenarios, reality will become more malleable and, although the future cannot be predicted, we can help set in place today factors that will increase the probability of more desirable futures happening (Dunne and Raby 2013: 2).

In my practice, speculative thinking started at architecture school, then at the Royal College of Art, London (RCA), where I used the opportunity to study by asking, "What does the world need from a relevant designer today?" As Bratton states, "Some may even conclude that the job of Design in the 21st century is to undo (much of) the Design of the 20th" (Bratton 2016).[1]

The Validation Junky

Speculative design facilitates the consideration that behind every object we use, and beyond a basic level of utility, an aesthetic function exists to illustrate its wearer or user, as defined in evolutionary biology, as "signaling theory" (Cronk 2005). I wanted a segment of my studio to operate as a form of "permission" and creative, experimental platform to investigate connections between consumer psychology, technology, and designed objects.

The "validation junky" is a phrase used by American clinical psychologist Alan Downs' book, *The Velvet Rage* (2012). In the book, Downs describes the psychology of gay men, "growing up gay in a straight world," and the associated deep-rooted anxiety of seeking validation through family and society through every turn in their consumer behavior. Downs' connection between anxiety and consumption was in some ways a eureka moment, and perhaps even explained many of my own motivations as to why I wanted to become a designer in the first place: "By the time the gay boy becomes a man, he is well practiced in the art of achieving validation for his actions that may be praiseworthy, but are inauthentic to him. He is, so to speak, a validation junky" (Downs 2012: 31).

This insight helped to contextualize how the objects, images, and brands that we choose to illustrate ourselves become embedded within an individual's own anxieties, complexities, and tensions, affecting consumption behaviors and taste. Consequently, The Validation Junky was borrowed as a title for my studio's critical lens, the outcomes of which continually shift to accommodate evolving, complex needs of the consumer, and the challenges faced when designing technology. Today, The Validation Junky collaborates with galleries, research labs, brands, and designers on projects that focus on technology and technology-driven sociocultural issues.

Underpinnings of The Genetics Gym

The Genetics Gym project originated as an investigation during my Masters study at the RCA, where two contrasting cultures, or perceptions of success influenced my design direction. First, the critical design education I was receiving on MA Design Interactions encouraged the questioning of each stage of decision making within what is designed, created, purchased, and worn. This contrasted with the image-led dynamics present within contemporary gay and queer culture, which is heavily guided by the internet as a tool for interaction. The use of the internet combined with self-photography celebrates the illustration of testosterone and apparent masculinity, using the given metrics embedded within the software to locate, select, and validate each other.

"Other gay men seek validation through sexual conquest and adoration. If this is you, you'll spend most of your spare time at the gym, building what you believe is the body that will one day earn you enough adoration to satisfy your craving for it" (Downs 2012: 32).

The Genetics Gym began with the question "Why do gay guys have such great bodies?" More specifically, I wanted to understand why the motivations toward gym use, bodybuilding, steroid use, and lean protein consumption exists at such scale within gay male culture. I wanted to explore how the existing identity and aesthetic trends within queer culture outlined as the "clone and the development of a masculine stereotype" (Cole 2000: 94) of the twentieth century was now heightened by technology and social media platforms within the twenty-first century.

The investigation quickly evolved into a series of subquestions not limited to queer culture, and relating to the role of the internet and social media on perceptions of male and female beauty, culminating in: "How will the continued use of digital media replace human interactions with a new system of technology-driven validation?" and ultimately "What can we improve in the way that we design technologies for human interaction by more fully understanding the way that the human brain perceives beauty and genetic strength?"

These questions laid the foundations of a wider topic, by using insights into queer culture as a way into researching how the internet, and more broadly designed technologies, are affecting consumer choices and perceptions of identity.

Fashion and genetics

What an evolutionary psychologist might term "strong genes," we call sexiness or appeal (Dawkins 1976). When a person looks at someone and finds them "sexy" or "attractive," their brain is "telling them" that if they were to reproduce with that person, they would produce strong, healthy, well-balanced offspring.

"Symmetry and balance matter so much to us because their opposites—facial asymmetry and imbalance—are markers of diseases contracted either in the womb or in the early years of life, at a time when the greater part of the self is still being shaped" (de Botton 2012: 85).

Certain viewed imagery stimulates the brain's responses to proportions, mathematics, colors, and signals, operating the subconscious, hardwired perception of a "selfish gene" (Dawkins 1976). The physiological/chemical reaction involves the sending of serotonin and dopamine, a brain format sugar or nectar, into the body system in calculated response to visuals, specific to the individual. Beyond the remit of viewing images online (Buss 1989), physical interactions lead to more complex sensorial interactions stimulated by pheromones, voice resonance, scent, and personality (Zuckerman, Miyake, and Hodgins 1991). However, this investigation observes only photographic-based visual communication as found within online interaction platforms such as YouTube, Instagram, Facebook, Tinder, or Grindr. The project therefore explores the motivation behind self-initiated body design, by seeking to understand more about an individual's subconscious perception of genetics, or genetic strength.

Genetics and cybernetics

The concept of quantifying the brain's perception of genetic strength becomes particularly compelling when we begin to imagine how designers might translate Dawkins' theory of genetic strength into software linked to digital photography, in the realm of cybernetics[2] (Wiener 1948). If we were able to program a machine to read the conditions that affect perceptions of genetic strength and frame the interaction within the understanding of genetic compatibility, we might program a machine to identify something attractive, compelling, or "sexy." This development would ultimately depend upon how the data was accrued and how the software was designed, and by whom. However, the underlying principle of learning more about how the human brain reads beauty on-screen in the era of online affirmation is what inspired the Genetics Gym inquiry to explore how we might enhance the way we coexist with designed technology. This work links to other research into the impact of technology-driven social behavior, from framing forecasts in fashion, design, marketing, and political trends through a blend of design, psychology, branding, and computer science.[3]

Epigenetics and body design

In 2014, it was widely reported that there had been a "breakthrough" alternative to chemotherapy in cancer treatment. The development of a specific genetic technology called epigenetics could potentially lead to "turning off" the cancer cells that had been "turned on" through environmental triggers (Saini 2014). This development made me question—what would happen if this technology, once developed to scale became a tangible commodity, harnessed by pharmaceutical corporations and packaged within mass-produced cosmetic consumer products? What would be the ethical implications in the future, if we could buy a shampoo, cream, or pill that over time would fine-tune our genes? This could be appropriate and potentially exciting as a method to change hair from straight to wavy—but what if we, as consumers, had the ability to edit the expression of other genetically inherited characteristics such as our sexualities, IQ levels, or certain racial characteristics such as eye shape and skin color?

Scoping The Genetics Gym

"It is not the strongest of species that survives, nor the most intelligent that survives. It is the one that is most adaptable to change."

Megginson 1963: 4, summarizing Charles Darwin

In 2016, I was awarded the Design Residency at the Fashion Space Gallery at London College of Fashion (LCF).[4] The open brief was "to work collaboratively bringing together the expertise of multidisciplinary individuals working within the world of design, technology, science and politics to produce visionary and poignant new work." I set out a framework over the year-long residency to research and develop the project focused on, "What would you do if you had the ability to design yourself in any way imaginable with epigenetic, or (still to be invented) genetic technology." This was not really a question of what genetic technology is capable of, but a philosophical question relating to where we want designed technologies to lead us, how the internet is currently affecting personal, physical aspirations and consumption behavior, and how these observations may impact the way we design technology for the future. This design inquiry builds on Dunne and Raby's design manifesto, in asking whether design today should "Change us to the suit the world," or "Change the world to suit us" (Dunne and Raby 2013: vii).

Project strategy

My core aim was to develop a methodology toward uncovering how the internet and image-based communication is affecting us psychologically, socially, and culturally. The project's objectives lie within its ability to give access to a multilayered philosophical discussion on the role of image-based technology development through the combined lenses of genetics, philosophy, cybernetics, branding/communication, and fashion design.

A component of the research phase was a research symposium entitled "Designing Sex" devised as an experimental stitching together of the different specialisms and observations that had been explored within the initial scoping of the project.

"Designing Sex" Symposium

Six expert panelists were invited to give ten-minute presentations of their research, to tell the story of a hypothetical Genetics Gym by describing how (and why) social observation on the effects of photographic digital technologies, an awareness of genetic and biomedical sciences and the human perception of attractiveness might culminate in a viable future product, realized through a cybernetic system.

Duncan Stephenson, Director of External Affairs at the Royal Society for Public Health, spoke on body talk, levels of body satisfaction, and influences on body image, noting weight stigmatization, disordered relationships with food, and health sacrificed for appearance noting, "one in seven gay men living in London would be happy to give up ten years of their life for their perfect body, now."[5]

Dr. Joyce Harper, Professor in Human Genetics and Embryology at University College, London (UCL), spoke on how to make a human using genetic technology, presenting an overview on reproductive genetics through preconception, pre-implantation, and prenatal and postnatal genetic testing. Harper concluded by outlining potential future procreation via reproduction without sex, reproductive and genetic classism, and gene editing.

Dr. Helen C. O'Neill, head of MSc. Women's Health and Fertility at UCL, presented "Designing the Body from Inside Out." O'Neill spoke on evolution, survival of the fittest, genetic diversity, genetics and epigenetics, and what causes gene mutation, and discussed the interplay between fashion and the perception of genes noting "biological fashion evolves with wealth." She highlighted that many of the body aesthetics desirable in fashion models are bad for fertility, concluding that "Change *is* evolution."

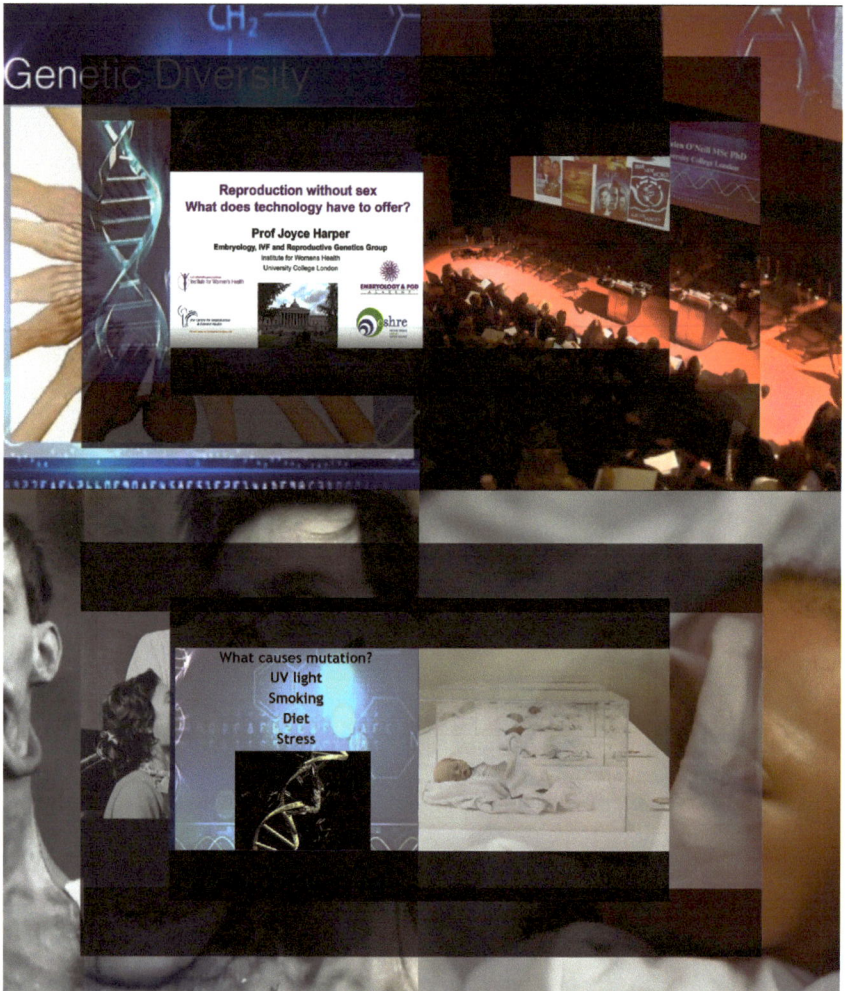

Figure 12.2 A composite image of the "Designing Sex" Symposium held at LCF, featuring presentations by Prof. Joyce Harper on "the future of applied genetic technology"; Dr. Helen C. O'Neill on "genetics and appeal," and Agi Haines on "designing babies with synthetic biology." Image © Adam Peacock 2016; displayed slides © Joyce Harper, Helen C. O'Neill, and Agi Haines.

Agi Haines, PhD student at the CogNovo Lab for Transtechnology Research, at Plymouth University, introduced the concept of surgical art and synthetic biology applied within speculative design. Haines presented a series of her works including a speculative range of edited human babies and organs that had been modified and biologically combined with different plant and animal genes to create enhanced functional abilities.

Dr. Barry M. Jones, consultant plastic and reconstructive surgeon and Hunterian Professor at the Royal College of Surgeons of England, spoke on how he might discuss what subjective beauty "is" and how he consults his patients to find out what "beauty" means and looks like to them.

Henrique Mathias, founder and programmer of threesome dating app Feeld, presented a brief history of internet dating from 1993 to the present day

Figure 12.3 Creative ideation by student participants from the Speculative Body Workshop: (clockwise from top left) Images by Siyang Meng, Jo Cope, and Voranida Rujekitnara. Composite image © Adam Peacock 2017.

(2016). Mathias noted the cultural ramifications and differences between the early days of internet dating and communication, where imagery was not widely used and partner selection was based on written text within chat forums and profile names, to present internet dating, which relies heavily upon image-based communication as a form of selection. Mathias highlighted that image-based communication and trends toward both enhancing bodies with gym use, makeup, or personal aesthetics/characters (using Computer Graphics (CG) software and filters, etc.) to gain online traction, is limiting the "colorfulness of character" as found in both analogue "real world" interactions and early online dating.

The evening, a post-disciplinary experiment between specialisms, was summarized by a shared sense of urgency to continue with these explorative conversations and creative actions to highlight the potential realities of applying such technologies.

The Speculative Body Workshop

Following the symposium, a "Speculative Body Workshop" was hosted at the Digital Learning Lab at LCF, inviting MA students from London College of Fashion (LCF) and UCL, selected from portfolio submissions across the disciplines of Fashion Design, Psychology, and Genetics.[6] The workshop built on the insights gained from the "Designing Sex" symposium, asking "What could you do if you had the ability to design yourself?" and "Why do we aspire to be anything other than who we currently are?" The primary aim of the design workshop was devised to both share with, and learn from an array of practitioners and experts, and to question my own preconceived ideas of how someone might "want" to redesign their body if they had the opportunity to change it.

The group observed the mathematical principles of the golden ratio 1.618 (phi/φ), the Fibonacci sequence, the waist-to-hip ratio of 0.7 and their combined relationships within observing genetic strength within subconscious image-based partner selection. The group noted a growing trend in celebrating biological or genetic differences among models within fashion publications, such as models Shaun Ross's[7] albinism and Winnie Harlow's[8] vitiligo and featured in *Vogue Italia* and *i-D Magazine*, with Ross modeling for Alexander McQueen and Givenchy.

The collaboration and discussion between disciplines raised uncomfortable parallels between the possibilities of editing of "the self" and issues found in *Vaught's Practical Character Reader*, such as: "an unreliable mother" defined by the prominence and formation of the rear of the head, highlighted for "men who would select wives who will make good mothers" (Vaught 1902: 25), and the differentiation between an "ambitious ear" and the "ear of the uncultivated" or the "ear of a selfish and tenacious of life" (Vaught 1902: 133). The group noted how pertinent it was that the validation and success embedded within photographic communication was, somewhat uncomfortably, leading us back to the research of the 1940s eugenics movement;[9] and highlighted the importance attached to ongoing debate to critique technology's impact on today's society.

Ideas raised in the workshop that were taken forward into the strategic development of the five characters in the Genetics Gym project included: altering genetic traits to "design" visual synesthesia (a perceptual phenomenon affecting how a person sees light), colour, and silhouettes, to designing bodies and faces that heightened the expression of neoteny[10]—larger features, such as eyes and noses close together in proportion to the head, identified as "cute" in babies or puppies.

Genetics and consumer culture

"The uses and abuses of genetic tests open a backdoor to eugenics."

Holzman 1991: 244

In progressing the practice, I was faced with the challenge of establishing a strategy encompassing the social and cultural insights and issues, raised in the "Designing Sex" symposium and Speculative Body workshop. The primary concern was an ethical one—that the project might be misinterpreted as a literal design proposal, rather than a conceptual idea formed to critique technology-driven consumer culture and to understand more about how internet-enabled interactions are affecting our sense of identity. Establishing an approach to ensure that the project's intent would be "read" accurately by a broad audience became paramount both strategically and artistically.

Working with the genetics team from UCL was helpful in terms of discussing and clarifying an ethical position, as follows. A geneticist would argue that it is important to understand the full breadth of what is possible within genetic technology, so that we can navigate the application and effect of such technologies carefully and with respect to the diversity and sustainability of humankind. Arguably, the best way to guide the journey of species-affecting technology is through open and wide discussion, observing, noting, and celebrating diverse perspectives upon where it should and could go next.

Perceptions of gene strength

Perceptions of what constitutes a "strong" or "weak" gene in a world where it is possible to use genetic engineering to design ourselves and our children differ between global, national, cultural, and individual contexts. Consideration of "difference" is critical within the scenario of programming a machine or AI to incorporate or act on perceptions of genetic strength. Taking homosexuality as an example, the debate is compelling when we consider that there is evidence of a series of genes associated with homosexuality (Sanders et al. 2015), and that, until 1973, homosexuality was considered a mental illness by the British Psychological Association (Butler, Moon, and Barker 2006), and that today, practicing homosexuality is still illegal in seventy-two countries (Duncan 2017). It could therefore be argued that in some cultures, this is a character trait with the potential to be "designed out." This is particularly alarming when we consider the claim that the first gene edited baby was born in China in 2018.[11]

The role of The Genetics Gym is not to support or dismiss any one view on how to define a strong or weak gene, but to adopt the position that there is a breadth of perspectives to consider as holistically as possible. However, if we were able to program a machine to read genetic semiotics within visuals, it would have to be programmed to account for a true representation of a range of ideologies. This, in observing the connection between genetic strength perception and consumption behaviors, would directly affect the type of products and brands we use to illustrate our aspirations.

To approach this consideration within consumption behavior, a matrix of "different perceptions of success" was developed graphically, to suggest a range of ideologies encompassing both left and right wing, progressive and traditional design sensibilities including Visionary and Populist on one axis, and Self-Centered and Community-Centered on the other.

Within this axiom, five "ideologies" were imagined as hypothetical brands, developed utilizing a brand development methodology of image-based publications used in marketing. The resulting brand ideologies, or "perceptions

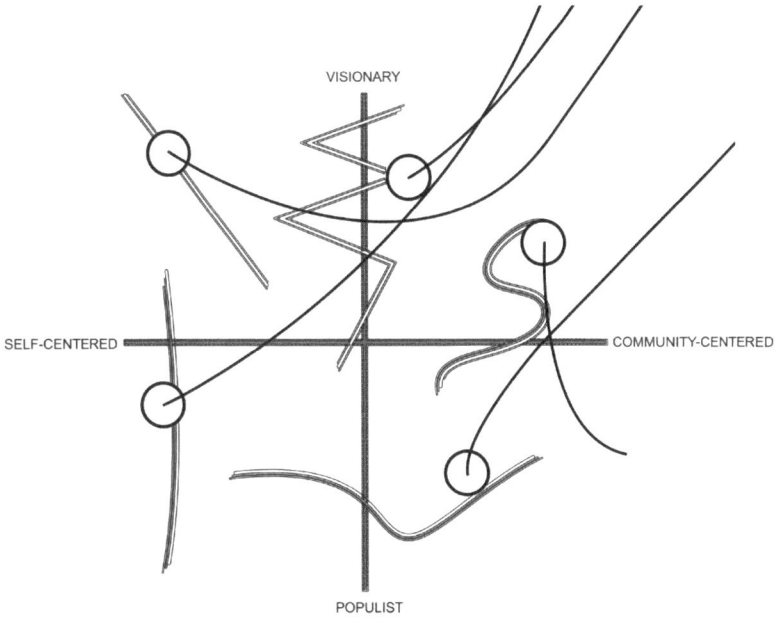

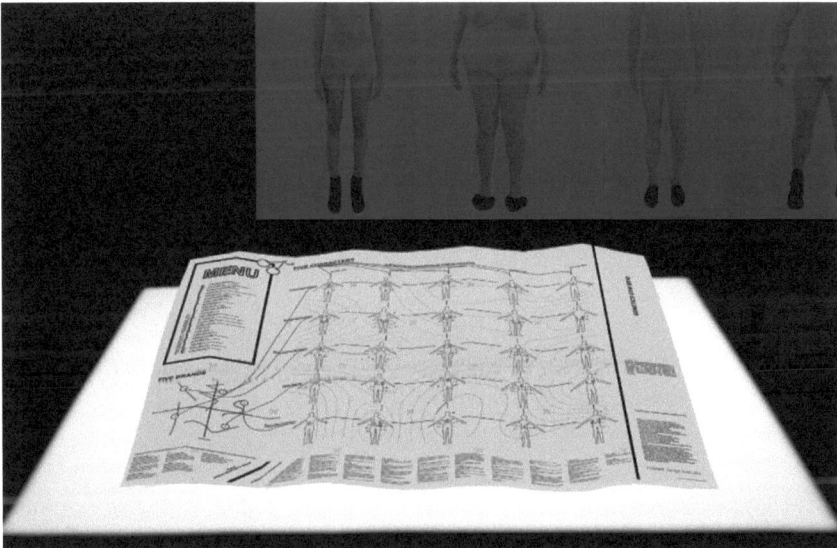

Figure 12.4 (top) Five brand outlines picked from two axes; (bottom) Research document showing brand outlines aligning with the five characters to create twenty-five portraits, including the "menu" of genetic components required for the body-morphs situated within the gallery installation. Images © Adam Peacock 2017.

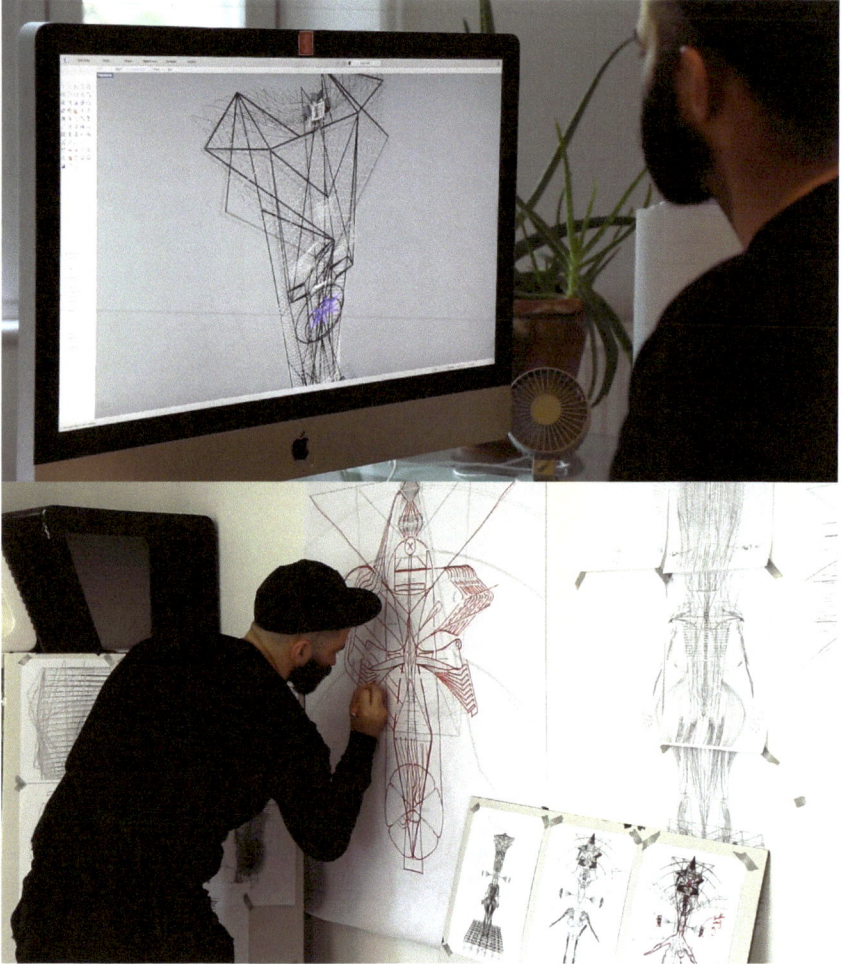

Figure 12.5 (top) Computer-drawn three-dimensional visualisation, imagining the mechanization of the human brain; (bottom) Illustration development as interplay between hand-drawn and computer-generated vector lines. Photographs John Duff. Image © Adam Peacock 2017.

of success" were named Self-Centered Populist, Manifesto-Visionaire, No-Substance-Visionaire, Basic-Pleaser, and Communo-Consumer, and formed the given consumption ideologies for the five characters to "change into." I took direct inspiration from Dunne and Raby's United Micro Kingdoms (UmK) project,[12] where they created four speculative characterizations and calculated fictions that allow us to look critically at contemporary society.

Project design and production

Taking the five brands imagined as different methods of approaching and interpreting consumer characteristics, it was my intention to develop five characters in their full complexity, imagining how each of them might interact and exhibit the five ideologies physically. Using different image-based methods (photography, film, graphic software, editing tools) I planned to illustrate the five characters in a ten-minute video, standing side by side, and morphing every two minutes in unison into each of the five brand ideologies. It would therefore be possible to observe how each character (with their own anxieties, tensions, and intricacies) would demonstrate the ideologies of the speculative brands. This would be achieved through interaction with each character's given genetics to illustrate "how and why" they would aspire to change themselves.

Illustration development

To illustrate the intricacies of different cognitive dispositions and sociocultural contexts of the imagined characters, I supplemented the video piece with an illustration for each character. The illustrations were an evolution of the original 2014 Validation Junky illustration (Figure 12.1). However, unlike the original illustration which was a blank template created to objectify the relationship between the human brain, the sociopolitical network, and the way we perceive our bodies, I wanted the illustration to evolve as if inhabited by the specific characters. Therefore, the illustrations would be updated to show the character's psychological dispositions interacting with different brand ideologies. These illustrations were developed over a series of conversations with Prof. Carolyn Mair[13] to discuss hardwired character cognition.[14]

An important component within the illustration is a three-dimensional mapping of the human brain,[15] conceptualising the character's different hardwired connections on three sliding scales. Scale 1: heterosexual, homosexual, and asexual, noting the sociocultural character implications of sexuality; Scale 2: cognitive testosterone and estrogen, noting the brain's hardwiring effect on gender identity and character expression; Scale 3: tension to resolve, illustrating that there is much of the brain still unexplained. The illustration was not intended to act as a scientifically accurate representation of cognitive dispositions, but as a tool for discussion on the types of drivers that might influence today's consumers.

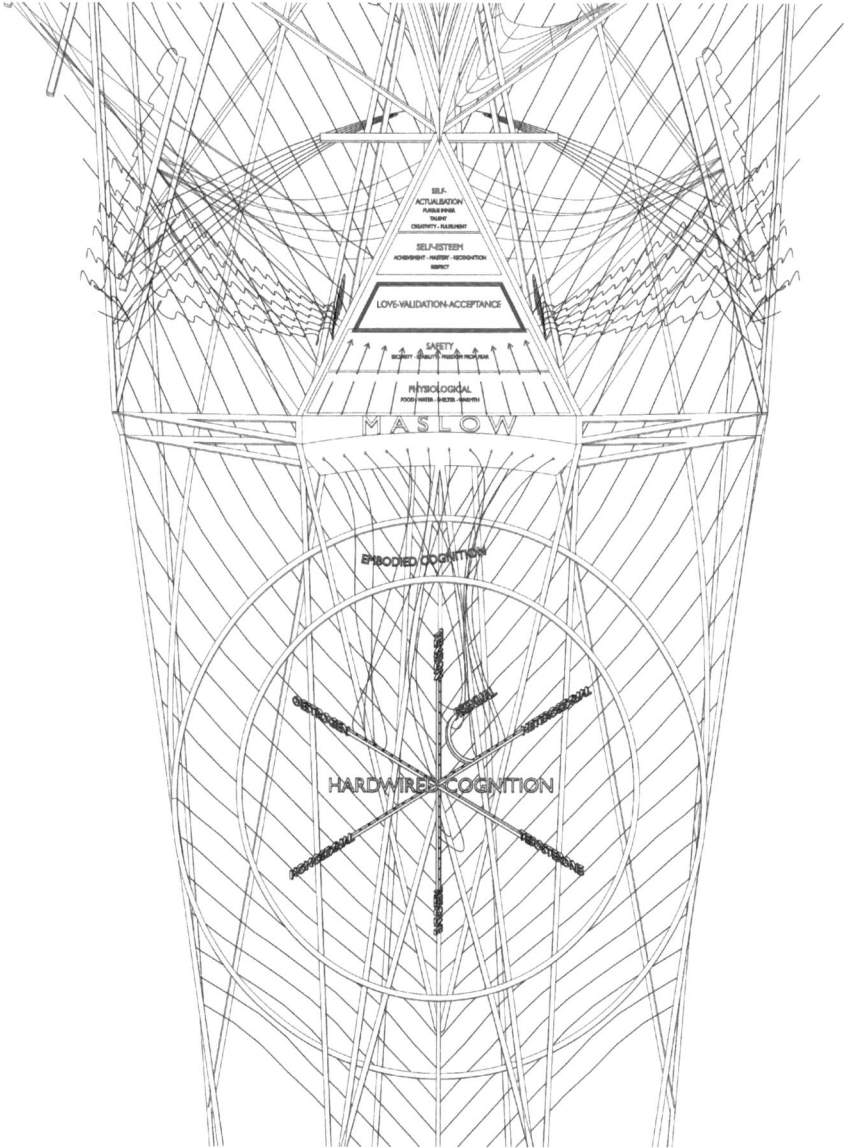

Figure 12.6 Illustration detail of a 3D interpretation of cognitive "hardwiring" within a sliding scale, linking to Maslow's hierarchy of needs as part of an algorithm of aesthetic taste. Image © Adam Peacock 2017.

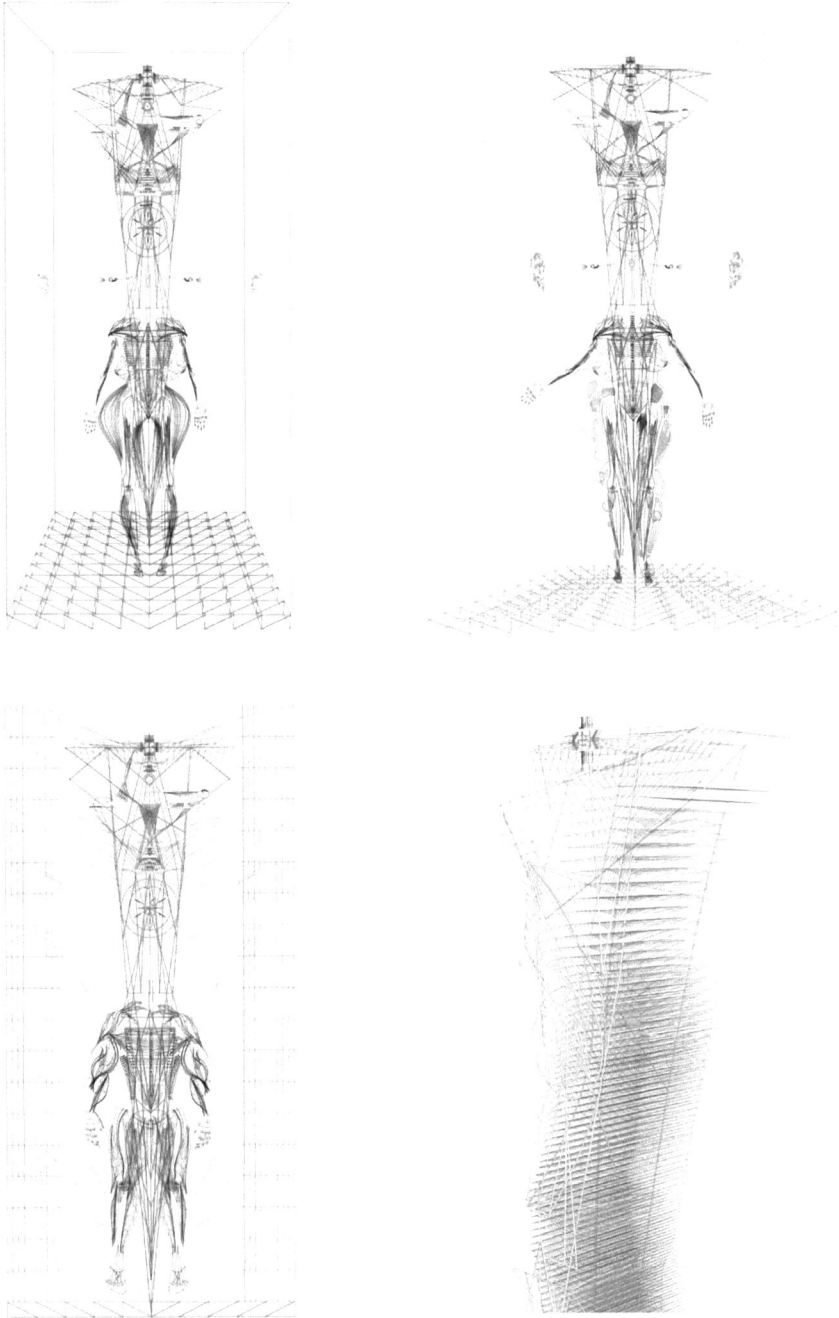

Figure 12.7 Four illustrations of characters, their hardwired cognitive dispositions, and sociopolitical responses within the graphic: (clockwise from top left) Character One, Character Two, Character Four, Character Five (with graphic focus on the cognitive mechanism as opposed to the body of Character Five, emphasizing personality and self-perception). Images © Adam Peacock 2017.

Character casting

Primarily, the challenge of casting characters lay within compromising between the aesthetic considerations of art direction and selecting models who would communicate the narrative according to the scientific and psychological principles in play. A significant consideration within the project was how to approach the artistic designing and editing of bodies from a human-centered, ethical, cultural, and political perspective, while maintaining creative license to explore the project.

I chose a range of individuals of different ethnicities, genders, and body types, who I felt could represent a contrasting range of both cognitive hardwiring and genetic characteristics in a controlled artistic environment. From observing initial test-shots from the interview stage, I selected an Asian female model from Hong Kong, with a toned slim build, a British Caucasian female model with a curvaceous build, a Caucasian-Asian Irish-Chinese male model with slim build, a British Caucasian red-haired male model with muscular build, and a Black-British male model with slim build. Their selection was based upon how well they understood and agreed with the project concept, how they held their body postures for the camera, and how their (edited) bodies and faces could illustrate the five narratives that were in development.

The reality of exploring internet-driven image-based communication means to explore narratives that might demonstrate prejudice toward individuals based on their age, disability, gender, relationships, race, religion or beliefs, sex or sexuality (HM Government 2010) within the developed character's physical expressions.

Through the developed system of exploring visual attraction as a "cognitive perception of genetic strength," I believe that it is possible to observe that what one person finds visually unattractive within someone, another person might find highly attractive. According to Dawkins' theories on evolution and sexual selection, how two different people's genes combine (to result in the potential of well-balanced offspring via procreation) are specific to an individual's genetic makeup. I attempted to integrate these narratives into the model lineup and across genders, ethnicities, and body types.

It is important to highlight that as a creative inquiry, The Genetics Gym is not limited to (my own) queer culture but is a lens to speculate upon how image-based communication, particularly digitally manipulated photography of the human body (Vainshtein 2019) is affecting human perceptions of identity and consumption behavior.

Scientific strategy

As a speculative design project, The Genetics Gym was not restricted to the scientific mechanics behind what "is" and "isn't" possible today, but more of an exploration of what genetic technology may be capable of in the future. Following the symposium and workshop, I collated the research and development, and translated the outcomes into the five characters and five brands, resulting in twenty-five individual portraits, using controlled art direction.

First, the models' bodies were developed as sketched silhouettes, exploring how five different characters might interact with five different consumption

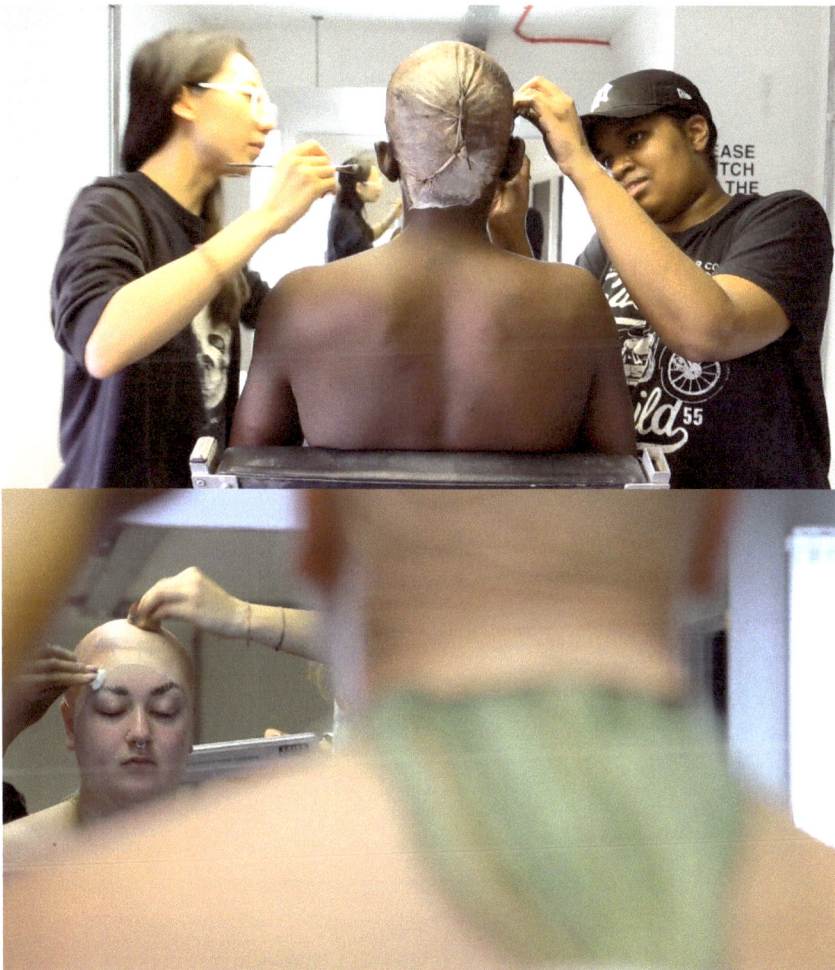

Figure 12.8 Models preparing for the photoshoot with prosthetic makeup artists. Photo credits: Dian-Jen Lin (top); Isabela Branca Gygax (bottom).

ideologies. Through discussion with the genetics team from UCL, the feasibility of making the genetic alterations that were illustrated were considered on a scale of 1 (impossible) to 5 (possible), using a "genetics menu" containing a total of twenty-three "offerings." Each offering was developed from scientific research, making it clear that some aspects of the project are not far from scientific possibility, such as Sex Hormone Changes, probability 4/5, Fat Reduction (probability 3.5/5) and the Ability to Put on Muscle Mass (probability 3.5/5), while others are scientifically unfeasible such as Instant Anti-Ageing (probability 0.5/5) and Neoteny / Cute Face (probability 1/5).

Art direction: Building the dystopia

Part of the success of the project would be defined by the emotive response from the audience. An aesthetic language was developed using a mixture of prosthetic makeup and Adobe Aftereffects to create smooth, hairless unified "skin," to emphasize ethnicity and body type. The models were filmed separately using 4K video,[16] and then edited into a collated ten-minute loop of all five characters standing side by side, stitched together in mathematical segments of footage featuring models' hands twitching, chests moving, breathing, and blinking while staring straight into the camera lens.

This allowed the characters to be understood as hyperreal human subjects, rather than manipulated images (Vainshtein 2019: 53) to heighten the connection between the audience and the imagined human conditions I wanted to express. Post-production included skin blend and color-grading to give the image a smooth "painted" surface quality. When developing this aesthetic, I was observing the light quality, similar to the still-life paintings from the sixteenth century, that inspired Nick Knight's "Flora" project (1993; see Schgaguler 2015), the faux–real mix of CGI (computer-generated images) and visuals prevalent within Reed + Rader's "Flowers" for *V Magazine* (2014), and observed the capturing of vulnerability present within the photography of Jan Hoek in "Sweet Crazies" (2011).

The art/creative direction included designing the ambience of the gallery to heighten the way that a viewer might experience the piece. I collaborated with sound-artist TWANG (aka Timothy Wang), resident at London's queer techno night KAOS, to respond to each of the five consumption strategies with abstract, mathematical sounds, playing alongside the video installation of the bodies slowly morphing and changing.

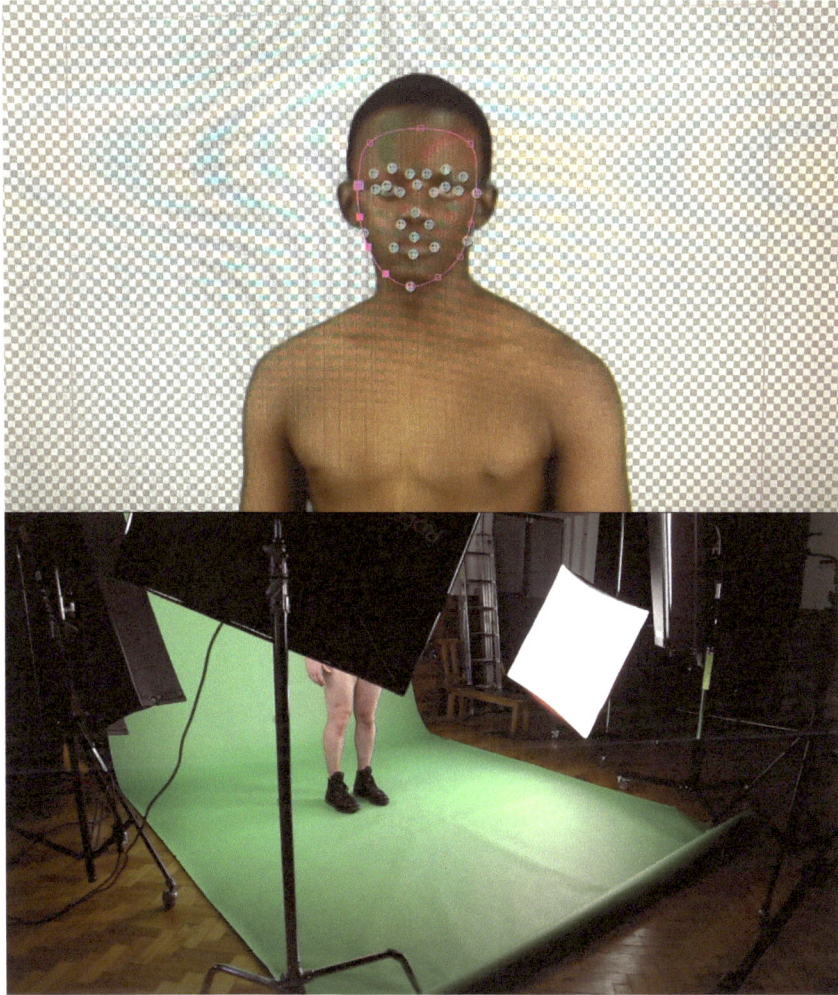

Figure 12.9 (top) Footage of model's facial features tracked for post-production editing; (bottom) Model recorded in 4K video on green screen. Photo credits: Adam Peacock (top); Isabela Branca Gygax (bottom).

Body design parameters

The bodies were digitally crafted according to a series of parameters including expression of ethnicity through eye and nose size and shape, expression of estrogen or testosterone through breast/chest, hip to waist ratio, lip size, cheek bone contours, brow and chin dominance, expression of body-fat quantity and location, and eye pupil size and dilation.

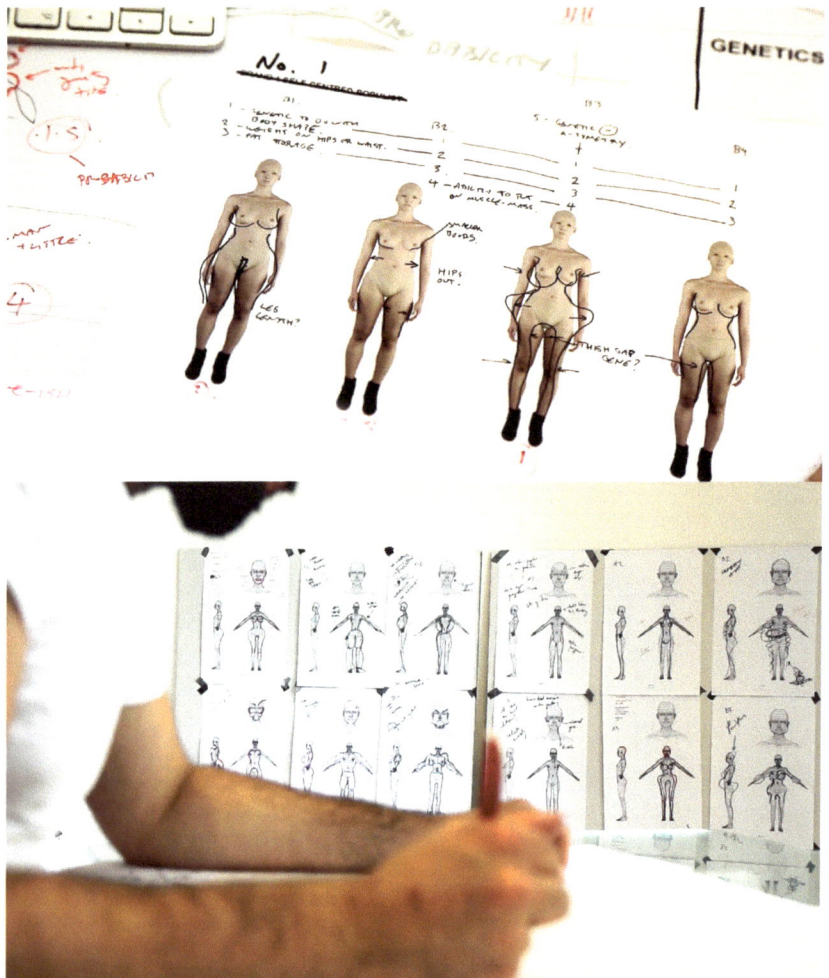

Figure 12.10 (top) The five brand-driven body manifestations of Character One are strategized by sketching onto unedited printouts of the model; (bottom) The twenty-five portraits were ideated by sketching onto printed wireframe bodies. Photographs by John Duff. © Adam Peacock 2017.

I wanted the viewer to observe and imagine themselves in the space. Who are you, who would you want to become if you could change yourself in any way imaginable? How is technology affecting who you want to be? How are the ideologies and communication strategies of brands playing into given anxieties, tensions, and personality? How can technologies be better designed for today by understanding how the human brain reads beauty and attractiveness?

Feedback

As part of the permissions process, I explained to the models that representations of their bodies would not be developed as a reflections of "themselves," but would be utilized purely as a source imagery, adjusted to the specifications of the constructed brand ideologies.

Character One was designed to embody a conventional fashionable aesthetic, a recognized cultural perspective of female beauty. The reactions to her (either reduced or exaggerated) bust led to discussions questioning the relevance of bust within expressions of contemporary femininity, noting successful figures in pop culture who embodied this. The expression of Character One's ethnicity was more dramatically manipulated—with the eye shape changing from almond (associated with Asian ethnicity), to more rounded (associated with Caucasian ethnicity). This prompted interesting conversations on the aesthetic of photo-filters in Snapchat, etc., and their embedded Caucasian ethnicity bias.

Of all the models who attended the opening, Character Two, featured in four brand expressions (Figure 12.11) was the most surprised by her representation and didn't recognize herself. The way her appearance was manipulated explored the idea that given the opportunity to reduce body fat genetically (to meet current conventions of beauty), a curvaceous woman might instead utilize science and technology to enhance or celebrate her shape. This controversial approach, to amplify, rather than minimize physiological features, understandably, received a mixed audience response.

The narrative of Character Three was built around androgyny through altering the expression of testosterone and estrogen through facial features and body silhouette. The model is of mixed Irish (Caucasian) and Chinese heritage, so provided an opportunity to explore Asian ethnicity through manipulating eye and nose shape and form. They were placed in the center (Figure 12.12) between the two characters easily identifiable as female, and the two characters easily identifiable as male to signal gender fluidity. Feedback from geneticists (who attended the "Designing Sex" symposium) suggested that this identity could potentially be "designed" with CRISPR-Cas9 genetic technology, leading to discussions about the feasibility of some of the ideas raised by The Genetics Gym.

Male gay friends visiting the exhibition found the exaggerated muscular form of Character Four (e.g., wide neck, chest, nose bridge) attractive. A (female) feminist visiting the exhibition said that while the outcomes were unsettling and "uncanny," they demonstrated the potential for visualizing the body in

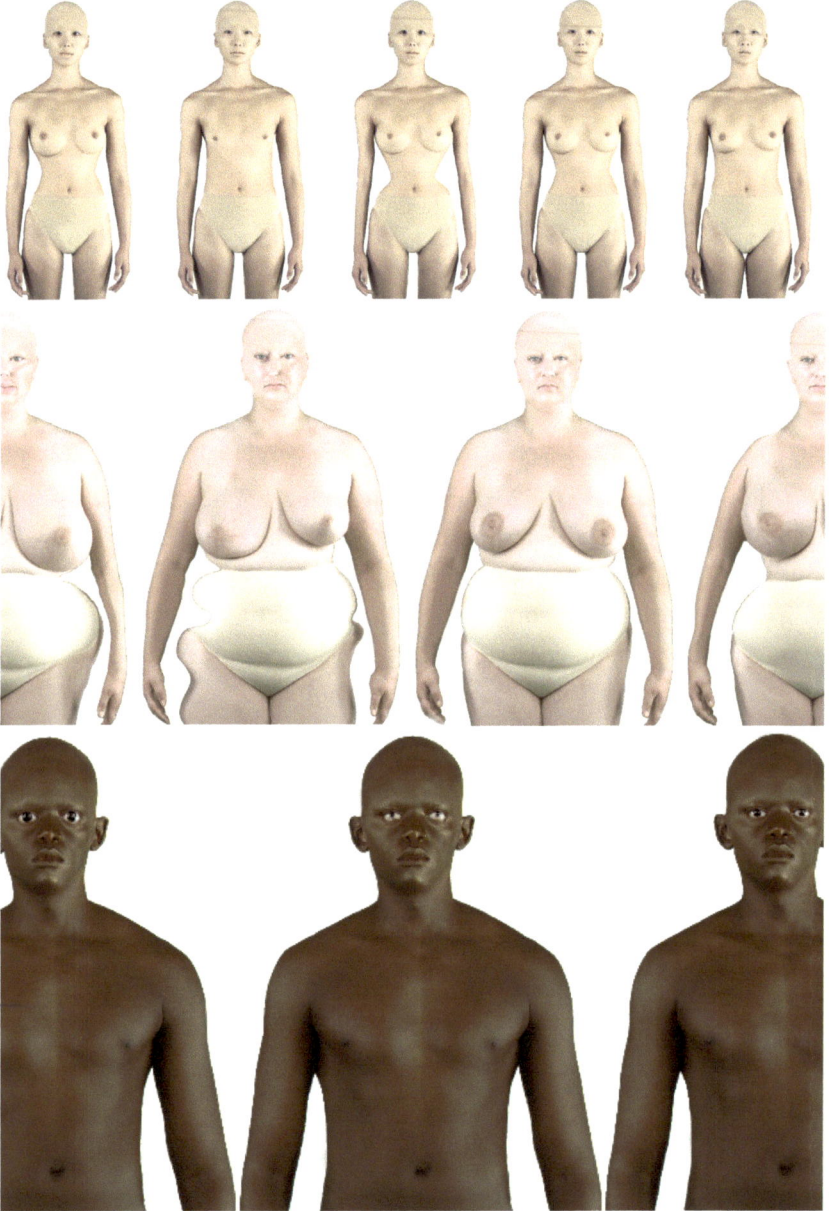

Figure 12.11 A selection of stills from the ten-minute gallery video, showing three character morphs from the twenty-five portraits: (top) Character One in all five brand expressions; left to right: A. "self-centered populist," B. "manifesto-visionaire," C. "no-substance-visionaire," D. "basic-pleaser," and E. "communo-consumer"; (middle) Character Two in four brand expressions A, C, D, E; (bottom) Character Five in three brand expressions B, A, D adjusting only pupil dilation illustrating cognitive and perceptual manipulation rather than physical silhouette alteration. Image © Adam Peacock 2017.

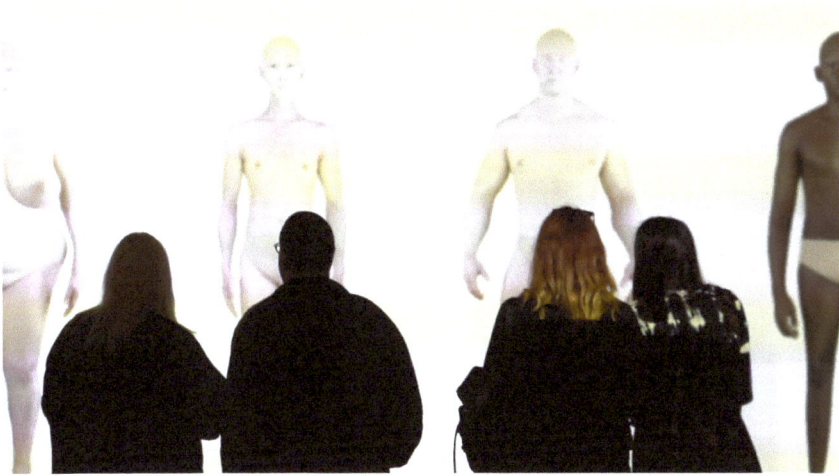

Figure 12.12 Gallery visitors observe the characters blinking, breathing, moving, and slowly morphing between the five different "perceptions of success." Photograph by Isabela Branca Gygax. Image © Adam Peacock 2017.

challenging ways to support future discussions around body positivity. Character Five's facial expressions were manipulated, as opposed to his physique, by altering the positioning and color of his eyes, the size of the iris, and direction of his gaze. This approach was informed by neoteny, making the model look younger, almost childlike in some of the morphs, as commented on by visitors.

The future of The Genetics Gym

The reaction to The Genetics Gym has varied; visitors to the gallery were left wondering what might happen when genetic engineering develops further, while new conversations were opened across disciplines into the future of applied technology and consumer behavior.

The Genetics Gym has been featured in: 'Punishing Industrial Techno from Hell', (Arcana 2017) and Fertility Fest 2018, London; Fashion Clash 2018, Maastricht, The Netherlands; *Perfection*, the Science Gallery, Melbourne (2018) and the Science Gallery, Dublin (2019). The project was awarded the 2018 Robert Garland Treseder Fellowship by the University of Melbourne, Australia;[17] featured in the BBC documentary, DNA+ Beauty (2018); as the keynote at the 'Product Innovation Apparel Conference: Genetics and AI' (2018) in Milan,

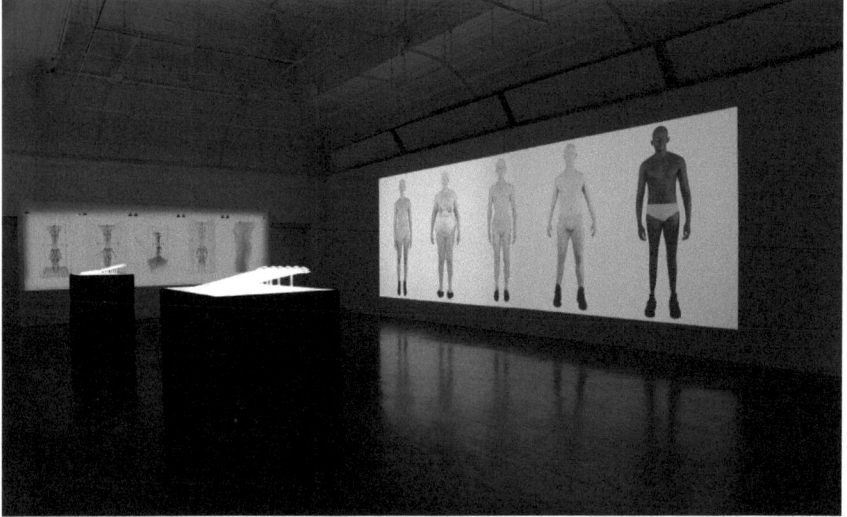

Figure 12.13 A gallery still of the five projected characters, the two research documents and five illustrations (2017). Photograph by Isabela Branca Gygax. Image © Adam Peacock 2017.

Italy, which questioned "what can we learn about our consumers that will enable more successful and impactful products?" and discussed in the context of marketing and apparel development in the 'Fashion Made' video series (2019).

The Genetics Gym has informed postgraduate curricula on the Speculative Prototyping Unit of MA Fashion Futures at LCF[18] and been developed into a MArch (Fashion/Architecture Studio) to broaden discourse across multidisciplinary paradigms at the University of Melbourne entitled 'The DNA of Perfection'.[19] The project outcomes have been presented to MA Fashion Design at the RCA via 'Digital Bodies + Validation Junkies' (2019), and on MFA Media Design Practices at The Art Centre College of Design in Los Angeles (2019), and the School of International Art (SIA) in Beijing (2018–19). In summer 2020, the project will inform a framework and open-call to international artists, designers, and researchers to explore sensibilities toward consumer behavior and technology entitled 'Validation+Norway'.

Based on this, I hope that some of the ideas highlighted by the Genetics Gym will continue to inspire new conversations and collaborations to explore and challenge the realisation of 'A Machine to Automate Taste'.

Within the relative complexities of cognitive disposition, and sexual and gender identity, sociocultural environments and commercial imperatives, humans (observed through the characters I have imagined and otherwise) share similar needs; to be loved, validated, and accepted (Maslow 1954). The desire, use, and choice of products, and images that we use to illustrate our identities will continue to play an important role in human validation, increasingly accessed via designed technologies.

Notes

1 Benjamin H. Bratton, Associate Professor of Visual Arts at the University of California, San Diego.

2 Norbert Wiener is considered to be the originator of the term *cybernetics*, describing the term in 1948 within his book *Cybernetics: Or, Study of Control and Communication in the Animal and the Machine.*

3 Other examples of technology-driven social behavior include IBM Watson and Google DeepMind.

4 The original Genetics Gym presentation took place over Skype with Fashion Space Gallery Director Ligaya Salazar, Digital Anthropology Lab Director Lynne Murray, Head of London College of Fashion Frances Corner, and Director of the Stanley Picker Gallery David Falkner.

5 Duncan Stephenson's research came from the YMCA / Centre for Appearance Research, University of West of England 2012.

6 The Speculative Body Design Workshop was held on Friday January 27, 2017. The group included Jo Cope, Hew Wang, Yuqing Lai, Voranida Rujekitnara, Siyang Meng, Dian-Jen Lin, James Boag, David Adams, Dr. Helen C. O'Neill, Liane Stein, Rachel Ho, Ashley Campbell, Anderson Dalle Laste, Prof. Roberta Degnore, and Celia Tang.

7 Shaun Ross is the first African-American model with albinism.

8 Winnie Harlow is a Canadian model diagnosed with the chronic skin condition vitiligo.

9 The term *eugenics* was coined by Sir Francis Galton in 1883 to encompass the idea of modification of natural selection through selective breeding for the improvement of humankind. Galton's use of the word meant "well-born," encouraging healthy, capable people, or "positive eugenics." The term has *since* become associated with Hitler, genocide, racism, and master-race theories.

10 "Retention of juvenile characteristics in adult life," 1898, from German *neotenie* (1884), from Greek *neos* "young" + *teinein* "to extend." See: https://www.etymonline.com/search?q=neoteny (accessed June 24, 2019).

11 He Jiankui is a researcher from the Southern University of Science and Technology in Shenzhen, China who claimed to have overseen the inception and birth of the first gene edited baby with HIV resistance.

12 See: http://unitedmicrokingdoms.org/.

13 Dr. Carolyn Mair is a consultant and academic and was Professor of Psychology for Fashion at University of the Arts London.

14 "Cognition" is defined as the mental action or process of acquiring knowledge and understanding through thought, experience, and the senses.

15 Inspired by a sketch by Zowie Broach called "three dimentional mapping of identity." See: https://www.are.na/the-validation-junky/digital-anthropology.

16 The production team included Tamara James-Dickson, Isabela Branca Gygax, Lara Gill, Dian-Jen Lin, Liane Stein, and Ashley Campbell.

17 The Robert Garland Treseder Fellowship is an annual award by The Faculty of Architecture, Building and Planning at Melbourne University.

18 The Speculative Prototyping unit for MA Fashion Futures at LCF is taught by Alex McIntosh, Adam Peacock, Tarang Bharti, and Julia Crew (2016–).

19 Studio 13, "The DNA of Perfection" at M.Arch Architecture at The University of Melbourne is jointly run by Dr. Isun Kazerani and Adam Peacock (2019).

References

Arcana (2017) "Punishing Industrial Techno from Hell." Available online: https://www.residentadvisor.net/events/1021337 (accessed March 1, 2019).

BBC Radio 1 (2018) "Could You Edit Your DNA to Look Hotter?" (at 4:37). Available at https://www.youtube.com/watch?v=jZIIh_VHjAw (accessed September 10, 2019).

Bratton, B. H. (2016) "Alternative Modernities: The Past, Present, and Future of Speculative Design," symposium, held at the University of California, San Diego, La Jolla. Available online: http://dismagazine.com/discussion/81971/on-speculative-design-benjamin-h-bratton/ (accessed January 28, 2019).

Buss, D. M. (1989) "Sex Differences in Human Mate Preferences: Evolutionary Hypotheses Tested in 37 Cultures," *Behavioral Brain Science*, 12(1): 1–49.

Butler, C., Moon, L., and Barker, M. (2006) "Sexuality Special Issue—Part One." *British Psychological Society: The Psychologist*, 19: 18–23. Available online: https://thepsychologist.bps.org.uk/volume-19/edition-1/sexuality-special-issue-part-one (accessed February 21, 2019).

Cole, S. (2000) *"Don We Now Our Gay Apparel": Gay Men's Dress in the Twentieth Century*, Oxford: Berg.

Cronk, L. (2005) "The Application of Animal Signaling Theory to Human Phenomena: Some Thoughts and Clarifications," *Social Science Information*, 44(4): 603–20.

Dawkins, R. (1976) *The Selfish Gene*, Oxford: Oxford University Press.

De Botton, A. (2012) *How to Think More About Sex*, Basingstoke: Macmillan.

Downs, A. (2012) *The Velvet Rage: Overcoming the Pain of Growing Up Gay in a Straight Man's World*, 2nd edn., Boston, MA: Da Capo Press.

Duncan, P. (2017) "Gay Relationships Are Still Criminalised in 72 Countries, Report Finds," *The Guardian*, July 27. Available online: https://www.theguardian.com/world/2017/jul/27/gay-relationships-still-criminalised-countries-report (accessed February 21, 2019).

Dunne, A. and Raby, F. (2013) "Speculative Everything: Design, Fiction, and Social Dreaming," Cambridge, MA: MIT Press.

Dupont, C., Armant, D. R., and Brenner, C. A. (2009) "Epigenetics: Definition, Mechanisms and Clinical Perspective," *Seminars in Reproductive Medicine*, 27(5): 351–7.

Duster, T. (2013) *Backdoor to Eugenics*, New York: Routledge.

Fashion Space Gallery (2016) "Design Residency—Fashion Space Gallery Design Resident 2016: Adam Peacock," February 5. Available online: www.fashionspacegallery.com/residency/fashion-space-gallery-design-resident-2016-adam-peacock/ (accessed January 28, 2019).

HM Government (2010) *Equality Act 2010*. Available online: http://www.legislation.gov.uk/ukpga/2010/15/pdfs/ukpga_20100015_en.pdf (accessed February 21, 2019).

Hoek, J. (2011) "Sweet Crazies." Available online: https://janhoek.net/sweet-crazys/ (accessed February 21, 2019).

Holtzman, N. A. (1991) "Review: *Backdoor to Eugenics* by Troy Duster," *Journal of Public Health Policy*, 12(2): 243–7.

Maslow, A. H. (1954) *Motivation and Personality*, New York: Harper & Brothers.

Megginson, L. C. (1963) "Lessons from Europe for American Business," *Southwestern Social Science Quarterly*, 44(1): 3–13.

Melbourne School of Design (2018) "London-based designer awarded Robert Garland Treseder Fellowship for 2018," September 13. Available online: https://msd.unimelb.edu.au/news/london-based-designer-awarded-robert-garland-treseder-fellowship-for-2018 (accessed March 1, 2019).

Reed + Rader (2014) "Flowers." Available online: www.reedandrader.com/work#/flowers/ (accessed February 21, 2019).

Saini, A. (2014) "Epigenetics: Genes, Environment and the Generation Game," *The Observer*, September 7. Available online: https://www.theguardian.com/science/2014/sep/07/epigenetics-heredity-diabetes-obesity-increased-cancer-risk (accessed January 28, 2019).

Sanders, A. R., Martin, E. R., Beecham, G. W., Guo, S., Dawood, K., Rieger, G., Badner, J. A., Gershon, E. S., Krishnappa, R. S., Kolundzija, A. B., Duan, J., Gejman, P. V., and Bailey, J. (2015) "Genome-Wide Scan Demonstrates Significant Linkage for Male Sexual Orientation," *Psychological Medicine*, 45(7): 1379–88.

Schgaguler, M. (2015) "Blurring the Line between Photography and Painting. Acclaimed fashion photographer Nick Knight is known for his edgy images and innovative techniques. In his latest works 'Flora' he shows off the final product of a project he started in 1993," *Panamy*, March 20. Available online: www.panamy.ch/nick-knight/ (accessed February 21, 2019).

Vainshtein, O. (2019) "Photography and the Body," in A. Geczy and V. Karaminas (eds.), *The End of Fashion: Clothing and Dress in the Age of Globalization*, 47–65, London: Bloomsbury.

Vaught, L. A. (1902) *Vaught's Practical Character Reader*, Chicago, IL: M. A. Donohue & Co.

Wiener, N. (1948) *Cybernetics: Or, Control and Communication in the Animal and the Machine*, Cambridge, MA: MIT Press.

Zuckerman, M., Miyake, K., and Hodgins, H. S. (1991) "Cross-Channel Effect of Vocal and Physical Attractiveness and Their Implications for Interpersonal Perception," *Journal of Personality and Social Psychology*, 60(4): 545–54.

13

The Body as Factory

A Post-Productivist Fashion Practice Through Film

Lara Torres

Introduction

This chapter builds upon the methodologies developed throughout a practice-based PhD at the London College of Fashion, University of the Arts London (UAL). Entitled "Towards a Practice of Unmaking: The Essay Film as Critical Discourse for Fashion in the Expanded Field," this artistic inquiry proposed a strategy for critical fashion practices in a research context at the intersection of fashion, fine arts, and film. The research started from a need to understand if there was a change to the role of the fashion designer in response to the growing concerns regarding sustainable fashion in the twenty-first century and, if so, what would that role comprise? As a fashion practitioner, I am looking at fashion[1] as Kawamura puts it, in its material and immaterial manifestations (Kawamura 2005: 1); but also, as a theoretical and methodological framework for understanding the complex dynamic relationship between the body, dress, and culture. I describe my practice as being rooted in fashion but no longer limited by its disciplinary boundaries.

A matter of memory

As fashion practitioners, our relation to materials is very significant. They provide the means through which we connect to our practice and communicate concepts. Materials allow us to engage on an aesthetic, emotional, and conceptual level. In 2005, when I began my own practice as a fashion designer, I was interested in developing a way of translating fashion's mechanisms of memory into form, because I believed that to understand fashion I would have to understand its relation to memory. The poetics of fashion were explored in processes where I would translate the notion of "forgetting" (via the physical erasure of shape and motifs and/or the destruction of some fabrics) and "remembering"—through collaging and stitching pieces together. My project Mimesis[2] emphasized the importance of process, or procedural stages of making (as opposed to completing a predetermined design composition or plan).

The question "What is fashion?" has constantly been foregrounded in my work. As a result, my fashion practice represents a departure from the traditional role of "designer as producer" toward an alternative form of creative production based on the exploration and embodiment of my own questions. I have constantly tried to redefine the territory of fashion practice, and my work is presented in a broad spectrum of media but follows a consistent conceptual path: to understand the nature of fashion. By experimenting at the borders of the discipline through the mediums of sculpture, performance, and film, I had to learn how to use unfamiliar media within a fashion practice allowing for a certain critical distance that came from applying other perspectives when looking at fashion. During the 1990s there were large exhibitions documenting conceptual approaches to fashion such as the Florence Fashion Biennial (1996) entitled *Looking at Fashion*, directed by Germano Celant, and the exhibition *Addressing the Century, 100 Years of Art & Fashion* (1998) at the Hayward Gallery in London, curated by Fiona Bradley, Julia Coates, and Ulrich Lehmann, which assembled 250 works of art, fashion, photography, video, and film.

However, the procedure that I have developed is different from that of former artists and fashion practitioners working through conceptual fashion insofar as I use film montage in order to assert fashion criticality. In my attempt to depict "thought in the process of being formed," I have used montage itself as a form of thinking fashion through film.

Archival practice: Crafting garments as objects of memory

By describing and recollecting remnants as in an archaeological station,[3] the results depend far more on the mode of inquiry and research methods than on the end result itself. Figure 13.1 depicts "archaeological cataloguing" used to document my working processes, allowing the audience to understand the manufacturing process—where the tasks undertaken were strongly connected

Figure 13.1 (top) Archive of project Mimesis (2008) from the catalogue *Collecting Collections and Concepts* for Guimarães European Capital of Culture (2012); (bottom) Porcelain t-shirt with V neck in archive of project Mimesis. Image credit and © Lara Torres.

to failure, repetition, and acceptance of failure, and as a result the relevance of experiments with materials, shapes, and forms in the fashion creation process.

During Mimesis, the importance of "trace as an archival form" (Merewether 2006: 10) was very significant. As in Walter Benjamin's model of thought that underlines the importance of the trace and its meaningfulness toward deciphering the debris of the world, archaeological cataloguing enabled the exhibition audience to dive into a complex manufacturing process by accessing information that was not usually available to the general public. As Neil Leach puts it in his Benjaminian reflection regarding mimesis, this accurately describes the author's approach:

Mimesis here should be understood not in the terms used, say, by Plato, to refer to simple "imitation." To reproduce something is to step beyond mere imitation. Here Benjamin challenges the inherited view of mimesis as an essentially compromised form of imitation that necessarily loses something of the original. For Benjamin "mimesis" alludes to a constructive reinterpretation of an original, which becomes a creative act in itself. . . To understand the meaning of mimesis in Benjamin we must recognise its origin in the process of modelling, of "making a copy of"

Leach 2006: 19–20

The project Mimesis and the exhibition *Fac-simile* (2008) were a turning point in my fashion practice.[4] During the making process, instead of copies, what was achieved more closely represented "specters" of the original pieces. In *The End of Fashion* (2019), Geczy and Karaminas refer to Elizabeth Wilson's understanding of garments as " 'congealed memories' of the past suspended like 'specters' in the mausoleums of culture, vestiges of a life once lived but now long gone" (Geczy and Karaminas 2019: 28). In their understanding, "Not only do garments function as signifiers of loss and absence, they also serve as a representation of death and as a reminder of the past that is lost. Garments in this sense become a substitute, a surrogate, or consolation for something that is missing" (ibid.).

This understanding is shared with the fashion historian Caroline Evans in her book *Fashion at the Edge* (Evans 2003: 43–73). This project marked a departure from a productivist to a post-productivist[5] fashion practice. The fashion objects were developed as ceramics, whereby clothes were dipped in liquid porcelain and crystallized at high temperatures; losing the original garment and leaving a new materialized form made of porcelain, a record of every detail of the garment such as the fabric's textures, folds, and wrinkles, while the original piece was lost in the fire.

In the case of latex "translations" (see Figure 13.2), the original garment was reproduced in latex, taking advantage of the material's ability to retain all surface detail to safeguard the object's memory. The reproduced pieces consisted of found objects that the participants of the project collected in their family homes in Portugal; there was a need to keep a record of these objects and, at the same time, an inevitable failure because we knew that the original items of clothing would disappear during the "remaking" process. The gesture of reproducing found objects, such as jewelry, accessories, and garments and its proximity to failure reproduced the mechanisms of memory, as memory often fails to reproduce an event.[6] The process of reproduction was approached through methods that used

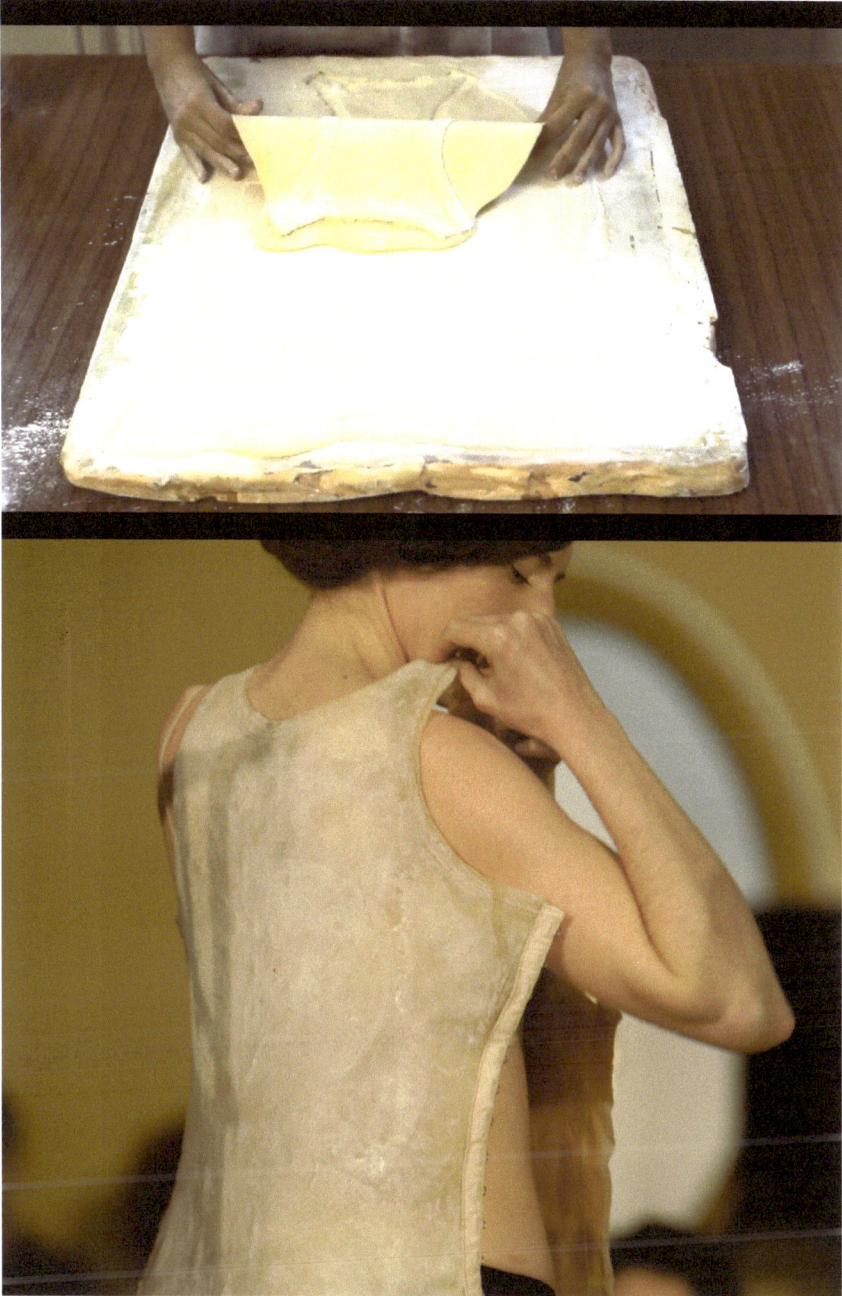

Figure 13.2 (top) Film still of latex reproduction technique (2014). Image credit and © Lara Torres; (bottom) Fashion performance at the Lisbon Fashion Week. Photo credit: Rogério Martins (2008). Reproduced courtesy of the artist.

both traditional plaster mold making techniques and innovative technical skills such as using liquid latex to reproduce garments, developed while searching for ways to translate the metaphor of memory into clothing.

Figure 13.3 Film stills from "An Impossible Wardrobe for the Invisible" (2011). Image credit and © Lara Torres.

Film as fashion matter

Traditionally, fashion explores both material and immaterial constructs. My film project, "An Impossible Wardrobe for the Invisible" (2011), translated this idea into an installation composed of seven films[7] documenting seven crafting actions discussing the importance of clothing and the transience of fashion. The project was based on the creation of "temporary clothes" produced with the aim of being destroyed. Made of a soluble material, these clothes would dissolve in contact with water, leaving only visual impressions of the pieces on film.

The process of disappearance highlights the ephemeral nature of fashion, acting as a metaphor for the speed of the contemporary fashion processes (i.e., fast fashion) and the current speed of the fashion system (Bhardwaj and Fairhurst 2009: 165–7). This process, a design process in itself, left sometimes only a drawing on the performer's body, the "skeleton" of a particular garment. The symbolic lines of the seams against the performer's body induce a sense of the intimacy of clothing, its facility to enhance personal agency and loss. In each of the seven situations filmed, a performer becomes

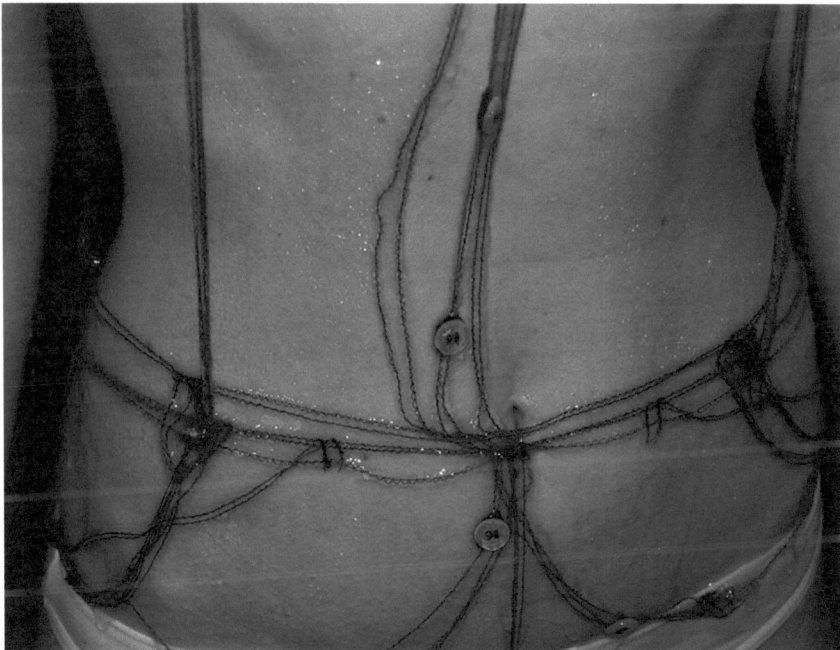

Figure 13.4 Documentation illustrating seams on the body after dissolution of the garments during the shooting of "An Impossible Wardrobe for the Invisible" (2011). Image credit and © Lara Torres.

an archetypal character that the audience can relate to while watching each film. The clothes relate to stereotypical garments that make the performers identifiable characters. The bodies represented in these films are not only an essential part of clothing, but also act as sites where fashion as an event takes place. These films morph the body and garment into one. After the dissolution of the garment, a body is left with seams and buttons added to the skin, a body-garment of sorts, in which there is no longer separation between subject and object.

Productive fashion bodies

In their book *The Productive Body* (2014), Guéry and Deleule ask how the human body and its labor have been expropriated through successive stages of capitalism. When Guéry and Deleule refer to the "productive body" in Marx and the capitalist "appropriation of the body's powers" (2014: 51, 63), it is in the sense of the subjugation of the organic body to capital, becoming the body of capital (Guéry and Deleule 2014). The productive body resonates with Joanne Entwistle in *The Fashioned Body* (2000: 1) where she states that "fashion is about bodies: it is produced, promoted and worn by bodies." Addressing the body from this sociological perspective, my film *Unmaking* (2016) depicts the relevance of bodies in fashion—both as a site of performance and production. This notion is central to my film's content, in creating sequences "of production," like in a factory production line. For example, in sequences 7 and 8 (see Figures 13.5 and 13.7), which depict hand gestures related to clothes, making is juxtaposed with women getting dressed or undressed, suggestive of a relation between the bodies that make our clothes, the dressed body, and a deconstruction of fashion, a disordering of the fashioned meaning. *Unmaking* was assembled as a composition of thoughts on the process of how we "make the body" through action, material, etc. Research into fashion is necessarily bonded to the concept of "being" due to fashion's own nature of materializing identity. As sociologist Joanne Finkelstein observes in *The Fashioned Self* (1991: 1): "We know that appearances are created and that dressing after a particular fashion, is done in order to convey a certain impression."

Michel Foucault is interested in how power is enacted through bodies; thus, his theories are particularly useful in an analysis of the practices and rituals around regulation clothing and everyday dress. Whatever private meanings clothes hold, they also have a profoundly social role. The choreographic aspect of activities that constitute fashion at different levels include dressing, producing, and consuming. As Entwistle writes in relation to Bryan S. Turner, a British and

Australian sociologist focusing on the development of sociology of the body: "there is an obvious fact about human beings, they have bodies and they are bodies" (Entwistle 2000: 6; see also Turner 1985: 33). These bodies, in fashion, are at the same time the bodies that produce, promote, and wear fashion, composing a system of bodies that together constitute the fashion system. For Foucault, the body is critical to how power works: its visible construction shapes social and political discourses (Tynan 2016: 186). For Finkelstein, "fashion is collective, systematised and prescriptive" (Finkelstein 2007: 211). Such perspective is Foucauldian; it is critical to note that manufacturing also bears down on the bodies of garment workers, "whose employment conditions are often made hazardous and precarious by a globalised fashion industry" (Tynan 2016: 190–1). Finding parallels across "discursive fields" prompts Foucault to consider social life in terms of systems of representation and their reproduction through the operation of institutional power. Thus, in her analysis of fast fashion, Tynan points to a major theme in Foucault's work: the concern with accountability. For me, within my film *Unmaking*, the matter of accountability is central and defines a political positioning of my fashion practice. *Unmaking* represents the several types of bodies in the fashion system—the bodies that wear, promote, and produce. The meaning of the film lies in the semiotics of fashion, in deconstructing the "sign of fashion" (Barthes 2010 [1983]) and the principle of signification itself, just as the alternative to political economy can only lie in the deconstruction of commodity and production itself.

The creation of meaning through film images: Critical discourse

My approach to generating visual images as a method for creating meaning in essay films is used not to illustrate ideas but to embody them, to actualize them in the film itself. Discourse, as developed in Foucault's *The Archaeology of Knowledge* (2004), refers to the creation and organization of knowledge, which determines how and what we know, both as individuals and as a society. In 2009 the sociologist and fashion theorist Agnès Rocamora, drawing on both Bourdieu and Foucault, developed the notion of a "fashion discourse." Rocamora explores the complex formation of texts, statements, and ideas articulated in the French fashion media to demonstrate how and where fashion discourses proliferate, and the social and material practices that give them life and meaning. Fashion discourse is critical to

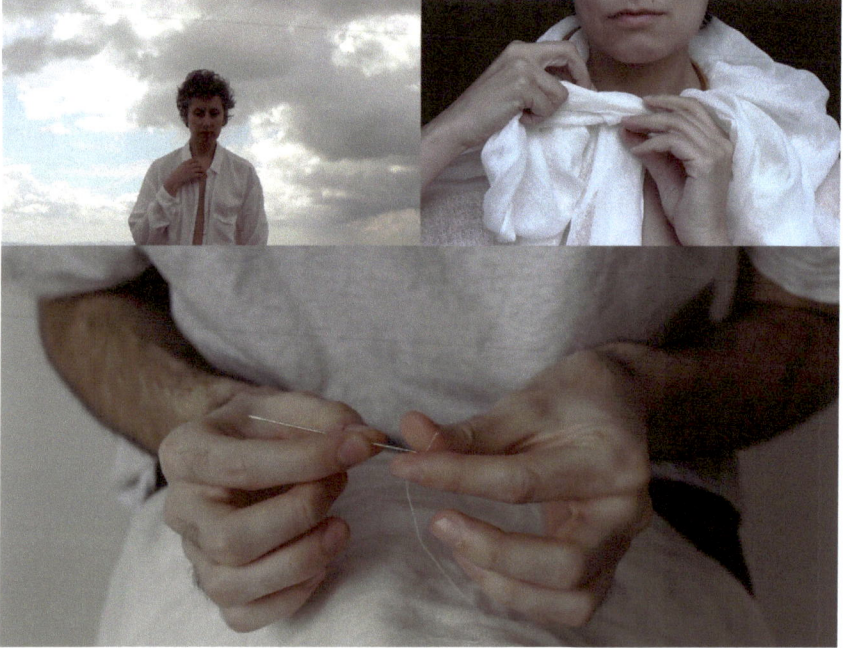

Figure 13.5 Editing sequences 1, 2, and 9 in "Dressing shirt" from *Unmaking* (2016). Image and © Lara Torres 2016.

the maintenance of the fashion system, through which fashion also "constructs dominant narratives about health, gender, sexuality, class and race, or at least, fashion colludes with dominant narratives in any given social framework" (Tynan 2016: 186). The creative development of *Unmaking* as a practice-based research method involves building on fashion discourse through layers of images and meaning, with a strong focus on the juxtaposition of image sequences; the film's narrative is used to discuss what fashion is by using images of the body dressing, sewing, and unraveling as thought, memory, and representation metaphors. The principle of montage is that a third meaning is created by the juxtaposition of two images (as shown in Figure 13.5, that simulates the editing process) rather than any immutable meaning inherent in each separate image frame.

Fashion film meaning-making: A critical fashion practice

Films are built on layers of images and meaning, the intervals between the images, the gaps through which the images can appear. The notion of the image as trace, memory, and representation has been central to my film practice. My films *Fragment* (2008) and in "An Impossible Wardrobe for the Invisible" document a performance and stand as traces of garments that no longer exist. In *Unmaking,* the parallel lines of the layered narrations lead to the "reveal," working like a mirror, pointing back at us as observer participants in our own fabrication. We are all bodies, we are all human, and both *Unmaking* and "An Impossible Wardrobe for the Invisible" seem, in the end, to talk about and to all of us, even if they seem to be about something or someone else. The fashion image is never a given, the fictitious reality of fashion only reveals its relationship to humanity, the body, and work in a crisis situation, like the present one in which human conditions, climate change, and environmental damage become clearer (Rockström et al. 2009; Zalasiewicz et al. 2011). In *Unmaking,* the fragmentary narrative makes it clear that no obvious answer will be given. No uniform meaning is intended to be given to the film's audience. The form would be defined by the relationship between the images. My intention when making the film was that this would better translate "thought" as the process that I intended to portray in the film. This simple process also contributed to the politics of reduction that I tried to keep in the making, with the use of minimum resources possible and "dematerialized practices" (Lippard 1997). The fashion apparatus deployed by fashion practitioners in recent decades has become mostly centered upon visual strategies, due to the internet and online communications (Wolbers 2019). Although I have been very reticent about providing an explanation of each sequence as I don't want to provide the audience one possible meaning—I prefer an open-ended narrative with room for speculation; I can, however, provide a declaration of my intentions toward each sequence and, perhaps inevitably, a speculative exercise where I interpret my own ideas in the film.

Unmaking: Film contents

In sequence 1, Dressing shirt (see Figure 13.5), the performer, a woman, stands in front of the camera with the sky as a backdrop during the seemingly banal gesture of putting on a shirt. Slowly, the performer buttons the shirt until it is entirely buttoned up. While the banality of this common gesture seems empty of meaning, my intention was to bring the audience close to the performer through a gesture that is familiar and relatable. By making the image so clean and technical I wanted to avoid the so-called "male gaze" (Mulvey 1975). I composed the frame carefully to reflect feminist video works such as Martha Rosler's

Semiotics of the Kitchen (1975), where the camera technically documents the action, placing the performer in the center of the frame captured by an objective still camera. Rosler's film is a feminist parody video and performance piece considered a critique of the commodified versions of traditional women's roles in modern society. In sequence 1, Dressing shirt, the images of dressing are juxtaposed with others of sewing and a spectral sequence of "imagined sewing" and "imagined dressing" that refer to bringing together productive bodies (Guéry and Deleule 2014) and dressed bodies. Montage brings the second sequence in Dressing shirt (see Figure 13.5) by mimicking gestures, the performer repeats the actions and positioning of sequence 1; she once again stands in front of the camera with the sky as set. Slowly, the performer pretends to button the shirt until it is entirely buttoned. My intention with this juxtaposition is to enhance the familiarity of the gesture of buttoning, because it has been repeated so many times we would be able to reproduce it by heart. Juxtaposing them with Sewing and Mimicking sewing and sequence 9, I intended to move between the actions of "real sewing" and mimicking sewing. The performer I chose was himself a maker, familiar with the actions he had to reproduce; I was interested in having a male figure doing the sewing and knitting actions because somehow these are activities usually related to traditional women's roles which I did not want to perpetuate as such because I wanted to move away from traditional stereotypes regarding women's roles. In sequence 7 What a factory might be: Fabric, refers to an idea from a William Morris pamphlet (Morris 1884) by expanding on the notion of factory. In Figure 13.5, on the right, the performer uses embroidery hoops as a "jewelry piece" to enact an idea for "what a factory might be," reducing the notion of "factory" to an extreme—as part of a simple mechanism where fabric is wrapped around the body (reminiscent of the ancient Greek *Chiton* or *Himation* or *Peplos* shapes), where a cloth is draped around the body and can afterward be undone, suggesting that we could put things together temporarily and undo them when necessary.

Sequence 8 (see Figure 13.6), Consumption, perhaps the most literal of the sequences, was filmed in Oxford Street[8] on a Saturday morning from walking up and down the street collecting images of the many people shopping and carrying bags of new things. The intention of this sequence was to record the movement of people in an area dedicated to consumption and to produce documentary images, bringing the film into contemporary reality and familiarity. Sequence 8 was juxtaposed with sequence 4 (see Figure 13.6), Overdressed, featuring the performer Liz Vahia: a still camera observes her as she dresses in a vast array of clothing items. It uses a largely static camera and her home as a set. Vahia

Figure 13.6 Film stills from *Unmaking* (2016): (clockwise from top left) sequences 6, 4, and 8. Image and © Lara Torres 2016.

navigates a lexicon of "dress objects" (Skjold 2016: 139). Else Skjold uses the term "dress objects" in her research referring to the "real garment" in the sense that she addresses the physical object of dress—the signified—from its signifier, the "written garment" or "image garment" (Barthes 2010 [1983]). Combining it with the wording "design object" highlights how people are affected by design characteristics of what they wear. In my film, Vahia's body is layered with her wardrobe: she begins with a skirt, adds another skirt, adds a dress . . . and by the end of the sequence, she can barely move due to the number of garments she has on, inducing laughter, giving the sequence a tone of parody (which is purposely very distinct from the rest of the film). The focus on the different garments is important, since I intended the film to suggest how diverse this wardrobe is (multiple identities). Vahia's own wardrobe is used in this sequence; initially it was intended to film Vahia putting on her entire wardrobe, but we had to abandon that idea as Vahia is a collector of vintage items and had an entire room as a wardrobe. Instead, she randomly selected pieces and did not predetermine an order, although she used tighter clothing for the start and larger outerwear for the ending. This sequence parallels today's excess of production, referring to someone's wardrobe, in this case a sort of archetypal wardrobe because it is made of vintage and contemporary outfits that translate a certain lack of temporality. The sequence is juxtaposed with sequence 6, with the woman unraveling a knitted dress (see Figure 13.7): Unraveling refers to the illustration of cyclical movement of production and destruction, so familiar to fashion in its transient nature. Recorded in Hilly Fields in South London with the intent of being a literal representation of unmaking, it was included to illustrate parallel movements of making and unmaking in fashion, juxtaposing this with the making of a thread structure over a body (see Figure 13.7), and gesture of hands knitting (Figure 13.7), connecting these three images in the idea of circular movement—where the thread becomes dress→is unraveled→becomes thread again→becomes structure and can be reknitted.

This is a simplification of the idea of "circular fashion" based on Niinimäki (2017). However, I believe that we can think about the circulatory movement of production (body as factory is how I see it—productive bodies) and explore how we could perform it and document it, philosophically. I am interested in the idea of production–destruction, as I explored previously—always a quiet gesture—but trying to understand how to reveal this "circular" movement of materialization and dematerialization through the action of the body itself. Sequence 6, Unraveling, originally juxtaposed with images of making, now acts as a huge contrast when juxtaposed with the documentary footage of Oxford Street in London, where people walk around with their shopping bags, resonating with Benjamin's or Baudelaire's notion of the urban *flâneur* (Benjamin 2002: 448). Both sequences 4 and 8 (see Figure 13.6) illustrate the excess of shopping and an exaggeration that gains a comedic tone in this desperate attempt of wearing multiple layers. It is a reminder of all the skins we put on, how they play with the construction of our identity and the self. This conjures a sequence of literal making and unmaking: a woman in a park unravels a knitted dress while another sequence constructs a structure of thread around her body. A "factory" made by her own hands that makes and unmakes, her body is displayed with numbered sections that evoke, in the minds of fashion designers and workers, the patterns that are used to make clothing.

In sequence 12, What a factory might be: Thread (see Figure 13.7), thread is wrapped around the body as if mimicking the places where seams could be; the structure becomes an almost nonexistent garment (film sequence 12, see Figure 13.7). Once again, the body is seen here as a tool and a site, a factory for making, but it is also the same body that is dressed. I was interested in the gestures of making the structure and representing the body as being both the producer and

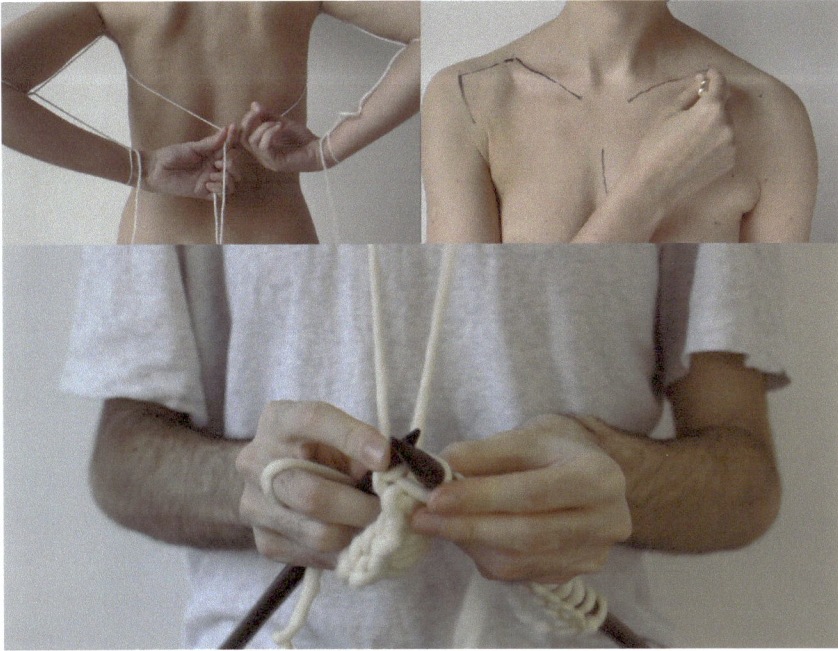

Figure 13.7 Film still from *Unmaking* (2016): (clockwise from top left) sequences 12, 11, and 10. Image and © Lara Torres 2016.

the consumer, in a reference to the invisibility of the bodies of producers in capitalist systems (Ehmann and Eshun 2009: 53). The gestures in sequence 12 (Figure 13.7) were filmed so that all the actions were recorded, and, in the end we filmed the body with the structure of thread "dressed" on the body. The intention of the film is to capture the presence of makers, *making*. The repetition of gestures, the implementation, choreographed movements, and the body itself become a signal system in themselves. In sequence 11, Pattern drawn on the body (see Figure 13.7), the sequence of pattern self-drawn on a female body could be said to be reminiscent of Croatian artist Sanja Iveković's video *Instructions No.1* (1976), where a close-up shot shows the artist as a young woman painting black arrows over the contours of her face, as a surgeon might when preparing her for cosmetic surgery. She then massages her face along the arrows, erasing them and leaving a smudged residue across her skin. As in Iveković's video, the performer draws on her own body with a dark pencil. Although in the sequence that I have created, while the performer's drawing refers to patterns for clothing, the reading is ambiguous and could be interpreted as marks for cosmetic surgery or to open up the body. It is a somewhat violent gesture to mark the body in this way even if done by oneself. Juxtaposed with sequence 10, Hand knitting (see Figure 13.7), in the same way as sequence 9 (see Figure 13.5), real knitting and mimicking knitting. In this sequence, the thread from the unraveling sequence 6 (Figure 13.6) is made again, introducing the notion of a cycle of deconstruction and reconstruction. This sequence makes a connection with "An Impossible Wardrobe for the Invisible" where clothes are also destroyed, except this time it is within a cycle of destruction and reconstruction (the woolen thread is reused later in sequence 10, see Figure 13.7). The dress was knitted with the intent of being destroyed, so its construction was planned as such; the movement of the performer was dictated by the unraveling gestures. The film is a parallel with Francis Alÿs' art project of 1995 Fairy Tales, where the artist documents the action of walking around the city in his unraveling blue sweater, leaving a trace everywhere he passes, like a trail of color, a drawing in the city landscape—a fable of loss, the thread becoming an urban drawing of his journey. The procedure that I developed is unique insofar as I have used montage to juxtapose these different sequences to assert a new fashion criticality. In my attempt to depict "thought in the process of being formed," I have used montage itself as a form of thinking in images. Although my film deals with recurrent "dress" themes, and unoriginal themes (represented throughout artistic and fashion practices), my original contribution lies in the dialogue established between the juxtaposed images via editing. The montage of these "leitmotifs" is what generates a critical understanding and stimulates questioning from the audience. Although I did not expect to receive formal feedback from audiences, they nevertheless responded to my film during screenings and exhibitions. Some of the insights I have received from viewers have related to the way the film reminds them of something they have experienced, and how it makes them question fashion's role and how they think about it.

Finally, a white shirt being put on by a male body seems to close the cycle but also connects the drawing of the body with the shapes of the shirt and the gesture of drawing with the gesture of dressing (drawing over the body), resonating with the making–unmaking aspect. The final section is layered with a text that connects bodies–identities–dress. In sequence 13, Dressing shirt (see Figure 13.8) the performer stands in front of the camera once again with the sky as scenery for the banal gesture of dressing in a shirt, once again connecting the film to the audience via common action. In the last sequence, sequence 14, Mimicking putting on imaginary shirt (see Figure 13.8, sequence 1) the male performer repeats the imagined gesture of putting on a nonexistent shirt,

Figure 13.8 Film stills from *Unmaking*: (left) sequences 13 and 14; (right) sequences 1 and 2. Image and © Lara Torres 2016.

resonating with the female performer in the earlier sequence. My film has a "very little almost nothing" approach in some of its "factories sequences," where you see the body of the performer working with a frame of thread around the body; the performer's body and hands becomes the factory and the product a simple thread with tied knots, being "very little almost nothing"; if we rethink production to the very minimum, maybe we could have a minimal factory of hands putting together frames.

Discussion

The use of film as a medium in the development of my fashion practice allows for reflexivity, using film editing as a language of thought: video-thought, proposing a conceptual framework for cinematic modes that acknowledge fashion film as "thought experiment." At once speculative and self-reflexive, film when understood as a thought experiment invites a variety of hermeneutic approaches, relating to the meaning of texts and the ways in which they are understood and permitted to "think the unthinkable," while generating rules that may redefine what we understand by "narrative." This strategy allows describing the relationships within the fashion system through metaphor and allegories that would allow a juxtaposition of meanings and content, using the minimum means possible, simplifying it, dismantling its parts. The matter of the linearity of the narrative became secondary as I became interested in the density of associations that an image allows, the idea of Benjamin's "dialectical image" (Pensky 2004). The questions posed when building a practice of fashion through the medium of film used montage to self-interrogate fashion, to ask the question of "What is fashion?" Understanding that "montage is conflict," as Eisenstein famously proclaimed (1949 [1929]: 38):

> Just as cells in their division form a phenomenon of another order, the organism or embryo, so, on the other side of the dialectical leap from the shot there is montage.
>
> By what, then is montage characterised and, consequently, its cell—the shot?
>
> By collision. By the conflict of two pieces in opposition to each other. By conflict. By collision.
>
> Eisenstein 1949 [1929]: 38

Fashion theorists like Hollander, Barnard, Entwistle, Finkelstein, Roach-Higgins, and Eicher attempted to define the words "fashion," "dress," and "clothing," words that are entangled in the "complicated network of similarities and criss-crossing" that the terms bring (Barnard 2002: 11). To me, this entanglement of ideas that form fashion could be represented through the conflict between images, through montage. The question "What is fashion?" has been posed endlessly by fashion theorists. According to Simmel, fashion is "a process that consists of balancing destruction and up building" and "its content acquires characteristics by destruction of an earlier form" (1957: 549). This notion is reflected in the process used in the making of my film—developed between the making of a series of scenes and then editing them together, every time unmaking the sequence and re-editing the whole video. This continuous deconstruction of the filmic sequence is, in a way, a form of reproducing the mechanisms of fashion in the same way I did previously with clothing items within my fashion design practice. In Deleuze and Guattari's *What Is Philosophy?* "The concept is a whole because it totalises its components, but it is a fragmentary whole" (Deleuze and Guattari 2014: 16); every concept has a history and there are no simple concepts, every concept has components and is defined by them. "There is no concept with only one component; they all have a multiplicity to them" (ibid.: 15). Fashion is a concept: it has a multiplicity and also has a becoming that involves its relationship with other concepts on the same plane, what Ludwig Wittgenstein calls a "family resemblance" (Wittgenstein 1968: 66–7; see also Barnard 2002: 10–11). While there is no single meaning that is common with all of them, each of the terms have something in common and draws together a family of terms: clothing, adornments, dress, and fashion. Barnard explains why this gives an idea of the "difficulty involved in, if not the impossibility of, trying to provide a rigid definition of the meanings of any of these words" (2002: 11). There is no stand-alone definition and, as Wilson has pointed out, fashion is like all cultural phenomena "especially of the symbolic or mythic kind, [which] are curiously resistant to being imprisoned in one 'meaning'" (Wilson 2003 [1985]: 10–11). Various sequences are joined together to create a system of meanings into which viewers may descend. We can find similar "becoming" in the film, and also in "unmaking," where I have tried to avoid the conventional approaches to linear narrative through the editing process, shaping the discontinuity of the discourse throughout the film, preventing the viewer from drawing on their conventional film habits to comprehend the meaning of the film.

Notes

1 In his book *Fashion-ology* (2005), Yuniya Kawamura describes the connection between fashion that is an immaterial object and clothing that is a material object, mentioning Brenninkmeyer's notes, "clothing and dress are the raw material from which fashion is formed. Fashion as a belief is manifested through clothing" (1963: 6). Kawamura adds: "People are wearing clothes, but they believe or wish to believe that it is fashion that they are wearing and that they are consuming fashion and not clothing" (2005: 1–2).

2 Developed in Lisbon between May 2007 and March 2008, the project Mimesis was an interdisciplinary project, between fashion, ceramics, and jewelry disciplines, making use of metalwork techniques and the age-old tradition of mold making using plaster, natural latex, and porcelain, to reproduce found clothing, jewelry, and accessories from their original form as a disruptive voice regarding functionality.

3 The visitors to the exhibition *Mimesis/Fac-simile* could see an account of the production process of the project Mimesis (2008), failures and experimentation. Like an archaeologist, I was trying to put together fragments to recover evidence of a long-lost form. The exhibition had vitrines with the contents displayed as

archaeologic findings. I did not work as a professional archaeologist, but in a similar way to an archaeologist, when they carefully collect and record fragments of old things "as a study of the human past as inferred from the surviving material remains" (Renfrew and Bahn: 11).

4   In the sense that my studio moved from being a traditional fashion studio producing small commercial collections into becoming an experimental, disruptive artist studio producing often dysfunctional, non-commercial series.

5   Victor Margolin cites the design theorist Clive Dilnot in the diagnosis of a "movement towards a 'post-product' society, i.e., to one distinguished by a more explicit social management of man–environment relations, is likely to bring back this historic sense of design's significance [as planning]. Design becomes once again a means of ordering the world rather than merely of shaping commodity." Dilnot quoted in Margolin (1998: 86).

6   In the 1970s, artists commonly used clothing for its symbolic content. Clothes were used by artists to translate someone's presence/absence or memory. The artwork "All the Clothes of a Woman" (1973) by the artist Hans Peter Feldman is a good example of such practices. It refers to seventy items of a woman's wardrobe photographed one by one and framed as one archival image as a reminder of her existence in her absence. Hans Peter Feldman's work displays something that seems to represent a specific woman whose identity is not revealed to the audience, but who is recreated in their minds by her clothing items. In 1972, Christian Boltanski made the artwork "Les habits de François C." ("The Clothes of François C.," 1970) that surveys Boltanski's main motifs of place, memory, and loss through clothing that represents someone's identity.

7   Available online: https://vimeo.com/album/1533464.

8   Oxford Street is one of the busiest shopping streets in the world, with 500,000 pedestrians walking every day, as of 2016. See https://www.london.gov.uk/press-releases/assembly/oxford-st-the-busiest-feet-street-in-the-world.

References

Barnard, M. (2002) *Fashion as Communication*, 2nd edn., Abingdon: Routledge.

Barthes, R. (2010 [1983]) *The Fashion System*, London: Vintage Classics.

Benjamin, W. (2002) *The Arcades Project*, trans. H. Eiland and K. McLaughlin, Cambridge, MA: Harvard University Press.

Bhardwaj, V. and Fairhurst, A. (2010) "Fast Fashion: Response to Changes in the Fashion Industry," *The International Review of Retail, Distribution and Consumer Research*, 20(1): 165–73.

Brenninkmeyer, I. (1963) *The Sociology of Fashion*, Opladen: Westdeutscher.

Deleuze, G. and Guattari, F. (2014) *What Is Philosophy?*, trans. J. Tomlinson and G. Burchell, New York: Columbia University Press.

Ehmann, A. and Eshun, K., eds. (2009) *Harun Farocki: Against What? Against Whom?*, London: Walther König.

Eisenstein, S. (1949 [1929]) "The Cinematographic Principle and the Ideogram," in S. Eisenstein (ed.), *Film Form*, trans. and ed. J. Leyda, reprinted edn., 37–70, New York: Harcourt, Brace and World.

Entwistle, J. (2000) *The Fashioned Body: Fashion, Dress and Modern Social Theory*, Cambridge: Polity Press.

Evans, C. (2003) *Fashion at the Edge: Spectacle, Modernity and Deathliness*, New Haven, CT: Yale University Press.

Finkelstein, J. (1991) *The Fashioned Self*, Cambridge: Polity Press.

Finkelstein, J. (2007) *The Art of Self Invention: Image and Identity in Popular Visual Culture*, London: I. B. Tauris.

Foucault, M. (2004) *The Archeology of Knowledge*, Abingdon: Routledge.

Geczy, A. and Karaminas, V. (2018) *The End of Fashion: Clothing and Dress in the Age of Globalization*, London: Bloomsbury.

Guéry, F. and Deleule, D. (2014) *The Productive Body*, trans. P. Barnard and S. Shapiro, Winchester: Zero Books.

Kawamura, Y. (2005) *Fashion-ology: An Introduction to Fashion Studies*, Oxford: Berg.

Leach, N. (2006) *Camouflage*, Cambridge, MA: MIT Press.

Lippard, L. R. (1997) *Six Years: The Dematerialization of the Art Object from 1966 to 1972*, London: Studio Vista.

Margolin, V. (1998) "Design for a Sustainable World," *Design Issues*, 14(2): 83–92.

Merewether, C. (2006) *The Archive: Documents of Contemporary Art*, London: Whitechapel Gallery.

Morris, W. (1884) *A Factory As It Might Be*. First published in *Justice*, April–May, 1884. Reproduced in *the informal education archives*. Available online: http://infed.org/ archives/e-texts/william_morris_a_factory_as_it_might_be_1884.htm (accessed February 24, 2019).

Mulvey, L. (1975) "Visual Pleasure and Narrative Cinema," *Screen*, 16(3): 6–18.

Niinimäki, K. (2017) "Fashion in a Circular Economy," in C. E. Henninger, P. J. Alevizou, H. Goworek, and D. Ryding (eds.), *Sustainability in Fashion: A Cradle to Upcycle Approach*, 151–69, Cham: Springer.

Pensky, M. (2004) "Method and Time: Benjamin's Dialectical Images," in D. S. Ferris (ed.), *The Cambridge Companion to Walter Benjamin*, 177–98, Cambridge: Cambridge University Press.

Renfrew, C. and Bahn, P. (1996) *Archaeology: Theories, Methods, Practice*, London: Thames & Hudson.

Rocamora, A. (2009) *Fashioning the City: Paris, Fashion and the Media*, London: I. B. Tauris.

Rockström, J., Steffen, W., Noone, K., Persson, Å., Chapin, F. S., III, Lambin, E. F., Lenton, T. M., Scheffer, M., Folke, C., Schellnhuber, H. J., Nykvist, B., de Wit, C. A., Hughes, T., van der Leeuw, S., Rodhe, H., Sörlin, S., Snyder, P. K., Costanza, R., Svedin, U., Falkenmark, M., Karlberg, L., Corell, R. W., Fabry, V. J., Hansen, J., Walker, B., Liverman, D., Richardson, K., Crutzen, P., and Foley, J. A. (2009) "A Safe Operating Space for Humanity," *Nature*, 461: 472–5.

Simmel, G. (1957) "Fashion," *American Journal of Sociology*, 62(6): 541–58.

Skjold, E. (2016) "Biographical Wardrobes: A Temporal View on Dress Practice," *Fashion Practice*, 8(1): 135–48.

Turner, B. S. (2008) *The Body and Society: Explorations in Social Theory*, 3rd edn., London: Sage.

Tynan, J. (2016) "Michel Foucault: Fashioning the Body Politic," in A. Rocamora and A. Smelik (eds.), *Thinking Through Fashion: A Guide to Key Theorists*, 184–99, London: I. B. Tauris.

Wilson, E. (2003 [1985]) *Adorned in Dreams: Fashion and Modernity*, revised and updated edn., London: I. B. Tauris.

Wittgenstein, L. (1968) *Philosophical Investigations*, Oxford: Basil Blackwell.

Wolbers, M. (2019) *Fashion and Media*, Bibliographical Guide, Bloomsbury Academic. Available online: https://www.bloomsburyfashioncentral.com/products/berg-fashion-library/article/bibliographical-guides/fashion-and-media (accessed August 21, 2019).

Zalasiewicz, J., Williams, M., Haywood, A., and Ellis, M. (2011) "Introduction: The Anthropocene: A New Epoch of Geological Time?," *Philosophical Transactions of the Royal Society A: Mathematical, Physical, and Engineering Sciences*, 369: 835–41.

Discussion

14

On Fashioning Anatomy

Joanne Entwistle and Katherine Townsend

Working with the material

Crafting Anatomies is a unique exploration into the crafted relationships between bodies, selves, technologies, and materials, which takes us on multi- and transdisciplinary journeys through the myriad different ways in which bodies are understood, experienced, configured, and made meaningful within fashion and material culture. Since much of the work has emerged from artistic research practice, the overall content is more exploratory, open-ended, and creative than is often the case in academic publications. Most chapters do not present neat and tidy conclusions so much as ask questions and raise issues. It is therefore a surprising book in many ways.

Textile and fashion practice have long attended to the physical body and there is now also a well-established tradition of theoretical scholarship focused on the many ways in which cloth and dress intervenes with and shapes the body (McDowell 2013; Vincent 2009). As Mary Douglas (1966) and other anthropological work on the body has shown, the body's boundaries are fluid; its physical, social, and cultural materials, complex. Consequently, much early fashion scholarship has explored textiles and dress as "social fabric" (Checinska and Watson 2016), the meeting point between the self and culture (Entwistle 2015; Entwistle and Wilson 2001). However, as research linking bodies to cloth and clothing continues to grow it demonstrates the difficulty in knowing where anatomy/nature ends, and its fabrication via cultural constructs begins (see, for example, Mauss 1973).

The "material turn" in design research and conservation has particularly influenced the approaches and outcomes in this collection, by drawing attention away from texts, images, and representations (of the fashioned body) toward the materiality of bodily practices between different actors, objects, experts, and techniques (Clever and Ruberg 2014). Where earlier academic studies of fashion were concerned with semiotics or the reading of representations (Barnard 2002; Jobling 1999; Barthes 1990) a growing interest in the somatic relationships enacted between bodies, cloth, and dress has begun to address the ontological nature and impact of textiles and clothing on bodies and personhood (Jenss and Hofmann 2019; Slater 2014). Further developments in "wardrobe research" have revealed the practical, embodied, *and* emotional decisions that individuals make when deciding what to wear and keep (Townsend and Sadkowska 2018; Fletcher and Klepp 2017; Woodward 2007; Guy, Green, and Banim 2003). Linked to this, a contemporary concern with affect to the senses has attuned us to the ways in which cloth and dress have deep emotive and sensory qualities, which reinforce the holistic interrelationship between body/self, and textiles/dress (Millar and Kettle 2018; Johnson and Foster 2007; Weber and Mitchell 2004).

Crafting Anatomies explores these and other material-based issues through methodologies integrating the craft of fashion with other domains, such as biomedical and clinical science, that similarly focus on and shape the body. Materializing the body beyond its usual arenas subverts established combinations and uses of technology, involving a confluence of fields (Oxman 2015). Some of the resulting socio-bio-medical assemblages make trouble at the edges of the body, by challenging common understandings and stable categories, while other outcomes literally intervene in the body, and, at times, confuse the margins between human/non-human, natural/artificial, the carbon and digital human.

What is particularly striking about this collection of essays, then, is how it evidences the myriad ways in which anatomies are fashioned within and without through hybrid approaches. Many of these art/science-based practices call for the individual to care, via co-designed strategies, for their own "disruptive" self/ body, positioning bodies at the center of politics (Foucault 1977). New wearable technologies, prosthetic hands, and footwear instigated by/for the human form, are just some of the practical interventions and devices explored to understand the multiple, ever-changing ways bodies are reconfigured. The following sections mirror those in the book via "Unarchiving the Body," "Between Nature and Culture," and "Fashioning the Future Body," by responding to the core themes raised in each chapter and pointing to the ramifications of this work.

Unarchiving the Body

The researchers featured in "The Archived Body" advocate a closer reading of artifacts (materials and associated technologies) that were once new, by re/

activating the visible and invisible evidence of embodied cognition through engagement with material things (Merleau-Ponty 1969). Occupying a body means learning, experiencing, and living within the constraints of our culture. However, "culture" and indeed "material culture" is not simply "there" as proposed by actor-network-theory (ANT) drawing on Latour (2005) and "material semiotics", which provides tools "sensibilities and methods of analysis that treat everything in the social and natural worlds as a continuously generated effect of the webs of relations within which they are located" (Law 2009: 141). Working in archives requires a leap of faith by researchers, to imagine the things, the social worlds, of people who once existed.

In "The Archived Lace Body," Briggs-Goode and Baxter explore four artists' responses to the action of the body on and through historical lace textiles. In "Worn" (2013), Joy Buttress interrogates how the evidence of domestic labour performed by Victorian women in service, can be traced on their cotton undergarments. Buttress employs the precise, skilled practice of hand embroidery on and across the internal seams of garments abraded and stained by the body, reinforcing the intimacy of the original wearer's and the artist's methodical marking of the cloth (Diamond 2015). Danica Maier's "Flowers of Chivalry" (2005) in Ñandutí lace, was also created by hand with the help of local lace makers, during an artist's residency in Paraguay. As discussed in Chapter 2, Maier's practice both replicates and subverts the traditions of domestic needlework. In *Bummock: The Lace Archive* (Bracey and Maier 2018), she utilizes overlooked acts of dexterity (required in machine-made lace making) such as technical instructions and hand-punched jacquard cards, which she develops as musical scores to fill the space left by these fragmentary, inconclusive records (Barnett in Bracey and Maier 2018: 60).

Buttress's and Maier's work raises parallels between the invisibility and silencing of women undertaking domestic and textile tasks (Bracey and Maier 2018: 64) and those involved in contemporary fashion production. So, while hand stitching/making/repair are being revalued as sustainable acts of craft *and* use (Fletcher 2016) the hiding of labor in fashion continues to be enacted as a culturally and systemically induced form of ignorance (von Busch et al. 2017). There are many forms of hidden labor in fashion, from sweatshops to interns and bloggers, whose "work" is currently being reimagined by activists who are reconceptualizing the making of fashion, inspired by Hannah Arendt's (1958) idea of praxis as "heroic" (von Busch et al.: 17).

Millar and Kettle (2018: 12) discuss how the body is "most present when it is glimpsed through lace, a semi-transparent surface that allows the imagination to wander between cloth and body." On the surface, this erotic definition of lace appears to have been exploited to the full by Mal Burkinshaw's "Silhouettes en Dentelle" (2014), first shown in *Beauty by Design: Fashioning the Renaissance*, an exhibition combining art historical research with contemporary fashion design to question beauty and body image ideals. These transparent, ghost-like garments, shown physically and projected digitally leave the viewer to imagine their wearers.

In contrast, in Cal Lane's "Covered" (2005) a woman's naked body is patterned in soil, and in "Disobedient Virtues" (2016) oversized lace knickers are cut from industrial steel. Both these decorative but dysfunctional artworks recall Douglas's (1966) work on purity and danger, by drawing attention to the body's barriers; revealing what occurs at the margins as unexpected, or even dangerous. Lane has taken a tool most often used by men in construction and turned it to deconstructive use in decorating reclaimed metal objects with lingerie motifs. Images of Lane sitting astride a giant oil-drum, welding-torch in hand, crafting a new sculpture from a redundant object overturn historical notions of "women's work" and "hand-made."

Bodies are inevitably caught within or entangled into various assemblages that remake and remodel them, as evidenced via the shoe/foot/body assemblages discussed by Cope and Reponen in "Disarmed" (Chapter 3). Feet are rarely left unshod (and if they are it is frequently a sign of being an "outcast"). Thus, shoes provide a means by which the body's posture, articulation, and movement is shaped. Shoes are potent interventions or devices for configuring the body which the body, in turn, configures, leaving "lasting" imprints (pun intended). Playful interactions are made possible in these assemblages, for example "Twisted Stiletto" (2016) represents a fictional shoe (for a fictional foot), the final component of Cope's "Love Triangle" installation. This is design as social commentary, allowing for it to hint at alternative realities to the idealized fashion stereotype. As a form of observational commentary, design speaks to the ways in which bodies are shaped by cultural ideals and allows for reflection on interior/subjective and exterior/objective experiences of the self. Cope's imaginative, sculptural artifacts play with notions of how parts of the body, such as feet and shoes, are the most fetishized objects in fashion (Edelkoort 2013: 6). Cope is currently using wearable performance scenarios to inform human-centered solutions such as the Bionic Boob project at Leicester De Montfort University; where the body is (re)crafted from emotionally driven design aesthetics that seek to replace more than what has been lost.

In Chapter 4, Sadkowska investigates the temporal nature of clothing (Skjold 2016) through an investigation into how men over sixty view their wardrobes as archives and how the objects within them embody their sense of identity and masculinity. The older men in the study feel overlooked by high fashion, so it is not surprising that they return to the clothing of their youth to express their sense of personal agency. Sadkowska's original contribution to "practice as research" is based on how she analyzes references to subcultures such as Mods and Punks to inform her own creative responses to these past "non-conformist" styles through a collection of "pioneering" jackets. The use of second-hand tailored jackets as the starting point for these rematerializations reveals them as (doubly) "suitable clothes" (Klepp and Rysst 2017) for the ageing male body.

Sadkowska's ongoing research includes "Emotional Fit," an investigation into the emotionally durable design needs of a group of older women (Townsend and Sadkowska 2018) based on their "wearer-worn engagements" with clothing (Valle-Noronha, 2019). The project involves the co-creation of textile designs and garment silhouettes to produce a collection of experimental "research tools" embodying personal associations with fabric qualities and individual, non-standardized notions of fit (Downing Peters 2019; Colls 2006). The user-centered methodology challenges the "normalization of the body" in fashion, highlighting the need for designers to focus more on "the semantics of clothing" in order to rethink garment design and production (Vicerial in Pecorari 2016).

In "The Electric Corset," Townsend, Kettley and Walker's research involved visiting a lace, textile, and costume collection to identify archived items of dress that could be rematerialized as contemporary, wearable "dress objects" (Skjold 2016). The team selected "accessories" and details that interfaced most directly with the edges of the body and garment (Vainshtein 2012), resulting in a collection of electronically networked "fragment toiles." The term "fragment" was used to convey the objects' meaning and functionality; part of a host garment, body, and ontology of things.

The fragments were devised in accordance with the material and conceptual dimensions of the original artifacts (e.g., collar, cuff, pocket, spat); their imagined and actual use by neck, wrist, hand, and foot through traces of previous wearers' bodily imprints (Freud in Derrida 1995). As such, the practice acknowledges the "material turn" and associated agency of the fashioned object based on its material (textile) and its immaterial (human) properties (Scaturro 2017). The "Electric Corset" methodology also references Margiela's remaking of "relics," deemed to be classic fashion items and the intentional integration of time and memory (*dure*) into new designs (Verhelst and Debo 2008). The work points to the need for a "postphenomenological approach" to wearable technology, whereby advanced textile materials can mediate and "co-shape" the relationship between human beings and the world (Van Dongen et al, 2019). As reiterated at

Textile Intersections (2019) fashion/textile designers and engineers need to continue to develop shared languages of making to inform more aesthetic, functional and sustainable products/experiences.

Between Nature and Culture

The implicit hypothesis underpinning the different approaches to crafting anatomies is evidenced through different forms of material intelligence that extend bodily tolerance and expression. Bodies are *both* nature and culture extant, and the body is a designed entity—whether co-created by engineers and medical or fashion and textile practitioners. This approach requires learning in and between (bio)medicine, fashion discourse, and practice, in an interdisciplinary dialogue about the body, opening more avenues for combined and integrated praxis, as discussed in "The Body in Dialogue."

In "Tissue Engineered Textiles" (Chapter 7) craft's role in the laboratory is revealed through the working relationship of textile designer Amy Congdon and scientist Lucy Di Silvio in an interview with Carole Collet. Here the highly specialist technique used to grow replacement body parts is synthesized with stitch, to augment cellular growth and create different kinds of hybrid "textile tissues." Congdon's conceptualization of a Biological Atelier speculates toward 2080, when we will grow our clothes (as well as everything else) using biotechnology and our own biomaterials, to literally turn our body into a factory. This concept is explored from an alternative perspective by Torres in Chapter 13.

Congdon is continuing her research at Modern Meadow, New York, alongside their Chief Creative Officer, Suzanne Lee, who launched her BioCouture label in 2004. At Modern Meadow, materials and tools are mapped from the "Stone Age to the Biofabrication Age," where wool, leather, and silk are replaced by microbial cellulose, victimless leather, and spider silk (Modern Meadow 2019). Carole Collet, who has worked with both Congdon and Lee, continues to research toward the bio-circular economy, where living systems will disrupt and recalibrate established models of fashion production (Collet 2018).

Interventions onto and into our bodies are not just acted *on* by materials, technologies, or the medical profession. An example of user-centered involvement in the crafting of individual prosthetics is discussed by Cook and Pullin in "Hands of X" (Chapter 6), where participants were given the opportunity to take ownership of the specification of their prosthetic hand. The hand is an important part of the body, functional and highly nuanced. Besides many everyday activities performed by hands, hands are deeply culturally meaningful and symbolic. Hands are offered in friendship (shaking of the hand or bowing with hands in prayer are global greetings), and they are places for decorative embellishment through jewelry, nail decoration, and tattooing, which transform them.

Prosthetic hands are typically made as either supposedly skin-colored silicone or PVC, to closely imitate a natural hand and designed to make the wearer "pass" as normal. Alternatively, the wearer can choose an obvious "bionic" hand of high performing materials like titanium and carbon fiber, styled in post-human, cyber-punk mode. Between these two extremes, we lose sight of the more nuanced and differently shaped and styled hands that many might prefer. Those whose identities and fashion sense don't fit with conventional medical aesthetic languages have little to no choice of sophisticated design languages between these extremes. The aim, in Cook and Pullin's work is to elaborate this language of the prosthetic hand and produce more complex forms that allow users to be more expressive with their hands, and selves.

This and the other user-centered practices disseminated in the "Body in Dialogue," edited by Solomon, are also reinforced by her current research into the use of clothing to broker dialogues between breast reconstruction patients and surgeons (Thimbleby, Wright, and Solomon 2018). In this work, the body is the meeting place for individuals to share phenomenological and biomedical experiences of reconstruction (Solomon 2019).

Speculative and innovative in design, these examples demonstrate new ways of communicating the lived experience of the body and intervening in how it is translated and mediated between medical discourses and ordinary experiences.

There is a historical tendency toward disciplinary silos, with medical practitioners dealing with the serious stuff of "ill" bodies, and fashion/product designers dealing with the less serious aspects of bodily expression. This division reproduces the nature/culture division once more: bodies are either sick and need treatment, or well and can fully participate in "culture," but one does not stop participating in cultural forms like fashion when one moves into a medical setting. The recent exhibition *Frida Kahlo: Making Her Self Up* at the V&A, London (2018) and the Brooklyn Museum, New York (2019) demonstrated this effectively, by showing how the artist used traditional Mexican dress and bespoke accessories such as decorated plaster corsets and non-matching boots to fashion her disabled, or "deviant body" (Klepp and Rysst 2017). In a similar vein, the research project and exhibition *Universal Materiality* (2019) at Parsons School of Design, New York, explored how ageing and disabled bodies require greater consideration by the fashion industry. These issues, along with size, race, and LGBTQ+, were explored in *Body Beautiful: Diversity on the Catwalk* (2019) at the National Museums of Scotland, Edinburgh, demonstrating an overdue shift in thinking about the fashioned body.

The intimate nature of our bodily processes and how they generate emotional responses and physical reactions is explored in Tomasello and Almeida's work on women's self-care (Chapter 9). The Future Flora project involved the design of intimate pads that reproduce healthy female biophilia as a restorative act of self-care to prevent the development of vaginal infection, making women into domestic scientists, able to grow their own healthy bacteria for health purposes.

Future Flora was awarded the STARTS Prize (2018) for Artistic Exploration "where appropriation by the arts has a strong potential to influence or alter the use, deployment or perception of technology." The jury noted:

> As Digital Ghosts, we are hallucinating about being almighty, even immortal under the sun of a God-like AI. Tomasello forces us to lower our gaze from the digital heaven to the most vulnerable female body part—the vagina. With Future Flora she demonstrates this vulnerability as a strength, using the embodied openness as a medium between internal and external organisms, . . . provid[ing] a clear and loud signal that "Future" is not only "Digital."
>
> Giulia Tomasello 2019

As this example illustrates, thinking about the "culture" of the body takes us from the self-evident human-centered idea of culture (in traditional cultural studies to refer to meanings and values and practices) to ideas of bacterial cultures. Once again, the body as a nature/culture entity is made evident and challenges our sense of ourselves as discrete entities, separate from nature. Such design and technological interventions extend our vocabulary and understanding of the body's capacities to demonstrate how these are not finite and complete, neither purely natural or purely culture, but a complex hybrid of both.

In "Mind–Body–Garment–Cloth," Holly McQuillan and Timo Rissanen (Chapter 8) discuss another kind of dialogue with the body, that of fashion's often overlooked mediator: pattern cutting. Using zero-waste and single-piece cutting, their work references historical notions of "fixed" as opposed to "modish" or, fashionable dress (Barnard 2002; see also Flügel 1930) whereby garment styles and volumes were determined by the type of loom and corresponding woven widths of cloth produced by a culture (Burnham 1973). This holistic approach to covering the body is still practiced by artisans in indigenous communities, as in parts of Central America where the backstrap loom and its handwoven narrow widths are pieced together to produce a wardrobe comprised of traditional dress, or traje (e.g., *huipil*, *corte*, and *faja* as worn by Kahlo). The construction of such bespoke, high-quality clothing directly impacts on the body of both maker and wearer. McQuillan and Rissanen's practice explores how similar connections between designers and consumers can be made in Western fashion by deviating from Fordism (Forty 1986) making creative and conscious use of every fragment to make clothing that impacts on the physical and mental "body." They cite Umberto Eco's (1986) essay "Lumbar Thought," the effect of his jeans on his very persona, a garment that provides its own narrative of wear (Townsend 2011).

Building on the crucial relationship between garment, body, and wearer Rissanen is undertaking collaborative research into "Designing Garments with Evolving Aesthetics." The projects asks: "What if a shirt were designed from the beginning as an integral part of a fashion service system? What if the design of both the product and the system enabled the object's aesthetic to evolve over time [along with the needs of the user]?" (Rissanen, Grose, and Riisberg 2018). McQuillan's PhD expands the concept of "zero-waste thinking" through hybrid pattern-cutting approaches that synthesize hand/CAD, 2D/3D draping/cutting with digital jacquard weaving toward "crafting composite garments" (Piper and Townsend 2015: 3) that work within the constraints of zero waste and the shape of the human form. "This reshaping of form-making has the potential to future-make the structure of the industry itself, and through that our social fabric" (McQuillan 2019: 807).

Fashioning the Future Body

Lara Torres (Chapter 13) also challenges Fordism and its damaging division of labor and effect on the global body politic. Her conception of the "body as a factory" presents a post-productivity model of clothing manufacture that reveals the body's methods of *making* itself through fashion. The etymology of the word "fashion" relates it to the Latin *factio*, meaning "making" or "doing." So, to "unmake" fashion's "productive body" (Guéry and Deleule 2014), as Torres proposes, presents a paradox. The craft approach adopted within her fashion practice happens in relation to the current juncture, where knowledge and experience of traditional crafts have been supplemented by the opportunities offered by digital technologies. By capturing the material and immaterial manifestations of clothing (Kawamura 2005: 1) through film, Torres highlights the complex dynamic relationship between the body, dress, and culture, beyond the limits of fashion's current discipline boundaries.

Some of Torres' films were recently shown in "If I Could, Unless We," a night walk through Manifattura Tabacchi (2019), curated by Linda Loppa for Pitti Uomo alongside installations by Bart Hess, Armando Chant, Moses Hamborg, Bernhard Willhelm, Clemens Thornquist, and Senjan Jansen (Linda Loppa Factory 2019). The emphasis of Torres' films resonated with the former manufacturing site, through concepts that un-craft fashion's mechanization, as a form of resistance and activism. The conference and exhibition *Everything and Everybody as Material: Beyond Fashion Design Methods* also challenged the dominant, linear fashion methodology by questioning what/who constitutes the materials of fashion, the shifting categories of these connected constructs and the role of the body that performs them (Thornquist and Bigolin 2017).

A different kind of productive body is proposed by Papastavrou, Ciokajlo, and Solomon who interrogate the bodily boundary of human "skin" (Chapter 10), positioning it both as a blueprint to inform archetypal design and "meeting place to connect design and medical perspectives of the corporeal." Through their consultancy, OurOwnsKIN, the materiality of the body is considered as a core reference point—not something to design for, but something to design from— inspiring 3D-printed footwear, using Additive Manufacturing technologies.

Dialogues between "man, matter and machine" are exposed through reflections on these "digital skins" (see Harris 2013) opening new possibilities of "fit" through mass customization, allowing greater acknowledgement of the uniqueness of bodies; concepts of "perfect fit" also being linked to the idealized and imagined bodies designed for by the fashion system (Barthes 1990). OurOwnsKIN's research into new form-fitting apparel that mimics the human body's own flexible structures (informed by knowledge from reconstructive plastic surgery disciplines) subverts homogenous systems of making and sizing, traversing the nature/culture divide.

New technologies that allow us to mimic living organisms therefore challenge us to question the very materiality of the body. Amy Winters' (Chapter 11) practice involves the development of technologies that sit at the surface (of the body), in the form of substrates that act like prosthetic extensions of human anatomy. Her "textiles" comprise sensory robotics inspired by and incorporating biomaterials to extend the body's expressive communicative capacities. However, as discussed earlier, developing materials with biological functionality requires a transdisciplinary lab approach, as adopted by the Mediated Matter Lab, at MIT, where they combine "computerised design, additive manufacturing, materials engineering and synthetic biology" (Oxman 2015). Winters' work therefore can be categorized within a developing field that seeks to fabricate the body through immersive, tangible, and "intangible matter," mediated through a somatic "fifth sense" which plays with "the balance between human craft and generated perfection" (Hardcastle 2019).

In "The Genetics Gym," Peacock (Chapter 12) challenges the notion of homogeneity through an art/science collaboration that pushes the concept of body manipulation and identity creation to a thought-provoking extreme. Using a combination of photography, film, and computer-generated image editing, he crafts the anatomies of his different participating "models" to accentuate their natural physical features, resulting in a group of individuals that ironically appear to deviate from "Western bodily ideals of thinness, fitness and no deviances" (Klepp and Rysst 2017: 79). The hand/digitally rendered appearance of these augmented humans highlights the utopian and dystopian possibilities inherent in constantly seeking physical perfection. The bleached photorealistic characters in Peacock's speculative Genetics Gym, communicate a constantly metamorphosing fashioned identity that is fluid, exists as a work in progress; "unfinished, incomplete, mechanical, serviceable and renewable" (Bradley Quinn in Pecorari 2016). Ultimately, the practice warns of the potential impact of biological intervention and the influence of photography on the body through "undecidable" virtual representations (Vainshtein 2019).

Conclusion

This book could not have been written ten or so years ago as many of the technologies described here were in speculative development, were not yet invented, or were in their infancy. That this book has emerged within the work of fashion and textiles also demonstrates how far innovative practice and scholarship has come in the last few years.

Early work on the body and fashion had to fight for space and recognition, perceived as "soft" or "fluffy," associated with the "feminine" and "frivolous." If any such prejudice still lingers today (within social sciences, for example), this collection of essays should be seen to challenge it. No longer on the margins of design practice, and no longer only seen as part of the realm of "feminine" consumption, this collection shows how fashion and textile technologies are at the center of contemporary debates about new technologies, and medical and computational abilities.

The articles here demonstrate the many collaborations and innovative conversations that can be had between different professions and practices. They champion the importance of understanding the role that fashion/textile, biological/material and science/clinical practices share in shaping the aesthetics, performance, and well-being of the body. These interdisciplinary conversations

Figure 14.1 Jeanne Vicerial for Clinique Vestimentaire (Dress Clinic): Robe-manteau (dress coat) made according to the muscular weaving of the human backbone from a single 150 km thread. Photo credit: Maxime Imbert (2015).

are likely to continue and become more relevant. Bodies are complex ecosystems of biological material but the point at which the biology ends and the cultural bits are added on is not clear; it never has been, but our increasing knowledge of bodies means we have even more complexity to add to our understandings of nature/culture. Craft—very broadly defined—provides a meeting point between practices that are situated on, or around, the body. This collection challenges us to think about what a body is, what a body can do, and how fashion and textiles provide creative ways to explore these questions.

We have selected an example of Jeanne Vicerial's work to illustrate this final chapter of *Crafting Anatomies*. Vicerial runs Clinique Vestimentaire (clothing clinic), a design, art, and research studio based in Paris. Following her master's, "Un corps sur-mesure," meaning "A tailor-made body," she developed a method for crafting sculptural garments based on mimicking the anatomical structure of the human form, using strings to imitate sinews; each piece made from a single, 466-kilometer-long thread. Her art/science methodology resonates with the material practices of the makers discussed here, through a systematic testing of the boundaries of fashion through a self-created discipline that exploits "the analogy between clothing and the body" (Hyland 2016).

References

Arendt, H. (1958) *The Human Condition*, 2nd edn., Chicago, IL: University of Chicago Press.

Barnard, M. (2002) *Fashion as Communication*, Abingdon: Routledge.

Barthes, R. (1990) *The Fashion System*, trans. M. Ward and R. Howard, Berkeley, CA: University of California Press.

Bracey, A. and Maier, D. (2018) *Bummock: The Lace Archive*, Waddington: Flipping the Bummock Press.

Burnham, D. K. (1973) *Cut My Cote*, Toronto: Royal Ontario Museum.

Checinska, C. and Watson, G. (2016) "Social Fabric: Textiles, Art, Society and Politics," in J. Jefferies, D. Wood Conroy, and H. Clark (eds.), *The Handbook of Textile Culture*, 279–92, London: Bloomsbury.

Clever, I. and Ruberg, W. (2014) "Beyond Cultural History? The Material Turn, Praxiography, and Body History," *Humanities*, 3(4): 546–66.

Collet, C. (2018) "Recalibrating Fashion and Textiles for the Emerging Bio-circular Economy," in *Fashion Tech Talks*, June 5, Fotografiscica, Stockholm. Available online: https://www.fashiontechtalks.com/ (accessed August 22, 2019).

Colls, R. (2006) "Outsize/Outside: Bodily Bignesses and the Emotional Experiences of British Women Shopping for Clothes," *Gender, Place and Culture*, 13(5): 529–45.

Derrida, J. (1995) "Archive Fever: A Freudian Impression," trans. E. Prenowitz, *Diacritics*, 25(2): 9–63.

Diamond, S. (2015) "The Fabric of Memory—Towards the Ontology of Contemporary Textiles," in J. Jefferies, D. Wood Conroy, and H. Clark (eds.), *The Handbook of Textile Culture*, 367–86, London: Bloomsbury.

Douglas, M. (1966) *Purity and Danger: An Analysis of Concepts of Pollution and Purity*, London: Routledge and Kegan Paul.

Downing Peters, L. (2019) "Flattering the Figure, Fitting In: The Design Discourses of Stoutwear, 1915–1930," *Fashion Theory*, 23(2): 167–94.

Eco, U. (1986) "Lumbar Thought," in U. Eco (ed.), *Travels in Hyperreality: Essays*, trans. W. Weaver, 191–6, San Diego, CA: Harcourt.

Edelkoort, L. (2013) *Fetishism in Fashion*, Amsterdam: Frame.

Entwistle, J. (2015) *The Fashioned Body: Fashion, Dress and Social Theory*, 2nd edn., Cambridge: Polity Press.

Entwistle, J. and Wilson, E. (2001) *Body Dressing: Dress, Body, Culture*, Oxford: Berg.

Fletcher, K. (2016) *Craft of Use: Post-Growth Fashion*, Abingdon: Routledge.

Fletcher, K. and Klepp, I. G., eds. (2017) *Opening Up the Wardrobe*, Oslo: Novus Press.

Flügel, J. C. (1930) *The Psychology of Clothes*, London: The Hogarth Press.

Forty, A. (1986) *Objects of Desire. Design and Society Since 1750*, London: Thames & Hudson.

Foucault, M. (1977) *Discipline and Punish: The Birth of the Prison*, trans. A. Sheridan, London: Penguin.

Guéry, F. and Deleule, D. (2014) *The Productive Body*, trans. P. Barnard and S. Shapiro, Winchester: Zero Books.

Guy, A., Green, E., and Banim, M. (2003) *Through the Wardrobe: Women's Relationships with Their Clothes*, Oxford: Berg.

Hardcastle, L. (2019) "The Fifth Sense." *I-D Magazine*. Available online: https://thefifthsense.i-d.co/ (accessed April 10, 2019).

Harris, J. (2013) "Digital Skin: How Developments in Digital Imaging Techniques and Culture Are Informing the Design of Futuristic Surface and Fabrication Concepts," *Textile: The Journal of Cloth and Culture*, 11(3): 242–61.

Hyland, V. (2016) "The Mad-Scientist Designer Making Clothes from a Single Thread," *The Cut*, September 30. Available online: https://www.thecut.com/2016/09/clinique-vestimentaires-designer-is-a-mad-scientist.html (accessed June 20 2019).

Jenss, H. and Hofmann, V., eds. (2019) *Fashion and Materiality: Cultural Practices in Global Contexts*, London: Bloomsbury.

Jobling, P. (1999) *Fashion Spreads: Word and Image in Fashion Photography Since 1980*, London: Bloomsbury.

Johnson, D. C. and Foster, H.B. (2007) *Dress Sense: Emotional and Sensory Experiences of the Body and Clothes*, Oxford: Berg.

Kawamura, Y. (2005) *Fashion-ology: An Introduction to Fashion Studies*, Oxford: Berg.

Klepp, I. G. and Rysst, M. (2017) "Deviant Bodies and Suitable Clothes," *Fashion Theory*, 21(1): 79–99.

Latour, B. (2005) *Reassembling the Social: An Introduction to Actor-Network-Theory*, Oxford: Oxford University Press.

Law, J. (2009) "Actor Network Theory and Material Semiotics," in B.S. Turner (ed.), *The New Blackwell Companion to Social Theory*, 141–58, Oxford: Wiley-Blackwell.

Linda Loppa Factory (2019) *Linda Loppa Factory*. Available online: http://www.lindaloppafactory.com/ (accessed June 20, 2019).

Mauss, M. (1973) "Techniques of the Body," *Economy and Society*, 2(1): 70–88.

McDowell, C. (2013) *The Anatomy of Fashion: Why We Dress the Way We Do*, London: Phaidon.

McQuillan, H. (2019) "Hybrid Zero Waste Design Practices: Zero Waste Pattern Cutting for Composite Garment Weaving and Its Implications," *The Design Journal*, 22(supp.1): 803–19.

Merleau-Ponty, M. (1969) *The Essential Writings of Merleau-Ponty*, ed. A.L. Fisher, New York: Harcourt, Brace and World.

Millar, L. and Kettle, A., eds. (2018) *The Erotic Cloth: Seduction and Fetishism in Textiles*, London: Bloomsbury.

Modern Meadow (2019) *Modern Meadow*. Available online: http://www.modernmeadow.com/ (accessed March 20, 2019).

Oxman, N. (2015) *Design at the Intersection of Technology and Biology*. Ted.com, March. Available online: https://www.ted.com/talks/neri_oxman_design_at_the_intersection_of_technology_and_biology?language=en (accessed June 22, 2017).

Pecorari, C. (2016) "Blocking: Between Composition and Tableau," *Contributor*, 16. Available online: https://contributormagazine.com/16-2/ (accessed April 10, 2019).

Piper, A. and Townsend, K. (2015) "Crafting the Composite Garment: The Role of Hand Weaving in Digital Creation," *Journal of Textile Design Research and Practice*, 3(1/2): 3–26.

Rissanen, T., Grose, L., and Riisberg, V. (2018) "Designing Garments with Evolving Aesthetics in Emergent Systems, What's Going On?," Global Fashion Conference 2018, London College of Fashion, London. Available online: http://gfc-conference.eu/wp-content/uploads/2018/12/RISSANEN-ET-AL_Designing-Garments-with-Evolving-Aesthetics-in-Emergent.pdf (accessed August 22, 2019).

Scaturro, S. (2017) "Confronting Fashion's Death Drive: Conservation, Ghost Labor and the Material Turn Within Fashion Curation," in A. Vänskä and H. Clark (eds.), *Fashion Curating: Critical Practice in the Museum and Beyond*, 21–38, London: Bloomsbury.

Skjold, E. (2016) "Biographical Wardrobes—A Temporal View on Dress Practice," *Fashion Practice*, 8(1): 135–48.

Slater, A. (2014) "Wearing in Memory: Materiality and Oral Histories of Dress," *Critical Studies in Fashion and Beauty*, 5(1): 125–39.

Solomon, R. (2019) *Rhian Solomon*. Available at: https://www.rhiansolomon.co.uk/ (accessed May 5, 2019).

Textile Intersections (2019) Conference and Exhibition, Loughborough University, London 12–14 September. Available online: http://www.textile-intersections.com/ proceedings/.

Thimbleby, P., Wright, S., and Solomon, R. (2018) "Reconstructing Ourselves: An Arts and Research Project Improving Patient Experience," *Journal of Applied Arts and Health*, 9(1): 113–24.

Thornquist, C. and Bigolin, R. (2017) "Everything and Everybody as Material: Beyond Fashion Design Methods," Borås, Sweden, June 7–9. Available at: http:// everythingeverybodyasmaterial.com/ (accessed June 7, 2019).

Tomasello, G. (2019) *Giulia Tomasello*. Available online: https://gitomasello.com/ (accessed June 20 2019).

Townsend, K. (2011) "The Denim Garment as Canvas: Exploring the Notion of Wear as a Fashion and Textile Narrative," *Textile: The Journal of Cloth and Culture*, 9(1): 90–107.

Townsend, K. and Sadkowska, A. (2018) "Textiles as Material Gestalt: Cloth as a Catalyst in the Co-designing Process," *Journal of Textile Design Research and Practice*, 5(2): 208–31.

Vainshtein, O. (2012) " 'I Have a Suitcase Just Full of Legs Because I Need Options for Different Clothing': Accessorizing Bodyscapes," *Fashion Theory*, 16(2): 139–69.

Vainshtein, O. (2019) "Photography and the Body," in A. Geczy and V. Karaminas (eds.), *The End of Fashion: Clothing and Dress in the Age of Globalization*, 47–65, London: Bloomsbury.

Valle-Noronha, J. (2019) Becoming with Clothes: Activating Weaer-Worn Engagements Through Design, PhD Thesis, Finland, Helsinki: Aalto University.

Van Dongen, P., Wakkary, R., Tomico, O., Wensveen, S. (2019): Towards a Postphenomenological Approach to Wearable Technology through Design Journeys, Conference contribution in *Textile Intersections 2019*, Loughborough University, London 12–14 September, pp. 1–12. Available online: https://doi.org/10.17028/rd. lboro.9724649.v1.

Verhelst, B. and Debo, K. (2008) *Maison Martin Margiela: 20: The Exhibition*, Antwerp: MoMu.

Vincent, S. J. (2009) *The Anatomy of Fashion: Dressing the Body from the Renaissance to Today*, Oxford: Berg.

Von Busch, O., Cuba, L., Gatzen, P., Moon, C., Rissanen, T., and Wissinger, E. (2017) *Animal Laborans: The Labor of Fashion*, New York: The Fashion Praxis Collective / Self Passage.

Weber, S. and Mitchell, C. (2004) *Not Just Any Dress: Narratives of Memory, Body and Identity*, New York: Peter Lang.

Woodward, S. (2007) *Why Women Wear What They Wear*, Oxford: Berg.

Contributors

Teresa Almeida is an Associate Professor in the Department of Informatics at Umeå University in Sweden and starting in 2022 at the Instituto Superior Técnico, University of Lisbon in Portugal. Her work is interdisciplinary and explores human-data interactions and design research practices with a focus on women's health and wellbeing. She is the founder of Bitness, a platform that aims to empower women and girls by applying research to improving quality of life and social equity through design.

Dr. Gail Baxter is Research Fellow in the Nottingham Trent University Lace Archive, UK. She specializes in the interpretation of lace in archives and museum collections; her expertise covers both hand- and machine-made laces. Gail is also a lace practitioner who has exhibited internationally. She has acted as lace consultant on a number of contemporary lace projects including Loop.pH "Luminous Lace" at Kensington Palace and Alice Kettle "The Garden of England (Flower Helix)" at the Queen's House, Greenwich. Gail was co-organizer of the international conference "Lace: The Transgressive Thread" at the University for the Creative Arts.

Amanda Briggs-Goode is Professor of Textiles, Head of Department for Fashion, Textiles, Knitwear Design and the Director of the Fashion and Textile Research Centre at Nottingham Trent University, UK. Her research and supervision has recently focused on the field of textile heritage and specifically the NTU Lace Archive of which she has published, curated and exhibited work, such as, lace:here:now by Black Dog (2013) and *Lace Unarchived* in Bonington Gallery (2018). She has recently collaborated on Textile Tales, a Heritage Lottery funded project (www.textiletales.co.uk), which engaged local communities to share their oral histories from working within the fashion and textiles industry of the east Midlands between 1980 and 2005. She has also published work on design pedagogy and the early art schools and the use of textile heritage as a catalyst for contemporary creative work. In 2013 she co-led on lace:here:now a season of lace related events across the city of Nottingham and published *Printed Textiles* with Laurence King, a key textbook in the field.

Liz Ciokajlo is a 3D and footwear designer, researcher, and educator. She is Co-director of the design consultancy OurOwnsKIN and a senior lecturer at Ravensbourne University London. She works as a design consultant, collaboratively with artists, designers, and science-based specialists on creative research projects, and speaks and exhibits internationally. Liz's practice sits at the conceptual end of design and aims to bring a fresh look at how natural and bio-materials and leading technologies can underpin and reshape fashion footwear at the most emotive levels, seeing this combination as futuristic and decisively female. Nominations, awards, and commissions include The Arts Foundation Material Innovation Fellowship 2014 shortlist, International Talent Support 2013 Accessories finalist, UAL SEED Fund Award, The DATO Jimmy Choo Cordwainers Award, Arts Council Awards, Museum of Modern Art New York commission, and shortlisted for The Design Museum London, Beazley Design of the Year 2018 Award.

Professor Carole Collet has dedicated her career to developing a new vision for sustainable design, and pioneered the discipline of Textile Futures in 2000. She is Professor in Design for Sustainable Futures at Central Saint Martins, University of the Arts, London, UK, where she currently holds two key roles. As CSM-LVMH Director of Sustainable Innovation, she has set up Maison/0 to act as a catalyst for creative sustainable innovation across the partnership. As Director of the Design & Living Systems Lab, she explores the interface of biological sciences and design to challenge established craft and manufacturing paradigms and propose news models to biofabricate materials and products of the future. One of Collet's characteristics is that she takes on different research roles, from designer to curator and educator. This enables her to develop an informed critique of both the design outputs and the design contexts, from making knowledge to framing knowledge. Her work has been published and featured in international exhibitions and she regularly contributes to conferences on the subject of textile futures, biodesign, biomimicry, synthetic biology, future manufacturing and biomateriality, sustainable design, and climate change.

Amy Congdon is a designer, researcher, and critical thinker who explores the boundaries between design, science, and technology. Congdon's formal art school education saw her specialize in textiles, yet her work straddles material design and innovation, through to scientific practice. She has worked within laboratories, such as the Tissue Engineering & Biophotonics department at King's College London, and SymbioticA at the University of Western Australia.

Amy has exhibited her work internationally in venues such as Somerset House, UK; Pratt Manhattan Gallery; EDF Fondation Paris; Salone De Mobile Milan; The National Centre for Craft and Design, UK; and the Victoria and Albert Museum London. Her work has been featured in publications including *WIRED*, *Motherboard*, *Vogue*, and in books such as *Biodesign* by William Myers and *Biomimicry for Designers* by Veronika Kapsali. In 2016, she was named a Leading Innovator by the UK Craft Council. Amy is currently Team Lead for Materials Design at Modern Meadow and Producer of the annual Biofabricate Summit.

Andrew Cook is a designer and researcher, with an interest in fashion and design for disability. His work straddles product, service and graphic design, as seen in the *Hands of X* project, on which he was lead designer. He has a PhD from DJCAD Dundee, where he now lectures in design, is founder of the eyewear brand *Laughing Stock* and co-founder of *Studio Ordinary*.

Jo Cope is a practicing artist, fashion lecturer, and guest speaker at numerous universities including London College of Fashion where she studied her Masters in Fashion Artifacts. Jo is a member of the MIND fashion collective and describes her work as part of an anti-superficial fashion movement, crossing the boundaries of Fashion, Art, and Craft. Her work draws from human psychology, social/cultural trend observations, and philosophy, and for over a decade has been exhibited in a diverse range of environments from London Craft Week to the Design Festival at the Venice Biennale. She has been involved in exhibitions in places including Buckingham Palace, the Budapest Museum of Art, and the Decorative Arts Museum Paris. Jo's work not only has been exhibited in numerous museums, galleries, and concept stores internationally but is regularly in demand by cutting-edge fashion magazines to illustrate futurist perspectives of fashion in many contexts, including more recently cross-overs between fashion and science.

Professor Lucy Di Silvio is Professor of Tissue Engineering and Head of Tissue Engineering & Biophotonics at King's College London Dental Institute, Guy's Hospital, UK. Lucy has over 28 years' experience in the field, and has published over 120 papers in peer-reviewed journals and numerous book chapters, and is Editor of *Cell Materials Interactions*. She leads a multidisciplinary group whose focus is tissue repair and regeneration; functionalized biomaterials for the directed differentiation of stem cells and vascularization, and translation of these concepts into novel regenerative medicine approaches. In 2012 she was awarded the Italian civil honor Cavaliere dell'Ordine della Stella d'Italia (Order of the Star of Italy) "to recognize those expatriates who have made an outstanding contribution to the preservation and promotion of national prestige abroad." In 2015 she was appointed Guest Professor at Zheijang University and in September 2018, she was awarded the European Society for Biomaterials Klaas de Groot award.

Dr. Joanne Entwistle is Reader in the Department of Culture, Media and Creative Industries, King's College, London, UK. She has published extensively on fashion, dress, and the body, including *The Fashioned Body: Fashion, Dress and Modern Social Theory* (2015), *The Aesthetic Economy Markets and Value in Clothing and Fashion Modelling* (2009, Bloomsbury). She is editor of *Body Dressing* (with Elizabeth Wilson, 2001, Bloomsbury) and *Fashioning Models: Image, Text and Industry* (with Elizabeth Wissinger, 2012, Bloomsbury). She is co-founder of Configuring Light / Staging the Social research group and her current research is on light and lighting design.

Catherine Harper is Deputy Vice-Chancellor at University of Chichester, UK. A visual artist before turning to writing, Catherine's sculpture, performance, and public arts practice has been exhibited in the UK, Ireland, and internationally from North America to Japan, and she has been Artist-in-Residence at the Irish Museum of Modern Art, the Canadian Banff Centre for the Arts, Finland's Nordiskt Konstcentrum, and the National Museum of Prague. Her work is held in many private and public collections, including those of the Irish Government, the UK's National Health Service Trust, and the Tyrone Guthrie Centre. As Professor of Textiles, she holds a PhD in Composite Textile Engineering (Ulster, supported by Ford Motors), and has been Editor-in-Chief of the journal *TEXTILE: Cloth and Culture* for over a decade. Currently developing a monograph titled *Oestrogen Rising: Stained and Bloodied Cloths of Ireland*, Catherine's previous monograph was *Intersex* (2007), and she has published most recently on clothing, erotic intimacy, and masculine mourning in Lesley Millar and Alice Kettle's *The Erotic Cloth* (Bloomsbury, 2017) and in *Social Identities: Journal for the Study of Race, Nation and Culture* (2016). She is author/ editor of the four-volume *Textiles: Critical and Primary Sources* (Bloomsbury, 2012), and currently in receipt of funding from the Marc Fitch Trust and the Society of Antiquaries, London.

Sarah Kettley holds a Chair in Material and Design Innovation at Edinburgh College of Art, the University of Edinburgh, UK. She leads the RAFT research group at ECA and convenes the Design Research Society special interest group in embedded, tangible, and networked technology (tentSIG), both of which seek to facilitate collaborations across disciplines to deconstruct and reconstruct design processes in response to new technologies. Sarah's own interests are in craft epistemology, craft as a methodology for the development of wearable technologies, and person-centered methodologies for ethical and participatory design.

Dr. Holly McQuillan is Assistant Professor in Materialising Futures at the Industrial Design Engineering department at TU Delft exploring sustainable textile-form systems, with a particular focus on animate materials in 2D to 3D woven structures and design for circularity. Her current research explores the design and development of complex interconnected fibre-yarn-textile-form systems as a means for transforming how we design, make, use, and recover textile-based forms. She seeks to use design, craft and prototyping as a means to develop holistic – or multimorphic – design practice methodologies.

Dr. Manolis Papastavrou is an Industrial Designer specializing in Additive Manufacturing and Computational Design who holds a keen interest in translating the principles of biological systems into design solutions. His algorithmic designs have appeared in speculative artworks of OurOwnsKIN for the Design Museum London, Museum of Modern Art New York and Somerset House, London. Manolis has completed a PhD in the area of 3D-printed bone tissue substitutes and his research has been featured in major medical and 3D printing-related online magazines and academic journals. He is passionate about the role of design as the main driver in the Additive Manufacturing revolution. As a result, he has co-founded Metamorphic, a design consultancy that helps organisations innovate through the use of 3D Printing.

Adam Peacock is a post-disciplinary artist, designer, and consultant. Founder of The Validation Junky, an experimental lens on how technology is changing who we aspire to become through brands and products, Adam is Lecturer of Design Strategy and Future Related Design at London College of Fashion for MA Fashion Futures, and co-runs a Master of Architecture Studio at the University of Melbourne. Adam's design work includes projects for Heatherwick Studio and Amanda Levete Architects and WilkinsonEyre. Commercial future design, innovation, branding, and communication strategy work includes projects with Stella McCartney, Lyst, Audi, and FIAT. Adam was awarded the 2018 Robert Garland Treseder Fellowship with Melbourne School of Design, University of Melbourne for his work on the Genetics Gym project. In 2016,

Adam held the Design Residency at The Fashion Space Gallery at London College of Fashion, University of the Arts London, and in 2015–16, Adam was the Artist Residence at The Visible Futures Lab, School of Visual Arts in New York City.

Graham Pullin is a designer and author of *Design Meets Disability*. At DJCAD University of Dundee he is Professor of Design and Disability and co-founded the interdisciplinary research centre Studio Ordinary (previously he was a studio head at the design consultancy IDEO). *Hands of X* explored everyday materials, choice and ownership in prosthetic hands, funded by the EPSRC and later through an exhibition at V&A Design Museum Dundee during a fellowship with The Healthcare Improvement Studies Institute. A Wellcome Trust humanities collaboration is *Imagining technologies for disability futures*, Dundee critically re-imagining augmentative and alternative communication with mentors who use AAC.

Johannes Reponen is a fashion scholar, critic, and consultant. Having previously led MA Fashion Media Practice and Criticism as well as MA Fashion Cultures courses at London College of Fashion, Johannes is currently working as the Program Director for MA Fashion Media Practice at Condé Nast College in London. He regularly writes for a variety of international publications such as *Vestoj*, *McGuffin*, and *Press&Fold* about fashion and media. He is currently completing his PhD in fashion criticism at London College of Fashion.

Dr. Timo Rissanen is an artist, designer, and educator. He is the associate professor of fashion and textiles at the University of Technology Sydney (UTS). He was at Parsons School of Design for a decade, most recently as the associate professor of fashion design and sustainability. He was born in Finland and trained as a fashion designer. Rissanen completed a practice-based PhD on zero-waste fashion design at UTS in 2013. As an artist he has focused on labour, politics, and love through installation, performance, and cross-stitched poetry. Rissanen co-curated *Fashioning Now* with Alison Gwilt in 2009 and *Yield* with Holly McQuillan in 2011, and he has co-published two books on fashion and sustainability, *Shaping Sustainable Fashion* with Gwilt in 2011 and *Zero Waste Fashion Design* with McQuillan in 2016.

Dr. Ania Sadkowska is a Fashion Designer, Senior Lecturer, and Researcher at Coventry University, UK. In the past she worked as a Lecturer and Research Fellow at Nottingham Trent University, UK. Her research explores the intersection of sociology and psychology with art and design practices. Current projects span a variety of topics including fashion and aging, masculinity, phenomenology, and art and design research methodologies. Ania has presented her work at various UK and international conferences and exhibitions including Italy, China, Sweden, and the USA. Since 2014 she has been involved in a co-creative research project titled Emotional Fit: Developing a New Fashion Methodology with Older Women.

Rhian Solomon is an Artist and Design Researcher exploring cultural perspectives of the body using clothing-centred approaches. Her research currently examines the relationship between a patient's wardrobe and their experiences of primary breast cancer. Rhian is also Co-Director of consultancy OurOwnsKIN – facilitating innovation projects across medical, material and design sectors – and is a lecturer at Nottingham Trent University and London College of Fashion, MA Fashion Artefact. Her work has been presented at organisations including Nike Design Kitchen, The Royal College of Art and The V&A and has been commissioned by The Wellcome Trust, King's College London and the Arts and Humanities Research Council.

Giulia Tomasello is an interaction designer specialized in women's healthcare combining biotechnology, interactive wearables, and innovation. She is the winner of the STARTS Prize 2018 from the European Commission honoring Innovation in Technology, Industry, and Society stimulated by the Arts. She considers herself an explorer, using materiality to question and communicate the boundaries between technology and our bodies. She questions our notions of well-being to develop innovative tools in the intersection of medical and social sciences.

Lara Torres has been Senior Lecturer at the Fashion and Textiles Department since 2016 and is a Course Leader for the MA Fashion and Textiles at the University of Portsmouth, UK. She holds a doctorate from University of Arts London, London College of Fashion with the thesis "Towards a Practice of Unmaking: The Essay Film as Critical Discourse for Fashion in the Expanded Field." Lara's research sits at the intersection of fashion, fine arts, and film practice and theory, and explores notions of an expanded field of fashion, critical fashion, and fashion film practices in the twenty-first century. Her fashion practice has been featured in international exhibitions, including "The Future of Fashion is Now" (2014/15) in the Museum Boijmans van Beuningen in Rotterdam; "Why-What-Who: 10 Years of Fashion Artefacts" at the Venice Biennale (2018); and "State of Fashion" in Arnhem (2018).

Katherine Townsend is Professor of Fashion and Textile Practice in the School of Art and Design and a member of the Design, and Clothing Sustainability groups in the Fashion and Textile Research Centre, Nottingham Trent University. Katherine's experience as a fashion designer informed her PhD, *Transforming Shape* (2003), in which she developed a 'simultaneous method' for conceptualising minimal waste, printed garments in relation to body shape, synthesizing hand and digital technologies. Her research and PhD supervision encompasses dress archives and wearables (*Electric Corset*), participatory methodologies (*Emotional Fit*) and sustainable design for social change (*Emmanuel House X NTU*). Funded investigations include 'Redesigning PPE: enhancing the comfort and safety of healthcare workers wearing isolation gowns to treat patients with Covid-19' (AHRC, 2021) and 'Learning from the diversification of Guatemalan artisans during the global pandemic to develop sustainable models of textile practice' (GCRF, 2021). Katherine's research into the role of embodied knowledge in the crafting and use of textile objects has been disseminated through artefacts, curated exhibitions, publications, and her co-editorship of *Craft Research*, Intellect, UK.

Sarah Walker is a lecturer and PhD candidate based in Innovation Management in the Nottingham Business School, Nottingham Trent University, UK. She previously completed an MA at Nottingham Trent University in Textile Design Innovation exploring the potentials of smart textiles to develop innovative e-textile applications. Her research investigates how meaningful collaborative relationships can be developed between the diverse disciplines that are brought together within the field of smart textiles. In her work, Sarah draws on heuristic research to apply a critical practice-led methodology to facilitate experiential and reflective thinking within interdisciplinary teams. As part of her research, Sarah has collaborated on funded research projects such as "An Internet of Soft Things" and "Electric Corset and Other Future Histories." She is an experienced workshop facilitator in e-textiles and is an active member of the ArcInTex and E-Fibre Networks.

Amy Winters is the founder of material-technology studio Rainbow Winters. She holds a PhD in Interactive Textiles (Royal College of Art, 2017) and a BA (Hons) Performance Design (Central Saint Martins, 2006). Rainbow Winters develops soft materials that interact with external influences such as light, sound, speed, and moisture. During her doctoral studies at the RCA, Winters identified and cultivated a design-led approach toward the invention of materials for soft robotics. "Why Does Soft Matter?" articulates this specific approach through critical making: a visceral and hands-on engagement with soft materials and technology. Amy Winters is featured in *WIRED*, *WWB*, *Vertu Magazine*, *Trend Hunter*, *Vice Style*, *Stylist*, *The Guardian*, and *Marie Claire*. Shows, exhibitions, and presentations include International CES; CREATE, Brown Thomas, Dublin; Made in Future, Milan; Clever Dressing, Dana Centre, London; Science Gallery, Dublin; Hacking Arts, MIT, Boston; and The House of Lords.

Index